Evaluation of Text and Speech Systems

Text, Speech and Language Technology

VOLUME 37

The titles published in this series are listed on www.springer.com.

Evaluation of Text and Speech Systems

Edited by

Laila Dybkjær
Natural Interactive Systems Laboratory
Odense
University of Southern Denmark

Holmer Hemsen
Natural Interactive Systems Laboratory
Odense
University of Southern Denmark

Wolfgang Minker
Institute for Information Technology
University of Ulm
Germany

elsnet

Springer

A C.I.P. Catalogue record for this book is available from the Library of Congress.

ISBN-13 978-1-4020-5815-8 (HB)
ISBN-13 978-1-4020-5817-2 (e-book)

Published by Springer,
P.O. Box 17, 3300 AA Dordrecht, The Netherlands.

www.springer.com

Printed on acid-free paper

Contents

Preface

This book has its point of departure in courses held at the Tenth European Language and Speech Network (ELSNET) Summer School on Language and Speech Communication which took place at NISLab in Odense, Denmark, in July 2002. The topic of the summer school was "Evaluation and Assessment of Text and Speech Systems".

Nine (groups of) lecturers contributed to the summer school with courses on evaluation of a range of important aspects of text and speech systems, including speaker recognition, speech synthesis, talking animated interface agents, part-of-speech tagging and parsing technologies, machine translation, question-answering and information retrieval systems, spoken dialogue systems, language resources, and methods and formats for the representation and annotation of language resources. Eight of these (groups of) lecturers agreed to contribute a chapter to the present book. Since we wanted to keep all the aspects covered by the summer school, an additional author was invited to address the area of speaker recognition and to add speech recognition, which we felt was important to include in the book. Although the point of departure for the book was the ELSNET summer school held in 2002, the decision to make a book was made considerably later. Thus the work on the chapters was only initiated in 2004. First drafts were submitted and reviewed in 2005 and final versions were ready in 2006.

The topic of evaluation has grown from an afterthought into an important part of systems development and a research topic of its own. The choice of evaluation of text and speech systems as the topic for the 2002 summer school was no doubt a timely one, and evaluation has not become less important since then. On the contrary, and probably fuelled by the increasing sophistication of text and speech systems, evaluation has moved to an even more central position. Thus we believe that time is opportune for a book that provides overviews of evaluation in most key areas within text and speech systems. The book targets not only graduate students and Ph.D. students but also academic and industrial researchers and practitioners more generally who are keen on getting an overview of the state of the art and best practice in evaluation in one or more of the aspects dealt with in this book. Since the evaluation area is constantly developing, it may be difficult, in particular for newcomers to the field, to get an overview of current and best practice. The book may therefore be suitable both as a course book if the purpose is to give graduate students an overview of text and speech systems and their evaluation, and as supplementary reading material for graduate courses on one or more particular areas of text and speech systems.

We would like to thank the many people who contributed one way or another to the ELSNET summer school in 2002, without which this book would not have been written. We are grateful to all those who helped us in preparing the book. In particular, we would like to express our gratitude to the following external reviewers for their valuable comments and criticism on first drafts of the nine chapters: John Aberdeen, Elisabeth André, Walter Daelemans, Christophe d'Alessandro, John Garofolo, Inger Karlsson, Adam Kilgariff, Alon Lavie, Chin-Yew Lin, Susann Luperfoy, Inderjeet Mani, Joseph Mariani, John Mason, Dominic Massaro, Sebastian Möller, Roberto Pieraccini, Alexander Rudnicky, Michael Wagner, and Andrew Wilson. A special thanks is also due to people at the Department of Information Technology in Ulm and at NISLab in Odense for their support in editing the book.

Laila DYBKJÆR

Holmer HEMSEN

Wolfgang MINKER

Contributing Authors

Niels Ole Bernsen is Professor at, and Director of, the Natural Interactive Systems Laboratory, the University of Southern Denmark. His research interests are spoken dialogue systems and natural interactive systems more generally, including embodied conversational agents, systems for learning, teaching, and entertainment, online user modelling, modality theory, systems and component evaluation, as well as usability evaluation, system simulation, corpus creation, coding schemes, and coding tools.

Nick Campbell is currently an Expert Researcher with the National Institute of Information and Communications Technology (NICT) and the ATR Spoken Language Communications Research Labs. He is also Visiting Professor at Kobe University and at the Nara Institute of Science & Technology in Japan. He received his Ph.D. in Experimental Psychology from the University of Sussex in the UK in 1990. His research interests include prosody processing, corpus collection and analysis, concatenative speech synthesis, and expressive speech processing. As co-founder of ISCA's Speech Synthesis Special Interest Group, he has a particular interest in furthering the capabilities and quality of speech synthesis.

Christopher Cieri is the Executive Director of the Linguistic Data Consortium where he has overseen dozens of data collection and annotation projects that have generated speech and text corpora in many languages to support basic research and human language technology research and development. He has also served as principal investigator on several projects in which LDC coordinated linguistic resources for multiple site, common task technology evaluations. His Ph.D. is in Linguistics from the University of Pennsylvania. His research interests revolve around corpus-based language description, especially in phonetics, phonology, and morphology as they interact with non-linguistic phenomena, for example, in studies of language contact and linguistic variation.

Laila Dybkjær is a Professor at NISLab, University of Southern Denmark. She holds a Ph.D. degree in Computer Science from Copenhagen University. Her research interests are topics concerning design, development, and evaluation of user interfaces, including development and evaluation of interactive speech systems and multimodal systems, design and development of intelligent user interfaces, usability design, dialogue model development, dialogue theory, and corpus analysis.

Sadaoki Furui is a Professor at Tokyo Institute of Technology, Department of Computer Science, Japan. He is engaged in a wide range of research on speech analysis, speech recognition, speaker recognition, speech synthesis, and multimodal human–computer interaction.

Björn Granström is Professor of Speech Communication at KTH in Stockholm and the Director of CTT, the Centre for Speech Technology. He has published numerous papers in speech research and technology. His present research interest is focused on multimodal speech communication, including applications in spoken dialogue systems, rehabilitation, and language learning.

David House is an Associate Professor at the Department of Speech, Music and Hearing, School of Computer Science and Communication, KTH, Stockholm, Sweden. He received his Ph.D. in Phonetics at Lund University, Sweden, in 1991, and has held positions at the Department of Linguistics and Phonetics, Lund University; Department of Logopedics and Phoniatrics, Lund University; and the Department of Languages, University of Skövde. His research interests include speech perception, prosody, tone and intonation, speech synthesis, spoken dialogue systems, and multimodal speech perception.

Nancy Ide is Professor of Computer Science at Vassar College and Chair of the Computer Science Department. She has worked in the field of computational linguistics in the areas of word sense disambiguation and discourse analysis, as well as the acquisition and representation of lexical knowledge. She has been involved in work on the representation of language data and its annotations since 1987, when she founded the Text Encoding Initiative. She is the developer of the Corpus Encoding Standard, and currently serves as Project Leader of the ISO TC37/SC4 Working Group to develop a Linguistic Annotation Framework. Currently, she is Technical Manager of the American National Corpus project, and co-edits both the journal *Language Resources and Evaluation* and the Springer book series on Text, Speech, and Language Technology.

Margaret King is an Emeritus Professor of the School of translation and Interpretation in the University of Geneva, where she was Head of the Multilingual Information Processing Department until 2006. She has worked in the field of semantics and in machine translation. For the last 15 years she has had a special interest in the evaluation of human language technology software, concentrating particularly on systems dealing with written text. She was Chair of the European Union EAGLES working group on evaluation, and continued in this role in ISLE, a joint project of the European Union and the US National Science Foundation.

Wolfgang Minker is a Professor at the University of Ulm, Department of Information Technology, Germany. He received his Ph.D. in Engineering Science from the University of Karlsruhe, Germany, in 1997 and his Ph.D. in Computer Science from the University of Paris-Sud, France, in 1998. He was a Researcher at the Laboratoire d'Informatique pour la Mécanique et les Sciences de l'Ingénieur (LIMSI-CNRS), France, from 1993 to 1999, and a member of the scientific staff at DaimlerChrysler, Research and Technology, Germany, from 2000 to 2002.

Patrick Paroubek is a research engineer at LIMSI, a laboratory of the Centre National de la Recherche Scientifique (CNRS). He obtained his Ph.D. in Computer Science in 1989 from P&M Curie University (Paris 6) and specialized shortly after in the study of Natural Language Processing (NLP) systems. He was involved in the organization of several large-scale evaluation campaigns, in particular for parsing systems.

Laurent Romary is current Director of Scientific Information (STI) at CNRS. He got his Ph.D. in computational linguistics in 1989 and his Habilitation thesis in 1999. For several years, he has led the Langue et Dialogue research team (http://www.loria.fr/equipes/led/) at Loria laboratory and conducted various projects on human–machine dialogue, multilingual document management, and linguistic engineering. He was the editor of ISO 16642 (TMF – Terminological Markup Framework) under ISO committee TC37/SC3, and is Chair of ISO committee TC37/SC4 on Language Resource Management. He is also a member of the TEI council (Text Encoding Initiative; http:// www.tei-c.org).

Simone Teufel is a Senior Lecturer in the Natural Language and Information Processing Group at Cambridge University's Computer Laboratory. Her research interests include large-scale, applied NLP, information retrieval (IR), summarization evaluation and discourse parsing. During a Postdoc position at Columbia University in 2000–2001, she was also working on medical information retrieval. Her Ph.D. research (1999, Edinburgh University) looked at the application of discourse learning for summarization; her first degree, in Computer Science, is from Stuttgart University.

Introduction

Laila Dybkjær
Natural Interactive Systems Laboratory
Odense, Denmark
laila@nis.sdu.dk

Holmer Hemsen
Natural Interactive Systems Laboratory
Odense, Denmark
hemsen@nis.sdu.dk

Wolfgang Minker
Department of Information Technology
University of Ulm, Germany
wolfgang.minker@uni-ulm.de

Evaluation has eventually become an important part of the general software development process and therefore also of text and speech systems development. The ELSNET summer school entitled "Evaluation and Assessment of Text and Speech Systems" in which this book has its origin, took place in 2002 and was seen as a timely event. Since then the interest in evaluation has continued to increase which we believe is a good reason for following up on the summer school with this book.

The field of text and speech systems is a very broad one comprising highly different types of systems and components. In addition, language resources play a central role in enabling the construction of such system and component types. It would take far more than a single two-weeks summer school or a single volume of a book to cover evaluation in the entire field of text and speech systems. We have therefore decided to let the book reflect the areas selected for the summer school that were meant to collectively illustrate the breadth of the field. They encompass both component, system, and data resource evaluation aspects and are among the most important areas in the field of text and speech systems.

A typical illustration of the architecture of a unimodal spoken dialogue system shows that it roughly consists of a speech recogniser, a natural language understanding component, a dialogue manager, a response or natural language generation component, and a speech output component. Evaluation of speech recognition and spoken output – not least if a synthetic voice is used – is very important because the performance of these two components strongly influences the user's perception of the system in which they are embedded. We have included a chapter on the evaluation of speech recognition (Chapter 1), as well as a chapter on evaluation of speech synthesis (Chapter 2). The chapter on speech recognition evaluation also deals with evaluation of speaker recognition.

Text-based systems do not include any speech components. Natural language understanding may be needed at a more or less sophisticated level as illustrated by, e.g., question-answering versus information retrieval systems, cf. Chapter 6. This is also true for systems with spoken input where non-task-oriented systems and advanced conversational systems may require a much more detailed and complex understanding than, e.g., a simple bank account system. Natural language understanding is in itself a complex task. Chapter 4 addresses two important aspects of natural language understanding and their evaluation, i.e., part of speech tagging and parsing.

Some text and speech systems need a dialogue manager while others do not. For instance, machine translation does not require a dialogue manager because no dialogue interaction is involved. Whenever some understanding of the user's intentions is needed to find an appropriate reply, there is typically a need for a dialogue manager. For example, spoken dialogue systems normally have a dialogue manager and so do chat bots with written interaction. For simple tasks the dialogue manager may be very simple, whereas the more natural we want to make the conversation with the user the more sophisticated dialogue management techniques are needed. There is no separate chapter on evaluation of dialogue management but aspects of such evaluation are addressed in Chapter 7.

Response or natural language generation is a broad category that may vary considerably in complexity. There are response generation components that use simple pre-defined templates and there are those which try to do sophisticated generation of surface language from semantic contents. Response generation also includes, e.g., the return of a set of documents as in information retrieval tasks. There is no chapter explicitly dedicated to evaluation of response generation, but Chapters 6 and 7 contain elements of such evaluation.

Some or all of the components mentioned above, and maybe other components not mentioned here, may be put together to form a large variety of text and speech systems. We have included examples of evaluation of important system types, i.e., information retrieval and question answering systems (but not summarisation) in Chapter 6, and spoken dialogue systems in Chapter 7. Chapter 5 includes examples of evaluation of machine translation and spell-checkers but has a major emphasis on user-oriented aspects in general. Thus

Chapter 5 is closely related to human factors aspects although there is no separate chapter devoted to human factors in general.

If we combine text or speech with other modalities we would need one or more new components for each modality since we need to recognise and understand input modalities and generate information in the respective output modalities, and may also need to handle fusion and fission of input and output in two or more modalities. This book concentrates on text and speech and only takes a small peep at the multimodal world by including a chapter on talking heads and their evaluation (Chapter 3) and by describing evaluation of two concrete multimodal spoken dialogue systems (Chapter 7).

Nearly all the chapters mentioned so far demonstrate a need for language resources, be it for training, development, or test. There is in general a huge demand for corpora when building text and speech systems. Corpora are in general very expensive to create, so if corpora could be easily accessible for reuse this would of course be of great benefit. Chapter 8 addresses the collection, annotation, quality evaluation, and distribution of language resources, while Chapter 9 discusses standardisation of annotation, which would strongly facilitate reuse. There is no separate discussion of annotation tools.

No common template has been applied across chapters, since this was not really considered advisable given the state-of-the-art in the various subfields. Thus, each of the nine chapters follows its own approach to form and contents. Some chapters address component evaluation, others evaluation at system level, while a third group is concerned with data resources, as described in more detail below.

Component Evaluation. The first four chapters address evaluation of components of text and speech systems, i.e., speech and speaker recognition (Chapter 1), speech synthesis (Chapter 2), audio-visual speech via talking heads (Chapter 3), and part of speech tagging and parsers (Chapter 4). Some of these components may actually also, in certain contexts, be considered entire systems themselves, e.g., a speech synthesizer, but they are often embedded as components in larger text or speech systems.

Chapter 1 by Furui covers speech recognition, as well as speaker recognition. The chapter provides an overview of principles of speech recognition and of techniques for evaluation of speech and speaker recognition.

Speech recognition tasks are categorised as overall belonging to four different groups targeting human–human dialogue, e.g., interviews and meeting summarisation, human–human monologue, e.g., broadcast news and lectures, human–computer dialogue, such as information retrieval and reservation dialogue, and human–computer monologue in terms of dictation, respectively. Each category imposes different challenges on speech recognition.

Regarding evaluation of speech recognition the chapter has its focus on objective performance parameters although subjective measures in terms of, e.g., general impression and intuitiveness are briefly mentioned. Some performance measures, such as word error rate or recognition accuracy, are generally used across application types, while others are particular to a certain category of tasks, e.g., dictation speed for dictation applications. To compare the performance of different speech recognition systems, one must evaluate and normalise the difficulty of the task each system is solving.

Speaker recognition tasks are basically either speaker verification or speaker identification tasks, the former being the more frequent. A serious problem for speaker recognition is that the speech signal usually varies over time or across sessions. To overcome problems relating to such variations, different described normalisation and adaptation techniques can be used. Typical performance evaluation measures for speaker verification are described, including, e.g., equal error rate.

Chapter 2 by Campbell provides an introduction to speech synthesis and its evaluation, and to some of the attempts made over the years to produce and evaluate synthetic speech. There are three main stages in generating speech corresponding to three main components, i.e., language processing, prosody processing, and waveform generation. Approaches and challenges related to these three stages are described. Evaluation of speech synthesis is done both component-wise, as well as at entire speech synthesis system level, using subjective and objective measures. Evaluation of the language processing component mainly concerns the correctness of mapping between text and evaluation. Prosody is often evaluated using the Mean Opinion Score on a team of at least 30 listeners to obtain statistically significant results. The Mean Opinion Score can also be used to evaluate the waveform component.

Intelligibility has been the primary measure used to evaluate synthetic speech at the overall level. However, since synthetic speech nowadays normally is intelligible, naturalness and likeability have moved into focus instead. However, despite progress over the years, synthetic voices are still not like human voices. Control of paralinguistic information is a next challenge, i.e., control of non-verbal elements of communication, which humans use to modify meaning and convey emotion.

The chapter furthermore addresses concerted evaluation events and organisations involved in or related to speech synthesis evaluation. At the end of the chapter an extensive literature list is included, which the interested reader may benefit from when looking for further references within the area of speech synthesis.

Chapter 3 by Granström and House combines spoken output with an animated head. Focus is on the use of talking heads in spoken dialogue applications and on the communicative function of the head. Inclusion of an animated face in a dialogue system affects the way in which users interact with the system. However, metrics for evaluating talking head technology are not yet well-established. In particular the need for a further exploration of the coherence between audio and visual parameters is stressed.

The chapter briefly explains face models and speech synthesis used at KTH and data collection aimed at a data-driven approach to talking heads. The rest of the chapter then describes various approaches to evaluation and a number of evaluation studies.

Speech intelligibility is important and studies show that it can be increased by adding an animated face. Not only lip movements play a role in a virtual face, but also eyebrow and head movements contribute to communication. Evaluation of these visual cues for prominence is described based on studies of their relation and individual importance.

Visual cues together with prosody seem to affect what users judge to be positive or negative feedback, respectively. A study is presented, which was used to evaluate the influence of these parameters on the users' perception of the feedback. A further study is reported in which the influence of visual cues and auditory cues on the perception of whether an utterance is a question or a statement was evaluated. Evaluation of emotion expressions of the animated face is also addressed together with prosody.

Finally, the chapter describes evaluation studies made with animated heads from two implemented dialogue systems. Evaluation among other things concerned socialising utterances, prosodic characteristics, and facial gestures for turntaking and feedback.

Chapter 4 by Paroubek deals with evaluation of part-of-speech (POS) taggers and natural language parsers both of which form part of natural language processing.

POS tagging is the process of annotating each word in the input text with its morpho-syntactic class based on lexical and contextual information. POS tagging is normally fully automated since tagging algorithms achieve nearly the same quality as human taggers do and perform the task much faster. Accuracy is the most frequently used performance measure for POS taggers. If taggers are allowed to propose partially disambiguated taggings, average tagging perplexity may be used as an appropriate measure. Also precision and recall are used for POS tagger evaluation and so is a combination of the two called the f-measure. Several other measures are also discussed, such as average ambiguity and kappa. There are further parameters, including processing speed, portability, and multilingualism that may be of interest in an evaluation, depending on its purpose.

Parsing is a much more complex task than POS tagging. Parsing may be deep or shallow, i.e., partial. For many tasks shallow parsing is entirely sufficient and may also be more robust than deep parsing. Common approaches to parsing are briefly presented. An overview of how evaluation of parsers has been approached is given together with a description of measures that have been used and possible problems related to them. Examples of performance measures mentioned are percentage of correct sentences and recall. Evaluation campaigns may be used with benefit to comparatively evaluate a number of parsers on the same test suites.

System Evaluation.   The following three chapters deal with evaluation at system level, including software evaluation standardisation with several linguistic examples, e.g., from machine translation (Chapter 5), information retrieval systems, and question answering systems (Chapter 6), and spoken dialogue systems (Chapter 7).

Chapter 5 by King presents general principles of user-oriented evaluation based on work done in the EAGLES and ISLE projects and on ISO standards, in particular ISO/IEC 9126 on software evaluation. Focus is not on individual metrics but rather on what needs to be considered or done before it makes sense to decide on particular metrics. A number of examples are given from the broad area of natural language software, e.g., machine translation.

Software quality must be evaluated in terms of whether the users' needs are satisfied. Therefore the users' needs must first be identified and evaluation criteria must be formulated that reflect their needs. User needs may differ widely depending on the task they need to carry out. Furthermore, the kind of evaluation to choose depends on the purpose of the evaluation. The kinds of evaluation mentioned include diagnostic evaluation, comparative evaluation, progress evaluation, and adequacy evaluation.

It may seem that every evaluation task is one of a kind. However, at a more abstract level there are characteristics, which are pertinent across evaluations of software quality. The six software quality characteristics from ISO/IEC 9126-1 are presented. They include functionality, reliability, usability, efficiency, maintainability, and portability. Each of these is further broken down into sub-characteristics, a few of which are explained in more detail. Software quality, as expressed via these (sub-)characteristics, influences quality in use, which in ISO/IEC 9126-1 is expressed in terms of effectiveness, productivity, safety, and satisfaction.

The ISO quality model may be specialised to take into account the particular software to be evaluated and made more concrete by relating it to the needs of the users. This is done by adding further levels of sub-characteristics. Not all sub-characteristics are equally important. The importance depends on the users and the task. Low importance may be reflected in a low user rating still being defined as satisfactory. The terminal nodes of the quality model must have metrics associated.

Chapter 6 by Teufel addresses evaluation of information retrieval (IR) and question answering (QA) in the context of the large-scale annual evaluation conference series TREC (Text REtrieval Conference), where many systems are evaluated on the same test collections. An IR system returns one or more entire documents considered relevant for the query. Perceived relevance is a problem here because it is subjective. A QA system is supposed to output a short piece of text in reply to a question. QA is a fairly new activity as opposed to IR and more difficult in the sense that a more thorough understanding of the query is needed. Nevertheless the best QA systems get close to the possible maximum score, which is far from the case for IR systems. In both cases evaluation is expensive due to the human effort involved.

On the IR side the chapter focuses on ad hoc document retrieval where queries are not refined. A fixed document collection is also assumed. Evaluation of IR systems is typically a performance evaluation, which involves a set of documents, a set of human generated queries, and a gold standard for what is relevant as decided on by a human judge. Real users are not involved. The primary metrics used are precision and recall, while accuracy is not a good measure. Recall poses a problem because it is basically impossible to go through perhaps a million documents to check that no relevant ones have been omitted. The pooling method may, however, be used to solve this problem.

Different question types are distinguished and included in TREC QA, e.g., factoid questions and list questions, whereas opinion questions are not included. All questions do not necessarily have an answer. There is no gold standard. Instead each answer is judged independently by two human assessors. Main metrics have changed over time from mean reciprocal rank over weighted confidence to average accuracy.

Chapter 7 by Bernsen, Dybkjær, and Minker concerns the evaluation of spoken dialogue systems. It first provides a general overview of evaluation methods and criteria and then describes evaluation approaches for two specific (multimodal) spoken dialogue systems in detail. The two systems addressed are the non-task-oriented Hans Christian Andersen (HCA) system and the in-car SENECA system, both developed in European projects.

Both systems are prototypes and they are described along the same lines, i.e., a brief system overview is provided followed by a description of the evaluation of the prototype, including test set-up, evaluation method, test users, and evaluation criteria.

For the HCA system technical, as well as usability evaluation criteria are mentioned. The technical criteria encompass criteria meant to evaluate more general system issues, e.g., real time performance and robustness, as well as criteria, which relate to specific components. The components addressed include speech recognition, gesture recognition, natural language understanding, gesture interpretation, input fusion, character module, response generation, graphical rendering, and text-to-speech each of which have specific criteria assigned, such as lexical coverage for natural language understanding and intelligibility for text-to-speech.

Most of the usability evaluation criteria address (parts of) the entire system rather than a single component. For the HCA system examples include speech understanding adequacy, frequency of interaction problems, naturalness of user speech and gesture, entertainment value, and user satisfaction.

For the SENECA system no technical evaluation criteria are mentioned. Examples of usability evaluation criteria are glance analysis, driving performance, and user satisfaction.

Data Resources and Evaluation.   The two last chapters address language resources and evaluation in terms of an overview of data resources and their creation (Chapter 8) and standardisation efforts regarding annotation of language resources (Chapter 9), respectively.

Chapter 8 by Cieri gives an overview of language resources. Data is known to be a crucial driving factor for the development and evaluation of text and speech systems and the current trend is that there is an increasing demand for ever more sophisticated, diverse, and large-scale data resources – a demand, which the data providers still fail to keep pace with. The data providers include researchers and research groups, as well as data centres. The most well-known data centres are probably the Linguistic Data Consortium (LDC) in the USA and the European Language Resources Association (ELRA) in Europe. These data centres create data but also distribute data created by others, e.g., by evaluation programmes and projects. A wide variety of resources are available via these centres, including data developed in support of speech recognition, speech synthesis, language and acoustic modelling, information retrieval, information extraction, summarisation, natural language processing, machine translation, speech to speech translation, and dialogue systems.

Data is used for development, training, and evaluation. If one can find and get access to available resources, this is normally cheaper than creating them from scratch. However, the suitability of the data must often be traded off against the cost of developing new data.

Data resources are costly to develop and several steps are involved. There is already a substantial effort in just collecting them and subsequently they are often annotated in various ways, which again requires a human effort. The challenges involved in collecting data differ depending on their type. Challenges in the collection of broadcast, telephone, and meeting data are discussed. These include, e.g., variable environments, multimodality, and overlapping speech. Subject recruitment is also discussed.

Several layers of annotation may be added to the collected raw data. Annotation may or may not require expert annotators but in many cases some level of expertise is necessary. Data quality is important and annotations must therefore be evaluated. Precision, recall, discrepancy, and structure are the parameters used to evaluate annotation quality.

Chapter 9 by Ide and Romary also addresses language resources but from the perspective of standardisation of their representation and annotation. The ISO TC37/SC4 committee on language resources management has been established with this kind of standardisation in mind. The goal is to achieve an internationally accepted standard that will enable a much more flexible use, reuse, comparison, and evaluation of language resources than is the case today.

The chapter provides an overview of earlier, as well as ongoing projects that have dealt with various aspects of language resource standardisation, such as TEI, MATE, EAGLES, ISLE, XML, and RDF/OWL. The ISO group is building on such previous and contemporary work. The idea is to allow people to continue to still use their preferred annotation representation format and structure to the extent that it can be mapped to an abstract data model using a rigid dump format. To this end the Linguistic Annotation Framework (LAF) has been established to provide a standard infrastructure for the representation of language resources and their annotation. The underlying abstract data model builds on a clear separation of structure and contents.

On the contents side ongoing work is presented on creating a Data Category Registry, which describes various data categories, such as gender and its values. Again the idea is that users may continue with their own categories, which it should then be possible to convert to the standard categories. New standard categories may be added if needed. The idea is not to impose any specific set of categories but rather to ensure well-defined semantic categories.

An illustrative example is provided to explain how the presented standardisation work may enable a person to reuse annotations from two other persons who used two different coding schemes.

Much work still remains to be done on standardisation of language resources. However, the American National Corpus project has chosen the LAF dump format for annotation representation, which may be seen as a step in the right direction.

Chapter 1

SPEECH AND SPEAKER RECOGNITION EVALUATION

Sadaoki Furui

Department of Computer Science, Tokyo Institute of Technology
Tokyo, Japan

furui@cs.titech.ac.jp

Abstract   This chapter overviews techniques for evaluating speech and speaker recognition systems. The chapter first describes principles of recognition methods, and specifies types of systems as well as their applications. The evaluation methods can be classified into subjective and objective methods, among which the chapter focuses on the latter methods. In order to compare/normalize performances of different speech recognition systems, test set perplexity is introduced as a measure of the difficulty of each task. Objective evaluation methods of spoken dialogue and transcription systems are respectively described. Speaker recognition can be classified into speaker identification and verification, and most of the application systems fall into the speaker verification category. Since variation of speech features over time is a serious problem in speaker recognition, normalization and adaptation techniques are also described. Speaker verification performance is typically measured by equal error rate, detection error trade-off (DET) curves, and a weighted cost value. The chapter concludes by summarizing various issues for future research.

Keywords   Speech recognition; Speaker recognition; Objective evaluation; Subjective evaluation; Perplexity; Accuracy; Correctness; Equal error rate; DET curve.

1   Introduction

Given the complexity of the human–computer interface, it is clear that evaluation protocols are required which address a large number of different types of spoken language systems, including speech recognition and speaker recognition components. The majority of research in the area of spoken language system evaluation has concentrated on evaluating system components, such as measuring the word recognition accuracy for a speech recognizer, rather than overall effectiveness measures for complete systems.

1

L. Dybkjær et al. (eds.), Evaluation of Text and Speech Systems, 1–27.

In the United States, a very efficient evaluation paradigm has been funded by the Defense Advanced Research Projects Agency (DARPA) which includes an efficient production line of "hub and spoke"-style experiments involving the coordination of design, production and verification of data, distribution through Linguistic Data Consortium (LDC), and design, administration and analysis of testing by National Institute of Standards and Technology (NIST). These organizations have strongly advocated the importance of establishing appropriate "benchmarks", either through the implementation of standard tests, or by reference to human performance or to reference algorithms.

In order to give the reader information on how to evaluate the performance of spoken language systems, this chapter first specifies the types of systems and their applications, since this is important for understanding and using the evaluation methods. The chapter next introduces various performance measures, followed by discussions of the parameters which affect the performance. The chapter then goes on to an evaluation framework which includes high-level metrics such as correction and transaction success.

To obtain a detailed description of various evaluation techniques for spoken language systems, readers are suggested to refer to the handbook by (Gibbon et al., 1998).

2.   Principles of Speech Recognition

In the state-of-the-art approach, human speech production as well as the recognition process is modelled through four stages: text generation, speech production, acoustic processing, and linguistic decoding, as shown in Figure 1

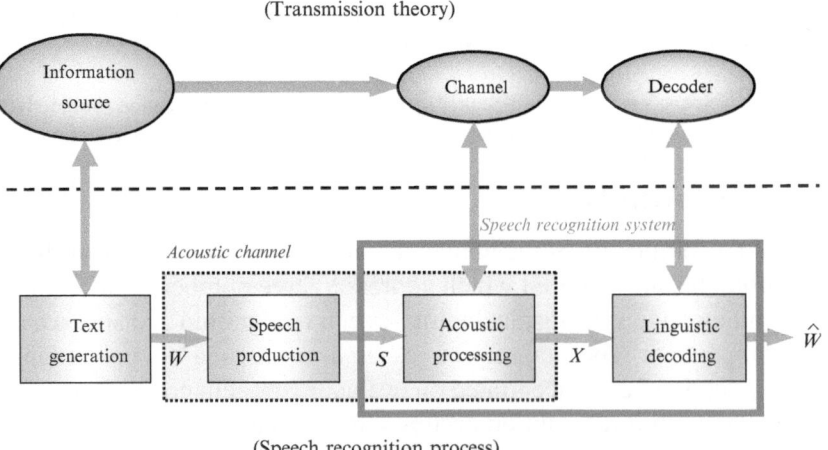

Figure 1.   Structure of the state-of-the-art speech recognition system.

(Furui, 2001). A speaker is represented as a transducer that transforms into speech the text of thoughts he/she intends to communicate (information source). Based on the information transmission theory, the sequence of processes is compared to an information transmission system, in which a word sequence W is converted into an acoustic observation sequence X, with a probability $P(W, X)$, through a noisy transmission channel, which is then decoded into an estimated sequence W. The goal of recognition is then to decode the word string, based on the acoustic observation sequence, so that the decoded string has the maximum a posteriori (MAP) probability (Rabiner and Juang, 1993; Young, 1996), i.e.,

$$\hat{W} = \arg \max_{W} P(W \,|\, X) \tag{1.1}$$

Using Bayes' rule, Eq. 1.1 can be written as

$$\hat{W} = \arg \max_{W} P(X \,|\, W) P(W) / P(X) \tag{1.2}$$

Since $P(X)$ is independent of W, the MAP decoding rule of Eq. 1.2 is converted into

$$\hat{W} = \arg \max_{W} P(X \,|\, W) P(W) \tag{1.3}$$

The first term in Eq. 1.3, $P(X|W)$, is generally called the acoustic model as it estimates the probability of a sequence of acoustic observations conditioned with the word string. The second term, $P(W)$, is generally called the language model since it describes the probability associated with a postulated sequence of words. Such language models can incorporate both syntactic and semantic constraints of the language and the recognition task. Often, when only syntactic constraints are used, the language model is called a grammar.

Hidden Markov Models (HMMs) and statistical language models are typically used as acoustic and language models, respectively. Figure 2 shows the information flow of the MAP decoding process given the parameterized acoustic signal X. The likelihood of the acoustic signal $P(X|W)$ is computed using a composite HMM representing W constructed from simple HMM phoneme models joined in sequence according to word pronunciations stored in a dictionary (lexicon).

3 Categories of Speech Recognition Tasks

Speech recognition tasks can be classified into four categories, as shown in Table 1, according to two criteria: whether it is targeting utterances from human to human or human to computer, and whether the utterances have a dialogue or monologue style (Furui, 2003). Table 1 lists typical tasks and data corpora that are representative for each category.

The Category I targets human-to-human dialogues, which are represented by the DARPA-sponsored recognition tasks using Switchboard and Call Home

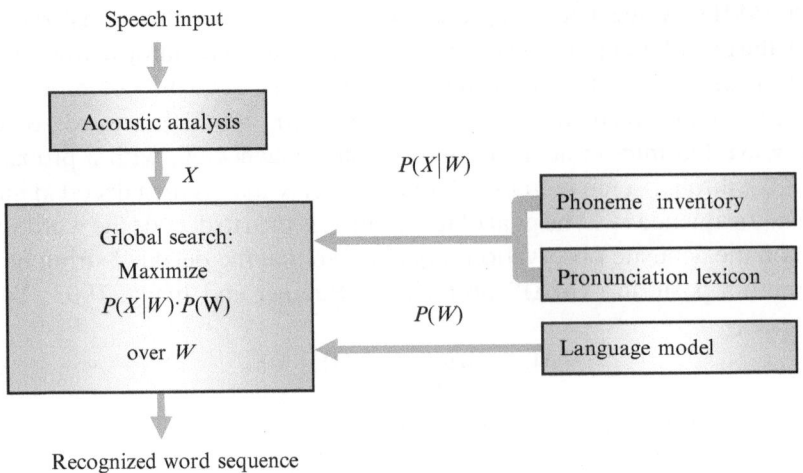

Figure 2.   Overview of statistical speech recognition.

Table 1. Categorization of speech recognition tasks.

	Dialogue	Monologue
Human to human	(Category I) Switchboard, Call Home (Hub5), meeting, interview	(Category II) Broadcast news (Hub 4), other programmes, lecture, presentation, voice mail
Human to machine	(Category III) ATIS, Communicator, information retrieval, reservation	(Category IV) Dictation

(Hub 5) corpora. Speech recognition research in this category aiming to produce minutes of meetings (e.g., Janin et al., 2004) has recently started. Waibel and Rogina (2003) have been developing a meeting browser that observes and tracks meetings for later review and summarization. Akita et al. (2003) have investigated techniques for archiving discussions. In their method, speakers are automatically indexed in an unsupervised way, and speech recognition is performed using the results of the indexing. Processing human–human conversational speech under unpredictable recording conditions and vocabularies presents new challenges for spoken language processing.

A relatively new task classified into this category is the Multilingual Access to Large spoken ArCHives (MALACH) project (Oard, 2004). Its goal is to advance the state-of-the-art technology for access to large multilingual collections of spontaneous conversational speech by exploiting an unmatched collection assembled by the Survivors of the Shoah Visual History Foundation (VHF). This collection presents a formidable challenge because of heavily accented, emotional, and old-age characteristics of the survivor's spontaneous speech. Named entity tagging, topic segmentation, and unsupervised topic classification are also being investigated.

Tasks belonging to Category II, which targets recognizing human–human monologues, are represented by transcription of broadcast news (Hub 4), news programmes, lectures, presentations, and voice mails (e.g., Hirschberg et al., 2001). Speech recognition research in this category has recently become very active. Since utterances in Category II are made with the expectation that the audience can correctly understand what he/she speaks in the one-way communication, they are relatively easier as a target of speech to recognize than utterances in the Category I. If a high recognition performance can be achieved for the utterances in Category II, a wide range of applications, such as making lecture notes, records of presentations and closed captions, archiving and retrieving these records, and retrieving voice mails, will be realized.

Most of the practical application systems widely used now are classified into Category III, recognizing utterances in human–computer dialogues, such as in airline information services tasks. DARPA-sponsored projects including ATIS and Communicator have laid the foundations of these systems. Unlike other categories, the systems in Category III are usually designed and developed after clearly defining the application/task. The machines that have been designed so far are, almost without exception, limited to the simple task of converting a speech signal into a word sequence and then determining from the word sequence a meaning that is "understandable". Here, the set of understandable messages is finite in number, each being associated with a particular action (e.g., route a call to a proper destination or issue a buy order for a particular stock). In this limited sense of speech communication, the focus is detection and recognition rather than inference and generation.

Various researches have made clear that utterances spoken by people talking to computers, such as those in Categories III and IV, especially when the people are conscious of computers, are acoustically, as well as linguistically, very different from utterances directed towards people, such as those in Categories I and II. One of the typical tasks belonging to Category IV, which targets the recognition of monologues performed when people are talking to computers, is dictation, and various commercial softwares for such purposes have been developed. Since the utterances in Category IV are made with the expectation that the utterances will be converted exactly into texts with correct characters, their spontaneity is much lower than those in Category III. Among the four categories, spontaneity is considered to be the highest in Category I and the lowest in Category IV.

Speech recognition tasks can also be classified according to whether it is isolated word recognition or continuous speech recognition and whether it is speaker-dependent or speaker-independent recognition. For isolated words, the beginning and the end of each word can be detected directly from the energy of the signal. This makes word boundary detection (segmentation) and recognition much easier than if the words are connected. However, in real applications where speech is contaminated by noise, it is not always easy to detect word boundaries by simply relying on the energy of the signal. Speaker-independent recognition is more difficult than speaker-dependent recognition, since the speech model must somehow be general enough to cover all types of voices and all possible ways of word pronunciations, and yet specific enough to discriminate between individual words. For a speaker-dependent system, training or adaptation of speech models is carried out by using utterances of each speaker. In speaker adaptation, the system is bootstrapped with speaker-independent models, and then gradually adapts to the specific aspects of the speaker.

4   Evaluation of Speech Recognition Systems

4.1   Classification of Evaluation Methods

Techniques for evaluating speech recognition methods/systems can be categorized depending on whether they use subjective or objective methods. The former directly involve human subjects during measurement, whereas the latter, typically using prerecorded speech, do not directly involve human subjects. Objective methods have the advantage of producing reproducible results and of lending themselves to being automated; thus, they are also more economical. The problem with objective methods for speech recognition application evaluation is that it is difficult to create methods with the capacity to cope easily with the complex processes required for evaluating speech understanding or interaction systems. On the other hand, subjective methods are more suited to evaluating applications with higher semantic or dialogue content, but they suffer from the fact that human subjects cannot reliably perform quality measurement and that they cannot handle fine-grained measurement scales, either. On average, a human subject uses gradation scales with 5–10 levels and no more.

In order to compare performances of different speech recognition systems, it is necessary to normalize the difficulty of the task of each system. For this purpose, the following task difficulty evaluation methods are used.

4.2   Evaluation of Task Difficulty

In order to reduce the effective number of words to select from, recognition systems are often equipped with some linguistic knowledge. This may vary from very strict syntax rules, in which the words that may follow one another are defined by certain rules, to probabilistic language models, in which the probability of the output sentence is taken into consideration, based on statistical knowledge of the language. An objective measure of the freedom of the language model is *perplexity*, which measures the average branching factor of the language model (Ney et al., 1997). The higher the perplexity, the more words to choose from at each instant, and hence the more difficult the task.

The perplexity is defined by

$$PP = 2^{H(L)} \tag{1.4}$$

where $H(L)$ is the *entropy* of the language model per word, which is defined by

$$H(L) = - \sum_{w_1 \ldots w_n} \frac{1}{n} P(w_1 \ldots w_n) \log P(w_1 \ldots w_n) \tag{1.5}$$

Here, $P(w_1 \ldots w_n)$ is the probability of producing a word sequence $w_1 \ldots w_n$ given the language model L. $H(L)$ indicates the amount of information (bits) necessary to specify a word produced by the language model. The perplexity defined above is often called language model perplexity.

Performance of a speech recognition system depends not only on its task but also on texts of a test set, i.e., a set of utterances to be used for a recognition test. Therefore, in order to evaluate the difficulty of the test set, the perplexity is often calculated for the test set, which is called *test set perplexity* or *corpus perplexity*. If we assume that the Ergodic feature exists for language, the entropy per word can be calculated as follows:

$$H(L) = -\frac{1}{Q} \log P_M(w_1 \ldots w_Q) \tag{1.6}$$

where $P_M(w_1 \ldots w_Q)$ is the probability of producing the test set word sequence $w_1 \ldots w_Q$. Therefore, the test set perplexity can be calculated as follows:

$$PP = 2^{H(L)} = P_M(w_1 \ldots w_Q)^{-\frac{1}{Q}} \tag{1.7}$$

The above equations show that the test set perplexity is the geometric average of the reciprocal probability over all Q words. Apart from the constant factor $(-1/Q)$, the perplexity is identical to the average conditional probability or likelihood. Therefore, minimizing the perplexity is the same as maximizing the log-likelihood function. Since the test set for recognition experiments should be separate from the corpus that is used to construct the language model, the language model perplexity and the test set perplexity are usually different.

When a formal grammar, such as finite automaton and context-free grammar, is used as the language model, every partially parsed tree up to word w_i

is made, and the number of words that can follow the word w_i is calculated. The test set perplexity is obtained as a geometric mean of the number of possible following words at each word w_i, assuming that every word is selected with equal probability.

The set of all words the recognition system has been set up to be able to recognize is called *vocabulary* V_L. The vocabulary size is one of the measures indicating the task difficulty. The test vocabulary V_R is defined as the set of words appearing in the evaluation test. A word w is called out-of-vocabulary (OOV) if it is present in the test vocabulary but not in the recognizer's vocabulary. The *OOV rate* is defined as the ratio of the number of words in the test set which are not included in V_L to the total number of words in the test set. In general, the larger the test vocabulary size V_R and the larger the OOV rate, the more difficult the task is.

The perplexity requires a closed vocabulary. If OOV exists, the perplexity definition may become problematic because it then becomes infinitely large. Therefore, usually OOV class <UNK> (unknown word class) is defined and the language model of OOV is calculated by

$$p'\left(<UNK>|h\right) = \frac{p\left(<UNK>|h\right)}{V_R - V_L} \tag{1.8}$$

where h is the history. Since there are $(V_R - V_L)$ kinds of OOV words to be recognized that are not included in the language model vocabulary, the OOV probability is divided by $(V_R - V_L)$.

The perplexity changes according to the vocabulary size. In general, the perplexity decreases by decreasing the vocabulary size V_L, since the probability allocated to each word becomes larger. However, if the test vocabulary size V_R is fixed and the language model vocabulary size V_L is decreased, the linguistic constraint becomes lower, since the number of OOV in the test set increases. Therefore, the test set perplexity cannot be used for comparing the difficulty of the tasks if the OOV rates of the language models are different. In order to solve this problem, *adjusted perplexity* (APP) has been proposed (Ueberla, 1994). In APP, by using the language model of the OOV words defined above and defining V_R as union of V_L and all the words appearing in the test set, the perplexity is adjusted by the total number of OOV words, o, and the number of different OOV words, m, in the test set as follows:

$$\log APP = -\frac{1}{Q}\log P_M\left(w_1 \ldots w_Q\right) + o\log m \tag{1.9}$$

Although the perplexity and the OOV rate measure the test source's complexity from the recognizer's point of view, they refer to written (e.g., transcribed) forms of language only and completely disregard acoustic–phonetic modelling. Difficulty of the recognition task also depends on the length of the sentences (average number of words) and average number of phonemes of which each word consists. Therefore, task difficulty needs to be measured by a combination of various factors covering both linguistic and acoustic complexity.

4.3   Objective Evaluation of General Recognition Performance

Isolated word scoring.   The *error rate* of speech recognition is defined as "the average fraction of items incorrectly recognized". Here, an item can be a word, a subword unit (e.g., a phone), or an entire utterance. For an isolated word recognition system, the error rate is defined as:

$$E = \frac{N_E}{N} \qquad (1.10)$$

Here, N is the number of words in the test utterance and N_E the number of words incorrectly recognized. The latter can be subdivided into substitution error, N_S, and deletion (incorrect rejection) error, N_D:

$$N_E = N_S + N_D \qquad (1.11)$$

Sometimes the fraction of correctly recognized words, $C = 1 - E$, called *correctness*, is used:

$$C = \frac{N_C}{N} = \frac{N - N_S - N_D}{N} \qquad (1.12)$$

These measures do not include so-called insertions, since it is assumed that the beginning and the end of each word can be detected directly from the energy of the signal. However, in real applications where speech is contaminated by noise, it is not always easy to detect word boundaries, and sometimes noise signals cause insertion errors. Therefore, in these practical conditions, the same measure as that used in continuous word scoring, which will be described later, is also used in the isolated recognition task.

For isolated word recognizers, a more specific measure than the various contributions to the error rate, a *confusion matrix*, has also been used, in which the class of substitutions is divided into all possible confusions between words. The confusion C_{ij} is defined as the probability that word i is recognized as word j. The value C_{ii} is the fraction of times word i is correctly recognized. These probabilities are estimated by measuring the number of times the confusion took place:

$$C_{ij} = \frac{N_{ij}}{\sum_{j'} N_{ij'}} \qquad (1.13)$$

where N_{ij} is the number of times word j is recognized on the input word i. The confusion matrix gives more detailed information than the error rates. Insertions and deletions can also be included in the matrix by adding a null word $i = 0$ (non-vocabulary word). Then, the row C_{0j} contains insertions, the column C_{i0} the deletions, and $C_{00} = 0$. Using this expanded confusion matrix, the error rate can be calculated from the diagonal elements, i.e., $E = 1 - \Sigma_i C_{ii} = \Sigma_{i \neq j} C_{ij}$. The elements C_{ij} for $i \neq j$ are called the off-diagonal elements.

Continuous word scoring.   In continuous speech recognition, the output words are generally not time-synchronous with the input utterance. Therefore, the output stream has to be aligned with the reference transcriptions. This means that classifications such as substitutions, deletions, words correct and insertions can no longer be identified with complete certainty. The actual measurement of the quantities through alignment is difficult. The alignment process uses a dynamic programming algorithm to minimize the misalignment of two strings of words (symbols): the reference sentence and the recognized sentence. The alignment depends on the relative weights of the contributions of the three types of errors: substitutions, insertions, and deletions. Hunt (1990) discussed the theory of word–symbol alignment and analysed several experiments on alignment. Usually, the three types of errors have equal weights. Depending on the application, one can assign different weights to the various kinds of errors.

Thus, the total number of errors is the summation of three types of errors:

$$N_E = N_S + N_I + N_D \qquad (1.14)$$

where N_S, N_I, and N_D are the numbers of substitutions, insertions, and deletions, respectively. The error rate is therefore

$$E = \frac{N_E}{N} = \frac{N_S + N_I + N_D}{N} \qquad (1.15)$$

Note that this error measure can become larger than 1 in cases of extremely bad recognition. Often, one defines the *accuracy* of a system as

$$A = 1 - E = \frac{N - N_S - N_I - N_D}{N} \qquad (1.16)$$

Note that this is not just the fraction C of words correctly recognized, because the latter does not include insertions.

NIST has developed freely available software for analysis of continuous speech recognition systems. It basically consists of two parts: an alignment program and a statistics package. The alignment program generates a file with all alignment information, which can be printed by another utility in various levels of detail. The statistics program can pairwise compare the results of different recognition systems and decide whether or not the difference in performance is significant.

Other scoring. The objective scores other than accuracy include percentage of successful task completions, the time taken to complete the task, or the number of interactions necessary per task.

Speaker variability. The variety of speech recognition performances is highly dependent on the speaker. Apparently, speakers can be classified as "goats" (low recognition scores) and "sheep" (high recognition scores) (Furui, 2001). Since knowledge of this classification is usually not available a priori, it is necessary to use many speakers for evaluation. A sufficient number of speakers allows estimation of the variance in score due to speaker variability, and significance can be tested using Student's *t*-test.

4.4 Objective Evaluation of Spoken Dialogue Systems

Performance measures that can be used for evaluating spoken dialogue systems are:

1. Recognition accuracy.

2. OOV rejection: a good system correctly rejects OOV words and asks the users to rephrase, instead of wrongly recognizing them as vocabulary words. This is actually a very difficult issue, since there is no perfect confidence measure for the recognition results.

3. Error recovery: both the system and the user are sources of errors. A good system allows the user to undo actions triggered by previous spoken commands.

4. Response time: important for good usability is the time it takes to respond to a spoken command, i.e., system reaction time. This is defined as the time from the end of the command utterance to the start of the action. Both the average time and the distribution of the response time are important parameters.

5. Situation awareness: users who give commands to a system have certain expectations about what they can say. The active vocabulary usually depends on the internal state of the system but if users are not aware of that state, it is said that they have lost their situational awareness. This can be expressed as the number of times a test subject uttered a command in a context where it was not allowed. A subjective impression by the tester or the subject can also be used as a measure. Suitable questions for the users could be:

   - Is the list of possible commands always clear?
   - Are special skills required?
   - Is on-line help useful?

To learn details of the issues for evaluating telephone-based spoken dialogue systems, readers are recommended to refer to the textbook by Möller (2005).

4.5   Objective Evaluation of Dictation Systems

Various commercial systems (software) for dictation using automatic speech recognition have been developed. The performance measures that can be used for evaluating these systems are:

1. Recognition accuracy

2. Dictation speed: number of words per minute that can be received

3. Error correction strategies: a good measure for the ease of error correction is the average time spent per correction

Dictation systems can be compared to other systems and also to human performance. Error rate and dictation speed are the most obvious performance measures for the human benchmark.

4.6   Subjective Evaluation Methods

In subjective evaluation, the test is designed in such a way that human subjects interact with the system. Subjective measures include level of intelligibility, general impression, annoyance, user-friendliness, intuitiveness, level of difficulty, and the subjective impression of system response time. The ultimate overall measure is: "Can the task be completed?" This is a measure that includes recognition, error recovery, situational awareness, and feedback. In this sense, the time required to complete the entire test might also be indicative of the quality of the system. General impressions of test subjects can be indicative of how the system performs.

5   Principles of Speaker Recognition

A technology closely related to speech recognition is speaker recognition, or the automatic recognition of a speaker (talker) through measurements of individual characteristics existing in the speaker's voice signal (Furui, 1997, 2001; Rosenberg and Soong, 1991). The actual realization of speaker recognition systems makes use of voice as the key tool for verifying the identity of a speaker for application to an extensive array of customer-demand services. In the near future, these services will include banking transactions and shopping using the telephone network as well as the Internet, voicemail, information retrieval services including personal information accessing, reservation services, remote access of computers, and security control for protecting confidential areas of concern.

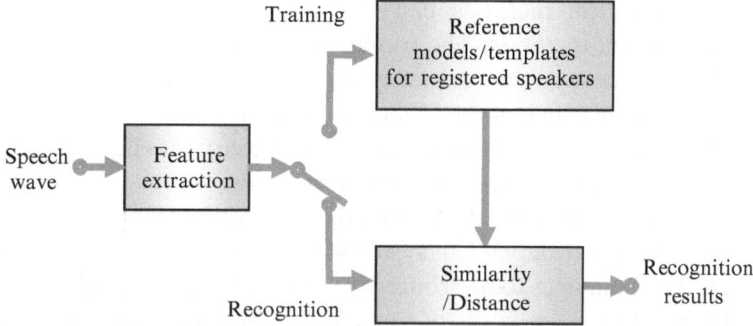

Figure 3. Principal structure of speaker recognition systems.

The common structure of speaker recognition systems is shown in Figure 3. Feature parameters extracted from a speech wave are compared with the stored templates or models for each registered speaker. The recognition decision is made according to the distance (or similarity) values. For speaker verification, input utterances with distances to the reference template/model smaller than the threshold are accepted as being utterances of the registered speaker (customer), while input utterances with distances larger than the threshold are rejected as being those of a different speaker (impostor). With speaker identification, the registered speaker whose reference template/model is nearest to the input utterance among all of the registered speakers is selected as the speaker of the input utterance.

6   Categories of Speaker Recognition Tasks

Speaker recognition can be principally divided into speaker verification and speaker identification. Speaker verification is the process of accepting or rejecting the identity claim of a speaker by comparing a set of measurements of the speaker's utterances with a reference set of measurements of the utterance of the person whose identity is being claimed. Speaker identification is the process of determining from which of the registered speakers a given utterance comes. The speaker identification process is similar to the spoken word recognition process in that both determine which reference model is closest to the input speech.

Speaker verification is applicable to various kinds of services using voice as the key input to confirming the identity claim of a speaker. Speaker identification is used in criminal investigations, for example, to determine which of the suspects produced a voice recorded at the scene of the crime. Since the possibility always exists that the actual criminal is not one of the suspects, however, the identification decision must be made through a combined process of speaker verification and speaker identification.

Speaker recognition methods can also be divided into text-dependent and text-independent methods. The former require the speaker to issue a predetermined utterance whereas the latter do not rely on a specific text being spoken. In general, because of the higher acoustic–phonetic variability of text-independent speech, more training material is necessary to reliably characterize (model) a speaker than with text-dependent methods.

Although several text-dependent methods use features of special phonemes, such as nasals, most text-dependent systems allow words (keywords, names, ID numbers, etc.) or sentences to be arbitrarily selected for each speaker. In the latter case, the differences in words or sentences between the speakers improves the accuracy of speaker recognition. When evaluating experimental systems, however, common keywords or sentences are usually used for every speaker.

Although keywords can be fixed for each speaker in many applications of speaker verification, utterances of the same words cannot always be compared in criminal investigations. In such cases, a text-independent method is essential. Difficulty in automatic speaker recognition varies depending on whether or not the speakers intend to have their identities verified. During actual speaker verification, speakers are usually expected to cooperate without intentionally changing their speaking rate or manner. It is well known, however, and expected that speakers are most often uncooperative in criminal investigations, consequently compounding the difficulty in correctly recognizing their voices.

Both text-dependent and text-independent methods have a serious weakness. These security systems can be circumvented, because someone can play back the recorded voice of a registered speaker uttering keywords or sentences into the microphone and be accepted as the registered speaker. Another problem is that people often do not like text-dependent systems because they do not like to utter their identification number, such as their social security number, within hearing distance of other people. To cope with these problems, some methods use a small set of words, such as digits as keywords, and each user is prompted to utter a given sequence of keywords which is randomly chosen every time the system is used (Rosenberg and Soong, 1987; Higgins et al., 1991). Yet even this method is not reliable enough, since it can be circumvented with advanced electronic recording equipment that can reproduce keywords in a requested order. Therefore, a text-prompted speaker recognition method has been proposed in which password sentences are completely changed every time (Matsui and Furui, 1993). The system accepts the input utterance only when it determines that the registered speaker uttered the prompted sentence. Because the vocabulary is unlimited, prospective impostors cannot know in advance the sentence they will be prompted to say. This method not only accurately recognizes speakers, but can also reject an utterance whose text differs from the prompted text, even if it is uttered by a registered speaker. Thus, the playback of a recorded voice can be correctly rejected.

7 Normalization and Adaptation Techniques

How can we normalize intraspeaker variation of likelihood (similarity) values in speaker verification? The most significant factor affecting automatic speaker recognition performance is variation in signal characteristics from trial to trial (intersession variability or variability over time). Variations arise from the speakers themselves, from differences in recording and transmission conditions, and from noise. Speakers cannot repeat an utterance in precisely the same way from trial to trial. It is well known that samples of the same utterance recorded in one session are much more correlated than tokens recorded in separate sessions. There are also long-term trends in voices with variation over several months and years (Furui et al., 1972; Furui, 1974).

It is important for speaker recognition systems to accommodate these variations. Adaptation of the reference model as well as the verification threshold for each speaker is indispensable to maintain a high recognition accuracy for a long period. In order to compensate for the variations, two types of normalization techniques have been tried: one in the parameter domain, and the other in the distance/similarity domain. The latter technique uses the likelihood ratio or a posteriori probability. To adapt HMMs for noisy conditions, various techniques, including the HMM composition (or parallel model combination: PMC) method (Gales and Young, 1993), have proved successful.

7.1 Parameter-Domain Normalization

As one typical normalization technique in the parameter domain, spectral equalization, the "blind equalization" method, has been confirmed to be effective in reducing linear channel effects and long-term spectral variation (Atal, 1974; Furui, 1981). This method is especially effective for text-dependent speaker recognition applications using sufficiently long utterances. In this method, cepstral coefficients are averaged over the duration of an entire utterance, and the averaged values are subtracted from the cepstral coefficients of each frame (cepstral mean subtraction: CMS). This method can compensate fairly well for additive variation in the log spectral domain. However, it unavoidably removes some text-dependent and speaker-specific features, so it is inappropriate for short utterances in speaker recognition applications. Time derivatives of cepstral coefficients (delta-cepstral coefficients) have been shown to be resistant to linear channel mismatches between training and testing (Furui, 1981; Soong and Rosenberg, 1988).

7.2 Likelihood Normalization

Higgins et al. (1991) proposed a normalization method for distance (similarity or likelihood) values that uses a likelihood ratio. The likelihood ratio is the ratio of the conditional probability of the observed measurements of the utterance, given the claimed identity is correct, to the conditional probability of the observed measurements, given the speaker is an impostor (normalization term). Generally, a positive log-likelihood ratio indicates a valid claim, whereas a negative value indicates an impostor. The likelihood ratio normalization approximates optimal scoring in Bayes' sense.

This normalization method is, however, unrealistic because conditional probabilities must be calculated for all the reference speakers, which requires large computational cost. Therefore, a set of speakers, "cohort speakers", who are representative of the population distribution near the claimed speaker, was chosen for calculating the normalization term (Rosenberg et al., 1992). Another approximation of using all the reference speakers is to use speakers who are typical of the general population. Reynolds (1994) reported that a randomly selected, gender-balanced background speaker population outperformed a population near the claimed speaker.

Matsui and Furui (1993, 1994) proposed a normalization method based on a posteriori probability. The difference between the normalization method based on the likelihood ratio and that based on *a posteriori* probability is whether or not the claimed speaker is included in the impostor speaker set for normalization. The cohort speaker set in the likelihood-ratio-based method does not include the claimed speaker, whereas the normalization term for the a posteriori probability-based method is calculated by using a set of speakers including the claimed speaker. Experimental results indicate that both normalization methods almost equally improve speaker separability and reduce the need for speaker-dependent or text-dependent thresholding, compared with scoring using only the model of the claimed speaker.

Carey and Paris (1992) proposed a method in which the normalization term is approximated by the likelihood for a "world model" representing the population in general. This method has the advantage that the computational cost for calculating the normalization term is much smaller than in the original method since it does not need to sum the likelihood values for cohort speakers. Matsui and Furui (1994) proposed a method based on tied-mixture HMMs in which the world model is made as a pooled mixture model representing the parameter distribution for all the registered speakers. The use of a single background model for calculating the normalization term has become the predominate approach used in speaker verification systems.

Since these normalization methods neglect absolute deviation between the claimed speaker's model and the input speech, they cannot differentiate highly dissimilar speakers. Higgins et al. (1991) reported that a multilayer network decision algorithm can make effective use of the relative and absolute scores obtained from the matching algorithm.

A family of normalization techniques has recently been proposed, in which the scores are normalized by subtracting the mean and then dividing by standard deviation, both terms having been estimated from the (pseudo) impostor score distribution. Different possibilities are available for computing the impostor score distribution: Znorm, Hnorm, Tnorm, Htnorm, Cnorm, and Dnorm (Bimbot et al., 2004). The state-of-the-art text-independent speaker verification techniques combine one or several parameterization level normalizations (CMS, feature variance normalization, feature warping, etc.) with a world model normalization and one or several score normalizations.

8 Evaluation of Speaker Recognition Systems

8.1 Evaluation of Speaker Verification Systems

The receiver operating characteristic (ROC) curve adopted from psychophysics is used for evaluating speaker verification systems. In speaker verification, two conditions are considered for the input utterances: s, the condition that the utterance belongs to the customer, and n, the opposite condition. Two decision conditions also exist: S, the condition that the utterance is accepted as being that of the customer, and N, the condition that the utterance is rejected.

These conditions combine to make up the four conditional probabilities as shown in Table 2. Specifically, $P(S|s)$ is the probability of correct acceptance; $P(S|n)$ the probability of false acceptance (FA), namely, the probabilities of accepting impostors; $P(N|s)$ the probability of false rejection (FR), or the probability of mistakenly rejecting the real customer; and $P(N|n)$ the probability of correct rejection.

Since the relationships

$$P\left(S\left|s\right.\right) + P\left(N\left|s\right.\right) = 1 \tag{1.17}$$

and

$$P\left(S\left|n\right.\right) + P\left(N\left|n\right.\right) = 1 \tag{1.18}$$

exist for the four probabilities, speaker verification systems can be evaluated using the two probabilities $P(S|s)$ and $P(S|n)$. If these two values are assigned to the vertical and horizontal axes respectively, and if the decision criterion (threshold) of accepting the speech as being that of the customer is varied, ROC curves as indicated in Figure 4 are obtained. This figure exemplifies the curves for three systems: A, B, and C. Clearly, the performance

Table 2. Four conditional probabilities in speaker verification.

Decision condition	Input utterance condition	
	$s(customer)$	$n(impostor)$
$S(accept)$	$P(S|s)$	$P(S|n)$
$N(reject)$	$P(N|s)$	$P(N|n)$

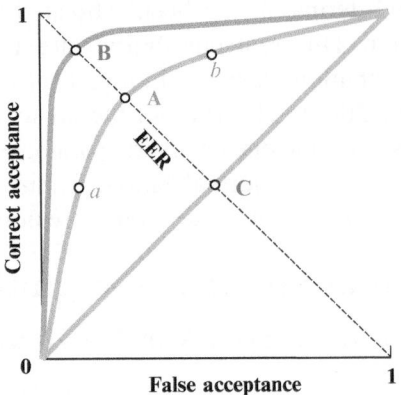

Figure 4. Receiver operating characteristic (ROC) curves; performance examples of three speaker verification systems: A, B, and C.

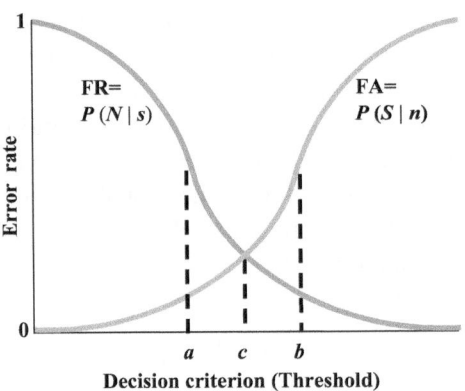

Figure 5. Relationship between error rate and decision criterion (threshold) in speaker verification.

of curve B is consistently superior to that of curve A; and C corresponds to the limiting case of purely chance performance. On the other hand, the relationship between the decision criterion and the two kinds of errors is presented in Figure 5. A "tight" decision criterion makes it difficult for impostors to be falsely accepted by the system. However, it increases the possibility of rejecting customers. Conversely, a "loose" criterion enables customers to be consistently accepted, while also falsely accepting impostors. Position a in Figures 4 and 5 corresponds to the case in which a strict decision criterion is employed, and position b corresponds to that wherein a lax criterion is used. To set the threshold at the desired level of FR and FA, it is necessary to know the distribution of customer and impostor scores as baseline information. The decision criterion in practical applications should be determined according to the consequences or risk of decision errors. This criterion can be determined based on a priori probabilities of a match, $P(s)$, on the cost values of the various decision results, and on the slope of the ROC curve. If the FR rate is specified, the corresponding FA rate is obtained as the intersection of the ROC curve with the vertical line indicating the FR rate. In experimental tests, equal error rate (EER), is a commonly accepted summary of system performance. It corresponds to a threshold at which the FR rate is equal to the FA rate as indicated by c in Figure 5. The criterion is usually set a posteriori for each individual speaker or for a set of test speakers. The EER point corresponds to the intersection of the ROC curve with the straight line of 45 degrees, indicated in Figure 4. Although the EER performance measure rarely corresponds to a realistic operating point, it is quite a popular measure of the ability of a system to separate impostors from customers. Another popular measure is the half total error rate (HTER), which is the average of the two error rates FR and FA. It can also be seen as the normalized cost function assuming equal costs for both errors.

It has recently become standard to plot the error curve on a normal deviate scale (Martin et al., 1997), in which case the curve is known as the detection error trade-offs (DETs) curve. With the normal deviate scale, a speaker verification system whose customer and impostor scores are normally distributed, regardless of variance, will result in a linear scale with a slope equal to -1. The better the system is, the closer to the origin the curve will be. In practice, the score distributions are not exactly Gaussian but are quite close to it. The DET curve representation is therefore more easily readable and allows for a comparison of the system's performances over a large range of operating conditions. Figure 6 shows a typical example of DET curves. EER corresponds to the intersection of the DET curve with the first bisector curve.

In NIST speaker recognition evaluations, a cost function defined as a weighted sum of the two types of errors has been chosen as the basic performance measure (Przybocki and Martin, 2002). This cost, referred to as the C_{DET} cost, is defined as:

$$C_{DET} = (C_{FR} \times P_{FR} \times P_C) + (C_{FA} \times P_{FA} \times (1 - P_C)) \qquad (1.19)$$

where P_{FR} and P_{FA} are FR and FA rates, respectively. The required parameters in this function are the cost of FR (C_{FR}), the cost of FA (C_{FA}), and the a priori probability of a customer (P_C).

8.2 Relationship between Error Rate and Number of Speakers

Let us assume that Z_N represents a population of N registered speakers, $X = (x_1, x_2, ..., x_n)$ is an n-dimensional feature vector representing the speech sample, and $P_i(X)$ is the probability density function of X for speaker

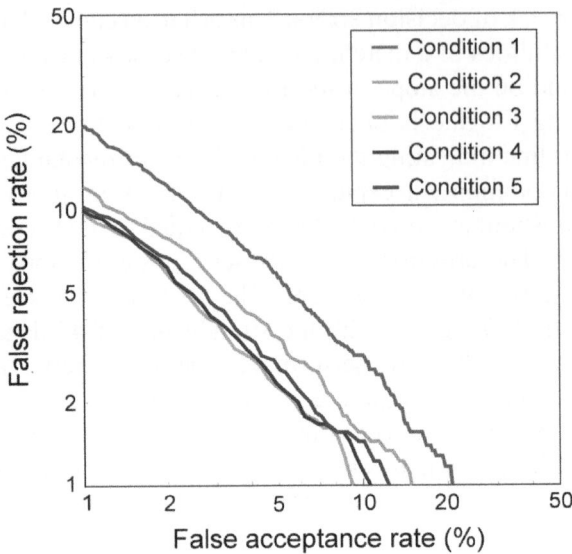

Figure 6. Examples of the DET curve.

i $(i \in Z_N)$. The chance probability density function of X within population Z_N can then be expressed as

$$P_Z(X) = \operatorname*{E}_{i \in Z_N} [P_i(X)]$$

(1.20)

$$= \sum_i P_i(X) \, Pr[i], \quad i \in Z_N$$

where $Pr[i]$ is the a priori chance probability of speaker i and E indicates expectation (Doddington, 1974).

In the case of speaker verification, the region of X which should be accepted as the voice of customer i is

$$R_{Vi} = \{ X \, | P_i(X) > C_i P_Z(X) \}$$

(1.21)

where C_i is chosen to achieve the desired balance between FA and FR errors. With Z_N constructed using randomly selected speakers, and with the a priori probability independent of the speaker, $Pr[i] = 1/N$, $P_Z(X)$ will approach a limiting density function independent of Z_N as N becomes large. Thus, FR and FA ratios are relatively unaffected by the size of the population, N, when it is large. From a practical perspective, $P_Z(X)$ is assumed to be constant since it is generally difficult to estimate this value precisely, and

$$R_{Vi} = \{ X \, | P_i(X) > k_i \}$$

(1.22)

is simply used as the acceptance region.

With speaker identification, the region of X, which should be judged as the voice of speaker i, is

$$R_{Ii} = \{ X \mid P_i(X) \quad > \quad P_j(X), \ \forall j \neq i \} \qquad (1.23)$$

The probability of error for speaker i then becomes

$$P_{Ei} = 1 - \prod_{\substack{k=1 \\ k \neq i}}^{N} Pr\left(P_i(X) \quad > \quad P_k(X)\right) \qquad (1.24)$$

With Z_N constructed by randomly selected speakers, the equations

$$\underset{Z_N}{\mathrm{E}}\left[P_{Ei}\right] = 1 - \underset{Z_N}{\mathrm{E}} \left\{ \prod_{\substack{k=1 \\ k \neq i}}^{N} Pr\left(P_i(X) \quad > \quad P_k(X)\right) \right\}$$

$$= 1 - \underset{i}{\mathrm{E}} \left\{ \prod_{\substack{k=1 \\ k \neq i}}^{N} \mathrm{E}\left[Pr\left(P_i(X) \quad > \quad P_k(X)\right)\right] \right\} \qquad (1.25)$$

$$= -\underset{i}{\mathrm{E}} \left\{ P_{Ai}^{N-1} \right\}$$

can be obtained, where P_{Ai} is the expected probability of not confusing speaker i with another speaker. Thus, the expected probability of correctly identifying a speaker decreases exponentially with the size of the population.

This is a consequence of the fact that the parameter space is bounded. Therefore, when the population of speakers increases, the probability that the distributions of two or more speakers are very close increases. Consequently, the effectiveness of speaker identification systems must be evaluated according to their targeted population size.

8.3   Long-Term Variability of Speech

As described in the previous section, even if the same words or sentences are spoken by the same speaker, speech characteristics are always varying, and there are also long-term trends. Samples recorded together in one session are much more highly correlated than those recorded in separate sessions. Therefore, the number of training sessions for making speaker models or templates and the time interval between those sessions, as well as training and testing sessions, are important factors. Several training sessions over a long period of time help to cope with long-term variability of speech. It is crucial to leave a gap of at least several weeks between the last training session and the testing session to obtain meaningful results in evaluating speaker recognition systems.

8.4   Individual Variability

A desirable feature for a practical speaker recognition system is a reasonably uniform performance across a population of speakers. Unfortunately, it is typical to observe in speaker recognition experiments a substantial discrepancy between the best performing individuals, the "sheep", and the worst, the "goats". This problem has been widely observed, but there are virtually no studies focusing on the cause of this phenomenon. Speakers with no observable speech pathologies, and for whom apparently good reference models have been obtained, are often observed to be "goats". It is possible that such speakers exhibit large amounts of trial-to-trial variability, beyond the ability of the system to provide adequate compensation.

This means that large test sets are required to be able to measure error rates accurately. For clear methodological reasons, it is crucial that none of the test speakers, whether customers or impostors, be in the training and development sets. This excludes, in particular, using the same speakers for the background model and for the tests. It may be possible to use speakers referenced in the test database as impostors. However, this should be avoided whenever discriminative training techniques are used or if cross-speaker normalization is performed since, in this case, using referenced speakers as impostors would introduce a bias in the results.

9   Factors Affecting the Performance and Evaluation Paradigm Design for Speech and Speaker Recognition Systems

There are several factors affecting the performance of speech recognition and speaker recognition systems. First, several factors have an impact on the quality of the speech material recorded. Among others, these factors are the environmental conditions at the time of the recording (background noise etc.), the type of microphone used, and the transmission channel bandwidth and compression if any (high bandwidth speech, landline and cell phone speech, etc.). Second, factors concerning the speakers themselves (see Sections 4.3 and 8.4) and the amount of training data available affect performance. The speaker factors include physical and emotional states (under stress or ill), speaker cooperativeness, and familiarity with the system. Finally, the system performance measure depends strongly on the test set complexity. Ideally, all these factors should be taken into account when designing evaluation paradigms or when comparing the performance of two systems on different databases. The excellent performance obtained in artificially good conditions (quiet environment, high-quality microphone, and consecutive recordings of the training and test material) rapidly degrades in real-life applications. Therefore, it is important to make an inventory of the acoustic environment in which the system is typically used. It is also important to know that for high noise conditions, such as higher than 60 dB(A), the Lombard effect (Furui, 2001) may change the level and voice of a speaker. In comparative testing, only a common subset of capabilities should be compared quantitatively.

10 System-Level Evaluation of Speech and Speaker Recognition

There are two complementary approaches to evaluate speech and speaker recognition systems: evaluation of the system components, and system-level evaluation. Evaluation of the system components can be performed using the methods described in the previous sections. Depending on the goal of evaluation, there are three broad categories of system-level evaluation (Cole et al., 1995):

1. Adequacy evaluations: determining the fitness of a system for a purpose: does it meet the requirements, and if so, how well and at what cost? The requirements are mainly determined by user needs.

2. Diagnostic evaluations: obtaining a profile of system performance with respect to possible utilization of a system.

3. Performance evaluations: measuring system performance in specific areas. There are three basic components of a performance evaluation that need to be defined prior to evaluating a system.

   - Criterion: characteristics or quality to be evaluated (e.g., speed, error rate, accuracy, learning)

   - Measure: specific system property for the chosen criterion (e.g., word accuracy)

   - Method: how to determine the appropriate value for a given measure (e.g., counting the number of substitution, insertion, and deletion errors after alignment)

For evaluation of multimodal human–computer dialogue systems, readers are recommended to refer to Dybkjær et al. (2005) and Whittaker and Walker (2005). Readers are also recommended to refer to textbooks on general designing and assessment of human–computer interaction (e.g., Dix et al., 1998).

11   Conclusion

Technology development and evaluation are two sides of the same coin; without having a good measure of progress, we cannot make useful progress. However, since the human–computer interface using speech is very complex, it is not easy to establish evaluation strategies. Although various investigations on evaluation methods have been conducted and various measures have been proposed, a truly comprehensive tool has not yet been developed. Since the target of speech recognition is now shifting from clean read speech to natural spontaneous speech contaminated by noise and distortions, evaluation of system performance is becoming increasingly difficult. The target is also shifting from recognition to understanding. Evaluation of speech understanding systems is far more difficult than that of speech recognition systems. Speech summarization is one interesting research domain that has recently emerged (Furui et al., 2004), but it is very difficult to find a way to objectively measure the quality of automatic summarization results (Hirohata et al., 2005). Thus, continued efforts are required to advance evaluation strategies for speech and speaker recognition systems.

References

Akita, Y., Nishida, M., and Kawahara, T. (2003). Automatic Transcription of Discussions Using Unsupervised Speaker Indexing. In *Proceedings of the IEEE Workshop on Spontaneous Speech Processing and Recognition*, pages 79–82, Tokyo, Japan.

Atal, B. (1974). Effectiveness of Linear Prediction Characteristics of the Speech Wave for Automatic Speaker Identification and Verification. *Journal of the Acoustical Society of America*, 55(6):1304–1312.

Bimbot, F., Bonastre, F., Fredouille, C., Gravier, G., Magrin-Chagnolleau, I., Meignier, S., Merlin, T., Ortega-Garcia, J., Petrovska-Delacretaz, D., and Reynolds, D. (2004). A Tutorial on Text-Independent Speaker Verification. *EURASIP Journal on Applied Signal Processing*, 2004(4):430–451.

Carey, M. J. and Paris, E. S. (1992). Speaker Verification Using Connected Words. *Proceedings of Institute of Acoustics*, 14(6):95–100.

Cole, R., Mariani, J., Uszkoreit, H., Zaenen, A., and Zue, V., editors (1995). *Survey of the State of the Art in Human Language Technology*. Center for Spoken Language Understanding (CSLU), Oregon, USA.

Dix, A. J., Finlay, J. E., Abowd, G. D., and Beale, R. (1998). *Human-Computer Interaction*. Prentice Hall, London, UK, 2nd edition.

Doddington, G. (1974). Speaker Verification. Technical Report RADC 74–179, Rome Air Development Center.

Dybkjær, L., Bernsen, N. O., and Minker, W. (2005). Overview of Evaluation and Usability. In Minker, W., Bühler, D., and Dybkjær, L., editors,

Spoken Multimodal Human-Computer Dialogue in Mobile Environments, pages 221–246. Springer, Dordrecht, The Netherlands.

Furui, S. (1974). An Analysis of Long-Term Variation of Feature Parameters of Speech and its Application to Talker Recognition. *Transactions of IECE, 57-A*, 12:880–887.

Furui, S. (1981). Cepstral Analysis Technique for Automatic Speaker Verification. *IEEE Transactions on Acoustics, Speech, and Signal Processing*, 29(2):254–272.

Furui, S. (1997). Recent Advances in Speaker Recognition. In *Proceedings of the First International Conference on Audio- and Video-based Biometric Person Authentication*, pages 237–252, Crans-Montana, Switzerland.

Furui, S. (2001). *Digital Speech Processing, Synthesis, and Recognition*. Marcel Dekker, New York, USA, 2nd edition.

Furui, S. (2003). Toward Spontaneous Speech Recognition and Understanding. In Chou, W. and Juang, B.-H., editors, *Pattern Recognition in Speech and Language Processing*, pages 191–227. CRC Press, New York, USA.

Furui, S., Itakura, F., and Saito, S. (1972). Talker Recognition by Longtime Averaged Speech Spectrum. *Transactions of IECE, 55-A*, 1(10):549–556.

Furui, S., Kikuchi, T., Shinnaka, Y., and Hori, C. (2004). Speech-to-text and Speech-to-speech Summarization of Spontaneous Speech. *IEEE Transactions on Speech and Audio Processing*, 12(4):401–408.

Gales, M. J. F. and Young, S. J. (1993). HMM Recognition in Noise Using Parallel Model Combination. In *Proceedings of the European Conference on Speech Communication and Technology (Eurospeech)*, volume 2, pages 837–840, Berlin, Germany.

Gibbon, D., Moore, R., and Winski, R., editors (1998). *Spoken Language System Assessment. Handbook of Standards and Resources for Spoken Language Systems*, volume 3. Mouton de Gruyter, Berlin, Germany.

Higgins, A., Bahler, L., and Porter, J. (1991). Speaker Verification Using Randomized Phrase Prompting. *Digital Signal Processing*, 1:89–106.

Hirohata, M., Shinnaka, Y., Iwano, K., and Furui, S. (2005). Sentence Extraction-based Presentation Summarization Techniques and Evaluation Metrics. In *Proceedings of International Conference on Acoustics, Speech and Signal Processing (ICASSP)*, pages 1065–1068, Philadelphia, USA.

Hirschberg, J., Bacchiani, M., Hindle, D., Isenhour, P., Rosenberg, A., Stark, L., Stead, L., S., S. W., and Zamchick, G. (2001). SCANMail: Browsing and Searching Speech Data by Content. In *Proceedings of the European Conference on Speech Communication and Technology (Eurospeech)*, pages 2377–2380, Aalborg, Denmark.

Hunt, M. (1990). Figures of Merit for Assessing Connected-word Recognizers. *Speech Communication*, 9:329–336.

Janin, A., Ang, J., Bhagat, S., Dhillon, R., Edwards, J., Macias-Guarasa, J., Morgan, N., Peskin, B., Shriberg, E., Stolcke, A., Wooters, C., and Wrede, B. (2004). The ICSI Meeting Project: Resources and Research. In *Proceedings of the NIST ICASSP Meeting Recognition Workshop*, Montreal, Canada.

Martin, A., Doddington, G., Kamm, T., Ordowski, M., and Przybocki, M. (1997). The DET Curve in Assessment of Detection Task Performance. In *Proceedings of the European Conference on Speech Communication and Technology (Eurospeech)*, volume 4, pages 1895–1898, Rhodes, Greece.

Matsui, T. and Furui, S. (1993). Concatenated Phoneme Models for Text-Variable Speaker Recognition. In *Proceedings of the IEEE International Conference on Acoustics, Speech, and Signal Processing*, volume 2, pages 391–394, Minneapolis, USA.

Matsui, T. and Furui, S. (1994). Similarity Normalization Method for Speaker Verification Based on a Posteriori Probability. In *Proceedings of the ESCA Workshop on Automatic Speaker Recognition, Identification and Verification*, pages 59–62, Martigny, Switzerland.

Möller, S. (2005). *Quality of Telephone-Based Spoken Dialogue Systems*. Springer, New York, USA.

Ney, H., Martin, S., and Wessel, F. (1997). Statistical Language Modeling Using Leaving-one-out. In Young, S. and Bloothooft, G., editors, *Corpus-based Methods in Language and Speech Processing*, pages 174–207. Kluwer Academic Publishers, The Netherlands.

Oard, D. W. (2004). Transforming Access to the Spoken Word. In *Proceedings of the International Symposium on Large-scale Knowledge Resources*, pages 57–59, Tokyo, Japan.

Przybocki, M. and Martin, A. (2002). NIST's Assessment of Text Independent Speaker Recognition Performance. In *Proceedings of the Advent of Biometrics on the Internet, A COST 275 Workshop*, Rome, Italy. http://www.nist.gov/speech/publications/index.htm.

Rabiner, L. R. and Juang, B.-H. (1993). *Fundamentals of Speech Recognition*. Prentice Hall, New Jersey, USA.

Reynolds, D. (1994). Speaker Identification and Verification Using Gaussian Mixture Speaker Models. In *Proceedings of the ESCA Workshop on Automatic Speaker Recognition, Identification and Verification*, pages 27–30, Martigny, Switzerland.

Rosenberg, A. E., DeLong, J., Lee, C.-H., Juang, B.-H., and Soong, F. (1992). The Use of Cohort Normalized Scores for Speaker Verification. In *Proceedings of the International Conference on Spoken Language Processing (ICSLP)*, pages 599–602, Banff, Canada.

Rosenberg, A. E. and Soong, F. K. (1987). Evaluation of a Vector Quantization Talker Recognition System in Text Independent and Text Dependent Modes. *Computer Speech and Language*, 22:143–157.

Rosenberg, A. E. and Soong, F. K. (1991). Recent Research in Automatic Speaker Recognition. In Furui, S. and Sondhi, M. M., editors, *Advances in Speech Signal Processing*, pages 701–737. Marcel Dekker, New York, USA.

Soong, F. K. and Rosenberg, A. E. (1988). On the Use of Instantaneous and Transitional Spectral Information in Speaker Recognition. *IEEE Transactions on Acoustics, Speech, and Signal Processing*, ASSP-36(6):871–879.

Ueberla, J. (1994). Analysing a Simple Language Model: Some General Conclusion for Language Models for Speech Recognition. *Computer Speech and Language*, 8(2):153–176.

Waibel, A. and Rogina, I. (2003). Advances on ISL's Lecture and Meeting Trackers. In *Proceedings of the IEEE Workshop on Spontaneous Speech Processing and Recognition*, pages 127–130, Tokyo, Japan.

Whittaker, S. and Walker, M. (2005). Evaluating Dialogue Strategies in Multimodal Dialogue Systems. In Minker, W., Bühler, D., and Dybkjær, L., editors, *Spoken Multimodal Human-Computer Dialogue in Mobile Environments*, pages 247–268. Springer, Dordrecht, The Netherlands.

Young, S. (1996). A Review of Large-vocabulary Continuous Speech Recognition. *IEEE Signal Processing Magazine*, 9:45–57.

Chapter 2

EVALUATION OF SPEECH SYNTHESIS

From Reading Machines to Talking Machines

Nick Campbell

National Institute of Information & Communications Technology,
and ATR Spoken Language Communication Labs,
Acoustics and Speech Research Department,
Keihanna Science City, Kyoto, Japan

nick@nict.go.jp

Abstract   This chapter discusses the evaluation of speech synthesis. It does not attempt to present an overview of all the techniques that may be used, or to cover the full history of previous evaluations, but instead it highlights some of the weaknesses of previous attempts, and points out areas where future development may be needed. It presents the view that speech synthesis should be judged not as a technology, but as a performance, since the actual intended listener presumably has less interest in the achievements of the developers than in the effect of the speech, its pleasantness, and its suitability to the various listening contexts.

Keywords   Speech synthesis; Human communication; Perception; Evaluation; Naturalness; Character; Expression of affect.

1   Introduction

Computer speech synthesis is the art and science of making machines speak or talk. At its inception, the focus of research was on producing reading machines as aids for the handicapped, but nowadays speech synthesis is likely to be encountered in more general situations such as customer care networks, replacing humans in telephone-based services, or providing information such as stock prices, car navigation directions, weather forecasts, and railway-station announcements.

The focus of this chapter is on the evaluation of computer speech systems and components, and it urges consideration of both the aesthetic and the scientific aspects of results when judging the acceptability of computer-generated

29

L. Dybkjær et al. (eds.), Evaluation of Text and Speech Systems, 29–64.
© 2007 *Springer.*

speech. The technology has now reached a stage at which intelligibility is no longer in question, but how should we now evaluate the naturalness and like-ability of synthesised speech? It is useful to consider here how we judge human speech; certainly not from the point of view of its technological achievements – those we take for granted – but rather by its effects. Perhaps by its expressivity?

We should start by defining some evaluation criteria. Here too, human speech might offer some useful parallels. Parents judge the developing speech of an infant by its intelligibility, recognising words amongst the babble, but computer speech comes already endowed with a full set of lexical rules from the start. Teachers judge the quality of foreign-learners' speech from a com-bination of intelligibility and naturalness, considering prosodic appropriacy alongside linguistic intelligibility. Actors judge prosodic expression first of all, determining whether the speech portrays the intended deeper meanings of its text when performed, and newscasters judge the personality as well as the expressiveness in a speaker's voice, evaluating not just the fit between words and expression but also the character of the speaker and whether the "tone" is appropriate for the desired station image. These are harsh criteria for evaluating computer speech, but unless we start from a framework in which human speech is likely to be judged, we are in danger of accepting unsatisfactory aspects of speech production and endorsing products that will be likely to cause frustration or dissatisfaction in the human listener.

2   Components of Computer Speech

It is generally agreed that there are three main stages in the production of computer-generated speech, whether from text or from concept. The first is the language-processing stage; producing a machine-readable representation of the input in a form that indicates both (a) the word sequence and its pronunciations, and (b) the relations between the words so that their intended meaning can be understood. The second stage is prosody processing, converting the abstract text-based representation of the speech into a sequence of parameters repre-senting the pitch, energy, duration, and voice quality of each acoustic segment. The third stage is waveform generation, a component that takes the parameter-based representation and converts it into a sequence of waveform segments that can be sent to an audio device for presentation to the listener.

It is common to evaluate each component stage separately, but it is also necessary to perform a holistic evaluation, since the interactions and depen-dencies between each component can also have an important effect on the acceptability of the resulting speech.

2.1   Text Pre-Processing

Producing a machine-readable representation of the input in a form that indicates both the word sequence in pronouncable form and the relations between the words.

The input to a computer speech synthesiser is commonly in the form of plain text. This text may be pre-existing in the outside world in the form of newspaper articles, books, etc., or from keyboard input, or it may be machine-generated, as in concept-to-speech systems.

In the former case, of pre-existing text, the speech-related information must be generated by the synthesis system. This processing takes two main forms: anomaly resolution and dependency relations.

In the latter case, the text does not have the requirement of being human-readable, and can be pre-annotated with various forms of speech-related information to aid in its disambiguation, pronunciation, and phrasing, in much the same way that the layout and format of a web page can be specified by the use of XML markup and style sheets.

The Speech Synthesis Markup Language (SSML) Version 1.0 home page (http://www.w3.org/TR/speech-synthesis/) of the World Wide Web Consortium summarises this goal as follows:

> The Voice Browser Working Group has sought to develop standards to enable access to the Web using spoken interaction. The Speech Synthesis Markup Language Specification is one of these standards and is designed to provide a rich, XML-based markup language for assisting the generation of synthetic speech in Web and other applications. The essential role of the markup language is to provide authors of synthesizable content a standard way to control aspects of speech such as pronunciation, volume, pitch, rate, etc. across different synthesis-capable platforms.

Note that no effort has yet been made to incorporate paralinguistic information, except by direct manipulation of the lowest-level acoustic parameters, making specification by the non-specialist rather difficult.

2.1.1 Making sense of the text: anomaly resolution.

Not all text that is clear to the eye is so easily converted into sounds; abbreviations such as "Mr." and "Dr." may be ambiguous (the latter, for example, typically representing "doctor" when coming before a proper name, and "drive" when coming after one) and common acronyms may require different pronunciation rules (IBM being pronounced as three separate letters, and JAL being pronounced as a single monosyllabic word, for example). Such textual anomalies must be converted into phonetic representations in this component of the speech synthesiser. Dictionary entries listing the possible pronunciations require complex rules to determine which is most appropriate in any given case.

Dependencies between words can require even more complex knowledge before their proper pronunciation can be determined; the simple text sequence "old men and women", for example, has a potential ambiguity in the scope of the adjective "old": does it refer to the men alone, or to both the men and the women? The former interpretation would require a short pause after "men", and a pitch reset before "women", but the latter would require that the words be reproduced as a single phrase with no prosodic reset. Considerable text analysis (and some world knowledge, usually represented in the form of statistical probabilities) is required before an appropriate pronunciation can be determined.

2.1.2   Differences between text and speech.   Text and speech have evolved differently and independently throughout human history, but there is nonetheless a common misconception that text can be simply converted into speech (and vice versa) through a process of media transformation, and that the two media differ primarily only in terms of their surface form. Speech, however, is by far the older medium (in terms of human evolution) and is usually conversational and interactive, one-to-one, directly signalling many more types of information than text does.

As well as carrying propositional content (and often instead of), speech contains many clues about the speaker's affective states, intentions, emotions, identity, health, and both short- and long-term relationships with the listener. Speech incorporates paralinguistic and extra-linguistic information that is not present (or relevant) in text. Text, on the other hand, has evolved for the eye rather than for the ear; being two-dimensional, it can be scanned from top to bottom, and from right to left, remaining present and (usually) unchanging on the page or screen to allow a more considered and analytical processing of its content. We typically scan more than one word at a time when reading text, but we receive spoken input linearly, as a one-dimensional sequence of sounds.

The speech signal decays with time, but speech makes full use of prosody to carry the information of this missing second dimension. The complex syntactic and semantic relations of a text must be converted into prosodic information before rendering it into speech, but this transformation is something which even many humans find difficult. The art of reading a text aloud requires considerable training, and very few "ordinary people" can do it well. Yet we expect a perfect enunciation from a speech synthesiser! Perhaps text-to-speech pre-processing remains the most challenging component of speech synthesis, but it can be done well only in the most uninteresting of cases. However, with annotated input, or marked-up text, the responsibility for determining the surface realisation of the utterance is passed back to the human author of the text, who has the best understanding of what the desired output rendering of each utterance should be.

2.2   Prosody Prediction

Converting the abstract representation of the speech into a sequence of parameters representing the pitch, energy, duration, and voice quality of each segment.

Prosody in speech is used to portray a complex bundle of information, the strands of which also include speaker identity, character, health, mood, interest, and emotion. At the same time, it serves also to distinguish nouns from verbs (e.g., "import", "record"), proper nouns from common nouns (e.g., "White House" vs "white house"), and to show syntactic relations and phrasing by means of pauses and pitch resets. The calculation of speech prosody for a given utterance is therefore a major component of speech synthesis, but one which relies on receiving adequate input from the text-processing component that precedes it.

2.2.1 Knowing the right answer.

One of the difficulties in evaluating the prosody of computer speech synthesis is that it requires prior knowledge of the intended interpretation of any synthesised utterance. Many prosodic contours may be appropriate, but only one of them correct for a given utterance in context. However, since sufficient world knowledge or context-related information is not always available to the text- and prosody-processing components, a so-called default prosody is often generated instead. This is the least-marked form that an utterance can take. The use of a so-called default may render mistaken interpretations less likely, but it also results in the flat and monotonous tone of much synthesised speech.

2.2.2 Four prosodic variables.

Prosody is typically realised first through manipulation of the fundamental frequency contour of a synthesised utterance. The second major prosodic variable is segmental duration, which can function instead of, or in conjunction with, the fundamental frequency contour to signal the intended interpretations of an utterance.

The manipulation of either pitch or duration requires either signal processing of the speech waveform (which can have damaging effects on its naturalness) or judicious selection of segments for concatenation (which in turn requires an inordinately large repository of sounds from which to make the selection).

Little research attention has been given to prosodic manipulation of the energy contour (traditionally considered to be the third prosodic variable), partly because it correlates quite closely with the fundamental-frequency information, and partly because the voice level of synthesised speech is usually held at a constant predetermined volume.

The fourth prosodic component, which is recently receiving more attention in the speech research communities, is voice quality, or manner of articulatory phonation, which can be varied to indicate emotion or speaker activation and interest, in addition to marking focus or emphasis and to showing characteristics related to phrasal and utterance position.

2.2.3   Acceptable variation in prosody.   Whereas the output of a text-pre-processing module can perhaps be evaluated in isolation, without resorting to synthesis, it is more difficult to evaluate prosody prediction in this way. There can be large differences in the physical measurement of the prosodic parameters that do not appear as perceptually relevant differences in the realisation of an utterance as speech. An obvious example is the difference in pitch (or more correctly fundamental frequency range) between the speech of men, women, and children, which human listeners appear to disregard unconsciously, since they pay less attention to these individual differences and hear instead the "intended prosody" of an utterance regardless of often very large differences in acoustic prosodic parameter values. This is not a claim that people do not hear these large differences, but rather that they can perceive utterances that have the same content as "the same" even though they may be spoken by different people.

A less obvious example is the raising or lowering of pitch in the speech of a single speaker; if all values for a given utterance are raised or lowered by the same amount, and if that amount is still within the normal speaking range of that speaker, then no difference in intended meaning will be perceived. Conversely, even a slight delay or advancement of a pitch peak in an utterance can result in a profound difference in perceived meaning of the utterance. Thus, simple numerical measures of, for example, difference between the prosody of a natural utterance and that of a synthesised one can be extremely difficult for the evaluator to interpret.

Furthermore, we observe considerable differences in the absolute values of the prosodic parameters in the speech of humans, all of which would be considered "natural" and "correct" by a listener, but often a much smaller difference in the output of a speech synthesiser is perceived as quite unnatural, or as presenting a different interpretation. This paradox is not yet well explained scientifically.

2.3   Waveform Generation

Taking the parameter-based representation and converting it into a sequence of waveform segments that can be sent to an audio device for presentation to the listener.

There are many ways to produce speech waveforms by computer; the simplest (perhaps) is by concatenation, just joining together segments selected from different parts of a larger database, and the most complex is by modelling the variations in the articulatory tract and voice-source parameters and then reproducing them by rule. The science of acoustics and the physics of wave propagation find practical application in this area, but psychology has yet to enter.

2.3.1 From phones to segments. The earliest attempts at computer modelling of speech employed formant approximations of the phones (and produced a smoothed interpolation between them) to replicate the acoustics of vowel and consonant differences as observed from spectrographic representations of human speech utterances. The works of Gunnar Fant, Ken Stevens, and Dennis Klatt contributed considerably to our understanding of the physics of speech production and formed the basis of much of modern speech synthesis.

Later contributions, most notably from Osamu Fujimura, Joe Olive, and Yoshinori Sagisaka, resulted in a different, non-phonemic view of speech segmentation, and led to the concatenative systems that are in more popular use today. Rather than modelling the "centres" of speech information and interpolating between them, they recorded the "transitions" (i.e., made use of dynamic rather than static information) and concatenated short segments of speech waveforms to produce the synthesised speech.

More recent improvements in concatenative speech synthesis have resulted in less need (often none at all) for signal processing to modify the recorded waveform segments, by enlarging the source-unit database, enriching it, instead of using a smaller unit-inventory and resorting to signal modifications to manipulate the prosody.

2.3.2 System size and output quality. Whereas articulatory modelling of speech may offer the most scientific benefit, it is still very far from being of practical use in real-time speech synthesis systems, and concatenative synthesis appears to offer a higher quality of speech output for the present time, leaving parametric synthesis (such as formant-based synthesis-by-rule) to offer a lower-quality but smaller-footprint synthesiser that may be more suitable for use in applications where speech quality is of lesser importance than price or memory requirements.

Of course, each of these synthesis systems has its own individual strengths and weaknesses, and each should be evaluated in situ, taking into account not just the overall quality of the resulting speech, but also its appropriateness for a given synthesis application. We should not think in terms of "one best system", but of a range of different methods that can be selected from, and possibly even switched between, according to the needs and preferences of the individual user.

Paradoxically, the smallest system may offer the most flexibility, being able to mimic many voices and speaking styles but at the cost of not being able to sound "human", and the most expensive (in terms of speech segment inventories) may be limited to the voice of only one speaker and one speaking style, though able to reproduce that with such a precision that it may be difficult or sometimes impossible to notice any difference from natural human speech.

Even among human speakers, there is a similar trade-off of talents, as very few professional speakers are able to master all modes of presentation equally well. A Shakespearean actor might make a very poor newsreader, for example, yet it is often assumed that computer speech synthesis will one day outperform them all! This is still an unrealistic assumption, and we should be looking instead for different methods that can match different expectations, rather than one global system that can excel at all.

3   Evaluation Methodologies

There are many different ways that a speech synthesiser can be evaluated: diagnostic or comparative, subjective or objective, modular or global, task-based or generic, etc., and probably as many different ways to perform the evaluation: web-based or live, over headphones or loudspeakers, with actual users or recruited listeners, specialist or naive, pairwise or in isolation, and whether or not human speech samples are included in the same evaluation with the synthesized speech.

Early speech synthesisers were evaluated primarily for intelligibility, using rhyme tests, anomalous sentences (e.g., the Haskins set which had the form "the *adj noun verb* the *noun*") and lists of words both in sentences and in isolation. The goal of such evaluation was phonetic discrimination, i.e., focussing on "intelligibility" rather than "naturalness".

Intelligibility is of course necessary, but naturalness is perhaps also desirable. As early as 1974, this point was being addressed:

> From our point of view it is not physical realism but psychological acceptability which is the proper evidence for correctness at the phonological and phonetic levels, just as it is on the syntactic level. *(I.G. Mattingly, 1974. Developing models of human speech.)*

However, whereas "naturalness" may be difficult to judge in synthesised speech, different synthesisers (or different settings of a given synthesiser) can be compared instead for *relative* naturalness. The need for human realism is variable; in some applications it is essential, while in others it is undesirable. Yet in all cases, the listener must endure the speech, so I here propose a third evaluation criterion: "likeability", in addition to the standard two above, as a measure of the degree to which extended listening becomes bearable, or even perhaps enjoyable.

3.1   Component-Based Evaluation

Whereas the listener (or "customer" perhaps) is primarily concerned with the overall quality, intelligibility, and likeability of the output speech, the developer is usually more concerned with testing one component at a time. Not all components can be run in isolation, so contrived input may be necessary for testing purposes, but in judging a speech synthesis system as a whole, it can be difficult to determine the source of any specific error, and small errors may be compounded as they cascade through later components.

3.1.1   Evaluating the text pre-processing component.

Because the mapping between a text and its pronunciation is deterministic, this component of the speech synthesiser is, paradoxically, perhaps the easiest to evaluate using objective measures. For example, the part of speech of a given word in a given context is a fact that may be difficult to estimate from limited knowledge in a computer program, but one which has a single right answer that can be checked.

Similarly, the pronunciation of a text sequence might vary with, for example, speaking rate, or dialect, but it is in general predetermined. For example, the letter sequence /b-a-s-s/ will be pronounced one way in the context of music, and another in the context of fishing, but in either case there is a "right" pronunciation. This is not the case with proper names, however, which can vary even according to personal whim, and for which no dictionary or rule set can provide a definitive answer.

Number strings require context-specific rules for their realisation as word sequences: telephone numbers having a different syntax from ordinals, as do special symbols (e.g., $N = "dollar-N" in a computer program, but "N-dollars" in a financial context), but again, these can be categorically judged for correctness.

Sometimes the input to the text preprocessor is by default ill-formed. The listings in a telephone directory, for example, are usually highly abbreviated and, although intelligible to a human reader, may be very difficult to disambiguate by rule, but again, there is usually one "right answer".

Dictionaries can be produced, and letter-to-sound rules trained on them so that only the exceptions need to be stored. The output of these rules, fall-back dictionaries, parsers, and morphological analysers can be evaluated objectively for a large subset of the language (that which excludes proper names, for example) and scores can be calculated to evaluate the component performance.

However, the remaining (almost infinite) subset of texts which contain lexical items whose pronunciation may be arbitrary, can only be evaluated subjectively. Since even humans will not always agree on, for example, the pronunciation of proper names, there can be no objective measure and scoring for "acceptability" rather than correctness will be needed. This work then becomes labour-intensive and expensive.

If the results are passed through the remaining modules of a synthesiser so that the test can be performed aurally, perhaps even over a telephone line, then the output is likely to be corrupted further by compounding of errors as they cascade through the system. However tedious it may be to perform, a text-based examination of the component output is therefore preferable to listening tests for evaluating the early stage of speech synthesis processing.

3.1.2   Evaluating the prosody component.

Given perfect input, the prosody component should be able to reliably produce the specifications for an unambiguous rendering of the text as speech when output by the waveform component. Its input can be modified if necessary, to represent the perfect output of a text pre-processing stage, but how is its output to be evaluated?

As mentioned above, there is tremendous variability in the prosody of human speech, much of which is perceptually insignificant or cognitively irrelevant, but some of which has the effect of changing the entire meaning of an utterance. The word "yes" for example, if spoken slowly and with a rise-fall-rise contour, can even signal "no" to a familiar listener.

Textual anomalies, such as "I saw Janet and John saw Fred" (where "Janet and John" might be a compound subject) must be resolved at an earlier stage and the disambiguating information passed as input, but in order to judge the correctness of predictions from the prosody component, the listener (or reviewer) must first know the *intended interpretation* of the utterance.

It is highly unlikely that any two speakers will produce the "same" utterance with identical prosodic contours, yet most human listeners would be able to judge whether or not there was an intended difference in meaning or nuance between any pair of utterances from different speakers. As a science, we do not yet have enough understanding of this flexible variability in perception or production to produce a model or technology that would enable its objective evaluation. Yet to assess the performance of a prosody component using aural perception requires passing it through a further stage of processing in which errors can be compounded (or hidden). This is the "catch-22" of prosody research; we need to know about both the speaker's intentions and the listener's perceptions of them, yet only in a very few "black-and-white" cases can these be categorically determined.

When we expand our goals beyond judging correctness, towards judging paralinguistic expression, the problem becomes even more difficult, but if a computer speech synthesiser is to be used in place of a human speaker in interactive discourse situations, the expression of paralinguistic and extra-linguistic information is as important (if not more so) as the expression of linguistic or propositional content.

Teams of listeners are required for an efficient evaluation, and in the case of the commonly used Mean Opinion Score (MOS) evaluations, a minimum of 30 listeners is necessary for a statistically significant result. ABX tests are common (comparing two versions to a target and indicating the closer one) as are preference tests, but it is very difficult for a listener to precisely identify the particular cause of a prosodic problem as the four elements of prosody are perceived as an integrated whole, and events occur too quickly for the ear to be able to identify their exact location. Diagnostic testing of prosody is therefore a difficult art.

3.1.3   Evaluating the waveform component.

In earlier times, the focus of output evaluation was on mechanical performance and particularly on the ability to mimic human phonetic sequences, so rhyme tests and dictation-type exercises were adequate to determine if a target phonetic sequence was correctly perceived. Nowadays, though, as technology progresses, we advance beyond segmental intelligibility and are more concerned with judging expressiveness and personality in computer speech.

The quality of audio on the web has now reached hi-fi performance but the quality of most synthetic speech is already lagging quite far behind. Again, the needs with respect to quality must be regarded as application-specific, and it is probably not necessary to provide broadcast-quality speech in a talking wristwatch or toaster, but the failure to meet the expectations of the ordinary person-in-the-street might be the main reason that speech synthesis technology has been so slow in getting accepted.

When evaluating the waveform generation component, we can assume that the rest of the system has functioned perfectly and provide it with (perhaps hand-crafted) ideal input as well as with input that has actually been generated by passing through the earlier components. In an ideal world, there will be no difference between the two, but any difference that is found at this stage can be attributed to earlier processing inadequacies and ignored for the sake of the evaluation.

Physical measures of waveform similarity are used in speech recognition and can be used similarly in speech synthesis for determining an objective measure of the distance between one speech waveform and another. Unfortunately, none of these measures matches human perception perfectly, and they either underestimate problems that human listeners might find noticeable, or raise an error on points that the human listener might not notice. If a measure that perfectly matched human perception could be found, the problems of concatenative speech synthesis would be over, for the minimisation of error could then be performed automatically.

As with prosody evaluation, waveform generation is best evaluated by subjective measures, and again, MOS (which is widely used in the telecommunications industry for speech-coder assessment) has proved to be a very good indicator of overall performance.

3.2   Evaluating the Complete System

Component evaluation is a necessary part of system development, and provides both feedback and diagnostic information to the researcher, but even if every component is working well, their integration can sometimes lead to problems, so a full system-level evaluation is also required. Of prime importance is intelligibility of the output, then its naturalness, and last, but by no means least, its likeability. People may buy synthesisers "off the shelf", and first impressions will have a strong influence on their decisions, but after repeated use, the character of the system becomes as important as its clarity. If people do not like a synthesiser's voice and speaking styles, they will soon cease to use it.

3.2.1   Intelligibility.   Tests of nonsense words and semantically anomalous sentences do provide a measure of the intelligibility of synthesised speech output, but not one that realistically represents everyday situated use. If the tests were carried out in a car, a helicopter cockpit, a busy shopping centre, or at home with a television and children playing in the background, they might be more useful, but this is rarely the case. Researchers seem to be more interested in evaluating topline performance than baseline reliability.

Now that the science of speech synthesis has progressed beyond the early stage of testing phonetic adequacy, perhaps we will begin to see more task-based evaluation. There have been some performance-based measures of fatigue and response time delays related to use of speech synthesisers in the performance of a real-world task, but this mode of testing, although it better reflects the actual needs of the end-user, seems to be the exception rather than the rule.

As speech synthesis becomes more expressive, particularly when used in place of a human voice, as in translation systems and communication aids, the variability of speaking style will require fast and even slurred speech to be produced if it is to faithfully represent the intentions of the original speaker. It is not yet known whether the present waveform generation methods will be robust against such intentional distortion of the clean-speech signal, so quantitative measures of degradation in intelligibility (both segmental and prosodic) will also be required.

3.2.2   Naturalness or believability.   Perhaps "believability" would be a better term to use instead of "naturalness", although it has not been seen much in the previous literature, because even an artificial-sounding voice (as in fictional cartoons, for example) can sound believably natural if the prosody is appropriate.

The world of Walt Disney is a perfect example of why "naturalness" may not be the best way of approaching this aspect of speech synthesis evaluation. Very few of the creatures in Disney films are photo-realistic, yet they are all very believable. So how should we measure believability in speech synthesis?

Fitting the voice and speaking style to the content and context of the message requires a flexibility in all three stages of synthesis design. The success of such an effort can be intuitively felt by many listeners, even if they cannot explicitly quantify it. The selection of telephone personnel, newsreaders, actors for roles, and characters in advertisements, is a very sensitive process involving delicate judgements about voice as well as role suitability and matching. This framework should be adapted for use in synthesis evaluation.

3.2.3 Likeability. The selection of an ideal voice for use in a concatenative speech synthesiser is a very lengthy process. Not only must the voice have characteristics that allow for easy joining between segments extracted from different parts of the database, but it must also have an appeal to the listener and a fit to the perceived or projected image of the company or product whose voice it is to become.

Whether produced by concatenation or signal processing, whether from a large source database or a small one, the resulting voice and the range of speaking styles that it is capable of will define the popularity of a synthesiser as much as technical ability in the processing of the various stages.

Current evaluation methodologies are biased towards accountability and reproducibility, favouring objective measures over subjective ones, but ultimately, the listener's feelings towards the synthesiser must also be allowed to play a role in the evaluation process. Likeability though is an aspect of synthesiser use that can easily change over time. What sounds fun and attractive on first listening may become irritating after prolonged use, or what is appealing in a quiet environment may become inadequate when used in noise. Long-term assessment is an issue that must be addressed if we are to produce a technology that is pleasant as well as efficient.

4   Organised Evaluations and Assessment

In this section we will examine some techniques that have been successfully used in the past and suggest some new ones that may better address the developing needs of the current technology.

4.1   Learning from the Past

Many scientific presentations concerning speech synthesis are accompanied by demonstrations of the resulting output, but these are usually demonstrations of carefully controlled samples that are limited in number and that do not necessarily give a fair impression of the overall performance of a given synthesis system as it might perform across a wide range of everyday application tasks.

Scientific research is rightly more concerned with raising the topline of achievements, as evidenced by the fact that negative findings are rarely reported at academic meetings, but the products of developers are evaluated by the customers throughout their full range of everyday use. While it is topline performance that is demonstrated at conferences, the owner/user of a synthesis system is usually more concerned about the baseline; i.e., not just how well a system can perform in the best of cases, but also how badly it might perform in the worst. A large part of the role of evaluation is to bridge this gap between scientists and developers and to bring the thoughts of the end-user into an earlier stage of the design process.

Evaluation of speech synthesis is by no means a well developed art. In comparison with the number of papers published reporting advances in speech synthesis, the number of papers describing how these advances might be evaluated is still remarkably few. At the recent ISCA Speech Synthesis Tutorial and Research Workshops, for example, there has been on average only 4% of papers explicitly addressing evaluation issues (SSW5, 2004: 3/46; SSW4, 2001: 1/62; SSW3, 1998: 3/60).

4.1.1   The Jenolan experience.

At the ESCA/COCOSDA Tutorial and Research Workshop on Speech Synthesis (SSW3), held in 1998 at Jenolan in the Blue Mountains near Sydney, Australia, a concerted evaluation of the then current speech synthesis systems was organised in an attempt to remedy this imbalance. The evaluation served three goals:

1. To give the participants first-hand experience with a wide range of current text-to-speech systems (altogether 70 system/language combinations were presented)

2. To stimulate discussion of speech synthesis evaluation procedures by offering direct experience to contributing participants, who function both as developers and as evaluators

3. To provide feedback to the system developers about some of the strong and weak points of their speech synthesisers

The evaluation was limited to full text-to-speech systems but employed several text types, ranging from newspaper text through semantically unpredictable sentences to telephone directory listings. The newspaper text sentences were further subdivided into "easy', using frequent words, and "hard", using sentence selection based on trigram-frequencies calculated from the Linguistic Data Consortium (LDC) text corpora.

The texts were automatically generated from large corpora for several languages (though not all), and were made available to participants via an interactive web site a very short time before the evaluation was carried out. Speech files had to be synthesised from the texts and returned via the same site to the organisers who then randomised them for presentation to participants at the workshop. Regardless of original sampling rate, all submitted waveform files were resampled to 11.25 kHz by the evaluation organisers before the comparisons were performed.

All participants in the workshop took part as participants in the listening tests. Utterances were presented to the listeners via headphones, and responses were entered using rating scales (from "poor" to "excellent") and also identifying problem areas. Since the listeners were mainly professional synthesis researchers, advantage was taken of their expertise for free input in the latter category, while the former included such scales as "overall voice quality", "naturalness", "wrong syllable stressed". Experimental design was blocked by text type within listeners, all listening to each text-to-speech system exactly once with each text item for a given language.

Full details of the evaluation procedure are still available at the original COCOSDA web site (http://www.slt.atr.co.jp/cocosda/evaltext.htm), but the results of the evaluation remain confidential as this became a condition of participation. There was concern that (a) system developers would refrain from participating otherwise, and (b) that the results of such a (necessarily) rushed evaluation might not be completely reliable. However, although the experience gained both by organisers and participants was considered valuable, the experiment has not been repeated.

4.2   Synthesis Assessment and Evaluation Centres

There is now no shortage of suitable organisations that could take on the role of assessment centres for synthesis systems in the various languages and world regions, but there is at present no such centre and currently no such effort that the author is aware of.

The LDC was very helpful in providing texts for the Jenolan evaluation and for a while afterwards the LDC maintained a speech synthesis evaluation web site to enable similar web-based comparisons. Unfortunately, at the present time, this site (the interactive speech synthesizer comparison site at http://www.ldc.upenn.edu/ltts/) does not appear to be supported.

The European Language Resources Association (ELRA; http://www.elda.fr/) is a sister organisation to the LDC, based in Europe. Their distribution agency (ELDA) actively participates in evaluation projects, and is beginning to include speech synthesis:

> In the near future, as we are getting more and more involved in the evaluation activity, ELRA & ELDA will add in its catalogue further resources and tools related to evaluation, and a new team, whose task will include the organisation of evaluation campaigns and every other aspects of the evaluation activity, will join the agency. (2005)

The International Committee for the Co-ordination and Standardisation of Speech Databases and Assessment Techniques for Speech Input/Output (COCOSDA; http://www.cocosda.org) organised the Jenolan Assessment, in conjunction with the International Speech Communication Association (ISCA (then ESCA); http://www.isca-speech.org/), but after more than 10 years of activity, this group, too, no longer participates in evaluation programmes, though their annual workshops stress the importance of assessment as part of technology development and form a central meeting place for such discussions and information exchange.

A spin-off from COCOSDA, the ISCA Special Interest Group for Speech Synthesis (SynSIG; http://feast.his.atr.jp/synsig/) has taken over the task of organising tutorial workshops related to speech synthesis, and would be the most likely independent (and fully international) organisation to coordinate future speech synthesis assessments, but a repeat of Jenolan is unlikely unless a committed team of volunteers is formed to ensure that the meticulous organisation and arrangement of details can be repeated.

In the Far East, the ChineseLDC (http://www.chineseldc.org/) and the GSK in Japan (Gengo Shigen Kyoyukiko is Japanese for Language Resource Consortium) both aim at developing, sharing, and distributing language resources for research into speech and natural language processing. Both groups are committed to facilitating speech research and will perhaps also take on an assessment and evaluation role in the near future.

4.3   More Recent Assessments

The Verbmobil project across Germany and the international TC-Star project for speech-to-speech translation both conducted end-to-end evaluations that included a speech synthesis component. Unfortunately, most speech-to-speech translation systems have yet to take expressiveness of the input speech as a relevant factor in the translation, and in both cases the output speech synthesis was considered to be a relatively minor component, with the bulk of the evaluations being performed at the level of text. Although both systems accepted human speech as input, as long as the translated text was rendered intelligibly the synthesis was considered to be satisfactory, and little attention was paid to voice quality or expressiveness of the output per se.

The European project COST 258 (http://www.icp.inpg.fr/cost258/), lasting from 1997 to 2001, was concerned with the naturalness of synthetic speech in concrete applications, with a particular focus on the improvements of sound quality and prosodic modelling. It recognised four priority topics for speech synthesis evaluation:

1. Prosodic and acoustic effects of focus and/or emphasis

2. Prosodic effects of speaking styles

3. Rhythm: what is rhythm, and how can it be synthesised?

4. Mark-up: what prosodic markers are needed at a linguistic (phonological) level?

Their book (published by Wiley, see below) can be considered essential reading on the topic.

Recently, from the United States and Japan, the Blizzard Challenge (http://www.festvox.org/blizzard) for evaluating corpus-based speech synthesis using common databases is becoming an example of the direction that future bottom-up assessment initiatives might take. The goal of this challenge is for different groups to each use the same publicly available speech databases to build a synthetic voices. Unknown sentences from an independent source will be generated and each participant will synthesize them with their system. The synthesised speech will then be put on the web for evaluation. The results are not available at this time of writing, but such an open evaluation of different methodologies using a common resource in the public arena is bound to be helpful.

5   Speaking to (and on Behalf of) People

To date, the knowledge underlying speech synthesis research has been that of phonetic science and its acoustic correlates, and there has perhaps been an undue emphasis upon the linguistic and segmental components of spoken language. Speech production per se rather than *communication* has been the goal. Yet in many of the current applications of speech synthesis, we find that machines are now acting in the place of people to impart information in an interactive conversational framework.

Recent studies of conversational speech have shown that only a small part of the total speech activity is devoted to the pure expression of propositional content, and that the larger part is devoted to maintaining successful discourse flow, expression of affect, expression of speaker–listener relationships, and revealing the speaker's attitude towards the content of the message. These expressions of paralinguistic information require more than just linguistically well-formed utterances, and place stricter demands for more sophisticated uses of prosody than current speech synthesis systems are capable of.

Synthesisers have traditionally been regarded as reading machines, and the term "text-to-speech" is often thought of as synonymous with "speech synthesis", but the emphasis is changing, and "talking machines" are beginning to appear. These machines will not just be required to talk, but also to laugh (for sure) and even to cry perhaps. They will be required to express more than just emotion, and to take part in an interaction where not just the content of the message is of importance, but also the tone of voice, and the manner of speaking. Computer speech will have to brush up on its interpersonal skills if it is to keep pace with the changes in society and technology.

6   Conclusion

This chapter has presented an overview of some of the main issues concerning current speech synthesis assessment and evaluation. Although there has been a tremendous amount of research into this subject in the past, it seems that the goalposts are always moving and that as the technology advances, so must the evaluation methodologies. Unfortunately there may still be a mismatch between the goals of the scientists and technicians who are developing the systems and the needs of the people-in-the-street who we hope will buy and benefit from their products. In spite of more than half a century of advanced research, few ordinary people yet use a speech synthesiser in their daily lives; at least, not unless they have to. This is the ultimate assessment of our technology.

Part of the problem is that we, as developers, necessarily see the system in terms of its component parts and then evaluate the performance of each on a limited set of criteria that are defined in terms of technological and methodological goals, rather than holistic perception targets. Speech is broken down into processes and sub-processes, and yet in its entirety, speech is more than the just sum of these parts.

What is missing from current speech synthesis technology is a model of interpersonal communication strategies. We have reached the stage at which we can successfully mimic and control many of the individual speech production processes, but we lack a way of evaluating how well they can be used to signal all of the integrated factors that combine to form human speech. We long ago mastered control of the linguistic component, and recently succeeded in incorporating extra-linguistic, speaker-specific information into the technology. What is still missing is a control of paralinguistic information, and a means to evaluate the subtle nuances and shifts of meaning that add richness to human speech. The challenge of modelling global weather systems and climatic effects is known to be a very difficult task, yet understanding and modelling the subtlety and beauty of human speech processes is a far more challenging one. It will perhaps keep us busy for many years to come.

Acknowledgements   The author wishes to express thanks to the National Institute of Information & Communications Technology, Japan, to the Japan Science & Technology Agency, and to the management and staff of the Advanced Telecommunications Research Institute in Kyoto for their kind support of this work.

Further Reading

There are already several excellent books on speech synthesis that the interested reader could use as a source for further information, though there is none that I know of which is dedicated solely to the topic of evaluation and assessment.

A comprehensive manual that does include much relevant information is the *Handbook of Standards and Resources for Spoken Language Systems*, by Dafydd Gibbon, Roger Moore, and Richard Winski (editors), published by Mouton de Gruyter (November 1997).

A collection of extended papers from the first ISCA ETRW on Speech Synthesis can be found in *Talking Machines: Theories, Models, and Designs*, by G. Bailly, C. Benoit, and T.R. Sawallis, published by North-Holland (1 May 1992) and a follow-up *Progress in Speech Synthesis*, by Jan P.H. Van Santen, Richard W. Sproat, Joseph P. Olive, and Julia Hirschberg, published by Springer-Verlag (15 January 1997).

No books have resulted from the subsequent ITRW speech synthesis workshops, but their proceedings are available on the web under the home pages of ISCA (http://isca-speech.org). For a more general introduction to the field, the following are recommended:

An Introduction to Text-to-Speech Synthesis, by Thierry Dutoit (Faculté Polytechnique de Mons), published by Kluwer Academic Publishers (Text, Speech and Language Technology series, edited by Nancy Ide and Jean Véronis, volume 3) (1997). *Improvements in Speech Synthesis: Cost 258: The Naturalness of Synthetic Speech,* by E. Keller, G. Bailly, A. Monaghan, J. Terken, and M. Huckvale (editors), published by Wiley (November 2001). *Text to Speech Synthesis: New Paradigms and Advances,* by Shrikanth Narayanan and Abeer Alwan, published by Prentice Hall IMSC Press Multimedia Series (2004).

For the specialist reader, the proceedings of the following workshops and conferences will contain papers of interest:

LREC, the International Language Resources and Evaluation Conference

ICASSP, the International Conference on Acoustics, Speech, and Signal Processing

Eurospeech, the European Conference on Speech Communication and Technology

ICSLP, the International Conference on Spoken Language Processing

ISCA ETRWs, the series of Speech Synthesis workshops organised by ISCA

COCOSDA, International Committee for the Co-ordination and Standardisation of Speech Databases and Assessment Techniques for Speech Input/Output.

Although a Google search will probably be more useful to the reader since it can be interactively directed and presents the very latest information, the following reference section summarises previous work that may not appear on the web. It presents a small sample of the types of research that have been conducted on the evaluation of speech synthesis systems, and in spite of this tremendous body of knowledge, we can still say that the science of speech synthesis evaluation is just at its beginning, and that the effective evaluation of synthesis systems has probably not even begun.

References

Akers, G. and Lennig, M. (1985). Intonation in Text-to-Speech Synthesis: Evaluation of Algorithms. *Journal of the Acoustical Society of America*, 77(6):2157–2165.

Benoit, C. and Pols, L. C. W. (1992). On the Assessment of Synthetic Speech. In Bailly, G., Benoit, C., and Sawallis, T., editors, *Talking Machines: Theories, Models and Designs*, pages 435–441, Elsevier, North Holland, Amsterdam, The Netherlands.

Benoit, C., van Erp, A., Grice, M., Hazan, V., and Jekosch, U. (1989). Multilingual Synthesiser Assessment Using Semantically Unpredictable Sentences. In *Proceedings of the European Conference on Speech Communication and Technology (Eurospeech)*, volume 2, pages 633–636, Paris, France.

Bernstein, J. (1982). Evaluating Synthetic Speech. In *Proceedings of the NBS Workshop on Standardization for Speech I/O Technology*, pages 87–91, Gaithersburg, Maryland, USA.

Bernstein, J. and Pisoni, D. B. (1980). Unlimited Text-to-Speech System: Description and Evaluation of a Microprocessor Based Device. In *Proceedings of the International Conference on Acoustics, Speech and Signal Processing (ICASSP)*, pages 576–579, Denver, Colorado, USA.

Bladon, A. (1990). Evaluating the Prosody of Text-to-Speech Synthesizers. In *Proceedings of Speech Tech*, pages 215–220, New York, USA.

Boeffard, O., Cherbonnel, B., Emerard, F., and White, S. (1993). Automatic Segmentation and Quality Evaluation of Speech Unit Inventories for Concatenation-Based, Multilingual PSOLA Text-to-Speech Systems. In *Proceedings of the European Conference on Speech Communication and Technology (Eurospeech)*, volume 2, pages 1449–1452, Berlin, Germany.

Boogaar, T. and Silverman, K. (1992). Evaluating the Overall Comprehensibility of Speech Synthesizers. In *Proceedings of the International Conference on Spoken Language Processing (ICSLP)*, pages 1207–1210, Banff, Canada.

Calliope (1989). Évaluation de la parole codée et synthétique. In *La parole et son traitement automatique, Collection scientifique et technique des Télécommunications*, pages 455–488, Masson, Paris, France.

Carlson, R. and Granström, B. (1989). Evaluation and Development of the KTH Text-to-Speech System on the Segmental Level. In *Proceedings of the ESCA Tutorial and Research Workshop on Speech Input/Output Assess-*

ment and Speech Databases, volume 2, pages 11–14, Noordwijkerhout, The Netherlands.

Carlson, R., Granström, B., and Larson, K. (1976). Evaluation of a Text-to-Speech System as a Reading Machine for the Blind. In *STL-QPSR 2-3, Quarterly Progress and Status Report*, pages 9–13, KTH, Stockholm, Sweden.

Carlson, R., Granström, B., Neovius, L., and Nord, L. (1992). The 'Listening Speed' Paradigm for Synthesis Evaluation. In *FONETIK, Sixth Swedish Phonetics Conference, Chalmers Technical Report No. 10*, pages 63–66, Gothenburg, Sweden. Department of Information Theory, Chalmers University of Technology.

Carlson, R., Granström, B., and Nord, L. (1990a). Results from the SAM Segmental Test for Synthetic and Natural Speech in Swedish (VCV, CV and VC). Internal Report, ESPRIT Project 2589 (SAM) Multi-Lingual Speech Input/Output, Assessment, Methodology and Standardization.

Carlson, R., Granström, B., and Nord, L. (1990b). Segmental Intelligibility of Synthetic and Natural Speech in Real and Nonsense Words. In *Proceedings of the International Conference on Spoken Language Processing (ICSLP)*, volume 2, pages 989–992, Kobe, Japan.

Cartier, M. and Gleiss, N. (1992). Synthetic Speech Quality Assessment for Telecommunication Purposes. In *Proceedings of the COCOSDA Meeting*, Banff, Canada.

Cartier, M., Karlsson, C., and Modena, G. (1989). Standardization of Synthetic Speech Quality for Telecommunication Purposes. In *Proceedings of the ESCA Tutorial and Research Workshop on Speech Input/Output Assessment and Speech Databases*, volume 2, pages 99–102, Noordwijkerhout, The Netherlands.

CCITT (1992a). *A Method for Subjective Performance Assessment of the Quality of Speech of Voice Output Devices*. Comité Consultatif International Téléphonique et Télégraphique, Draft Recommendation P.8S of Working Party XII/2, Special Rapporteur for Question 5/XII edition. Available upon request. International Telecommunications Union, Geneva, Switzerland.

CCITT (1992b). *Experiment in Assessing the Quality of Synthetic Speech*. Comité Consultatif International Téléphonique et Télégraphique, Temporary Document No. 70-E of Working Party XII/2 edition. Special Rapporteur for Question 5/XII. International Telecommunications Union, Geneva, Switzerland.

Delogu, C., Conte, S., Paoloni, A., and Sementina, C. (1992a). Comprehension of Synthetic Speech in Good and in Adverse Conditions. In *Proceedings of the ESCA Workshop on Speech Processing in Adverse Conditions*, pages 53–56, Cannes-Mandelieu, France.

Delogu, C., Conte, S., Paoloni, A., and Sementina, C. (1992b). Two Different Methodologies for Evaluating the Comprehension of Synthetic Passages. In *Proceedings of the International Conference on Spoken Language Processing (ICSLP)*, volume 2, pages 1231–1234, Banff, Canada.

Delogu, C., Di Carlo, A., Sementina, C., and Stecconi, S. (1993a). A Methodology for Evaluating Human-Machine Spoken Language Interaction. In *Proceedings of the European Conference on Speech Communication and Technology (Eurospeech)*, pages 1427–1430, Berlin, Germany.

Delogu, C., Falcone, M., Paoloni, A., Ridolfi, P., and Vagges, K. (1992c). Intelligibility of Italian Text-to-Speech Synthesizers in Adverse Conditions. In *Proceedings of the ESCA Workshop on Speech Processing in Adverse Conditions*, pages 57–60, Cannes-Mandelieu, France.

Delogu, C., Paoloni, A., and Pocci, P. (1991a). New Directions in the Evaluation of Voice Input/Output Systems. *IEEE Journal on Selected Areas in Communications*, 9(4):566–573.

Delogu, C., Paoloni, A., Pocci, P., and Sementina, C. (1991b). Quality Evaluation of Text-to-Speech Synthesizers Using Magnitude Estimation, Categorical Estimation, Pair Comparison, and Reaction Time Methods. In *Proceedings of the European Conference on Speech Communication and Technology (Eurospeech)*, pages 353–356, Genova, Italy.

Delogu, C., Paoloni, A., Ridolfi, P., and Vagges, K. (1993b). Intelligibility of Speech Produced by Text-to-Speech Synthesizers Over the Orthophonic and Telephonic Channel. In *Proceedings of the European Conference on Speech Communication and Technology (Eurospeech)*, pages 1893–1896, Berlin, Germany.

Delogu, C. and Sementina, C. (1993). Towards a More Realistic Evaluation of Synthetic Speech: A Cognitive Perspective. In *Proceedings of the NATO-ASI Workshop on New Advances and Trends in Speech Recognition and Coding*, Bubion, Granada, Spain.

Falaschi, A. (1992). Segmental Quality Assessment by Pseudo-Words. In Bailly, G., Benoit, C., and Sawallis, T., editors, *Talking Machines: Theories, Models and Designs*, pages 455–472, Elsevier, North Holland, Amsterdam, The Netherlands.

Fourcin, A. (1992). Assessment of Synthetic Speech. In Bailly, G., Benoit, C., and Sawallis, T., editors, *Talking Machines: Theories, Models and Designs*, pages 431–434, Elsevier, North Holland, Amsterdam, The Netherlands.

Fourcin, A. J., Harland, G., Barry, W., and Hazan, V., editors (1989). *Speech Input and Output Assessment. Multilingual Methods and Standards*. Ellis Horwood Ltd., Chichester, UK.

French PTT (1987). *An 'Objective' Evaluation of Difficulty in Understanding Voice Synthesis Devices*. Comité Consultatif International Téléphonique et Télégraphique, International Telecommunications Union, Geneva,

Switzerland. CCITT Com. XII, Study Group XII, Contribution No. FR4-E.

Garnier-Rizet, M. (1993). Evaluation of a Rule-Based Text-to-Speech System for French at the Segmental Level. In *Proceedings of the European Conference on Speech Communication and Technology (Eurospeech)*, pages 1889–1892, Berlin, Germany.

Goldstein, M., Lindström, B., and Till, O. (1992). Assessing Global Performance of Speech Synthesizers: Context Effects When Assessing Naturalness of Swedish Sentence Pairs Generated by 4 Systems Using 3 Different Assessment Procedures (Free Number Magnitude Estimation, 5-and 11-Point Category Scales). ESPRIT Project 2589 (SAM), Multilingual Speech Input/Output Assessment, Methodology and Standardization. Part of SAM Final Report, University College London, UK, 19 pages.

Graillot, P. (1983). Synthèse de la parole: Évaluation de la qualité en recette. I. S. F., Le Traitement Automatique de la Parole, CNET (French Telecom), Paris, France.

Graillot, P., Emerard, F., and Le Bras, J. (1983). Tests de rime appliqués a des systèmes de synthèse par diphones. Note Technique CNET, NT/LAA/TSS/180, CNET (French Telecom), 55 pages.

Granström, B. and Nord, L. (1989). A Report on Swedish Phonotactic Structures and Constraints. Interim Report, Year One, ESPRIT Project 2589 (SAM) Multi-Lingual Speech Input/Output, Assessment, Methodology and Standardization, pages 135–156.

Greene, B. G., Manous, L. M., and Pisoni, D. B. (1984). Perceptual Evaluation of DECtalk: A First Report on Perfect Paul. Speech Research Laboratory Technical Note No. 84-03, Speech Research Laboratory, Indiana University, Bloomington, USA.

Hampshire, B., Ruden, J., Carlson, R., and Granström, B. (1982). Evaluation of Centrally Produced and Distributed Synthetic Speech. In *STL-QPSR 2-3, Quarterly Progress and Status Report*, pages 18–23, KTH, Stockholm, Sweden.

House, J., MacDermid, C., McGlashan, S., Simpson, A., and Youd, N. J. (1993). Evaluating Synthesised Prosody in Simulations of an Automated Telephone Enquiry Service. In *Proceedings of the European Conference on Speech Communication and Technology (Eurospeech)*, pages 901–904, Berlin, Germany.

House, J. and Youd, N. J. (1992). Evaluating the Prosody of Synthesised Utterances within a Dialogue System. In *Proceedings of the International Conference on Spoken Language Processing (ICSLP)*, pages 1175–1178, Banff, Canada.

Houtgast, T. and Steeneken, H. J. M. (1971). Evaluation of Speech Transmission Channels by Using Artificial Signals. *Acustica*, 25:355–367.

Houtgast, T. and Steeneken, H. J. M. (1984). A Multi-Lingual Evaluation of the Rasti-Method for Estimating Speech Intelligibility in Auditoria. *Acustica*, 54(1):85–199.

Houtgast, T. and Verhave, J. A. (1991). A Physical Approach to Speech Quality Assessment: Correlation Patterns in the Speech Spectrogram. In *Proceedings of the European Conference on Speech Communication and Technology (Eurospeech)*, volume 1, pages 285–288, Genova, Italy.

Houtgast, T. and Verhave, J. A. (1992). An Objective Approach to Speech Quality. ESPRIT Project 2589 (SAM), Multilingual Speech Input/Output Assessment, Methodology and Standardization. Part of SAM Final Report, University College London, UK, 17 pages.

Howard-Jones, P. (1992). SOAP, Speech Output Assessment Package, Version 4.0. ESPRIT Project 2589 (SAM) Report, University College London, UK.

Jekosch, U. (1989). The Cluster-Based Rhyme Test: A Segmental Synthesis Test For Open Vocabulary. In *Proceedings of the ESCA Tutorial and Research Workshop on Speech Input/Output Assessment and Speech Databases*, volume 2, pages 15–18, Noordwijkerhout, The Netherlands.

Jekosch, U. (1990). A Weighted Intelligibility Measure for Speech Assessment. In *Proceedings of the International Conference on Spoken Language Processing (ICSLP)*, volume 2, pages 973–976, Kobe, Japan.

Jekosch, U. (1992). The Cluster-Identification Test. In *Proceedings of the International Conference on Spoken Language Processing (ICSLP)*, volume I, pages 205–209, Banff, Canada.

Jekosch, U. (1993). Cluster-Similarity: A Useful Database for Speech Processing. In *Proceedings of the European Conference on Speech Communication and Technology (Eurospeech)*, pages 195–198, Berlin, Germany.

Karlsson, I. (1992). Evaluations of Acoustic Differences Between Male and Female Voices: A Pilot Study. In *STL-QPSR 1, Quarterly Progress and Status Report*, pages 19–31, KTH, Stockholm, Sweden.

Kasuya, H. (1993). Significance of Suitability Assessment in Speech Synthesis Applications. *IEICE Transactions on Fundamentals of Electronics Communications and Computer Sciences*, E76-A(11):1893–1897.

Kasuya, H. and Kasuya, S. (1992). Relationships between Syllable, Word and Sentence Intelligibilities of Synthetic Speech. In *Proceedings of the International Conference on Spoken Language Processing (ICSLP)*, pages 1215–1218, Banff, Canada.

Kitawaki, N. (1991). Quality Assessment of Coded Speech. In Furui, S. and Sondhi, M. M., editors, *Advances in Speech Signal Processing*, chapter 12, pages 357–385, Marcel Dekker, New York, USA.

Kitawaki, N. and Nagabuchi, H. (1988). Quality Assessment of Speech Coding and Speech Synthesis Systems. *IEEE Communications Magazine*, 26(10):36–44.

Klaus, H., Klix, H., Sotscheck, J., and Fellbaum, K. (1993). An Evaluation System for Ascertaining the Quality of Synthetic Speech Based on Subjective Category Rating Tests. In *Proceedings of the European Conference on Speech Communication and Technology (Eurospeech)*, pages 1679–1682, Berlin, Germany.

Logan, J. S. and Greene, B. G. (1985). Perceptual Evaluation of DECtalk V1.8: Identification of Isolated Phonetically Balanced (PB) Words. Speech Research Laboratory Technical Note No. 85-04, Speech Research Laboratory, Indiana University, Bloomington, USA.

Logan, J. S., Greene, B. G., and Pisoni, D. B. (1985a). Perceptual Evaluation of the Prose 3.0. Text-to-Speech System: Phoneme Intelligibility Measured Using the MRT. Speech Research Laboratory Technical Note No. 85-05, Speech Research Laboratory, Indiana University, Bloomington, USA.

Logan, J. S., Greene, B. G., and Pisoni, D. B. (1989a). Measuring the Segmental Intelligibility of Synthetic Speech Produced by Ten Text-to-Speech Systems. *Journal of the Acoustical Society of America*, 86:566–581.

Logan, J. S., Greene, B. G., and Pisoni, D. B. (1989b). Segmental Intelligibility of Synthetic Speech Produced by Rule. *Journal of the Acoustical Society of America*, 86(2):566–581.

Logan, J. S. and Pisoni, D. B. (1986a). Intelligibility of Phoneme Specific Sentences Using Three Text-to-Speech Systems and a Natural Speech Control. In *Research on Speech Perception, Progress Report 12*, pages 319–333, Speech Research Laboratory, Indiana University, Bloomington, USA.

Logan, J. S. and Pisoni, D. B. (1986b). Preference Judgements Comparing Different Synthetic Voices. In *Research on Speech Perception, Progress Report 12*, pages 263–289, Speech Research Laboratory, Indiana University, Bloomington, USA.

Logan, J. S., Pisoni, D. B., and Greene, B. G. (1985b). Measuring the Segmental Intelligibility of Synthetic Speech: Results from Eight Text-to-Speech Systems. In *Research on Speech Perception, Progress Report 11*, pages 3–31, Speech Research Laboratory, Indiana University, Bloomington, USA.

Lopez-Gonzalo, E., Olaszy, G., and Nemeth, G. (1993). Improvements of the Spanish Version of the Multivox Text-to-Speech System. In *Proceedings of the European Conference on Speech Communication and Technology (Eurospeech)*, pages 869–872, Berlin, Germany.

Manous, L. M., Greene, B. G., and Pisoni, D. B. (1984). Perceptual Evaluation of Prose - the Speech Plus Text-to-Speech System: I. Phoneme Intelligibility and Word Recognition in Meaningful Sentences. Speech Research Laboratory Technical Note 84-04, Speech Research Laboratory, Indiana University, Bloomington, USA.

Manous, L. M. and Pisoni, D. B. (1984). Effects of Signal Duration on the Perception of Natural and Synthetic Speech. In *Research on Speech Perception,*

Progress Report 10, pages 311–321, Speech Research Laboratory, Indiana University, Bloomington, USA.

Manous, L. M., Pisoni, D. B., Dedina, M. J., and Nusbaum, H. C. (1985). Comprehension of Natural and Synthetic Speech Using a Sentence Verification Task. In *Research on Speech Perception, Progress Report 11*, pages 33–57, Speech Research Laboratory, Indiana University, Bloomington, USA.

Mariniak, A. (1993). A Global Framework for the Assessment of Synthetic Speech without Subjects. In *Proceedings of the European Conference on Speech Communication and Technology (Eurospeech)*, pages 1683–1686, Berlin, Germany.

Monaghan, A. I. C. (1989). Evaluating Intonation in the CSTR Text-to-Speech System. In *Proceedings of the ESCA Tutorial and Research Workshop on Speech Input/Output Assessment and Speech Databases*, volume 2, pages 111–114, Noordwijkerhout, the Netherlands.

Monaghan, A. I. C. and Ladd, D. R. (1990). Symbolic Output as the Basis for Evaluating Intonation in Text-to-Speech Systems. *Speech Communication*, 9(4):305–314.

Nusbaum, H. C., Dedina, M. J., and Pisoni, D. B. (1984a). Perceptual Confusions of Consonants in Natural and Synthetic CV Syllables. Speech Research Laboratory Technical Note 84-02, Speech Research Laboratory, Indiana University, Bloomington, USA.

Nusbaum, H. C., Greenspan, S. L., and Pisoni, D. B. (1986). Perceptual Attention in Monitoring Natural and Synthetic Speech. In *Research on Speech Perception, Progress Report 12*, pages 307–318, Speech Research Laboratory, Indiana University, Bloomington, USA.

Nusbaum, H. C. and Pisoni, D. B. (1984). Perceptual Evaluation of Synthetic Speech Generated by Rule. In *Proceedings of the Fourth Voice Data Entry Systems Applications Conference*, Sunnyvale, California, USA.

Nusbaum, H. C., Pisoni, D. B., Schwab, E. C., Luce, P. A., and Slowiaczek, L. M. (1983a). Perception of Synthetic Speech under high Cognitive Load. Paper presented at the Voice SubTAG Meeting, Fort Monmouth, New Jersey, USA.

Nusbaum, H. C., Schwab, E. C., and Pisoni, D. B. (1983b). Perceptual Evaluation of Synthetic Speech: Some Constraints on the Use of Voice Response Systems. In *Research on Speech Perception, Progress Report 9*, pages 283–294, Speech Research Laboratory, Indiana University, Bloomington, USA. Also published in *Proceedings of the Voice Data Entry Systems Application Conference,* pages 1–14, Chicago, USA.

Nusbaum, H. C., Schwab, E. C., and Pisoni, D. B. (1984b). Subjective Evaluation of Synthetic Speech: Measuring Preference, Naturalness and Acceptibility. In *Research on Speech Perception, Progress Report 10*, pages

391–407, Speech Research Laboratory, Indiana University, Bloomington, USA.

Nye, P. W. and Gaitenby, J. H. (1973). Consonant Intelligibility in Synthetic Speech and in Natural Speech Control (Modified Rhyme Test Results). In *Haskins Laboratories Status Report on Speech Research, SR-33*, pages 77–91.

Nye, P. W. and Gaitenby, J. H. (1974). The Intelligibility of Synthetic Monosyllabic Words in Short Syntactically Normal Sentences. In *Haskins Laboratories Status Report on Speech Research, SR-37/38*, pages 169–190.

Nye, P. W., Ingemann, F., and Donald, L. (1975). Synthetic Speech Comprehension: A Comparison of Listener Performances with and Preferences among Different Forms. In *Haskins Laboratories Status Report on Speech Research, SR-41*, pages 117–126.

O'Malley, M. H. and Caisse, M. (1987). How to Evaluate Text-to-Speech Systems. *Speech Technology*, 3(4):66–75.

Ozawa, K. and Logan, J. S. (1989). Perceptual Evaluation of Two Speech Coding Methods by Native and Non-native Speakers of English. *Computer Speech and Language*, 3:53–59.

Pallett, D. H., editor (1982). *Proceedings of the NBS Workshop on Standardization for Speech I/O Technology*, Gaithersburg, Maryland, USA.

Pascal, D. (1987). Méthodologies d'évaluation subjective de la qualité des systèmes de communication. In *Dossier: La qualité des services de communication*. Bulletin No. 28 de l'Institut pour le Développement et l'Amenagement des Télécommunications et de l'Économie, Montpellier, France.

Pascal, D. and Combescure, P. (1988). Évaluation de la qualité de la transmission vocale. L'Écho des Recherches, 132: 31–40.

Pavlovic, C. V. (1987). Derivation of Primary Parameters and Procedures for Use in Speech Intelligibility Predictions. *Journal of the Acoustical Society of America*, 82:413–422.

Pavlovic, C. V. and Rossi, M. (1990). Quality Assessment of Synthesized Speech: Status Report, Systematization, and Recommendations. In *Esprit Project 2589 (SAM), Interim Report, Year One*, pages 354–361.

Pavlovic, C. V., Rossi, M., and Espesser, R. (1989a). A Pilot Study on the Possibility of Using the ESNR Method for Assessing Text-to-Speech Synthesis Systems. In *Final Report, Extension Phase, ESPRIT Project 1542 (SAM)*, pages 40–42.

Pavlovic, C. V., Rossi, M., and Espesser, R. (1989b). Direct Scaling of the Performance of Text-to-Speech Synthesis Systems. In *Proceedings of the European Conference on Speech Communication and Technology (Eurospeech)*, volume 2, pages 644–647, Paris, France.

Pavlovic, C. V., Rossi, M., and Espesser, R. (1989c). Subjective Assessment of Acceptability, Intelligibility and Naturalness of Text-to-Speech Synthesis. In *Proceedings of the ESCA Tutorial and Research Workshop on Speech Input/Output Assessment and Speech Databases*, volume 2, pages 94–98, Noordwijkerhout, The Netherlands.

Pavlovic, C. V., Rossi, M., and Espesser, R. (1990). Use of the Magnitude Estimation Technique for Assessing the Performance of Text-to-Speech Synthesis Systems. In *Interim Report, Year One, Esprit Project 2589 (SAM)*, pages 362–380.

Pavlovic, C. V., Rossi, M., and Espesser, R. (1991a). Definition of Assessment Methodology for Overall Quality of Synthetic Speech. Stage Report 3, Year 2, Interim Report, SAM-UCL-G003, ESPRIT Project 2589 (SAM).

Pavlovic, C. V., Rossi, M., and Espesser, R. (1991b). Methods for Reducing Context Effects in the Subjective Assessment of Synthetic Speech. In *Proceedings of the 12th International Congress on Phonetic Sciences*, pages 82–85, Aix-en-Provence, France.

Picone, J., Goudie-Marshall, K. M., Doddington, G. R., and Fisher, W. (1986). Automatic Text Alignment for Speech Systems Evaluation. *IEEE Transactions on Acoustics, Speech, and Signal Processing (ASSP)*, 34(4):780–784.

Pisoni, D. B. (1989). Perceptual Evaluation of Synthetic Speech: A Tutorial Review. In *Proceedings of the ESCA Tutorial and Research Workshop on Speech Input/Output Assessment and Speech Databases*, Noordwijkerhout, The Netherlands, 13 pages.

Pisoni, D. B. and Dedina, M. J. (1986). Comprehension of Digitally Encoded Natural Speech Using a Sentence Verification Task (SVT): A First Report. In *Research on Speech Perception, Progress Report 12*, pages 3–18, Speech Research Laboratory, Indiana University, Bloomington, USA.

Pisoni, D. B. and Greene, B. G. (1990). The Role of Cognitive Factors in the Perception of Synthetic Speech. In Fujisaki, H., editor, *International Symposium on International Coordination and Standardization of Speech Database and Assessment Techniques for Speech Input/Output*, pages 3–25, Kobe, Japan.

Pisoni, D. B., Greene, B. G., and Logan, J. S. (1989). An Overview of Ten Years of Research on the Perception of Synthetic Speech. In *Proceedings of the ESCA Tutorial and Research Workshop on Speech Input/Output Assessment and Speech Databases*, volume 2, pages 1–4, Noordwijkerhout, The Netherlands.

Pisoni, D. B., Greene, B. G., and Nusbaum, H. C. (1985a). Some Human Factors Issues in the Perception of Synthetic Speech. In *Proceedings of Speech Tech*, pages 57–61, New York, USA.

Pisoni, D. B. and Hunnicutt, S. (1980). Perceptual Evaluation of MITalk: The MIT Unrestricted Text-to-Speech System. In *Proceedings of the Interna-*

tional Conference on Acoustics, Speech and Signal Processing (ICASSP), pages 572–575, Denver, Colorado, USA.

Pisoni, D. B. and Koen, E. (1981). Some Comparison of Intelligibility of Synthetic and Natural Speech at Different Speech-to-Noise Ratios. In *Research on Speech Perception, Progress Report 7*, pages 243–253, Speech Research Laboratory, Indiana University, Bloomington, USA.

Pisoni, D. B., Manous, L. M., and Dedina, M. J. (1986). Comprehension of Natural and Synthetic Speech: II. Effects of Predictability on Verification of Sentences Controlled for Intelligibility. In *Research on Speech Perception, Progress Report 12*, pages 19–41, Speech Research Laboratory, Indiana University, Bloomington, USA.

Pisoni, D. B., Nusbaum, H., and Greene, B. G. (1985b). Perception of Synthetic Speech Generated by Rule. In *Proceedings of the Institute of Electrical and Electronics Engineers (IEEE)*, 73(11): 1665–1676.

Pisoni, D. B. and Nusbaum, H. C. (1986). Developing Methods for Assessing the Performance of Speech Synthesis and Recognition Systems. In *Proceedings of the Human Factors Society*, volume 2, pages 1344–1348, Santa Monica, California, USA. Human Factors Society. (Also appeared in Speech Research Laboratory Publications and Reports 12, Indiana University, Bloomington, USA, 1986.).

Pisoni, D. B., Nusbaum, H. C., Luce, P. A., and Schwab, E. C. (1983). Perceptual Evaluation of Synthetic Speech: Some Considerations of the User/System Interface. In *Proceedings of the International Conference on Acoustics, Speech and Signal Processing (ICASSP)*, pages 535–538, Boston, USA.

Pisoni, D. B., Ralston, J. V., and Lively, S. E. (1990). Some New Directions in Research on Comprehension of Synthetic Speech. In Fujisaki, H., editor, *International Symposium on International Coordination and Standardization of Speech Database and Assessment Techniques for Speech Input/Output*, pages 29–42, Kobe, Japan.

Plomp, R. and Mimpen, A. M. (1979). Improving the Reliability of Testing the Speech Reception Threshold for Sentences. *Audiology*, 8:43–52.

Pols, L. C. W. (1974). Intelligibility of Speech Resynthesized by Using a Dimensional Spectral Representation. In *Speech Communication Seminar*, pages 87–95, Stockholm, Sweden.

Pols, L. C. W. (1975). Analysis and Synthesis of Speech Using a Broad-Band Spectral Representation. In Fant, G. and Tatham, M. A., editors, *Symposium on Auditory Analysis and Perception of Speech*, pages 23–36, Leningrad, Russia. Academic Press.

Pols, L. C. W. (1979a). Consonant Intelligibility of Speech Produced by Dyadic Rule Synthesis. British Telecom Laboratories Technical Memorandum, TM-79-1228-5, 21 pages.

Pols, L. C. W. (1979b). Intelligibility of Intervocalic Consonants in Noise. In *Proceedings of the International Conference on Acoustics, Speech and Signal Processing (ICASSP)*, pages 460–463, Washington DC, USA. Also IZF Report 1978-C25 (expanded version).

Pols, L. C. W. (1986). Assessing the Performance of Speech Technology Systems. In Clark, J. E., editor, *An Introduction to Speech Science*, chapter 5, pages 18–20, First Australian Conference on Speech Science and Technology, Canberra, Australia.

Pols, L. C. W. (1987). Quality Evaluation of Text-to-Speech Synthesis Systems. In *Multilingual Speech Input-Output Assessment, Methodology, and Standardization*. Deliverable of ESPRIT-project 1541. Also IFA Report No. 94, 31 pages.

Pols, L. C. W. (1988). Improving Synthetic Speech Quality by Systematic Evaluation. In *Proceedings of the Institute of Phonetic Sciences, Amsterdam (IFA) 12*, pages 19–27, Amsterdam, The Netherlands. Also in Preprints of the Second Symposium on Advanced Man-Machine Interface Through Spoken Language, November, Makaha, Oahu, Hawaii, USA, 17.1–17.9.

Pols, L. C. W. (1989a). Assessment of Text-to-Speech Synthesis Systems. In Fourcin, A., Harland, G., Barry, W., and Hazan, V., editors, *Speech Input and Output Assessment. Multilingual Methods and Standards*, chapter III, pages 53–81 and 251–266, Ellis Horwoord, Chichester, UK.

Pols, L. C. W. (1989b). ESCA Tutorial Day and Workshop on Speech Input/Output Assessment and Speech Databases. *Speech Communication*, 8(4):379–380.

Pols, L. C. W. (1990a). Assessing the Speech Quality of Text-to-Speech Synthesizers. In *Proceedings of VERBA, International Conference on Speech Technology*, pages 295–302, Rome, Italy.

Pols, L. C. W. (1990b). Does Improved Performance also Contribute to more Phonetic Knowledge? In *Proceedings of the ESCA Tutorial Day on Speech Synthesis*, pages 49–54, Autrans, France.

Pols, L. C. W. (1990c). How Useful are Speech Databases for Rule Synthesis Development and Assessment? In *Proceedings of the International Conference on Spoken Language Processing (ICSLP)*, volume 2, pages 1289–1292, Kobe, Japan.

Pols, L. C. W. (1990d). Improving Synthetic Speech Quality by Systematic Evaluation. In Fujisaki, H., editor, *Recent Research Toward Advanced Man-Machine Interface Through Spoken Language*, pages 445–453, Tokyo, Japan.

Pols, L. C. W. (1990e). Special Issue on Speech Input/Output Assessment and Speech Databases. *Speech Communication*, 9(4):263–388.

Pols, L. C. W. (1990f). 'Standardized' Synthesis Evaluation Methods. In *Proceedings of the International Workshop on International Coordination and*

Standardization of Speech Database and Assessment Techniques for Speech Input/Output, pages 53–60, Kobe, Japan.

Pols, L. C. W. (1991a). Evaluating the Performance of Speech Input/Output Systems. A Report on the ESPRIT-SAM Project. In *Proceedings of Tagung der Deutschen Arbeitsgemeinschaft für Akustik (DAGA)*, pages 139–150, Bochum, Germany.

Pols, L. C. W. (1991b). Evaluating the Performance of Speech Technology Systems. In *Proceedings of the Institute of Phonetic Sciences, Amsterdam (IFA) 15*, pages 27–41, Amsterdam, The Netherlands.

Pols, L. C. W. (1991c). Quality Assessment of Text-to-Speech Synthesis-by-Rule. In Furui, S. and Sondhi, M. M., editors, *Advances in Speech Signal Processing*, chapter 13, pages 387–416, Marcel Dekker, New York, USA.

Pols, L. C. W. (1994). Speech Technology Systems: Performance and Evaluation. In *Encyclopedia of Language & Linguistics*, volume 8, pages 4289–4296, Pergamon Press, Oxford, UK.

Pols, L. C. W. and Boxelaar, G. W. (1986). Comparative Evaluation of the Speech Quality of Speech Coders and Text-to-Speech Synthesizers. In *Proceedings of the International Conference on Acoustics, Speech and Signal Processing (ICASSP)*, pages 901–904, Tokyo, Japan.

Pols, L. C. W., Lefevre, J. P., Boxelaar, G., and van Son, N. (1987). Word Intelligibility of a Rule Synthesis System for French. In *Proceedings of the European Conference on Speech Technology*, volume 1, pages 179–182, Edinburgh, UK.

Pols, L. C. W. and Olive, J. P. (1983). Intelligibility of Consonants in CVC Utterances Produced by Dyadic Rule Synthesis. *Speech Communication*, 2(1):3–13.

Pols, L. C. W. and SAM-partners (1992). Multi-Lingual Synthesis Evaluation Methods. In *Proceedings of the International Conference on Spoken Language Processing (ICSLP)*, volume 1, pages 181–184, Banff, Canada.

Pols, L. C. W. and van Bezooijen, R. (1991). Gaining Phonetic Knowledge whilst Improving Synthetic Speech Quality? *Journal of Phonetics*, 19(1):139–146.

Pols, L. C. W. and van Rooijen, J. N. M. (1974). Intelligibility of Speech Resynthesized by Using a Dimensional Spectral Representation. In *Proceedings of the Eighth International Conference on Acoustics (ICA)*, page 297, London, UK.

Portele, T. (1993). Evaluation der segmentalen Verständlichkeit des Sprachsynthesesystems HADIFIX mit der SAM-Testprozedur. In *Proceedings of Tagung der Deutschen Arbeitsgemeinschaft für Akustik (DAGA)*, pages 1032–1035, Frankfurt, Germany.

Pratt, R. L. (1984). The Assessment of Speech Intelligibility at RSRE. In *Proceedings of the Instititute of Acoustics*, volume 6, Part 4, pages 439–443.

Pratt, R. L. (1986). On the Intelligibility of Synthetic Speech. In *Proceedings of the Instititute of Acoustics*, volume 8, Part 7, pages 183–192.

Pratt, R. L. (1987). Quantifying the Performance of Text-to-Speech Synthesizers. *Speech Technology*, 3(4):54–64.

Purdy, S. C. and Pavlovic, C. V. (1991). Scaling of Speech Intelligibility Using Magnitude Estimation and Category Estimation and Paired Comparisons. In *Proceedings of the 12th International Congress on Phonetic Sciences Sciences*, pages 434–437, Aix-en-Provence, France.

Purdy, S. C. and Pavlovic, C. V. (1992). Reliability, Sensitivity and Validity of Magnitude Estimation, Category Scaling and Paired-Comparison Judgments of Speech Intelligibility by Older Listeners. *Audiology*, 31:254–271.

Robert, J.-M., Choiniere, A., and Descout, R. (1989). Subjective Evaluation of Naturalness and Acceptability of Three Text-to-Speech Systems in French. In *Proceedings of the European Conference on Speech Communication and Technology (Eurospeech)*, volume 2, pages 640–643, Paris, France.

Rossi, M., Espesser, R., and Pavlovic, C. V. (1991a). Subjective Rating of Text-to-Speech Synthesis: The Effects of an Internal Reference and Cross-Modality Matching. *VERBUM, Tome XIV, fascicule 2-3-4*, pages 367–377.

Rossi, M., Espesser, R., and Pavlovic, C. V. (1991b). The Effects of an Internal Reference System and Cross-Modality Matching on the Subjective Rating of Speech Synthesisers. In *Proceedings of the European Conference on Speech Communication and Technology (Eurospeech)*, volume 1, pages 273–276, Genova, Italy.

Rossi, M., Pavlovic, C., and Espesser, R. (1989). Magnitude Estimation Technique in Evaluating Text-to-Speech Synthesis. In *Proceedings of the 13th International Congress on Acoustics*, volume 2, pages 479–482, Belgrade, Yugoslavia.

Rosson, M. B. (1985). Listener Training for Speech-Output Applications. In Borman, L. and Curtis, B., editors, *Proceedings of the Conference on Human Factors in Computing Systems*, pages 193–196, New York, USA. ACM.

Salza, P. L., Sandri, S., and Foti, E. (1987). Evaluation of Experimental Diphones for Text-to-Speech Synthesis. In *Proceedings of the European Conference on Speech Technology*, volume 1, pages 63–66, Edinburgh, UK.

Schnabel, B. (1986). Évaluation de la qualité de l'allemand synthétisé par diphones. In *15èmes Journées d'Etudes sur la Parole, GALF*, pages 19–20, Aix-en-Provence, France.

Schwab, E. C., Nusbaum, H. C., and Pisoni, D. B. (1983). Some Effects of Training on the Perception of Synthetic Speech. In *Research on Speech Perception, Progress Report 9*, pages 39–77, Indiana University, USA.

Schwab, E. C. and Pisoni, D. B. (1983). The Effects of Training on the Intelligibility of Synthetic Speech: I. Pre-Test and Post-Test Data. *Journal of the Acoustical Society of America*, 73, S3 (A).

Silverman, K., Basson, S., and Levas, S. (1990). Evaluating Synthesis Performance: Is Segmental Intelligibility Enough? In *Proceedings of the International Conference on Spoken Language Processing (ICSLP)*, pages 981–984, Kobe, Japan.

Sorin, C. (1982/83). Évaluation de la contribution de F0 a l'intelligibilité. *Recherches Acoustiques, CNET*, 7:141–155.

Sorin, C., Benoit, C., Charpentier, F., Emerard, F., and Schnabel, B. (1988). Évaluation de systèmes de synthèse. Contribution CNET au Projet Esprit SAM-Speech Assessment Methods, France.

Spiegel, M. F., Altom, M. J., Macchi, M. J., and Wallace, K. L. (1990). Comprehensive Assessment of the Telephone Intelligibility of Synthesized and Natural Speech. *Speech Communications*, 9:279–292.

Steeneken, H. J. M. (1982). Ontwikkeling en toetsing van een Nederlandstalige diagnostische rijmtest voor het testen van spraakkommunikatiekanalen. IZF Report 1982-13, TNO Institute for Perception, Soesterberg, The Netherlands (in Dutch).

Steeneken, H. J. M. (1987a). Comparison among Three Subjective and One Objective Intelligibility Test. IZF Report 1987-8, TNO Institute for Perception, Soesterberg, The Netherlands.

Steeneken, H. J. M. (1987b). Diagnostic Information of Subjective Intelligibility Tests. In *Proceedings of the International Conference on Acoustics, Speech and Signal Processing (ICASSP)*, pages 131–134, Dallas, USA.

Steeneken, H. J. M. (1992a). *On Measuring and Predicting Speech Intelligibility*. Doctoral thesis, University of Amsterdam, The Netherlands.

Steeneken, H. J. M. (1992b). Quality Evaluation of Speech Processing Systems. In Ince, N., editor, *Digital Speech Coding: Speech Coding, Synthesis and Recognition*, chapter 5, pages 127–160, Kluwer, Norwell, USA.

Steeneken, H. J. M. and Geurtsen, F. W. M. (1988). Description of the RSG-10 Noise Data-Base. IZF Report 1988-3, TNO Institute for Perception, Soesterberg, The Netherlands.

Steeneken, H. J. M., Geurtsen, F. W. M., and Agterhuis, E. (1990). Speech Data-Base for Intelligibility and Speech Quality Measurements. IZF Report 1990 A-13, TNO Institute for Perception, Soesterberg, The Netherlands.

Steeneken, H. J. M. and Houtgast, T. (1973). Intelligibility in Telecommunication Derived from Physical Measurements. In *Proceedings of the Symposium on Intelligibilité de la Parole*, pages 73–80, Liège, Belgium.

Steeneken, H. J. M. and Houtgast, T. (1978). Comparison of some Methods for Measuring Speech Levels. IZF Report 1978-22, TNO Institute for Perception, Soesterberg, The Netherlands.

Steeneken, H. J. M. and Houtgast, T. (1980). A Physical Method for Measuring Speech-Transmission Quality. *Journal of the Acoustical Society of America*, 67:318–326.

Steeneken, H. J. M. and Houtgast, T. (1991). On the Mutual Dependency of Octave-Band Specific Contributions to Speech Intelligibility. In *Proceedings of the European Conference on Speech Communication and Technology (Eurospeech)*, pages 1133–1136, Genova, Italy.

Steeneken, H. J. M. and van Velden, J. G. (1991). RAMOS Recognizer Assessment by Means of Manipulation of Speech Applied to Connected Speech Recognition. In *Proceedings of the European Conference on Speech Communication and Technology (Eurospeech)*, pages 529–532, Genova, Italy.

Steeneken, H. J. M., Verhave, J. A., and Houtgast, T. (1993). Objective Assessment of Speech Communication Systems. In *Proceedings of the European Conference on Speech Communication and Technology (Eurospeech)*, pages 203–206, Berlin, Germany.

Sydeserff, H. A., Caley, R. J., Isard, S. D., Jack, M. A., Monaghan, A. I. C., and Verhoeven, J. (1991). Evaluation of Synthetic Speech Techniques in a Comprehension Task. In *Proceedings of the European Conference on Speech Communication and Technology (Eurospeech)*, volume 1, pages 277–280, Genova, Italy.

Syrdal, A. K. (1987). Methods for a Detailed Analysis of Dynastat DRT Results. Technical Memorandum, AT&T Bell Laboratories.

Syrdal, A. K. and Sciacca, B. A. (1993). A Diagnostic Text-to-Speech Intelligibility Test. *Journal of the Acoustical Society of America*, 94:paper 4aSP9, 1842–1843 (A).

van Bezooijen, R. (1988). Evaluation of the Quality of Consonant Clusters in Two Synthesis Systems for Dutch. In *Proceedings of Speech'88, Seventh FASE Symposium*, volume 2, pages 445–452, Edinburgh, UK.

van Bezooijen, R. and Jongenburger, W. (1993). Evaluation of an Electronic Newspaper for the Blind in the Netherlands. In Granström, B., Hunnicutt, S., and Spens, E., editors, *Proceedings of the ESCA Workshop on Speech and Language Technology for Disabled Persons*, pages 195–198, Stockholm, Sweden.

van Bezooijen, R. and Pols, L. C. W. (1987). Evaluation of Two Synthesis-by-Rule Systems for Dutch. In *Proceedings of the European Conference on Speech Technology*, volume 1, pages 183–186, Edinburgh, UK.

van Bezooijen, R. and Pols, L. C. W. (1989a). Evaluation of a Sentence Accentuation Algorithm for a Dutch Text-to-Speech System. In *Proceedings of the European Conference on Speech Communication and Technology (Eurospeech)*, volume 1, pages 218–221, Paris, France.

van Bezooijen, R. and Pols, L. C. W. (1989b). Evaluation of Text-to-Speech Conversion for Dutch: From Segment to Text. In *Proceedings of the ESCA Tutorial and Research Workshop on Speech Input/Output Assessment and Speech Databases*, volume 2, pages 103–106, Noordwijkerhout, The Netherlands.

van Bezooijen, R. and Pols, L. C. W. (1990). Evaluating Text-to-Speech Systems: Some Methodological Aspects. *Speech Communication*, 9(4): 263–270.

van Bezooijen, R. and Pols, L. C. W. (1991a). Evaluation of Allophone and Diphone Based Text-to-Speech Conversion at the Paragraph Level. In *Proceedings of the 12th International Congress on Phonetic Sciences*, volume 3, pages 498–501, Aix-en-Provence, France.

van Bezooijen, R. and Pols, L. C. W. (1991b). Performance of Text-to-Speech Conversion for Dutch: A Comparative Evaluation of Allophone and Diphone Based Synthesis at the Level of the Segment, the Word, and the Paragraph. In *Proceedings of the European Conference on Speech Communication and Technology (Eurospeech)*, volume 2, pages 871–874, Genova, Italy.

van Bezooijen, R. and Pols, L. C. W. (1993). Evaluation of Text-to-Speech Conversion for Dutch. In van Heuven, V. J. and Pols, L. C. W., editors, *Analysis and Synthesis of Speech. Strategic Research Towards High-Quality Text-to-Speech Generation*, pages 339–360, Mouton de Gruyter, Berlin, Germany.

van Santen, J. P. H. (1992). Diagnostic Perceptual Experiments for Text-to-Speech System Evaluation. In *Proceedings of the International Conference on Spoken Language Processing (ICSLP)*, volume 1, pages 555–558, Banff, Canada.

van Santen, J. P. H. (1993). Perceptual Experiments for Diagnostic Testing of Text-to-Speech Systems. *Computer Speech and Language*, 7(1):49–100.

van Son, N. and Pols, L. C. W. (1989a). Final Evaluation of Three Multipulse LPC Coders: CVC Intelligibility, Quality Assessment and Speaker Identification. ESPRIT-SPIN Deliverable, IZF Report 17, IFA Report No. 103, 68 pages.

van Son, N. and Pols, L. C. W. (1989b). First Quality Evaluation of a Diphone-Based Synthesis System for Italian. ESPRIT-SPIN Deliverable, IZF Report 15, IFA Report No. 105, 47 pages.

van Son, N. and Pols, L. C. W. (1989c). Intelligibility of Words in Isolation and Words in Semantically Unpredictable Sentences. A Study of Two Diphone-Based Speech Synthesis Systems in French. ESPRIT-SPIN Deliverable, 20 pages + app.

van Son, N. and Pols, L. C. W. (1989d). Review of Synthesis Evaluation Activities during Five ESPRIT/SPIN Years. ESPRIT-SPIN Deliverable, 25 pages.

van Son, N. and Pols, L. C. W. (1989e). Second Quality Evaluation of a French Diphone-Based Synthesis System: Identification and Quality Ratings of Consonant Clusters. ESPRIT-SPIN Deliverable, IZF Report 16, IFA Report No. 104, 51 pages.

van Son, N., Pols, L. C. W., Sandri, S., and Salza, P. L. (1988). First Quality Evaluation of a Diphone-Based Speech Synthesis System for Italian. In *Proceedings of Speech'88, Seventh FASE Symposium*, volume 2, pages 429–436, Edinburgh, UK.

Voiers, W. D. (1977). Diagnostic Evaluation of Speech Intelligibility. In Hawley, M., editor, *Benchmark Papers in Acoustics, Speech Intelligibility and Speaker Recognition*, volume 11, pages 374–387, Dowden, Hutinson, & Ross, Stroudsburg, USA.

Voiers, W. D. (1982). Measurement of Intrinsic Deficiency in Transmitted Speech: The Diagnostic Discrimination Test. In *Proceedings of the International Conference on Acoustics, Speech and Signal Processing (ICASSP)*, pages 1004–1007, Paris, France.

Voiers, W. D. (1983). Evaluating Processed Speech Using the Diagnostic Rhyme Test. *Speech Technology*, 1(4):30–39.

Vonwiller, J., King, R., Stevens, K., and Latimer, C. (1990). Comprehension of Prosody in Synthesised Speech. In *Proceedings of the Third Australian International Conference on Speech Science and Technology (SST)*, pages 244–249, Melbourne, Australia.

Wery, B. W. M. and Steeneken, H. J. M. (1993). Intelligibility Evaluation of 4-5 KBPS CELP and MBE Vocoders: The Hermes Program Experiment. In *Proceedings of the European Conference on Speech Communication and Technology (Eurospeech)*, pages 67–70, Berlin, Germany.

Zhou, K. C. (1986). Preliminary Evaluation of a Chinese Text-to-Speech System. In *Proceedings of the First Australian International Conference on Speech Science and Technology (SST)*, pages 162–167, Canberra, Australia.

This list is, of course, not complete, but it supplies some relevant keywords for a further search and presents a snapshot of the types of work that have been carried out in the past. For a more complete and up-to-date listing of relevant papers, please consult (and contribute to) the web pages of the ISCA Speech Synthesis Special Interest Group.

Chapter 3

MODELLING AND EVALUATING VERBAL AND NON-VERBAL COMMUNICATION IN TALKING ANIMATED INTERFACE AGENTS

Björn Granström and David House

KTH (Royal Institute of Technology)
Stockholm, Sweden

bjorn@speech.kth.se, davidh@speech.kth.se

Abstract   The use of animated talking agents is a novel feature of many multimodal experimental spoken dialogue systems. The addition and integration of a virtual talking head has direct implications for the way in which users approach and interact with such systems. Established techniques for evaluating the quality, efficiency, and other impacts of this technology have not yet appeared in standard textbooks. The focus of this chapter is to look into the communicative function of the agent, both the capability to increase intelligibility of the spoken interaction and the possibility to make the flow of the dialogue smoother, through different kinds of communicative gestures such as gestures for emphatic stress, emotions, turntaking, and negative or positive system feedback. The chapter reviews state-of-the-art animated agent technologies and their applications primarily in dialogue systems. The chapter also includes examples of methods of evaluating communicative gestures in different contexts.

Keywords   Audio-visual speech synthesis; Talking heads; Animated agents; Spoken dialogue systems; Visual prosody.

1   Introduction

In our interaction with others, we easily and naturally use all of our sensory modalities as we communicate and exchange information. Our senses are exceptionally well adapted for these tasks, and our brain enables us to effortlessly integrate information from different modalities fusing data to optimally meet the current communication needs. As we attempt to take advantage of

65

L. Dybkjær et al. (eds.), Evaluation of Text and Speech Systems, 65–98.

the effective communication potential of human conversation, we see an increasing need to embody the conversational partner using audio-visual verbal and non-verbal communication in the form of animated talking agents. The use of animated talking agents is currently a novel feature of many multimodal experimental spoken dialogue systems. The addition and integration of a virtual talking head has direct implications for the way in which users approach and interact with such systems (Cassell et al., 2000). However, established techniques for evaluating the quality, efficiency, and other impacts of this technology have not yet appeared in standard textbooks.

Effective interaction in dialogue systems involves both the presentation of information and the flow of interactive dialogue. A talking animated agent can provide the user with an interactive partner whose goal is to take the role of the human agent. An effective agent is one who is capable of supplying the user with relevant information, can fluently answer questions concerning complex user requirements, and can ultimately assist the user in a decision-making process through the interactive flow of conversation. One way to achieve believability is through the use of a talking head where information is transformed through text into speech, articulator movements, speech-related gestures, and conversational gestures. Useful applications of talking heads include aids for the hearing impaired, educational software, audio-visual human perception experiments (Massaro, 1998), entertainment, and high-quality audio-visual text-to-speech synthesis for applications such as news-reading. The use of the talking head aims at increasing effectiveness by building on the user's social skills to improve the flow of the dialogue (Bickmore and Cassell, 2005). Visual cues to feedback, turntaking, and signalling the system's internal state are key aspects of effective interaction. There is also currently much interest in the use of visual cues as a means to ensure that participants in a conversation share an understanding of what has been said, i.e. a common ground (Nakano et al., 2003).

The talking head developed at KTH is based on text-to-speech synthesis. Audio speech synthesis is generated from a text representation in synchrony with visual articulator movements of the lips, tongue, and jaw. Linguistic information in the text is used to generate visual cues for relevant prosodic categories such as prominence, phrasing, and emphasis. These cues generally take the form of eyebrow and head movements which we have termed "visual prosody" (Granström et al., 2001). These types of visual cues with the addition of, for example, a smiling or frowning face are also used as conversational gestures to signal such things as positive or negative feedback, turntaking regulation, and the system's internal state. In addition, the head can visually signal attitudes and emotions. Recently, we have been exploring data-driven methods to model articulation and facial parameters of major importance for conveying social signals and emotion.

The focus of this chapter is to look into the communicative function of the agent, both the capability to increase intelligibility of the spoken interaction and the possibility to make the flow of the dialogue smoother, through different kinds of communicative gestures such as gestures for emphatic stress, emotions, turntaking, and negative or positive system feedback. The chapter reviews state-of-the-art animated agent technologies and their applications primarily in dialogue systems. The chapter also includes some examples of methods of evaluating communicative gestures in different contexts.

2 KTH Parametric Multimodal Speech Synthesis

Animated synthetic talking faces and characters have been developed using a number of different techniques and for a variety of purposes for more than two decades. Historically, our approach is based on parameterised, deformable 3D facial models, controlled by rules within a text-to-speech framework (Carlson and Granström, 1997). The rules generate the parameter tracks for the face from a representation of the text, taking coarticulation into account (Beskow, 1995). We employ a generalised parameterisation technique to adapt a static 3D wireframe of a face for visual speech animation (Beskow, 1997). Based on concepts first introduced by Parke (1982), we define a set of parameters that will deform the wireframe by applying weighted transformations to its vertices. One critical difference from Parke's system, however, is that we have decoupled the model definitions from the animation engine. The animation engine uses different definition files that are created for each face. This greatly increases flexibility, allowing models with different topologies to be animated from the same control parameter program, such as a text-to-speech system.

The models are made up of polygon surfaces that are rendered in 3D using standard computer graphics techniques. The surfaces can be articulated and deformed under the control of a number of parameters. The parameters are designed to allow for intuitive interactive or rule-based control. For the purposes of animation, parameters can be roughly divided into two (overlapping) categories: those controlling speech articulation and those used for non-articulatory cues and emotions. The articulatory parameters include jaw rotation, lip rounding, bilabial occlusion, labiodental occlusion, and tongue tip elevation. The non-articulatory category includes eyebrow raising, eyebrow shape, smile, gaze direction, and head orientation. Furthermore, some of the articulatory parameters such as jaw rotation can be useful in signalling non-verbal elements such as certain emotions. The display can be chosen to show only the surfaces or the polygons for the different components of the face. The surfaces can be made (semi-)transparent to display the internal parts of the model,

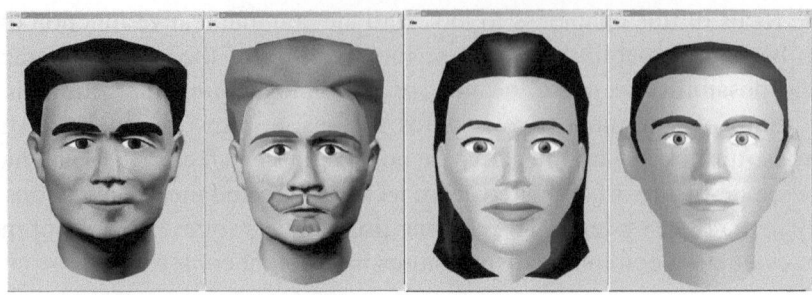

Figure 1.   Some different versions of the KTH talking head.

including the tongue, palate, jaw, and teeth (Engwall, 2003). The internal parts are based on articulatory measurements using magnetic resonance imaging, electromagnetic articulography, and electropalatography, in order to ensure that the model's physiology and movements are realistic. This is of importance for language learning situations, where the transparency of the skin may be used to explain non-visible articulations (Cole et al., 1999; Massaro et al., 2003; Massaro and Light, 2003; Bälter et al., 2005). Several face models have been developed for different applications, and some of them can be seen in Figure 1. All can be parametrically controlled by the same articulation rules.

For stimuli preparation and explorative investigations, we have developed a control interface that allows fine-grained control over the trajectories for acoustic as well as visual parameters. The interface is implemented as an extension to the WaveSurfer application (http://www.speech.kth.se/wavesurfer) (Sjölander and Beskow, 2000), which is a freeware tool for recording, playing, editing, viewing, printing, and labelling audio data.

The interface makes it possible to start with an utterance synthesised from text, with the articulatory parameters generated by rule, and then interactively edit the parameter tracks for F0, visual (non-articulatory) parameters as well as the durations of individual segments in the utterance to produce specific cues. An example of the user interface is shown in Figure 2. In the top box a text can be entered in Swedish or English. The selection of language triggers separate text-to-speech systems with different phoneme definitions and rules, built in the Rulsys notation (Carlson and Granström, 1997). One example of language-dependent rules are the rules for visual realisation of interdentals in English which do not apply to Swedish. The generated phonetic transcription can be edited. On pushing "Synthesize", rule-generated parameters will be created and displayed in different panes below. The selection of parameters is user-controlled. The lower section contains segmentation and the acoustic waveform. A talking face is displayed in a separate window. The acoustic synthesis can be exchanged for a natural utterance and synchronised to the face

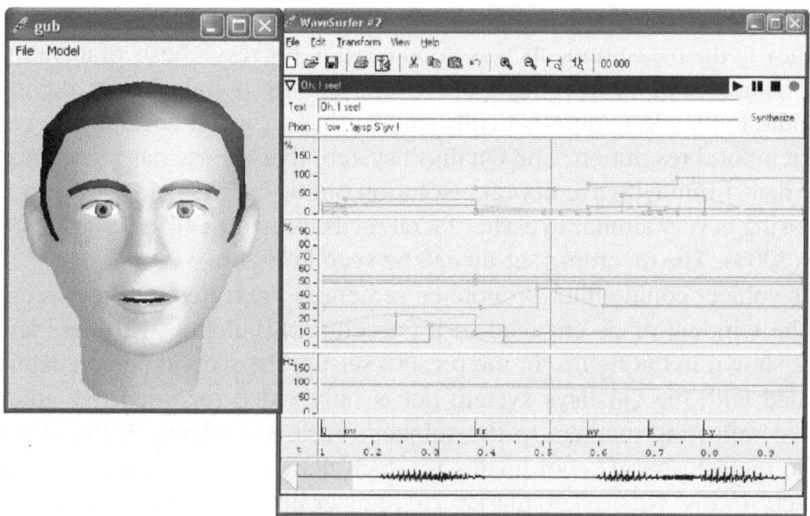

Figure 2. The WaveSurfer user interface for parametric manipulation of the multimodal synthesis.

synthesis on a segment-by-segment basis by running the face synthesis with phoneme durations from the natural utterance. This requires a segmentation of the natural utterance which can be done (semi-)automatically in, for example, WaveSurfer. The combination of natural and synthetic speech is useful for different experiments on multimodal integration and has been used in the Synface/Teleface project (see below). In language learning applications this feature could be used to add to the naturalness of the tutor's voice in cases when the acoustic synthesis is judged to be inappropriate. The parametric manipulation tool is used to experiment with, and define, gestures. Using this tool we have constructed a library of gestures that can be invoked via XML markup in the output text.

3 Data Collection and Data-Driven Visual Synthesis

More recently, we have begun experimenting with data-driven visual synthesis using a newly developed MPEG-4 compatible talking head (Beskow and Nordenberg, 2005). A data-driven approach enables us to capture the interaction between facial expression and articulation. This is especially important when trying to synthesize emotional expressions (cf. Nordstrand et al., 2004).

To automatically extract important facial movements we have employed a motion capture procedure. We wanted to be able to obtain both articulatory data as well as other facial movements at the same time, and it was crucial that the accuracy in the measurements was good enough for resynthesis of an animated head. Optical motion tracking systems are gaining popularity for being able to handle the tracking automatically and for having good accuracy as well as good temporal resolution. The Qualisys system that we use has an accuracy of better than 1 mm with a temporal resolution of 60 Hz. The data acquisition and processing is very similar to earlier facial measurements carried out by Beskow et al. (2003). The recording set-up can be seen in Figure 3.

The subject could either pronounce sentences presented on the screen outside the window or be engaged in a (structured) dialogue with another person as shown in the figure. In the present set-up, the second person cannot be recorded with the Qualisys system but is only video recorded. By attaching infrared reflecting markers to the subject's face, see Figure 3, the system is able to register the 3D coordinates for each marker at a frame rate of 60 Hz, i.e. every 17 ms. We used 30 markers to register lip movements as well as other facial movements such as eyebrows, cheek, chin, and eyelids. Additionally we placed three markers on the chest to register head movements with respect to the torso. A pair of spectacles with four markers attached was used as a reference to be able to factor out head and body movements when looking at the facial movements specifically.

The databases we have thus far collected have enabled us to analyse speech movements such as articulatory variation in expressive speech (Nordstrand et al., 2004) in addition to providing us with data with which to develop data-driven visual synthesis. The data has also been used to directly drive synthetic 3D face models which adhere to the MPEG-4 Facial Animation (FA) standard (Pandzic and Forchheimer, 2002) enabling us to perform comparative

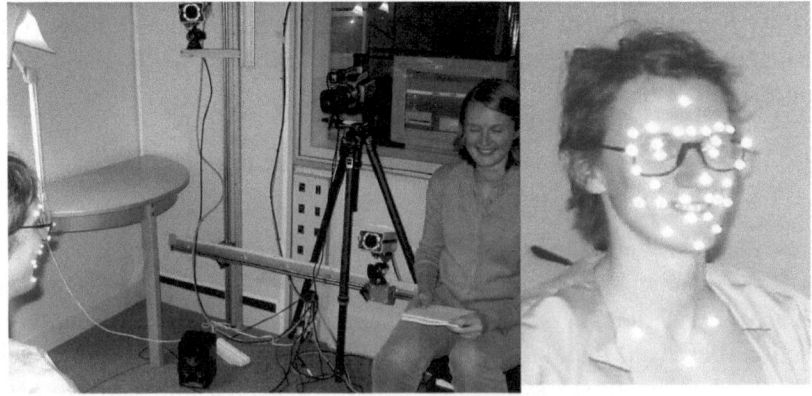

Figure 3.   Data collection set-up with video and IR-cameras, microphone and a screen for prompts (left), and test subject with the IR-reflecting markers glued to the face (right).

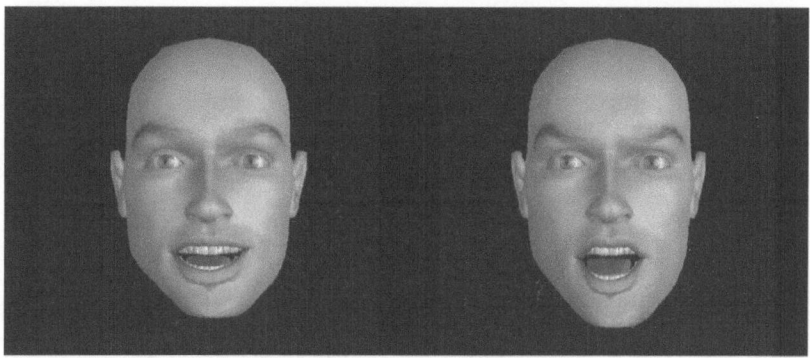

Figure 4. Visual stimuli generated by data-driven synthesis from the happy database (left) and the angry database (right) using the MPEG-4 compatible talking head.

evaluation studies of different animated faces within the EU-funded PF-Star project (Beskow et al., 2004a, b).

The new talking head is based on the MPEG-4 FA standard and is a textured 3D model of a male face comprising around 15,000 polygons. Current work on data-driven visual synthesis is aimed at synthesising visual speech articulation for different emotions (Beskow and Nordenberg, 2005). The database consists of recordings of a male native Swedish amateur actor who was instructed to produce 75 short sentences with the six emotions happiness, sadness, surprise, disgust, fear, and anger plus neutral (Beskow et al., 2004c). Using the data-bases of different emotions results in talking head animations which differ in articulation and visual expression. The audio synthesis used at present is the same as that for the parametric synthesis. Examples of the new head displaying two different emotions taken from the database are shown in Figure 4.

4 Evaluating Intelligibility and Information Presentation

One of the more striking examples of improvement and effectiveness in speech intelligibility is taken from the Synface project which aims at improving telephone communication for the hearing impaired (Agelfors et al., 1998). A demonstrator of the system for telephony with a synthetic face that articulates in synchrony with a natural voice has now been implemented as a result of the project. The telephone interface used in the demonstrator is shown in Figure 5.

Evaluation studies within this project were mainly oriented towards investigating differences in intelligibility between speech alone and speech with the addition of a talking head. These evaluation studies were performed off-line: e.g. the speech material was manually labelled so that the visible speech

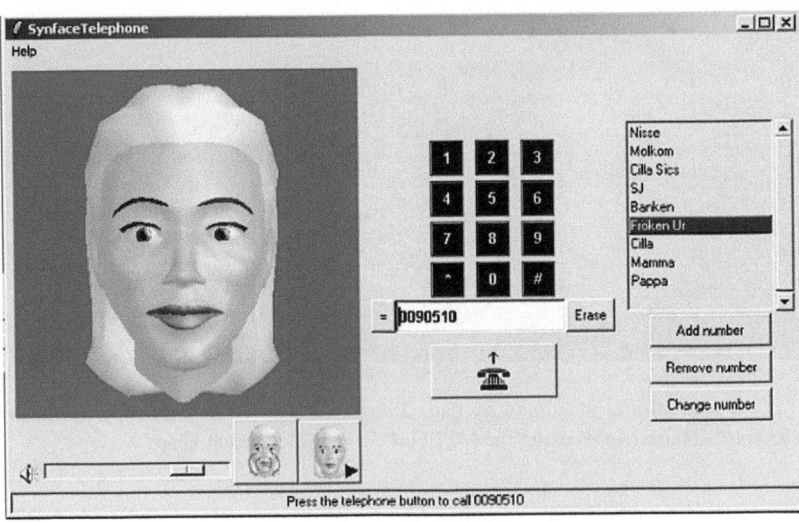

Figure 5. Telephone interface for Synface.

synthesis always generated the correct phonemes rather than being generated from the Synface recogniser, which can introduce recognition errors. The results of a series of tests using vowel-consonant-vowel (VCV) words and hearing-impaired subjects showed a significant gain in intelligibility when the talking head was added to a natural voice. With the synthetic face, consonant identification improved from 29% to 54% correct responses. This compares to the 57% correct response result obtained by using the natural face. In certain cases, notably the consonants consisting of lip movement (i.e., the bilabial and labiodental consonants), the response results were in fact better for the synthetic face than for the natural face. This points to the possibility of using over-articulation strategies for the talking face in these kinds of applications. Recent results indicate that a certain degree of overarticulation can be advantageous in improving intelligibility (Beskow et al., 2002b).

Similar intelligibility tests have been run using normal hearing subjects where the audio signal was degraded by adding white noise (Agelfors et al., 1998). Similar results were obtained. For example, for a synthetic male voice, consonant identification improved from 31% without the face to 45% with the face.

Hearing-impaired persons often subjectively report that some speakers are much easier to speech-read than others. It is reasonable to hypothesise that this variation depends on a large number of factors, such as rate of speaking, amplitude and dynamics of the articulatory movements, orofacial anatomy of the speaker, presence of facial hair, and so on. Using traditional techniques, however, it is difficult to isolate these factors to get a quantitative measure of their relative contribution to readability. In an attempt to address this issue, we employ a synthetic talking head that allows us to generate stimuli where each variable can be studied in isolation. In this section we focus on a factor that we will refer to as articulation strength, which is implemented as a global scaling of the amplitude of the articulatory movements.

In one experiment the articulation strength has been adjusted by applying a global scaling factor to the parameters marked with an x in Table 1. They can all be varied between 25% and 200% of normal. Normal is defined as the default articulation produced by the rules, which are hand-tuned to match a target person's articulation.

The default parameter settings are chosen to optimise perceived similarity between a target speaker and the synthetic faces. However, it is difficult to know whether these settings are optimal in a lip-reading situation for hearing-impaired persons. An informal experiment was pursued to find out the preferred articulation strength and its variance. Twenty-four subjects all closely connected to the field of aural rehabilitation either professionally or as hearing impaired were asked to choose the most intelligible face out of eight recordings of the Swedish sentence "De skrattade mycket högt" (They laughed very loudly). The subjects viewed the eight versions in eight separate windows on a computer screen and were allowed to watch and compare the versions as many times as they wished by clicking on each respective window to activate the recordings. The recordings had 25%, 50%, 75%, 100%, 112%, 125%, 150% and 175% of the default strength of articulation. The default strength of articulation is based on the phoneme parameter settings for visual speech synthesis as developed by Beskow (1997). The different articulation strengths were implemented as a global scaling of the amplitude of the articulatory movements. The amount of co-articulation was not altered.

The average preferred hyperarticulation was found to be 24%, given the task to optimise the subjective ability to lip-read. The highest and lowest preferred

Table 1. Parameters used for articulatory control of the face. The second column indicates which ones are adjusted in the experiments described here.

Parameter	Adjusted in experiment
Jaw rotation	x
Labiodental occlusion	
Bilabial occlusion	
Lip rounding	
Lip protrusion	x
Mouth spread	x
Tongue tip elevation	x

values were 150% and 90% respectively with a standard deviation of 16%. The option of setting the articulation strength to the user's subjective preference could be included in the Synface application. The question of whether or not the preferred setting genuinely optimises intelligibility and naturalness was also studied as is described below.

Experiment 1: Audio-visual consonant identification.   To test the possible quantitative impact of articulation strength, as defined in the previous section, we performed a VCV test. Three different articulation strengths were used: 75%, 100%, and 125% of the default articulation strength for the visual speech synthesis. Stimuli consisted of nonsense words in the form of VCV combinations. Seventeen consonants were used: /p, b, m, f, v, t, d, n, s, l, r, k, g, ng, sj, tj, j/ in two symmetric vowel contexts /a, U/ yielding a total of 34 different VCV words. The task was to identify the consonant. (The consonants are given in Swedish orthography – the non-obvious IPA correspondences are: ng=/ŋ/, sj=/ɧ/, tj= /ç/.) Each word was presented with each of the three levels of articulation strength. The list was randomised. To avoid starting and ending effects, five extra stimuli were inserted at the beginning and two at the end.

Stimuli were presented audio-visually by the synthetic talking head. The audio was taken from the test material from the Teleface project recordings of natural speech from a male speaker (Agelfors et al., 1998). The audio had previously been segmented and labelled, allowing us to generate control parameter tracks for facial animation using the visual synthesis rules.

The nonsense words were presented in white masking noise at a signal-to-noise ratio of 3 dB.

Twenty-four subjects participated in the experiment. They were all undergraduate students at KTH. The experiments were run in plenary by presenting the animations on a large screen using an overhead projector. The subjects responded on pre-printed answer sheets.

The mean results for the different conditions can be seen in Table 2. For the /a/ context there are only minor differences in the identification rate, while the

Table 2.   Percent correct consonant identification in the VCV test with respect to place of articulation, presented according to vowel context and articulation strength.

Articulation strength (%)	/aCa/	/UCU/
75	78.7	50.5
100	75.2	62.2
125	80.9	58.1

results for the /U/ context are generally worse, especially for the 75% articulation rate condition. A plausible reason for this difference lies in the better visibility of tongue articulations in the more open /a/ vowel context than in the context of the rounded /U/ vowel. It can also be speculated that movements observed on the outside of the face can add to the superior readability of consonants in the /a/ context. However, we could not find evidence for this in a study based on simultaneous recordings of face and tongue movements (Beskow et al., 2003; Engwall and Beskow, 2003). In general, the contribution of articulation strength to intelligibility might be different with other speech material such as connected sentences.

Experiment 2: Rating of naturalness. Eighteen sentences from the Teleface project (Agelfors et al., 1998) were used for a small preference test. Each sentence was played twice: once with standard articulation (100%) and once with smaller (75%) or greater (125%) articulation strength. The set of subjects, presentation method, and noise masking of the audio was the same as in experiment 1 (the VCV test). The subjects were asked to report which of the two variants seemed more natural or if they were judged to be of equal quality. The test consisted of 15 stimuli pairs, presented to 24 subjects. To avoid starting and ending effects, two extra pairs were inserted at the beginning and one at the end. The results can be seen in Table 3. The only significant preference was for the 75% version contrary to the initial informal experiment. However, the criterion in the initial test was readability rather than naturalness.

The multimodal synthesis software together with a control interface based on the WaveSurfer platform (Sjölander and Beskow, 2000) allows for the easy production of material addressing the articulation strength issue. There is a possible conflict in producing the most natural and the most easily lip-read face. However, under some conditions it might be favourable to trade off some naturalness for better readability. For example, the dental viseme cluster [r, n, t, d, s, and l] could possibly gain discriminability in connection with closed vowels if tongue movements could be to some extent hyperarticulated and well rendered. Of course the closed vowels should be as open as possible without jeopardising the overall vowel discriminability.

The optimum trade-off between readability and naturalness is certainly also a personal characteristic. It seems likely that hearing-impaired people would

Table 3. Judged naturalness compared to the default (100%) articulation strength.

Articulation strength(%)	Less natural	Equal	More natural
75	31.67	23.33	45.00
125	41.67	19.17	39.17

emphasise readability before naturalness. Therefore it could be considered that in certain applications like in the Synface software, users could be given the option of setting the articulation strength themselves.

Experiment 3: Targeted audio.   A different type of application which can potentially benefit from a talking head in terms of improved intelligibility is targeted audio. To transmit highly directional sound, targeted audio makes use of a technique known as "parametric array" (Westervelt, 1963). This type of highly directed sound can be used to communicate a voice message to a single person within a group of people (e.g., in a meeting situation or at a museum exhibit) without disturbing the other people. Within the framework of the EU project CHIL, experiments have been run to evaluate intelligibility of such targeted audio combined with a talking head (Svanfeldt and Olszewski, 2005).

Using an intelligibility test similar to the ones described above, listeners were asked to identify the consonant in a series of VCV words. The seven consonants to be identified were [f, s, m, n, k, p, t] uttered in an [aCa] frame using both audio and audio-visual speech synthesis. Four conditions were tested. Two audio conditions with and without the talking head were tested, one which targeted the audio directly towards the listener (the 0° condition) and one which targeted the audio 45° away from the listener (the 45° condition). The subjects were seated in front of a computer screen with the target audio device next to the screen. See Figure 6.

The addition of the talking head increased listener recognition accuracy from 77% to 93% in the 0° condition and even more dramatically from 58% to 88% in the 45° condition. Thus the talking head can serve to increase intelligibility and even help to compensate for situations in which the listener may be moving or not located optimally in the audio beam.

A more detailed analysis of the data revealed that consonant confusions in the audio-only condition tended to occur between [p] and [f] and between [m] and [n]. These confusions were largely resolved by the addition of the talking

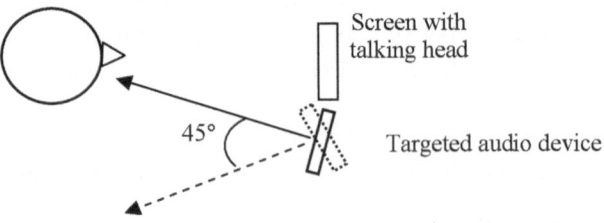

Figure 6.   Schematic view of the experimental set-up (Svanfeldt and Olszewski, 2005).

head. This is as could be expected since the addition of the visual modality provides place of articulation information for the labial articulation.

5   Evaluating Visual Cues for Prominence

Another quite different example of the contribution of the talking head to information presentation is taken from the results of perception studies in which the percept of emphasis and syllable prominence is enhanced by eyebrow and head movements. In an experiment investigating the contribution of eyebrow movement to the perception of prominence in Swedish (Granström et al., 1999), a test sentence was created using our audio-visual text-to-speech synthesis in which the acoustic cues and lower-face visual cues were the same for all stimuli. Articulatory movements were created by using the text-to-speech rule system. The upper-face cues were eyebrow movement where the eyebrows were raised on successive words in the sentence. The movements were created by hand-editing the eyebrow parameter. The degree of eyebrow raising was chosen to create a subtle movement that was distinctive although not too obvious. The total duration of movement was 500 ms and comprised a 100 ms dynamic raising part, a 200 ms static raised portion, and a 200 ms dynamic lowering part. In the stimuli, the acoustic signal was always the same, and the sentence was synthesized as one phrase. Six versions were included in the experiment: one with no eyebrow movement and five where eyebrow raising was placed on one of the five content words in the test sentence. The words with concomitant eyebrow movement were generally perceived as more prominent than words without the movement. This tendency was even greater for a subgroup of non-native (L2) listeners. The mean increase in prominence response following an eyebrow movement was 24% for the Swedish native (L1) listeners and 39% for the L2 group. One example result is shown in Figure 7. Similar results have also been obtained for Dutch by Krahmer et al. (2002a).

In another study (House et al., 2001) both eyebrow and head movements were tested as potential cues to prominence. The goal of the study was twofold. First of all, we wanted to see if head movement (nodding) is a more powerful cue to prominence than is eyebrow movement by virtue of a larger movement. Secondly, we wanted to test the perceptual sensitivity to the timing of both eyebrow and head movement in relationship to the syllable.

As in the previous experiment, our rule-based audio-visual synthesiser was used for stimuli preparation. The test sentence used to create the stimuli for the experiment was the same as that used in an earlier perception experiment designed to test acoustic cues only (House, 2001). The sentence, *Jag vill bara flyga om vädret är perfekt* (I only want to fly if the weather is perfect) was synthesized with focal accent rises on both *flyga* (fly) (Accent 2) and *vädret* (weather) (Accent 1). The F0 rise excursions corresponded to the stimulus

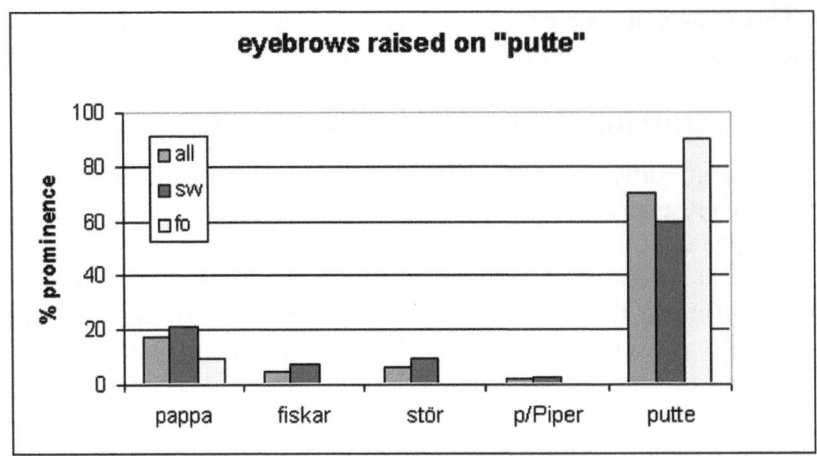

Figure 7.   Prominence responses in percent for each content word for the acoustically neutral reading of the stimulus sentence "När pappa fiskar stör p/Piper Putte", with eyebrow movement on "Putte". Subjects are grouped as all, Swedish (sw), and foreign (fo).

in the earlier experiment which elicited nearly equal responses for *flyga* and *vädret* in terms of the most prominent word in the sentence. The voice used was the Infovox 330 Ingmar MBROLA voice.

Eyebrow and head movements were then created by hand-editing the respective parameters. The eyebrows were raised to create a subtle movement that was distinctive although not too obvious. In quantitative terms the movement comprised 4% of the total possible movement. The head movement was a slight vertical lowering comprising 3% of the total possible vertical head rotation. Statically, the displacement is difficult to perceive, while dynamically, the movement is quite distinct. The total duration of both eyebrow and head movement was 300 ms and comprised a 100 ms dynamic onset, a 100 ms static portion, and a 100 ms dynamic offset.

Two sets of stimuli were created: set 1 in which both eyebrow and head movement occurred simultaneously, and set 2 in which the movements were separated and potentially conflicting with each other. In set 1, six stimuli were created by synchronizing the movement in stimulus 1 with the stressed vowel of *flyga*. This movement was successively shifted in intervals of 100 ms towards *vädret* resulting in the movement in stimulus 6 being synchronized with the stressed vowel of *vädret*. In set 2, stimuli 1–3 were created by fixing the head movement to synchronize with the stressed vowel of *vädret* and successively shifting the eyebrow movements from the stressed vowel of *flyga* towards *vädret* in steps of 100 ms. Stimuli 4–6 were created by fixing the eyebrow movement to *vädret* and shifting the head movement from *flyga* towards *vädret*. The acoustic signal and articulatory movements were the same for all stimuli. A schematic illustration of the stimuli is presented in Figure 8.

Jag vill bara FLYGA   om   VÄDRET är perfekt.

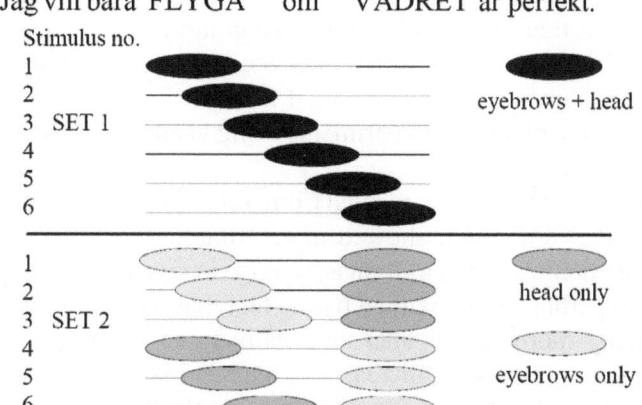

Figure 8. Schematic illustration of face gesture timing.

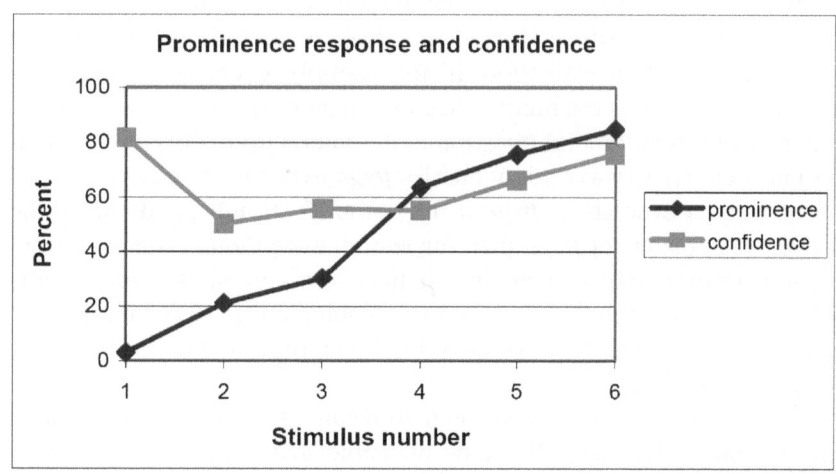

Figure 9. Results for stimulus set 1 showing prominence response for *vädret* and confidence in percent.

The results from stimulus set 1 where eyebrow and head movements occurred simultaneously clearly reflect the timing aspect of these stimuli as can be seen in Figure 9 where percent votes for *vädret* increase successively as movement is shifted in time from *flyga* to *vädret*.

It is clear from the results that combined head and eyebrow movements of the scope used in the experiment are powerful cues to prominence when synchronized with the stressed vowel of the potentially prominent word and when no conflicting acoustic cue is present. The results demonstrate a general sensitivity to the timing of these movements at least on the order of 100 ms as the prominence response moves successively from the word *flyga* to the word *vädret*. However, there is a tendency for integration of the movements to the nearest potentially prominent word, thus accounting for the jump in prominence response between stimulus 3 and 4 in set 1. This integration is consistent with the results of similar experiments using visual and auditory segmental cues (Massaro et al., 1996).

As could be expected, the results from set 2, where eyebrow and head movements were in conflict, showed more stimulus ambiguity. Head movement, however, demonstrated a slight advantage in signalling prominence. This advantage can perhaps be explained by the fact that the movement of the head may be visually more salient than the relatively subtle eyebrow movement. The advantage might even be increased if the head is observed from a greater distance. In an informal demonstration, where observers were further away from the computer screen than the subjects in the experiment, head-movement advantage was quite pronounced.

A number of questions remain to be answered, as a perception experiment of this type is necessarily restricted in scope. Amplitude of movement was not addressed in this investigation. If, for example, eyebrow movement were exaggerated, would this counterbalance the greater power of head movement? A perhaps even more crucial question is the interaction between the acoustic and visual cues. There was a slight bias for *flyga* to be perceived as more prominent (one subject even chose *flyga* in 11 of the 12 stimuli), and indeed the F0 excursion was greater for *flyga* than for *vädret*, even though this was ambiguous in the previous experiment. In practical terms of multimodal synthesis, however, it will probably be sufficient to combine cues, even though it would be helpful to have some form of quantified weighting factor for the different acoustic and visual cues.

Duration of the eyebrow and head movements is another consideration which was not tested here. It seems plausible that similar onset and offset durations (100 ms) combined with substantially longer static displacements would serve as conversational signals rather than as cues to prominence. In this way, non-synchronous eyebrow and head movements can be combined to signal both prominence and, for example feedback giving or seeking. Some of the subjects also commented that the face seemed to convey a certain degree of irony in some of the stimuli in set 2, most likely in those stimuli with non-synchronous eyebrow movement. Experimentation with, and evaluation of, potential cues for feedback seeking was pursued in the study reported on in Section 6.

6   Evaluating Prosody and Interaction

The use of a believable talking head can trigger the user's social skills such as using greetings, addressing the agent by name, and generally socially chatting with the agent. This was clearly shown by the results of the public use of the August system (Bell and Gustafson, 1999a) during a period of 6 months (see Section 9). These promising results have led to more specific studies on visual cues for feedback (e.g., Granström et al., 2002), in which smile, for example, was found to be the strongest cue for affirmative feedback. Further detailed work on turntaking regulation, feedback seeking and giving, and signalling of the system's internal state will enable us to improve the gesture library available for the animated talking head and continue to improve the effectiveness of multimodal dialogue systems. One of the central claims in many theories of conversation is that dialogue partners seek and provide evidence about the success of their interaction (Clark and Schaeffer, 1989; Traum, 1994; Brennan, 1990). That is, partners tend to follow a proof procedure to check whether their utterances were understood correctly or not and constantly exchange specific forms of feedback that can be affirmative ("go on") or negative ("do not go on"). Previous research has brought to light that conversation partners can monitor the dialogue this way on the basis of at least two kinds of features not encoded in the lexico-syntactic structure of a sentence: namely, prosodic and visual features. First, utterances that function as negative signals appear to differ prosodically from affirmative ones in that they are produced with more "marked" settings (e.g., higher, louder, slower) (Shimojima et al., 2002; Krahmer et al., 2002b). Second, other studies reveal that, in face-to-face interactions, people signal by means of facial expressions and specific body gestures whether or not an utterance was correctly understood (Gill et al., 1999).

Given that current spoken dialogue systems are prone to error, mainly because of problems in the automatic speech recognition (ASR) engine of these systems, a sophisticated use of feedback cues from the system to the user is potentially very helpful to improve human–machine interactions as well (e.g., Hirschberg et al., 2001). There are currently a number of advanced multimodal user interfaces in the form of talking heads that can generate audio-visual speech along with different facial expressions (Beskow, 1995, 1997; Beskow et al., 2001; Granström et al., 2001; Massaro, 2002; Pelachaud, 2002; Tisato et al., 2005). However, while such interfaces can be accurately modified in terms of a number of prosodic and visual parameters, there are as yet no formal models that make explicit how exactly these need to be manipulated to synthesise convincing affirmative and negative cues.

One interesting question, for instance, is what the strength relation is between the potential prosodic and visual cues. The goal of one study (Granström et al., 2002) was to gain more insight into the relative importance of specific prosodic and visual parameters for giving feedback on the success of the interaction. In this study, use is made of a talking head whose prosodic and visual features are orthogonally varied in order to create stimuli that are presented to subjects who have to respond to these stimuli and judge them as affirmative or negative backchannelling signals.

The stimuli consisted of an exchange between a human, who was intended to represent a client, and the face, representing a travel agent. An observer of these stimuli could only hear the client's voice, but could both see and hear the face. The human utterance was a natural speech recording and was exactly the same in all exchanges, whereas the speech and the facial expressions of the travel agent were synthetic and variable. The fragment that was manipulated, always consisted of the following two utterances:

Human:	"Jag vill åka från Stockholm till Linköping."
	("I want to go from Stockholm to Linköping.")
Head:	"Linköping."

The stimuli were created by orthogonally varying six parameters, shown in Table 4, using two possible settings for each parameter: one which was hypothesised to lead to affirmative feedback responses, and one which was hypothesised to lead to negative responses.

The parameter settings were largely created by intuition and observing human productions. However, the affirmative and negative F0 contours were based on two natural utterances. In Figure 10 an example of the all-negative and all-affirmative face can be seen.

The actual testing was done via a group experiment using a projected image on a large screen. The task was to respond to this dialogue exchange in terms of whether the head signals that he understands and accepts the human utterance, or rather signals that the head is uncertain about the human utterance. In addition, the subjects were required to express on a 5-point scale how confident they were about their response. A detailed description of the experiment and the analysis can be found in Granstroöm et al. (2002). Here, we would only like to highlight the strength of the different acoustic and visual cues. In Figure 11

Table 4.   Different parameters and parameter settings used to create different stimuli.

	Affirmative setting	Negative setting
Smile	Head smiles	Neutral expression
Head move	Head nods	Head leans back
Eyebrows	Eyebrows rise	Eyebrows frown
Eye closure	Eyes narrow slightly	Eyes open wide
F0 contour	Declarative	Interrogative
Delay	Immediate reply	Delayed reply

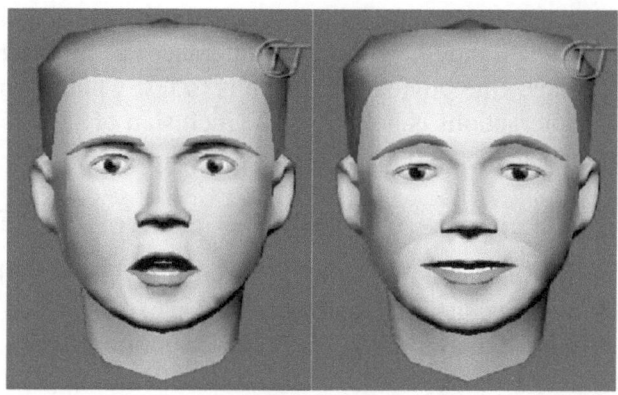

Figure 10. The all-negative and all-affirmative faces sampled in the end of the first syllable of Linköping.

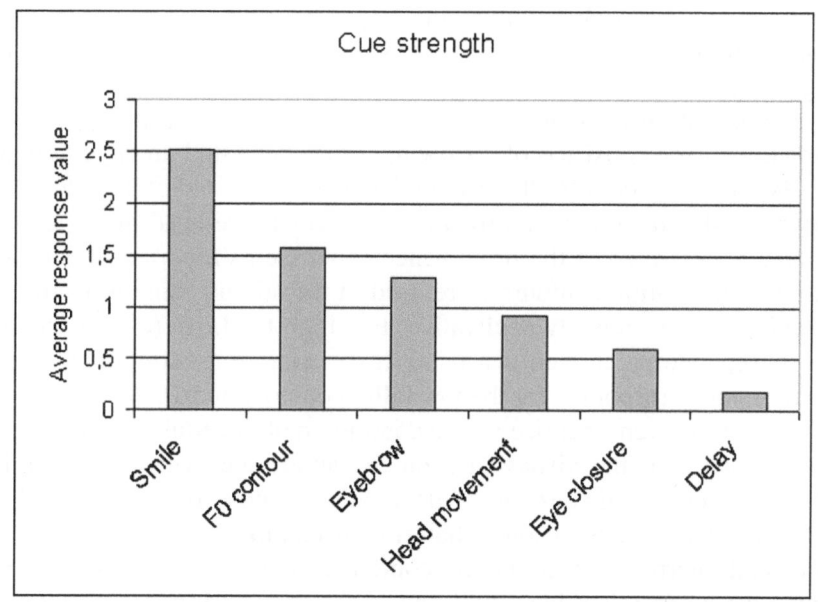

Figure 11. The mean response value difference for stimuli with the indicated cues set to their affirmative and negative value.

the mean difference in response value (the response weighted by the subjects' confidence ratings) is presented for negative and affirmative settings of the different parameters. The effects of Eye closure and Delay are not significant, but the trends observed in the means are clearly in the expected direction. There appears to be a strength order with Smile being the most important factor, followed by F0 contour, Eyebrow, Head movement, Eye closure, and Delay.

This study clearly shows that subjects are sensitive to both acoustic and visual parameters when they have to judge utterances as affirmative or negative feedback signals. One obvious next step is to test whether the fluency of human–machine interactions is helped by the inclusion of such feedback cues in the dialogue management component of a system.

7   Evaluating Visual Cues to Sentence Mode

In distinguishing questions from statements, prosody has a well-established role, especially in cases such as echo questions where there is no syntactic cue to the interrogative mode. Almost without exception this has been shown only for the auditory modality. Inspired by the results of the positive and negative feedback experiment presented in Section 6, an experiment was carried out to test if similar visual cues could influence the perception of question and statement intonation in Swedish (House, 2002). Parameters were hand manipulated to create two configurations: one expected to elicit more interrogative responses and the other expected to elicit more declarative responses. These configurations were similar, although not identical, to the positive and negative configurations used in the feedback experiment. Hypothesised cues for the interrogative mode consisted of a slow up–down head nod and eyebrow lowering. Hypothesised cues for the declarative mode consisted of a smile, a short up–down head nod, and eye narrowing. The declarative head nod was of the same type as was used in the prominence experiments reported in Section 5. 12 different intonation contours were used in the stimuli ranging from a low final falling contour (clearly declarative) to a high final rise (clearly interrogative). A separate perception test using these audio-only stimuli resulted in 100% declarative responses for the low falling contour and 100% interrogative responses for the high final rise with a continuum of uncertainty in between.

The influence of the visual cues on the audio cues was only marginal. While the hypothesised cues for the declarative mode (smile, short head nod, and eye narrowing) elicited somewhat more declarative responses for the ambiguous and interrogative intonation contours, the hypothesized cues for the interrogative mode (slow head nod and eyebrow lowering) led to more uncertainty in the responses for both the declarative intonation contours and the interrogative intonation contours (i.e., responses for the declarative contours were only slightly more interrogative than in the audio-only condition while responses for the interrogative contours were actually more declarative). Similar results were obtained for English by Srinivasan and Massaro (2003). Although they were able to demonstrate that the visual cues of eyebrow raising and head tilting synthesised based on a natural model reliably conveyed question intonation, their experiments showed a weak visual effect relative to a strong audio effect of intonation. This weak visual effect remained despite attempts to enhance the visual cues and make the audio information more ambiguous.

The dominance of the audio cues in the context of these question/statement experiments may indicate that question intonation may be less variable than visual cues for questions, or we simply may not yet know enough about the combination of visual cues and their timing in signalling question mode to successfully override the audio cues. Moreover, a final high rising intonation is generally a very robust cue to question intonation, especially in the context of perception experiments with binary response alternatives.

8   Evaluation of Agent Expressiveness and Attitude

In conjunction with the development of data-driven visual synthesis as reported in Section 3, two different evaluation studies have been carried out. One was designed to evaluate expressive visual speech synthesis in the framework of a virtual language tutor (cf. Granström, 2004). The experiment, reported in detail (Beskow and Cerrato, 2006), used a method similar to the one reported on in Section 6. The talking head had the role of a language tutor who was engaged in helping a student of Swedish improve her pronunciation. Each interaction consisted of the student's pronunciation of a sentence including a mispronounced word. The virtual tutor responds by correcting the mispronunciation after which the student makes a new attempt in one of three ways: with the correct pronunciation, with the same mistake, or with a new mistake. The test subjects hear the student's pronunciation and both see and hear the tutor. The task was to judge which emotion the talking head expressed in its final turn of the interaction.

Visual synthesis derived from a happy, angry, sad, and neutral database was used to drive the new MPEG-4 compatible talking head as described in Section 3. For the audio part of the stimuli, a pre-recorded human voice was used to portray the three emotions since we have not yet developed suitable audio data-driven synthesis with different emotions. All possible combinations of audio and visual stimuli were tested. The results indicated that for stimuli where the audio and visual emotion matched, listener recognition of each emotion was quite good: 87% for neutral and happy, 70% for sad, and 93% for angry. For the mismatched stimuli, the visual elements seemed to have a stronger influence than the audio elements. These results point to the importance of matching audio and visual emotional content and show that subjects attend to the visual element to a large degree when judging agent expressiveness and attitude.

In another experiment reported on in House (2006), the new talking head was evaluated in terms of degrees of friendliness. Databases of angry, happy, and neutral emotions were used to synthesise the utterance *Vad heter du?* (What is your name?). Samples of the three versions of the visual stimuli are presented in Figure 12. The three versions of the visual synthesis were combined with two audio configurations: low, early pitch peak; and high, late pitch

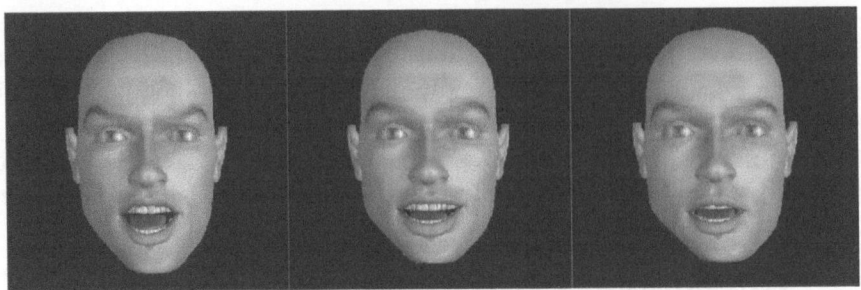

Figure 12.   Visual stimuli generated by data-driven synthesis from the angry database (left), the happy database (middle), and the neutral database (right). All samples are taken from the middle of the second vowel of the utterance *Vad heter du?* (What is your name?).

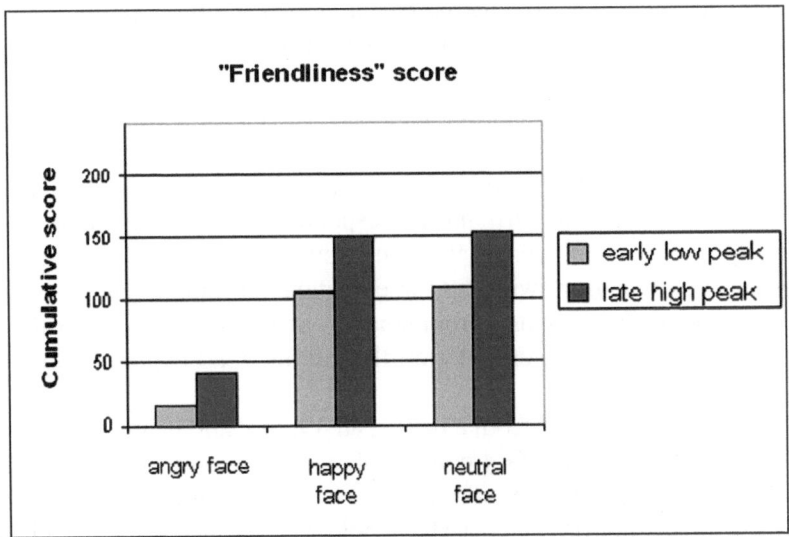

Figure 13.   Results from the data-driven synthesis test showing the cumulative "friendliness" score" for each stimulus.

peak, resulting in six stimuli. Previous experiments showed that the high, late pitch peak elicited more friendly responses (House, 2005). A perception test using these six stimuli was carried out by asking 27 subjects to indicate on a 4-point scale how friendly they felt the agent was.

The results are presented in Figure 13. It is quite clear that the face synthesised from the angry database elicited the lowest friendliness score. However, there is still evidence of interaction from the audio, as the angry face with the late, high peak received a higher friendliness score than did the angry face with the early, low peak. The faces from the other databases (happy and neutral) elicited more friendliness responses, but neither combination of face and audio received a particularly high friendliness score. The happy face did not elicit more friendliness responses than did the neutral face, but the influence of the audio stimuli remained consistent for all the visual stimuli. Nevertheless, the results show that the visual modality can be a powerful signal of attitude. Moreover, the effects of the audio cues for friendliness indicate that subjects make use of both modalities in judging speaker attitude. These results stress the need to carefully consider both the visual and audio aspects of expressive synthesis.

9   Agent and System Evaluation Studies

The main emphasis of the evaluation studies reported on in this chapter has been the evaluation of the intelligibility and the dialogue functions of the talking head agent as presented to subjects in experimental test situations. During the last decade, however, a number of experimental applications using the talking head have been developed at KTH (see Gustafson, 2002 for a review). Two examples that will be mentioned here are the August project, which was a dialogue system in public use, and the Adapt multimodal real-estate agent. Finally, we will also report on some studies aimed at evaluating user satisfaction in general during exposure to the August and the Adapt dialogue systems.

9.1   The August System

The Swedish author, August Strindberg, provided inspiration to create the animated talking agent used in a dialogue system that was on display during 1998 as part of the activities celebrating Stockholm as the Cultural Capital of Europe (Gustafson et al., 1999). The system was a fully automatic dialogue system using modules for speech recognition and audio-visual speech synthesis. This dialogue system made it possible to combine several domains, thanks to the modular functionality of the architecture. Each domain had its own dialogue manager, and an example-based topic spotter was used to relay the user utterances to the appropriate dialogue manager. In this system, the animated agent "August" presents different tasks such as taking the visitors on a trip through the Department of Speech, Music, and Hearing, giving street directions, and also reciting short excerpts from the works of August Strindberg, when waiting for someone to talk to. The system was built into a kiosk and placed in public in central Stockholm for a period of 6 months. One of the main challenges of this arrangement was the open situation with no explicit instructions being given to the visitor. A simple visual "visitor detector" made August start talking about one of his knowledge domains.

To ensure that the recorded user utterances were actually directed to the system, a push-to-talk button was used to initiate the recordings. The speech recordings resulted in a database consisting of 10,058 utterances from 2,685 speakers. The utterances were transcribed orthographically and labelled for speaker characteristics and utterance types by Bell and Gustafson (1999a,b; see also Gustafson, 2002 and Bell, 2003 for recent reviews of this work). The resulting transcribed and labelled database has subsequently been used as the basis for a number of studies evaluating user behaviour when interacting with the animated agent in this open environment.

Gustafson and Bell (2000) present a study showing that about half the utterances in the database can be classified as socially oriented while the other half is information-seeking. Children used a greater proportion of socialising utterances than did adults. The large proportion of socialising utterances is explained by the presence of an animated agent, and by the fact that the system was designed to handle and respond to social utterances such as greetings and queries concerning some basic facts about the life of Strindberg. Furthermore, it was found that users who received an accurate response to a socialising utterance continued to use the system for a greater number of turns than did those users who were searching for information or those who did not receive an appropriate response to a socially oriented utterance.

In another study concerning phrase-final prosodic characteristics of user utterances comprising wh-questions, House (2005) found that final rises were present in over 20% of the questions. Final rises can indicate a more friendly type of question attitude and were often present in social-oriented questions. However, rises were also found in information-oriented questions. This could indicate that the intention to continue a social type of contact with the agent may not be restricted to questions that are semantically categorized as social questions. The social intention can also be present in information-oriented questions. Finally children's wh-question utterances as a group contained the greatest proportion of final rises followed by women's utterances, with men's utterances containing the lowest proportion of final rises. This could also reflect trends in social intent. These results can be compared to findings by Oviatt and Adams (2000) where children interacting with animated undersea animals in a computer application used personal pronouns with about one-third of the exchanges comprising social questions about the animal's name, birthday, friends, family, etc.

9.2   The Adapt Multimodal Real-Estate Agent

The practical goal of the Adapt project was to build a system in which a user could collaborate with an animated agent to solve complicated tasks (Gustafson et al., 2000). We chose a domain in which multimodal interaction is highly useful, and which is known to engage a wide variety of people in our surroundings, namely, finding available apartments in Stockholm. In the Adapt project, the agent was given the role of asking questions and providing

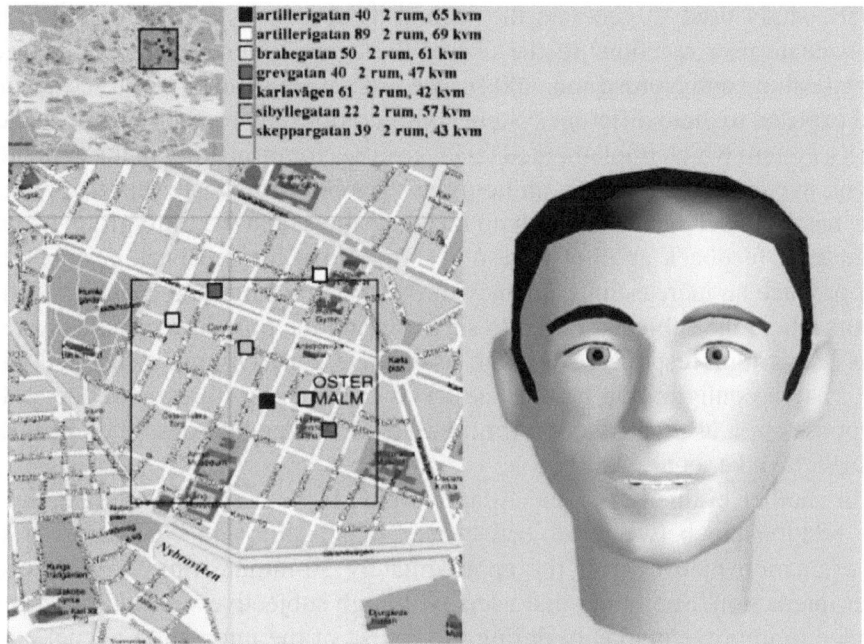

Figure 14. The agent Urban in the Adapt apartment domain.

guidance by retrieving detailed authentic information about apartments. The user interface can be seen in Figure 14.

Because of the conversational nature of the Adapt domain, the demand was great for appropriate interactive signals (both verbal and visual) for encouragement, affirmation, confirmation, and turntaking (Cassell et al., 2000; Pelachaud et al., 1996). As generation of prosodically grammatical utterances (e.g., correct focus assignment with regard to the information structure and dialogue state) was also one of the goals of the system, it was important to maintain modality consistency by simultaneous use of both visual and verbal prosodic and conversational cues (Nass and Gong, 1999). In particular, facial gestures for turntaking were implemented in which the agent indicated such states as attention, end-of-speech detection, continued attention, and preparing an answer (Beskow et al., 2002a; Gustafson, 2002).

Two different sets of data were collected from the Adapt system. The first collection was carried out by means of a Wizard-of-Oz simulation to obtain data for an evaluation of the prototype system under development. This first database represents 32 users and contains 1,845 utterances. The second database was collected in a study where 26 users interacted with a fully automated Adapt system. The second database comprises 3,939 utterances (Gustafson, 2002).

The study used to generate the second database was carried out in order to evaluate user reactions to the use of the agent's facial gestures for feedback (Edlund and Nordstrand, 2002). The users were split up into three groups and exposed to three different system configurations. One group was presented with a system which implemented facial gestures for turntaking in the animated agent, the second group saw an hourglass symbol to indicate that the system was busy but were provided with no facial gestures, and the third group had no turntaking feedback at all. The results showed that the feedback gestures did not produce an increase in efficiency of the system as measured by turntaking errors where the subjects started to speak during the time in which the system was preparing a response. However, users were generally more satisfied with the system configuration having the facial feedback gestures as reflected by responses in a user satisfaction form based on the method described in PARADISE (Walker et al., 2000).

In another evaluation of the Adapt corpus, Hjalmarsson (2005) examined the relationship between subjective user satisfaction and changes in a set of evaluation metrics over the approximately 30-minute time span of each user interaction. She found that users with high subjective satisfaction ratings tended to improve markedly during the course of the interaction as measured by task success. Users with low subjective satisfaction ratings showed a smaller initial improvement, which was followed by a deterioration in task success.

9.3   A Comparative Evaluation of the Two Systems

In a study designed to test new metrics for the evaluation of multimodal dialogue systems using animated agents, Cerrato and Ekeklint (2004) compared a subset of the August corpus with the Adapt Wizard-of-Oz simulation. Their hypothesis was that the way in which users ended their dialogues (both semantically and prosodically) would reveal important aspects of user satisfaction and dialogue success. The general characteristics of the dialogues differed substantially between the systems. The August dialogues were characterised by a small number of turns and frequent dialogue errors, while the dialogues in the Adapt simulations were much longer and relatively unproblematic. The final user utterances from both systems were analysed and classified as social closures or non-social closures. The social closures were then grouped into subcategories such as farewell, thanks, other courtesy expressions such as "nice talking to you", and non-courtesy expressions such as insults.

The comparison presented in Figure 15 shows a much greater percent of thanking expressions in the Adapt interactions than in those from the August corpus. While there were no insults ending Adapt interactions, insults and non-courtesy expressions comprised a fair proportion of the final utterances in the August interactions.

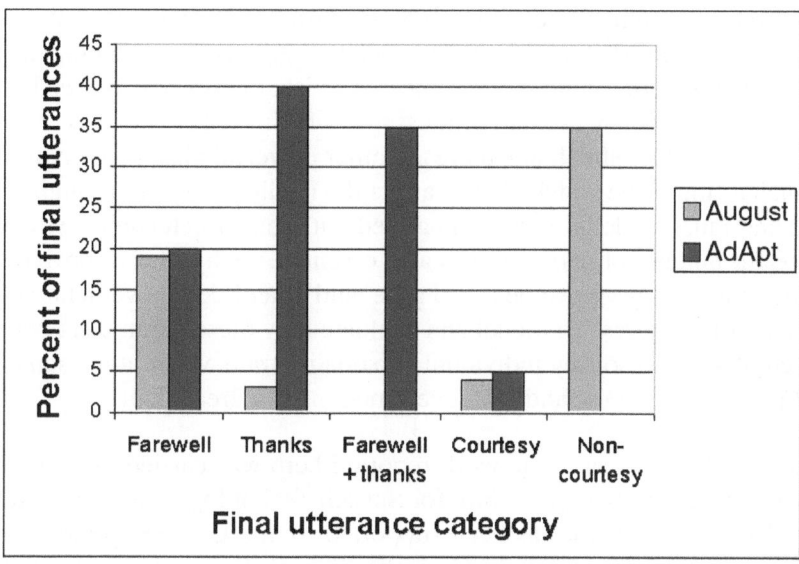

Figure 15. Distribution of social subcategories of the final utterances in the August and Adapt corpus. (Adapted from Cerrato and Ekeklint, 2004).

In addition to the category of final utterance, Cerrato and Ekeklint (2004) also analysed prosodic characteristics of the final utterances from the farewell and thanks category. They found a tendency for a farewell or thanks to have a rising intonation contour following a successful interaction with the system. They also found a tendency for users to end with a falling intonation, higher intensity, or greater duration in those cases where there had not been a successful interaction with the system.

10   Future Challenges in Modelling and Evaluation

In this chapter, we have presented an overview of some of the recent work in audio-visual synthesis, primarily at KTH, regarding data collection methods, modelling and evaluation experiments, and implementation in animated talking agents for dialogue systems. From this point of departure, we can see that many challenges remain before we will be able to create a believable, animated talking agent based on knowledge concerning how audio and visual signals interact in verbal and non-verbal communication. In terms of modelling and evaluation, there is a great need to explore in more detail the coherence between audio and visual prosodic expressions, especially regarding different functional dimensions. As we demonstrated in the section on prominence above, head nods which strengthen the percept of prominence tend to be integrated with the nearest candidate syllable resulting in audio-visual coherence. However, head nods which indicate dialogue functions such as feedback or turntaking may not be integrated with the audio in the same way. Visual gestures can even be used to contradict or qualify the verbal message, which is often the case in ironic expressions. On the other hand, there are other powerful visual communicative cues such as the smile which clearly affect the resulting audio (through articulation) and must by definition be integrated with the speech signal. Modelling of a greater number of parameters is also essential, such as head movement in more dimensions, eye movement and gaze, and other body movements such as hand and arm gestures. To model and evaluate how these parameters combine in different ways to convey individual personality traits while at the same time signalling basic prosodic and dialogue functions is a great challenge.

Acknowledgements   The work reported here was carried out by a large number of researchers at the Centre for Speech Technology which is gratefully acknowledged. The work has been supported by the EU/IST (projects SYN-FACE and PF-Star), and CTT, the Centre for Speech Technology, a competence centre at KTH, supported by VINNOVA, KTH, and participating Swedish companies and organisations. Marc Swerts collaborated on the feedback study while he was a guest at CTT.

References

Agelfors, E., Beskow, J., Dahlquist, M., Granström, B., Lundeberg, M., Spens, K.-E., and Öhman, T. (1998). Synthetic Faces as a Lipreading Support. In *Proceedings of the International Conference on Spoken Language Processing (ICSLP)*, pages 3047–3050, Sydney, Australia.

Bälter, O., Engwall, O., Öster, A.-M., and Kjellström, H. (2005). Wizard-of-Oz Test of ARTUR – a Computer-Based Speech Training System with Articulation Correction. In *Proceedings of the Seventh International ACM SIGACCESS Conference on Computers and Accessibility*, pages 36–43, Baltimore, Maryland, USA.

Bell, L. (2003). *Linguistic Adaptations in Spoken Human-Computer Dialogues; Empirical Studies of User Behavior*. Doctoral dissertation, Department of Speech, Music and Hearing, KTH, Stockholm, Sweden.

Bell, L. and Gustafson, J. (1999a). Interacting with an Animated Agent: An Analysis of a Swedish Database of Spontaneous Computer Directed Speech. In *Proceedings of the European Conference on Speech Communication and Technology (Eurospeech)*, pages 1143–1146, Budapest, Hungary.

Bell, L. and Gustafson, J. (1999b). Utterance Types in the August System. In *Proceedings of the ESCA Tutorial and Research Workshop on Interactive Dialogue in Multi-Modal Systems (IDS)*, pages 81–84, Kloster Irsee, Germany.

Beskow, J. (1995). Rule-based Visual Speech Synthesis. In *Proceedings of the European Conference on Speech Communication and Technology (Eurospeech)*, pages 299–302, Madrid, Spain.

Beskow, J. (1997). Animation of Talking Agents. In *Proceedings of ESCA Workshop on Audio-Visual Speech Processing (AVSP)*, pages 149–152, Rhodes, Greece.

Beskow, J. and Cerrato, L. (2006). Evaluation of the Expressivity of a Swedish Talking Head in the Context of Human-Machine Interaction. In *Proceedings of Gruppo di Studio della Comunicazione Parlata (GSCP)*, Padova, Italy.

Beskow, J., Cerrato, L., Cosi, P., Costantini, E., Nordstrand, M., Pianesi, F., Prete, M., and Svanfeldt, G. (2004a). Preliminary Cross-cultural Evaluation of Expressiveness in Synthetic Faces. In André, E., Dybkjær, L., Minker, W., and Heisterkamp, P., editors, *Affective Dialogue Systems. Proceedings of the Irsee Tutorial and Research Workshop on Affective Dialogue Systems*, volume 3068 of *LNAI*, pages 301–304, Springer.

Beskow, J., Cerrato, L., Granström, B., House, D., Nordenberg, M., Nordstrand, M., and Svanfeldt, G. (2004b). Expressive Animated Agents for Affective Dialogue Systems. In André, E., Dybkjær, L., Minker, W., and Heisterkamp, P., editors, *Affective Dialogue Systems. Proceedings of the Irsee Tutorial and Research Workshop on Affective Dialogue Systems*, volume 3068 of *LNAI*, pages 240–243, Springer.

Beskow, J., Cerrato, L., Granström, B., House, D., Nordstrand, M., and Svanfeldt, G. (2004c). The Swedish PF-Star Multimodal Corpora. In *Proceedings of the LREC Workshop on Multimodal Corpora: Models of Human Behaviour for the Specification and Evaluation of Multimodal Input and Output Interfaces*, pages 34–37, Lisbon, Portugal.

Beskow, J., Edlund, J., and Nordstrand, M. (2002a). Specification and Realisation of Multimodal Output in Dialogue Systems. In *Proceedings of the International Conference on Spoken Language Processing (ICSLP)*, pages 181–184, Denver, Colorado, USA.

Beskow, J., Engwall, O., and Granström, B. (2003). Resynthesis of Facial and Intraoral Articulation from Simultaneous Measurements. In *Proceedings of the International Congresses of Phonetic Sciences (ICPhS)*, pages 431–434, Barcelona, Spain.

Beskow, J., Granström, B., and House, D. (2001). A Multimodal Speech Synthesis Tool Applied to Audio-Visual Prosody. In Keller, E., Bailly, G., Monaghan, A., Terken, J., and Huckvale, M., editors, *Improvements in Speech Synthesis*, pages 372–382, John Wiley, New York, USA.

Beskow, J., Granström, B., and Spens, K.-E. (2002b). Articulation Strength - Readability Experiments with a Synthetic Talking Face. In *The Quarterly Progress and Status Report of the Department of Speech, Music and Hearing (TMH-QPSR)*, volume 44, pages 97–100, KTH, Stockholm, Sweden.

Beskow, J. and Nordenberg, M. (2005). Data-driven Synthesis of Expressive Visual Speech using an MPEG-4 Talking Head. In *Proceedings of the European Conference on Speech Communication and Technology (Interspeech)*, pages 793–796, Lisbon, Portugal.

Bickmore, T. and Cassell, J. (2005). Social Dialogue with Embodied Conversational Agents. In van Kuppevelt, J., Dybkjær, L., and Bernsen, N. O., editors, *Advances in Natural Multimodal Dialogue Systems*, pages 23–54, Springer, Dordrecht, The Netherlands.

Brennan, S. E. (1990). *Seeking and Providing Evidence for Mutual Understanding*. Unpublished doctoral dissertation, Stanford University, Stanford, California, USA.

Carlson, R. and Granström, B. (1997). Speech synthesis. In Hardcastle, W. and Laver, J., editors, *The Handbook of Phonetic Sciences*, pages 768–788, Blackwell Publishers, Oxford, UK.

Cassell, J., Bickmore, T., Campbell, L., Hannes, V., and Yan, H. (2000). Conversation as a System Framework: Designing Embodied Conversational Agents. In Cassell, J., Sullivan, J., Prevost, S., and Churchill, E., editors, *Embodied Conversational Agents*, pages 29–63, MIT Press, Cambridge, Massachusetts, USA.

Cerrato, L. and Ekeklint, S. (2004). Evaluating Users' Reactions to Human-like Interfaces: Prosodic and Paralinguistic Features as Measures of User Satisfaction. In Ruttkay, Z. and Pelachaud, C., editors, *From Brows to Trust: Evaluating Embodied Conversational Agents*, pages 101–124, Kluwer Academic Publishers, Dordrecht, The Netherlands.

Clark, H. H. and Schaeffer, E. F. (1989). Contributing to Discourse. *Cognitive Science*, 13:259–294.

Cole, R., Massaro, D. W., de Villiers, J., Rundle, B., Shobaki, K., Wouters, J., Cohen, M., Beskow, J., Stone, P., Connors, P., Tarachow, A., and Solcher, D. (1999). New Tools for Interactive Speech and Language Training: Using Animated Conversational Agents in the Classrooms of Profoundly Deaf Children. In *Proceedings of the ESCA/Socrates Workshop on Method and Tool Innovations for Speech Science Education (MATISSE)*, pages 45–52, University College London, London, UK.

Edlund, J. and Nordstrand, M. (2002). Turn-taking Gestures and Hour-Glasses in a Multi-modal Dialogue System. In *Proceedings of the ISCA Workshop on Multi-Modal Dialogue in Mobile Environments*, pages 181–184, Kloster Irsee, Germany.

Engwall, O. (2003). Combining MRI, EMA and EPG Measurements in a Three-Dimensional Tongue Model. *Speech Communication*, 41(2–3): 303–329.

Engwall, O. and Beskow, J. (2003). Resynthesis of 3D Tongue Movements from Facial Data. In *Proceedings of the European Conference on Speech*

Communication and Technology (Eurospeech), pages 2261–2264, Geneva, Switzerland.

Gill, S. P., Kawamori, M., Katagiri, Y., and Shimojima, A. (1999). Pragmatics of Body Moves. In *Proceedings of the Third International Cognitive Technology Conference*, pages 345–358, San Francisco, USA.

Granström, B. (2004). Towards a Virtual Language Tutor. In *Proceedings of the InSTIL/ICALL Symposium: NLP and Speech Technologies in Advanced Language Learning Systems*, pages 1–8, Venice, Italy.

Granström, B., House, D., Beskow, J., and Lundeberg, M. (2001). Verbal and Visual Prosody in Multimodal Speech Perception. In von Dommelen, W. and Fretheim, T., editors, *Nordic Prosody: Proceedings of the Eighth Conference, Trondheim 2000*, pages 77–88, Peter Lang, Frankfurt am Main, Germany.

Granström, B., House, D., and Lundeberg, M. (1999). Prosodic Cues in Multimodal Speech Perception. In *Proceedings of the International Congress of Phonetic Sciences (ICPhS)*, pages 655–658, San Francisco, USA.

Granström, B., House, D., and Swerts, M. G. (2002). Multimodal Feedback Cues in Human-Machine Interactions. In Bel, B. and Marlien, I., editors, *Proceedings of the Speech Prosody Conference*, pages 347–350, Laboratoire Parole et Langage, Aix-en-Provence, France.

Gustafson, J. (2002). *Developing Multimodal Spoken Dialogue Systems; Empirical Studies of Spoken Human-Computer Interaction*. Doctoral dissertation, Department of Speech, Music and Hearing, KTH, Stockholm, Sweden.

Gustafson, J. and Bell, L. (2000). Speech Technology on Trial: Experiences from the August System. *Natural Language Engineering*, 6(3–4):273–296.

Gustafson, J., Bell, L., Beskow, J., Boye, J., Carlson, R., Edlund, J., Granström, B., House, D., and Wirén, M. (2000). Adapt – a Multimodal Conversational Dialogue System in an Apartment Domain. In *Proceedings of the International Conference on Spoken Language Processing (ICSLP)*, volume 2, pages 134–137, Beijing, China.

Gustafson, J., Lindberg, N., and Lundeberg, M. (1999). The August Spoken Dialogue System. In *Proceedings of the European Conference on Speech Communication and Technology (Eurospeech)*, pages 1151–1154, Budapest, Hungary.

Hirschberg, J., Litman, D., and Swerts, M. (2001). Identifying User Corrections Automatically in Spoken Dialogue Systems. In *Proceedings of the North American Chapter of the Association for Computational Linguistics (NAACL)*, pages 208–215, Pittsburg, USA.

Hjalmarsson, A. (2005). Towards User Modelling in Conversational Dialogue Systems: A Qualitative Study of the Dynamics of Dialogue Parameters.

In *Proceedings of the European Conference on Speech Communication and Technology (Interspeech)*, pages 869–872, Lisbon, Portugal.

House, D. (2001). Focal Accent in Swedish: Perception of Rise Properties for Accent 1. In van Dommelen, W. and Fretheim, T., editors, *Nordic Prosody 2000: Proceedings of the Eighth Conference*, pages 127–136, Trondheim, Norway.

House, D. (2002). Intonational and Visual Cues in the Perception of Interrogative Mode in Swedish. In *Proceedings of the International Conference on Spoken Language Processing (ICSLP)*, pages 1957–1960, Denver, Colorado, USA.

House, D. (2005). Phrase-final Rises as a Prosodic Feature in Wh-Questions in Swedish Human-Machine Dialogue. *Speech Communication*, 46:268–283.

House, D. (2006). On the Interaction of Audio and Visual Cues to Friendliness in Interrogative Prosody. In *Proceedings of the Second Nordic Conference on Multimodal Communication*, pages 201–213, Gothenburg University, Sweden.

House, D., Beskow, J., and Granström, B. (2001). Timing and Interaction of Visual Cues for Prominence in Audiovisual Speech Perception. In *Proceedings of the European Conference on Speech Communication and Technology (Eurospeech)*, pages 387–390, Aalborg, Denmark.

Krahmer, E., Ruttkay, Z., Swerts, M., and Wesselink, W. (2002a). Perceptual Evaluation of Audiovisual Cues for Prominence. In *Proceedings of the International Conference on Spoken Language Processing (ICSLP)*, pages 1933–1936, Denver, Colorado, USA.

Krahmer, E., Swerts, M., Theune, M., and Weegels, M. (2002b). The Dual of Denial: Two Uses of Disconfirmations in Dialogue and their Prosodic Correlates. *Speech Communication*, 36(1–2):133–145.

Massaro, D. W. (1998). *Perceiving Talking Faces: From Speech Perception to a Behavioural Principle*. MIT Press, Cambridge, Massachusetts, USA.

Massaro, D. W. (2002). Multimodal Speech Perception: A Paradigm for Speech Science. In Granström, B., House, D., and Karlsson, I., editors, *Multimodality in Language and Speech Systems*, pages 45–71. Kluwer Academic Publishers, The Netherlands.

Massaro, D. W., Bosseler, A., and Light, J. (2003). Development and Evaluation of a Computer-Animated Tutor for Language and Vocabulary Learning. In *Proceedings of the 15th International Congress of Phonetic Sciences (ICPhS)*, pages 143–146, Barcelona, Spain.

Massaro, D. W., Cohen, M. M., and Smeele, P. M. T. (1996). Perception of Asynchronous and Conflicting Visual and Auditory Speech. *Journal of the Acoustical Society of America*, 100(3):1777–1786.

Massaro, D. W. and Light, J. (2003). Read My Tongue Movements: Bimodal Learning to Perceive and Produce Non-Native Speech /r/ and /l/.

In *Proceedings of the European Conference on Speech Communication and Technology (Eurospeech)*, pages 2249–2252, Geneva, Switzerland.

Nakano, Y., Reinstein, G., Stocky, T., and Cassell, J. (2003). Towards a Model of Face-to-Face Grounding. In *Proceedings of the 43rd Annual Meeting of the Association of Computational Linguistics (ACL)*, pages 553–561, Sapporo, Japan.

Nass, C. and Gong, L. (1999). Maximized Modality or Constrained Consistency? In *Proceedings of Auditory-Visual Speech Processing (AVSP)*, pages 1–5, Santa Cruz, USA.

Nordstrand, M., Svanfeldt, G., Granström, and House, D. (2004). Measurements of Articulatory Variation in Expressive Speech for a Set of Swedish Vowels. In *Speech Communication*, volume 44, pages 187–196.

Oviatt, S. L. and Adams, B. (2000). Designing and Evaluating Conversational Interfaces with Animated Characters. In *Embodied Conversational Agents*, pages 319–343, MIT Press, Cambridge, Massachusetts, USA.

Pandzic, I. S. and Forchheimer, R., editors (2002). *MPEG Facial Animation – The Standard, Implementation and Applications*. John Wiley Chichester, UK.

Parke, F. I. (1982). Parameterized Models for Facial Animation. *IEEE Computer Graphics*, 2(9):61–68.

Pelachaud, C. (2002). Visual Text-to-Speech. In Pandzic, I. S. and Forchheimer, R., editors, *MPEG-4 Facial Animation – The Standard, Implementation and Applications*. John Wiley, Chichester, UK.

Pelachaud, C., Badler, N. I., and Steedman, M. (1996). Generating Facial Expressions for Speech. *Cognitive Science*, 28:1–46.

Shimojima, A., Katagiri, Y., Koiso, H., and Swerts, M. (2002). Informational and Dialogue-Coordinating Functions of Prosodic Features of Japanese Echoic Responses. *Speech Communication*, 36(1–2):113–132.

Sjölander, K. and Beskow, J. (2000). WaveSurfer – an Open Source Speech Tool. In *Proceedings of the International Conference on Spoken Language Processing (ICSLP)*, volume 4, pages 464–467, Beijing, China.

Srinivasan, R. J. and Massaro, D. W. (2003). Perceiving Prosody from the Face and Voice: Distinguishing Statements from Echoic Questions in English. *Language and Speech*, 46(1):1–22.

Svanfeldt, G. and Olszewski, D. (2005). Perception Experiment Combining a Parametric Loudspeaker and a Synthetic Talking Head. In *Proceedings of the European Conference on Speech Communication and Technology (Interspeech)*, pages 1721–1724, Lisbon, Portugal.

Tisato, G., Cosi, P., Drioli, C., and Tesser, F. (2005). INTERFACE: A New Tool for Building Emotive/Expressive Talking Heads. In *Proceedings of the European Conference on Speech Communication and Technology (Interspeech)*, pages 781–784, Lisbon, Portugal.

Traum, D. R. (1994). *A Computational Theory of Grounding in Natural Language Conversation*. PhD thesis, Rochester, USA.

Walker, M. A., Kamm, C. A., and Litman, D. J. (2000). Towards Developing General Models of Usability with PARADISE. *Natural Language Engineering*, 6(3–4):363–377.

Westervelt, P. J. (1963). Parametric Acoustic Array. *Journal of the Acoustical Society of America*, 35:535–537.

Chapter 4

EVALUATING PART-OF-SPEECH TAGGING AND PARSING

On the Evaluation of Automatic Parsing of Natural Language

Patrick Paroubek

Laboratoire d'Informatique pour la Mécanique et les Sciences de l'Ingénieur
LIMSI-CNRS, Orsay, France

pap@limsi.fr

Abstract   The aim of this chapter is to introduce the reader to the evaluation of part-of-speech (POS) taggers and parsers. After a presentation of both POS tagging and parsing, describing the tasks and the existing formalisms, we introduce general considerations about evaluation of Natural Language Processing (NLP). Then we raise a point about the issue of input data segmentation into linguistic units, a crucial step in any evaluation related to language processing. We conclude by a review of the current evaluation methodologies and average levels of performance generally achieved for POS tagging and parsing.

Keywords   Natural language processing; Evaluation; Part-of-speech (POS) tagging; Parsing.

1   POS Tagging

Part-of-speech (POS) tagging is the identification of the morphosyntactic class of each word form using lexical and contextual information. Here is how Brill's tagger (Brill, 1995) tags the first sentence of this paragraph. Each line holds respectively: a token number, a word form, a POS tag, and a short tag description.

```
0 part-of-speech tagging VBG  verb, gerund or present participle
1 is VBZ  verb, present tense, 3rd person, singular
2 the DT  determiner
3 identification NN  noun, singular or mass
4 of IN  preposition or subordinating conjunction
```

L. Dybkjær et al. (eds.), Evaluation of Text and Speech Systems, 99–124.

© 2007 *Springer.*

```
 5 the DT  determiner
 6 morphosyntactic JJ  adjective
 7 class NN  noun, singular or mass
 8 of IN  preposition or subordinating conjunction
 9 each DT  determiner
10 word NN  noun, singular or mass
11 form NN  noun, singular or mass
12 using VBG  verb, gerund or present participle
13 lexical JJ  adjective
14 and CC  conjunction, coordinating
15 contextual JJ  adjective
16 information NN  noun, singular or mass
```

Brill's tagger uses the Penn Treebank[1] tagset (Marcus et al., 1993). The tagset regroups all the tags used to represent the various word classes. Ideally, a tagset should have the capacity to integrate all the morphosyntactic information present in the lexical descriptions of the words, if any is available. It should also have the capacity to encode the information needed to disambiguate POS tags in context, and last of all, it should have the capacity to represent the information that will be needed by the linguistic processing to which POS tagging is a preliminary processing phase. We give below a short description of the 36 tags of the Penn Treebank tagset (Marcus et al., 1993).

```
 1. CC  Coordinating conjunction
 2. CD  Cardinal number
 3. DT  Determiner
 4. EX  Existential there
 5. FW  Foreign word
 6. IN  Preposition or subordinating conjunction
 7. JJ  Adjective
 8. JJR Adjective, comparative
 9. JJS Adjective, superlative
10. LS  List item marker
11. MD  Modal
12. NN  Noun, singular or mass
13. NNS Noun, plural
14. NP  Proper noun, singular
15. NPS Proper noun, plural
16. PDT Predeterminer
17. POS Possessive ending
18. PP  Personal pronoun
19. PP$ Possessive pronoun
20. RB  Adverb
21. RBR Adverb, comparative
```

```
22. RBS Adverb, superlative
23. RP  Particle
24. SYM Symbol
25. TO  to
26. UH  Interjection
27. VB  Verb, base form
28. VBD Verb, past tense
29. VBG Verb, gerund or present participle
30. VBN Verb, past participle
31. VBP Verb, non-third person singular present
32. VBZ Verb, third person singular present
33. WDT Wh-determiner
34. WP  Wh-pronoun
35. WP$ Possessive wh-pronoun
36. WRB Wh-adverb
```

The selection of the linguistic features from the lexical descriptions and how they are associated to POS tags is always a difficult choice. Arbitrary linguistic choices, the application for which tagging is done, the performance expected of the tagger, and finally the disambiguation power offered by the current language technology are all important factors in determining lexical feature selection. For instance, Chanod and Tapanainen (1995) have shown that one way to improve the performance of a POS tagger for French, is to exclude the gender information from the tags of nouns and adjectives (there is less ambiguity to solve, and therefore less chance for the tagger to make an error). The gender information can be recovered afterwards by means of a lexicon and a few rules (Tufis, 1999).

It is very difficult to draw a precise boundary around the morphosyntactic information associated with POS tags, since it concerns morphology (e.g., verb tense), morphosyntax (e.g., noun/verb distinction), syntax (e.g., identification of the case for pronouns, accusative versus dative), and semantics (e.g., distinction between common and proper noun). Often it is represented by *lexical descriptions* which make explicit the way linguistic features are organised into a hierarchy and the constraints that exist between them (some features are defined only for some specific morphosyntactic categories, like the notion of tense which is restricted to the category of verbs). Here is an example of a lexical description of the word form "results":

```
[ word form = ``results''
       [ category = noun
                 subcategory = common
             morphology = [ number = plural
                             gender = neuter²
                                    lemma = ``result'' ]]
```

```
[ category = verb
        subcategory = main
    morphology = [ form = indicative
                        tense = present
                        number = singular
                        person = third
                            lemma = ``result'']]]
```

POS tagging is said to be one of the easiest linguistic tasks to implement, since the performance level that one can get with simple algorithms is several orders of magnitude above human performance in terms of speed and very near the level of human performance in terms of quality. Most of the complex linguistic phenomena that lie beyond the range of the current language technology occur relatively rarely. In fact, the apparent high performance level displayed by taggers in general is slightly misleading, since it is the result of the preponderant number of unambiguous word forms over the ambiguous ones in natural language. For instance, when we look at the performance on a per tag basis of one the best systems in the GRACE (Adda et al., 1999) evaluation campaign of French POS taggers, the error rate is 0.03% (4 tagging errors over 13,246 occurrences) for the punctuation category, while it goes up to 7% (1,449 tagging errors over 20,491 occurrences) for the noun category. Charniak et al. (1993) showed that the simple strategy of selecting the most likely tag for each word correctly tagged 90% of the word forms present in its data. The difficulty of POS tagging also varies greatly with the language considered; for instance, the fact that nouns are capitalized in German texts helps a lot. But problems arise from the morphological productivity of German, which results in a large number of lexical parameters, at least in the standard Markov model approach (Schmid, 1995). How to measure the performance of POS taggers is precisely the topic addressed in Section 4.

2   Parsing

Parsing is an analysis task aiming at identifying any constraint that controls the arrangement of the various linguistic units into sentences, and hence the ordering of words. An automatic parser tries to extract from the textual data it is given as input a description of the organization and function of the linguistic elements it finds in the data. The syntactic description can then be used by the application for which the parser was developed.

In Natural Language Processing (NLP), parsing has been studied since the early 1960s, first to develop theoretical models of human language syntax and general "deep"[3] parsers. After a period during which the formalisms have evolved to take into account more and more lexical information (linguistic descriptions anchored in words), the last decade has seen a regain of interest in "shallow parsers" since for many applications deep configurational analyses of a sentence are completely irrelevant. Often shallow parsers are qualified in the literature as "robust". But one should not think that robustness is implied by a shallow analysis. It is true that since the function of a shallow parser is not to produce a full analysis, the number of constraints it must satisfy ought to be less than for a deep parser. Consequently, its chances of producing a valid analysis ought to be better. However, for any system this reasoning remains a hypothesis until proper tests have been conducted to assess the robustness of the parser considered. In parallel, the past few years have seen the emergence of the concept of a "treebank", a large corpus, fully annotated with deep syntactic information (see Cieri, Chapter 8, this volume), and of great value for machine learning and evaluation.

Today parsing a sentence can be approached from two different directions: first, there are the *constituent*-based models, which put the emphasis on categorial aspects of the linguistic units; second, there are the *dependency*-based models, for which the elements of interest are the syntactic functions of the linguistic units.

With constituent-based analysis, the structure of a sentence is represented by nested constituents, tagged with their syntactic category (noun phrase, verb phrase, etc.) In this model, the syntactic functions are derived from the relations existing in the constituents structure. For each syntactic function there is a particular constituent configuration: for instance, the derivation of a noun phrase (NP) from a sentence constituent indicates that the NP has the subject function. Here is an example of constituent annotation from Monceaux, (2002) (translation: *Jean looks like Paul*):

$$[^S [^{NP} \text{Jean}] [^{VP} [^V \text{ressemble}] [^{PP} [^{Prep} \text{à}] [^{NP} \text{Paul}]]]]$$

In the dependency model introduced by Tesnière (1966), structural connections between the words fall into two classes: dependency relations (subordination) and junction relations (coordination). A dependency relationship is established between two words or linguistic units as soon as the syntactic and semantic features of one word constrain the possibilities for the other to co-occur. In this model, syntactic analysis is performed from left to right, and syntactic functions are carried out by specific words, i.e., the heads, and not by the constituents, as is the case with the constituent-based model. Figure 1 shows an example of dependency annotation.

Constituent models and dependency models are considered globally complementary since they offer two different points of view on the same data, and equivalent since it is theoretically possible to perform an automatic conversion (Bohnet and Seniv, 2004) in both directions, but sometimes this conversion is quite complex. We will now briefly present a few syntactic formalisms among the ones encountered most frequently in the literature, without in any way trying to be exhaustive. Ait-Mokhtar and Chanod (1997)

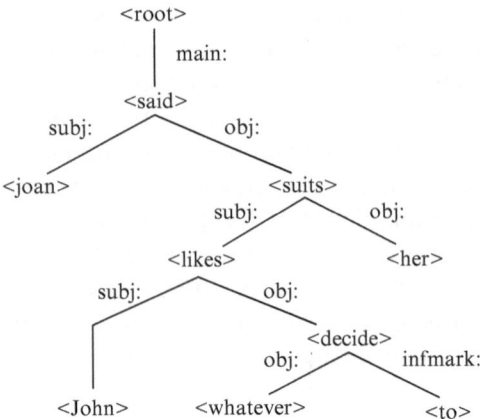

Figure 1. An example of dependency annotation of the sentence "John likes to decide whatever suits her" from Monceaux (2002).

describe a parser realised with finite state automata. An introduction to the use of statistical methods for parsing is proposed in Manning and Schütze (2002). A presentation of the various approaches that have been tried for parsing along with the main milestones of the domain is given in Wehrli (1997) and Abeillé and Blache (2000); in Abeillé (1993) we find a description of all the formalisms that were inspired from logic programming (based on unification operation) like the "lexical functional grammar" (LFG), the "generalized phrase structure grammar" (GPSG), the "head-driven phrase structure grammar" (HPSG), and the "tree adjoining grammar" (TAG).

LFG is a lexical theory that represents grammatical structure by means of two kinds of objects linked together by correspondences: the functional structures (f-structures), which express grammatical relations by means of attribute-value pairs (attributes may be features such as tense, or functions such as subject); and the constituent structures (c-structures), which have the form of phrase structure trees. Information about the c-structure category of each word as well as its f-structure is stored in the lexicon. The grammar rules encode constraints between the f-structure of any non-terminal node and the f-structures of its daughter nodes. The functional structure must validate the completeness and coherence condition: all grammatical functions required by a predicate must be present but no other grammatical function may be present.

In GPSG, phrase structure is encoded by means of context-free rules, which are divided into immediate dominance rules and linear precedence rules. The formalism is equipped with the so-called slash feature to handle unbounded movements in a context-free fashion. GPSG offers a high level, compact representation of language at the cost of sometimes problematic computation.

HPSG is a lexical formalism, in which language is a system of types of linguistic objects (word, phrase, clause, etc.) rather than a collection of sentences. HPSG represents grammar by declarative constraints. A grammar is a multiple-inheritance hierarchy of linguistic types. The lexicon is a subhierarchy in the grammar. A linguistic object type is represented by an underspecified feature structure, while a fully specified one identifies a unique linguistic object of the type considered. Constraints are resolved by feature structure unification.

TAG is a lightly context-sensitive formalism that represents grammar with two types of syntactic trees: elementary and auxiliary. Elementary trees hold the lexical information. In each elementary tree, a unique lexical item is attached to a leaf node. Auxiliary trees encode constraints on phrase structures. Trees are combined by means of two operations: substitution (replacement of a leaf node by a tree) and adjunction (replacement of a non-leaf node by a tree). Substitution and adjunction are constrained both by the labels of the nodes involved and by unification of the linguistic information stored in the feature structures associated to nodes.

A state-of-the-art description of dependency grammar is presented in Kahane (2000). Blache (2001) explores the contribution of contraint solving to parsing. Clément (2003) presents the latest development in parsing research. Vergne (2002) presents a multilingual parser that uses very few linguistic resources.

Parsing is an attempt at linking the linguistic phenomena naturally occurring in corpora with their encoding in a given syntactic formalism. We will see in Section 5 how evaluation attempts to qualify the way such linking is done.

3 Evaluation and Natural Language Processing

The purpose of evaluation is to provide an assessment of the value of a solution to a given problem; in our case, the purpose is to determine the performance of the POS tagging function or of the parsing function used in an application. When evaluating, we need to identify precisely the subject of evaluation. However, for NLP it is rather difficult to identify in a complete system, independent variables representative of the function to be observed. Often in NLP systems, the various functions involved are tightly coupled. When evaluating, the need to take into account the operational set-up adds an extra factor of complexity. This is why Sparck Jones and Galliers (1995), in their analysis and review of NLP system evaluation, stress the importance of distinguishing evaluation criteria relating to the language-processing goal (*intrinsic* criteria) from the ones relating to its role with respects to the purpose of the whole set-up (*extrinsic* criteria). One of the key questions is whether the operational set-up requires the help of a human, in which case, evaluation will also have to take into account human variability in the test conditions. The European project

EAGLES (King and Maegaard, 1998) used the role of the human operator as a guide to recast the question of evaluation in terms of users' perspective. The resulting evaluation methodology is centred on the consumer report paradigm. EAGLES distinguishes three kinds of evaluation:

1. *Progress evaluation*, where the current state of a system is assessed against a desired target state

2. *Adequacy evaluation*, where the adequacy of a system for some intended use is assessed

3. *Diagnostic evaluation*, where the assessment of the system is used to find where it fails and why

Among the other general characterisation of evaluation encountered in the literature, we retained the following ones, useful for comparing evaluation methodologies:

1. *Blackbox* or *whitebox* evaluation – whether only the global function performed between the input and output of a systems is accessible, or whether all its subfunctions are also accessible for investigation

2. *Subjective* or *objective* evaluation – whether the measurement is performed directly on data produced by the process under test, or whether it is based on the perception that human beings have of the process under test

3. *Qualitative* or *quantitative* evaluation – whether the result is a label descriptive of the behaviour of a system or whether it is the value resulting from the measurement of a particular variable

4. *Technology* or *user-oriented* evaluation (see King, Chapter 5, this volume) – whether one measures the performance of a system on a generic task (the specific aspects of any application, environment, culture, and language being abstracted as much as possible from the task), or whether one considers the actual performance of a system in the framework of a specific application, environment, culture, and language, in which case, not only technical aspects are compared, but also usability criteria like the human/machine synergy

An important point is whether the performance of a language-processing system is measured against a theoretical objective (the maximal performance value defined by the evaluation metrics), or rather against the performance level displayed by a human performing the task under consideration, as Peak (2001) proposes to do when evaluating spoken language dialogue systems.

Since the goal of evaluation is to provide answers to questions raised about the working of a given information-processing system, it is very likely that some decisive questions may have nothing to do with the ability to process a particular language. They may concern issues like software portability (choice of programming language, operating system compatibility, interoperability with other modules), or the capability of the system to handle various languages. On one occasion, decision makers preferred to select a unique multilingual system over a set of monolingual systems, for maintainability reasons, even though the multilingual system displayed lower performance on some language than its specific counterpart.

Finally we can say that any evaluation dealing with language processing resolves itself to proposing (partial) answers to the following three questions:

1. Which linguistic phenomena need to be taken into account and how frequently do they occur?

2. What kind of analysis is performed on them?

3. How will the result of their analysis be used by the application considered?

Note that, in practice, the question of which linguistic phenomena to adopt not only concerns the phenomena subject to the language processing considered, but also deals with the definition of more basic elements like affixes, word stems, types, lemmas, syntactic chunks, phrases, sentences, paragraphs, or even documents. Unfortunately, no standard exists for these.

Very often the evaluation process is based on a corpus[4] (Kilgarriff and Grefenstette, 2003). Thus we can have reproducible tests, if no human intervention is required by the application under test. If the latter cannot be achieved, a solution is to record the human intervention and reuse it at a later time. Thus the working of the application can be reproduced exactly. Fortunately, there is now enough knowledge available from corpus linguistics to ensure that a given corpus is representative of the language phenomena corresponding to the evaluation task.

The aim of this chapter is to introduce the reader to the evaluation of POS taggers and parsers for natural language textual data.[5] We will look at both POS tagging and parsing, two kinds of analysis almost always brought into play when processing natural language data.

With the current state of NLP technology, POS tagging and parsing deal essentially with the appearance of words, relegating semantic and pragmatic issues to other processing stages. Note that POS taggers and parsers are among the more readily available kinds of NLP software.

More precisely, by POS tagging is usually meant the identification of the morphosyntactic class of each word form[6] using lexical and contextual information. The classes are either a refinement of the ones inherited from the Latin grammar (where, for instance, the class of nouns regroups the words designating entities, objects, notions, and concepts), inferred from statistical data according to an arbitrary feature set, or a mix of both of the previous cases.

By definition, the task of parsing aims at identifying any constraint that controls the arrangement of the various linguistic units into sentences, and hence the ordering of words.

If we use basic linguistic terminology in the example of "The program prints results", POS tagging will identify the word form "prints" as a verb, at the third person singular of the indicative present tense (and not as a noun), and parsing will tell that the form "program" is the subject of the verb form "prints", and that the form "results" is the direct object complement of the verb form "prints".

Note that the majority of parsing algorithms require the result of a preliminary POS tagging analysis or incorporate a POS tagging function. Note also, that the definitions we have just given of POS tagging and parsing rely on the definition of what constitutes a word, a not so trivial task as we will see in Section 3.1.

3.1   Identifying the Boundaries of Basic Linguistic Units

"What is a word?" (Grefenstette and Tapanainen, 1994) is a trivial question, it seems, but we will see that it is not the case. Usually, the transformation of a character stream into the sequence of basic units that any analysis requires is called *tokenisation*, and the basic units *tokens*. They are built on the basis of purely orthographic considerations, taking into account exclusive character classes, namely separators versus non-separators (Habert et al., 1998; Manning and Schütze, 2002). However, no one-to-one correspondence exists between the tokens and the word forms (Adda et al., 1997). Despite the help provided by separator characters (for the languages whose written form has them[7]), the correct identification of the various word forms cannot be done only on the basis of their appearance because language is ambiguous by nature. To perform word segmentation, the use of syntactic or semantic and sometimes even pragmatic knowledge may be required. Such knowledge is generally not available during tokenisation, since it implies the prior identification of the various word forms present. For instance, in the following examples recourse to syntax and semantics is required to distinguish between the two analyses of"of course", a noun preceded by a preposition in the first excerpt, and an adverb in the second one:

1. Early parental absence as an indicator ⎡of⎤ ⎡course⎤ and outcome in chronic schizophrenia.

2. This is an impossibility ⎡of course⎤ and the manufacturers admit so in private.

Since evaluation generally implies comparing several systems or different versions of the same system, it is very likely that each will use its own specific word segmentation. Segmentation variation could have an impact either on the POS tagging or parsing process (i.e., different segmentations produce different analyses), or on the performance measurement (i.e., different word segmentations entail different performance measures). Providing different specific reference data for each system to limit the influence of word segmentation would be too costly in addition to raising questions about the universality of the evaluation results. Nevertheless, to limit the influence of word segmentation, it is possible either to take an average performance measurement across all the possible segmentations, or to choose arbitrarily a reference word segmentation, but if so, which one? Alternatively, the various word segmentations can be mapped onto a common underlying token segmentation that serves as the reference segmentation. Adda et al. (1999) propose to represent explicitly the word segmentation information through indices associated to the tokens,[8] which Cloeren (1999) calls *ditto* tags. With this scheme, any word segmentation can be represented, provided that the smallest word of any segmentation has a size equal to, or larger than, the one of the smallest token.

However, using the token segmentation instead of the word segmentation for counting correct/incorrect events distorts the counts. For instance, with such a scheme an erroneous word made of two tokens will be counted twice instead of once (see Table 1). In general, the distortion introduced by the change of segmentation is somehow compensated by the fact that it applies to both the erroneous cases and the correct ones. Thus, even though the values of the event counts are different for each of the two segmentations, the relative positions of the various systems in the performance graph are often preserved across segmentation change.

The problem of splicing the input stream is not limited to small linguistic units like word forms, but concerns also larger units like sentences. Neither

Table 1. Example of error amplification when using token segmentation instead of word segmentation (2 errors instead of one).

System output	[of course] adjective	1 error
Normalised system output	[of] adjective/1.2 [course] adjective/2.2	2 errors
Reference	[of] adverb/1.2 [course] adverb/2.2	–

a standard nor a clearly established definition of what constitutes a sentence exists. Furthermore, sentence segmentation may or may not be part of the function performed by a parser. For instance, Brill's tagger (Brill, 1995) expects to receive input that is already segmented into sentences. The quality of the sentence segmentation has a direct bearing on the quality of the parsing, since the beginning and end of sentences are elements of context that strongly determine parsing. If sentence segmentation is considered solved by some (Mikheev, 2000), this holds only for written language of good quality where punctuation marks obey typographic rules most of the time. It is quite another thing for emails or speech transcriptions. For instance, in the EASY-EVALDA evaluation campaign for parsers of French of the TECH-NOLANGUE program (Mapelli et al., 2004), the sentence boundaries for the manual speech transcription[9] data had to be set by hand only after the reference syntactic annotation had been done, since the annotators needed the syntactic information to assign end-of-sentence markers in a consistent manner.

Sometimes, it may even be the document boundary which is problematic, for instance when segmenting a continuous audio stream (Gauvain et al., 2001), where the limits of the different programmes (news, advertising, shows, etc.) need to be identified.

4   POS Tagging Evaluation Methodology

Accuracy is certainly the most intuitive and the most used among the performance measures mentioned in the literature. It is defined as the ratio of the number of word forms correctly tagged over the total number of word forms tagged.[10] Note that the exact signification of this measure depends on what is meant exactly by "correct" tagging, the simplest definition of which requires that the following two conditions be met:

1. The word segmentation convention used by the tagger must be the same as the one used for the reference data, otherwise there is a need to deploy realignment procedures (cf. Adda et al., 1999).

2. The tagset used by the tagger must be the same as the one used to annotate the reference data, otherwise specific mapping procedures need to be applied (cf. Adda et al., 1999).

For POS tagging, everybody agrees that the *accuracy* of a tagger cannot be properly evaluated without a comparison with an annotated reference corpus, which has a distribution of linguistic phenomena that is representative of the POS tagger target application. A test suite can give interesting insights on the way the tagger handles particular linguistic phenomena. However, the relatively small size of the test suites (up to a few thousand words in general), compared to the one of a corpus (at least a million words; Paroubek and

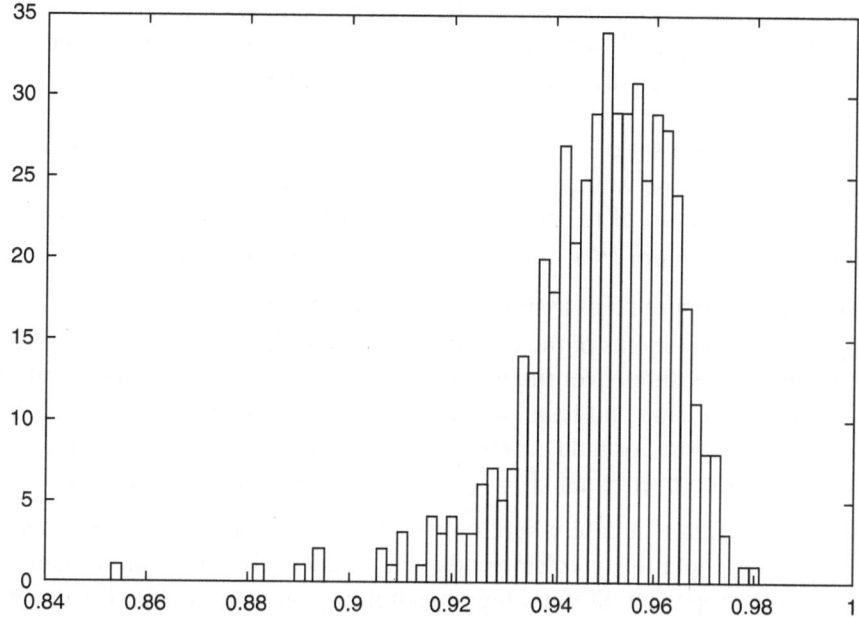

Figure 2. Variation of POS tagging accuracy depending on text genre. The graph (Illouz, 2000) gives the number of texts of a given genre (ordinate) in function of tagging precision (abscissa), measured on the Brown corpus (500 texts of 2000 words), with the Tree Tagger using the Penn Treebank tagset.

Rajman, 2002) does not permit to obtain enough information either on the language coverage or on the robustness of the tagger.

Not only the size of the corpus, but also its type can have an influence on the accuracy measure. To show how the performance of a POS tagger varies depending on the kind of data it processes, we give in Figure 2 the variation of tagging accuracy of the Tree Tagger (a freely available probabilistic POS tagger which uses the Penn Treebank tagset) as a function of the text genre, measured on the Brown corpus (500 texts of 2,000 words each). The accuracy varies from 85% to 98% with an average value of 94.6% (Illouz, 2000). Of course, it is recommended for testing to use material different from that which served for training of the system, since performance will invariably be better on the training material (van Halteren, 1999).

Things get more complicated as soon as we start considering cases other than the one in which both the tagger and the reference data assign only one tag per token. Then the accuracy measure no longer permits a fair comparison between different taggers, if they are allowed to propose partially disambiguated taggings. Van Halteren (1999) proposes in such cases to use the *average tagging perplexity*, i.e., the average number of tags per word assigned by the system,[11] or to have recourse to *precision* and *recall*, the now well-known evaluation measures from Information Retrieval.

Let us denote with t_i the set of tags assigned to the ith word form w_i by a tagger and r_i the set of tags assigned to the same word form in the reference annotations. The value of the precision and recall for this word form are, respectively, the ratio of the number of correct tags over the number of tags assigned by the system $P(w_i) = \frac{|t_i \cap r_i|}{|t_i|}$, and the ratio of the number of correct tags over the number of tags assigned in the reference $R(w_i) = \frac{|t_i \cap r_i|}{|r_i|}$. By averaging the respective sums of the two previous quantities for all the word forms, we obtain the measures over the whole corpus $P = \frac{1}{N} \sum_{i=1}^{N} p_i$ and similarly for R. Often precision and recall are combined together into one single value, the *f-measure* whose formula accepts as parameter α the relative importance[12] given to precision over recall, $F = \frac{1}{\frac{\alpha}{P} + \frac{(1-\alpha)}{R}}$ (Manning and Schütze, 2002).

In the very frequent case where only one tag per word form is assigned in the reference annotation, precision and recall take very intuitive interpretations. Recall is the proportion of word taggings holding one correct tag. Precision is the ratio between the recall and the average number of tags assigned per word by the tagger. This second measure is relatively close to the *average ambiguity* (Tufis and Mason, 1998), the average number of tags assigned by a lexicon to the words of a corpus. It integrates both the a priori ambiguity of the corpus and the *delicacy*[13] of the tagset used in the lexicon. Average ambiguity can be used to quantify the relative difficulty offered by the task of tagging the corpus, i.e., how much ambiguity remains to be solved, since some word forms have already an unambiguous tagging in the lexicon.

Note that precision is a global performance measurement which does not give any information about the error distribution over the various linguistic phenomena or the various genres of text, or on the types of error. It is not because two taggers have similar precision values that they make the same errors at the same locations. Therefore, it may be of interest to quantify the similarity between two taggings of the same text. There exists a measure initially developed for this very purpose, but for human annotators. It is the κ (kappa) coefficient (Carletta, 1996), which compensates for the cases where the two taggings agree by chance.

Other approaches use measures from Information Theory (Resnik and Yarowsky, 1997), like the per word cross-entropy, which measures the distance between a stochastic process q and a reference stochastic process p. In this approach, tagging is considered to be a stochastic process which associates to each word form a probability distribution over the set of tags. If we suppose that the reference process is stationary[14] and ergodic,[15] and that two subsequent taggings are two independent events, then for a sufficiently large corpus, the cross-entropy can be easily computed (Cover and Thomas, 1991).

Let us mention another set of measures which has been used in the GRACE evaluation campaign (Adda et al., 1999): precision and decision. The precision measures the number of times a word was assigned a single correct tag. The decision measures the ratio between the number of words which have been assigned a single tag and the total number of words. The originality of this measure lies with the possibility to plot the whole range of performance values reachable by a system, if one were to attempt to disambiguate some or all of the taggings that were left ambiguous by the tagger.

In the literature, most of the results mention precision values which are almost always greater than 90% and sometimes reach 99%. Already in de Rose (1988), the Volsunga tagger had achieved 96% precision for English on the Brown corpus. The best result in the GRACE evaluation of French taggers was 97.8% precision on a corpus of classic literature and the *Le Monde* newspaper. In the same evaluation, a lexical tagging (assigning all the tags found in the lexicon associated to the considered word form) achieved 88% precision. This result dropped to 59% precision[16] when a few contextual rule files were applied to try to artificially reduce the ambiguous taggings to one single tag per word. But let us remind the reader that all these measures must be considered with caution since they highly depend on the size and composition of the tagset as well as on the segmentation algorithms and on the genre of the text processed. Furthermore, evaluation results are given on a per word basis, which is not necessarily an appropriate unit for some applications where units like the sentence, the paragraph, or the document are often more pertinent. For instance, for a 15-word sentence and a tagging precision of 96% at the word level, we only get a tagging precision of 54.2% at the sentence level, i.e., almost 1 sentence in 2 contains a tagging error. Conversely, to achieve a 95% tagging precision at the sentence level, we would need to have a tagger which would achieve a 99.67% precision at the word level.

Although POS tagging seems to be a task far simpler than parsing, a POS tagger is a complex system combining several functions (tokeniser, word/sentence segmenter, context-free tagger, POS tag disambiguator) which may use external linguistic resources like a lexicon and a tagset. Evaluating such systems implies clear choices about the criteria that will be effectively taken into account during evaluation. Evaluation cannot resume itself to the simple measurement of tagging accuracy; factors like the processing speed (number of words tagged per second), the software portability (on which operating system can the tagger run, how easily can it be integrated with other modules), its robustness (is the system tolerant to large variations of the input data characteristics), the delicacy of the tagset (how fine a linguistic distinction can be made between two word classes), and the multilingualism of the system all constitute different dimensions of the evaluation space, the importance of which varies depending on the purpose of evaluation.

5   Methodology and Evaluation Measures for Parsing

Historically, the first comparative evaluation of the output of automatic parsers has been done by human experts, who formulated a diagnostics based on the processing of a set of test sentences. Very often this way of performing evaluation implies the use of an analysis grid (Blache and Morin, 2003) that lists evaluation features. To our knowledge the first publication on the subject for French is from Abbeillé (1991). In order to limit the bias introduced by the views of a particular expert and to promote reuse of linguistic knowledge, the community started to devise test suites compare, for instance, the European project TSNLP (Oepen et al., 1996). It produced a syntactic test suite for several European languages, with each test suite containing both positive and negative examples of annotations, classified by linguistic phenomena. Although they are of a great help to experts, test suites have nevertheless several drawbacks. First, they do not reflect the statistical distribution of the phenomena encountered in real corpora and they are also too small to be reused for evaluation (except for non-regression tests), because once they have been disclosed, it is relatively easy to customise any parser for the specific examples contained in the test suite. The second drawback concerns the formalism, because very likely the test suite and the parser under test will use different syntactic formalisms; thus a mapping between the formalisms will be required, which may generate some information loss. To answer this criticism, a new approach inspired by statistics and machine learning has emerged, helped by the recent progress in NLP and the development of standards for mark-up, i.e., the treebanks. A treebank is a relatively large corpus (at least more than 1 million word forms), completely annotated with a particular formalism in a consistent way. The first and certainly the most famous is the Penn Treebank (Marcus et al., 1993), which has inspired other developments like Brant et al. (2002) and Abbillé et al. (2000) for French. However, while treebanks provide a solution to the problem of language coverage, they do not solve the main problem of parsing evaluation, i.e., which pivot formalism should we use to obtain a faithful evaluation? A faithful evaluation is an evaluation that preserves both the information present in the reference data and in the data output by the parser. It should also provide the means to describe all the linguistic phenomena of the test data. Defining such a formalism is precisely one of the objectives of parsing, i.e., providing a universal formalism for all the phenomena of a language.

Up to now many propositions have been made in that direction. Some use annotation mappings (Gaizauskas et al., 1998); others propose to compare information quantity (Musillo and Simaán, 2002), which unfortunately obliges one to build a parallel corpus per formalism; and others again propose to use automatic grammar-learning procedures (Xia and Palmer, 2000) or computations based on the "edit" distance (Roark, 2002). The oldest approach (Black et al., 1991) focused on evaluation measures and used the constituent boundaries to compare parsers by measuring the percentage of crossing brackets (number of constituent boundaries output by the parser that cross[17] a constituent boundary of the reference) and recall (number of constituent boundaries output by the parser that exist in the reference data). Precision was added to the two previous measures to constitute what was called the GEIG[18] scheme (Srinivas et al., 1996) or PARSEVAL measures (Carroll et al., 2002). Unfortunately these measures were applicable in practice only on unlabelled constituents, i.e., without any information as to which category the constituent belongs to, since the output of the parsers that participated in these experiments was too diverse to allow for the use of such information. The PARSEVAL scheme takes into account only part of the information produced by a parser. Furthermore, it is more easily applied to constituent-based parsers.

To try to solve this problem, Lin (1998) suggested to use dependencies rather than constituents for evaluation. Briscoe et al. (2002) and Caroll et al. (1998, 2003) propose to go even further by annotating tagged grammatical relations between lemmatised lexical heads, in order to work on both the logic and grammatical relations that are present in the sentence, instead of looking at the topological details of a parse tree. The most recent developments in large-scale evaluation effort concern French with the TECH-NOLANGUE program (Mapelli et al., 2004) and its evaluation campaign for parsers, EASY (Vilnat et al., 2003) of the EVALDA project, which proposes to use an annotation formalism inspired by Carroll et al. (2003) with an initial level of constituents and grammatical relations, but without any explicit notion of head (Gendner et al., 2003; Vilnat et al., 2003).

The EASY annotation scheme recognises 6 types of syntactic chunks and 14 functional relations. The xml-like tags (cf.) Figure 3 indicate syntactic

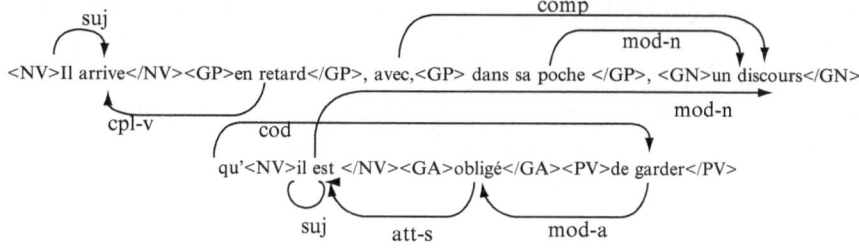

Figure 3. Example of reference annotation of the EASY evaluation campaign for the sentence: "He arrives late, with in his pocket, a discourse which he must keep."

chunks: NV = verb chunk, including clitics, as in "Il arrive" "He comes"; GP = prepositional chunk; GN = nominal chunk; GA = adjectival chunk; PV = prepositional-verbal chunk (i.e., for infinitive forms introduced by a preposition). The arrows indicate the functional relations, relating either syntactic chunks or tokens; *suj* means subject; *comp* represents "complementiser" mainly for conjunctive subordinates, with the subordinate conjunction and the verbal chunk of the subordinate as arguments, but it is also used, like here, to annotate the relation between a preposition and a nominal chunk or verbal chunk when they cannot be annotated as GP or PV, for instance, in the presence of an insertion ("dans sa poche", "in his pocket"); *cpl-v* means verb complement; *cod* encodes direct object; *mod-n* stands for noun modifier; *mod-a* for adjective modifier; *atb-s* means subject attribute.

5.1   Which Performance can Current Parsing Technology Achieve

Because there are many more different formalisms and these vary more than the ones used for POS tagging, the amount of reliable, widely available parsing software is smaller than for taggers. Even more so, since the analysis to perform is much more complex in the case of parsing. With the same reservation as for what was said about POS tagging, we will now give some results indicative of the level of performance achievable by current parsing technologies, without any claim of being exhaustive.

Black (1993) gives for five systems a percentage of correct sentences (without any constituent boundary crossing) varying from 29% to 78%. He gives for two systems respective values of 38% and 51% of exact match between the constituent boundaries of the parsers and the ones of the reference annotation. Similarly, John Carroll (Carroll et al., 2002) mentions, that describes a comparative evaluation done by the GEIG in 1992, recall measures on constituent boundaries varying from 45% to 64%, a mean rate of constituent boundary crossing between 3.17 and 1.84, and a sentence percentage, for which the best analysis contains at least one constituent boundary crossing, between 84% and 34%.

Srinivas et al. (1998) report that the XTAG (Doran et al., 1994) analyses correctly 61.4% of the sentences of the TSNLP test suite (Oepen et al., 1996) and 89.6% of the sentences of a weather forecast bulletin corpus. Srinivas et al. (1998) have achieved a precision value of 84.2% for another version of the same parser, measured on the dependencies extracted from the Penn Treebank, and Xia and Palmer (2000) computed on the same corpus a value of 97.2% of structure similarity for the syntactic patterns. Crouch et al. (2002) present values of f-measure lying between 73% and 79%, measured on the Penn Treebank for an LFG parser enhanced with a stochastic disambiguating mechanism.

Table 2. Performance range of four parsers of French and their combination, on questions of the Question and Answer TREC track corpus.

	Precision	Recall
Noun phrase	from 31.5% to 86.6%	from 38.7% to 86.6%
Verb phrase	from 85.6% to 98.6%	from 80.5% to 98.6%
Prepositional phrase	from 60.5% to 100%	from 60.5% to 100%

For a Category Combinatory Grammar (CCG), Clark and Hochenmaier (2002) give PARSEVAL results of 85.5% precision for unlabelled constituents (and 81.6% for labelled ones) and 85.9% recall on unlabelled constituents (and 81.9% on labelled constituents).

For French, Francopoulo and Blache (2003) have obtained a value of 74% for the f-measure with a chunk parser. Monceaux (2002) and Monceaux and Vilnat (2003) have studied the combination of parsers for the analysis of questions. The performance ranges of the four parsers and their combination are presented in Table 2.

As we have just seen, getting a clear idea of the level of performance achievable by the current parsing technology is rather difficult since the formalisms vary greatly and the results of evaluation display important differences, depending on the evaluation procedure applied and on the reference data used, even more so since evaluation results are scarce for languages other than English.

6   Conclusion

When POS taggers and parsers are integrated in an application, only quantitative blackbox methodologies are available to gauge their performance. This approach is characteristic for technology-oriented evaluation, which interests mostly integrators and developers, contrary to user-oriented evaluation, for which the interaction with the final user is a key element of the evaluation process.

Although the corpus-based automatic evaluation procedures do provide most of the information useful for assessing the performance of a POS tagger or parser, the recourse to the opinion of an expert of the domain is essential, not only to provide an interpretation of the results returned by the automatic evaluation procedures, but also to provide the knowledge needed to define the conditions under which the evaluation measures will be taken.

POS tagging evaluation methodology is now mature, and there exist enough results in the literature to be able to compare POS taggers on grounds sufficiently sound if one has the proper evaluation tools and an annotated corpus, the cost of which is rather high, not only because of the manpower needed, but also because of the annotation quality required.

For parsing, the situation is less clear, possibly only because of the greater variety of the syntactic formalisms and of the analysis algorithms. It is very difficult to compare on a fair basis systems that use different formalisms. However, the situation begins to change with the emergence of new evaluation protocols based on grammatical relations (Carroll et al., 2003) instead of constituents, and large-scale evaluation campaigns, like the French EASY-EVALDA of the TECHNOLANGUE program for parsers of French (Vilnat et al., 2003).

Notes

1. A Treebank is a large corpus completely annotated with syntactic information (trees) in a consistent way.

2. In English, gender for nouns is only useful for analysing constructions with pronouns.

3. A "deep" parser describes for all the word forms of a sentence, in a complete and consistent way, the various linguistic elements present in the sentence and the structures they form; on the contrary, a "shallow" parser only provides a partial description of the structures.

4. This is particularly true of any batch-processing activity like POS tagging and parsing.

5. Of all kinds, including emails or produced by automatic speech transcription.

6. We will refrain from using the term *type* to refer to word forms, to avoid any confusion with other meanings of this term.

7. Languages like Chinese are written without separators.

8. Tokens are indexed with indices made of the position of the current token in the compound word, associated with the total number of tokens in the compound, e.g., of/1.2 course/2.2.

9. Transcription of oral dialogues, recorded in various everyday life situations.

10. The error rate is simply the 1's complement of the accuracy.

11. Note that this measure takes all its sense when given with the corresponding measure of the standard deviation.

12. In general $\alpha = 0.5$.

13. The level of refinement in linguistic distinction offered by the tagset, in general, correlated with the number of tags: the finer the distinctions, the larger the tagset.

14. A stochastic process is stationary when its statistical characteristics do not depend on the initial conditions.

15. Observations made at any time over a succession of process states are the same as the observations made over the same states but on a large number of realisations.

16. The precision decreases, because as the ambiguous taggings are resolved, they become unambiguous and thus are taken into account in the computation of the precision, while before they were only taken into account in the measurement of the decision.

17. Here is an example where the A parentheses cross the B parentheses: $(A (B A)B)$.

18. Grammar Evaluation Interest Group.

References

Abeillé, A. (1991). Analyseurs syntaxiques du français. *Bulletin Semestriel de l'Association pour le Traitement Automatique des Langues*, 32:107–120.

Abeillé, A. (1993). *Les nouvelles syntaxes*. Armand Colin, Paris, France.

Abeillé, A. and Blache, P. (2000). *Grammaires et analyseurs syntaxiques*, pages 61–76, Ingénierie des langues, Hermes Science Publication, Paris, France.

Abeillé, A., Clément, L., and Kinyon, A. (2000). Building a Treebank for French. In *Proceedings of the Second International Conference on Language Ressources and Evaluation (LREC)*, pages 1251–1254, Athens, Greece.

Adda, G., Adda-Decker, M., Gauvain, J.-L., and Lamel, L. (1997). Text Normalization and Speech Recognition in French. In *Proceedings of the European Conference on Speech Communication and Technology (Eurospeech)*, volume 5, pages 2711–2714, Rhodes, Greece.

Adda, G., Mariani, J., Paroubek, P., Rajman, M., and Lecomte, J. (1999). L'action grace d'évaluation de l'assignation des parties du discours pour le français. *Langues*, 2(2):119–129.

Ait-Mokhtar, S. and Chanod, J.-P. (1997). Incremental Finite-State Parsing. In *Proceedings of the Fifth Conference on Applied Natural Language Processing*, pages 72–79, Washington, DC, USA.

Blache, P. (2001). *Les grammaires de propriétés: des contraintes pour le traitement automatique des langues*, Hermes Science Publication, Paris, France.

Blache, P. and Morin, J.-Y. (2003). Une grille d'évaluation pour les analyseurs syntaxiques. In *Acte de l'atelier sur l'Evaluation des Analyseurs Syntaxiques dans les actes de la 10ᵉ Conférence Annuelle sur le Traitement Automatique des Langues Naturelles (TALN)*, volume II, pages 77–86, Batz-sur-Mer, France.

Black, E. (1993). Parsing English by Computer: The State of the Art. In *Proceedings of the International Symposium on Spoken Dialog*, pages 77–81, Tokyo, Japan.

Black, E., Abney, S., Flickenger, D., Gdaniec, C., Grishman, R., Harison, P., Hindle, D., Ingria, R., Jelineck, F., Klavan, J., Liberman, M., Marcus, M., Roukos, S., Santorini, B., and Strzalkowski, T. (1991). A Procedure for Quantitatively Comparing the Syntactic Coverage of English Grammars. In *Proceedings of the Fourth DARPA Speech and Natural Language Workshop*, pages 306–311, Morgan Kaufman, Pacific Grove, California, USA.

Bohnet, B. and Seniv, H. (2004). Mapping Dependency Structures to Phrase Structures and the Automatic Acquisition of Mapping Rules. In *Proceedings of the Fourth International Conference on Language Resources and Evaluation (LREC)*, pages 855–858, Lisboa, Portugal.

Brant, S., Dipper, S., Hansen, S., Lezius, W., and Smith, G. (2002). The TIGER Treebank. In *Proceedings of the First Workshop on Treebank and Linguistics Thories (TLT)*, pages 24–41, Sozopol, Bulgaria.

Brill, E. (1995). Transformation-Based Error Driven Learning and Natural Language Processing: A Case Study in Part of Speech Tagging. *Computational Linguistics*, 21(4):543–565.

Briscoe, E., Carroll, J., Grayham, J., and Copestake, A. (2002). Relational Evaluation Schemes. In *Proceedings of the Workshop Beyond Parseval – Towards Improved Evaluation Measures for Parsing Systems at the Third International Conference on Language Resources and Evaluation (LREC)*, pages 4–8, ELRA, Las Palmas, Gran Canaria, Spain.

Carletta, J. (1996). Assessing Agreement on Classification Tasks: The Kappa Statistics. *Computational Linguistics*, 22(2):249–254.

Carroll, J., Briscoe, T., and Sanfilipo, A. (1998). Parser Evaluation: A Survey and a New Proposal. In *Proceedings of the First International Conference on Linguistic Resources and Evaluation (LREC)*, pages 447–454, Granada, Spain.

Carroll, J., Frank, A., Lin, D., Prescher, D., and Uszkoreit, H. (2002). Beyond Parseval – Towards Improved Evaluation Measures for Parsing Systems. In Carroll, J., editor, *Proceedings of the Workshop Beyond Parseval – Towards Improved Evaluation Measures for Parsing Systems at the Third International Conference on Language Resources and Evaluation (LREC)*, pages 1–3, ELRA, Las Palmas, Gran Canaria, Spain.

Carroll, J., Minnen, G., and Briscoe, E. (2003). *Parser Evaluation Using a Grammtical Relation Annotation Scheme*, pages 299–316, Treebanks: Building and Using Parsed Corpora, Kluwer, Dordrecht, The Netherlands.

Chanod, J.-P. and Tapanainen, P. (1995). Creating a Tagset, Lexicon and Guesser for a French Tagger. In *Proceedings of the ACL SIGDAT Workshop From Text to Tags: Issues in Multilingual Analysis*, pages 58–64, University College, Dublin, Ireland.

Charniak, E., Hendrickson, C., Jacobson, N., and Perkowitz, M. (1993). Equations for Part of Speech Tagging. In *Proceedings of the the 11th Conference of the American Association for Artificial Intelligence (AAAI)*, pages 784–789, Washington DC, USA.

Clark, S. and Hochenmaier, J. (2002). Evaluating a Wide-Coverage CCG Parser. In *Proceedings of the Workshop Beyond Parseval – Towards Improved Evaluation Measures for Parsing Systems at the Third International Conference on Language Resources and Evaluation (LREC)*, pages 60–66, ELRA, Las Palmas, Gran Canaria, Spain.

Clément, L. (2003). Evolution en analyse syntaxique. *Revue TAL*, 44(3). Hermes Science Publication, Paris, France.

Cloeren, J. (1999). Tagsets. In van Halteren, H., editor, *Syntactic Wordclass Tagging*, chapter 4, pages 37–54, Kluwer Academic Publishers, Dordrecht, The Netherlands.

Cover, T. M. and Thomas, J. A. (1991). *Elements of Information Theory.* John Wiley, New York, USA.

Crouch, R., Kaplan, R., King, T., and Riezler, S. (2002). Comparison of Evaluation Metrics for a Broad Coverage Stochastic Parser. In *Proceedings of the Workshop Beyond Parseval – Towards Improved Evaluation Measures for Parsing Systems at the Third International Conference on Language Resources and Evaluation (LREC)*, pages 67–74, ELRA, Las Palmas, Gran Canaria, Spain.

de Rose, S. J. (1988). Grammatical Category Disambiguation by Statistical Optimization. *Computational Linguistics*, 14(1):31–39.

Doran, C., Egedi, D., Hockey, B., Srinivas, B., and Zaidel, M. (1994). XTAG System – A Wide Coverage Grammar for English. In *Proceedings of the 17th International Conference on Computational Linguistics (COLING)*, pages 922–928, Kyoto, Japan.

Francopoulo, G. and Blache, P. (2003). Tag chunker, mécanisme de construction et évaluation. In *Acte de l'atelier sur l'Evaluation des Analyseurs Syntaxiques dans les actes de la 10e Conférence Annuelle sur le Traitement Automatique des Langues Naturelles (TALN)*, pages 95–104, Batz-sur-Mer, France.

Gaizauskas, R., Hepple, M., and Huyck, C. (1998). Modifying Existing Annotated Corpora for General Comparative Evaluation of Parsing. In *Proceedings of the Workshop on Evaluation of Parsing Systems in the Proceedings of the First International Conference on Language Resources and Evaluation (LREC)*, pages 21–28, Granada, Spain.

Gauvain, J.-L., Lamel, L., and Adda, G. (2001). Audio Partitioning and Transcription for Broadcast Data Indexation. *MTAP Journal*, 14(2):187–200.

Gendner, V., Illouz, G., Jardino, M., Monceaux, L., Paroubek, P., Robba, I., and Vilnat, A. (2003). Peas, the First Instantiation of a Comparative Framework for Evaluating Parsers of French. In *Proceedings of the Tenth Conference of the European Chapter of the Association for Computational Linguistics (EACL)*, pages 95–98, Budapest, Hungary. Companion Volume.

Grefenstette, G. and Tapanainen, P. (1994). What is a Word, What is a Sentence? Problems of Tokenization. In *Proceedings of the Third International Conference on Computational Lexicography*, pages 79–87, Budapest, Hungary.

Habert, B., Adda, G., Adda-Decker, M., de Mareuil, P. B., Ferrari, S., Ferret, O., Illouz, G., and Paroubek, P. (1998). The Need for Tokenization Evaluation. In *Proceedings of the First International Conference on Language Resources and Evaluation (LREC)*, volume 1, pages 427–431, Granada, Spain.

Illouz, G. (2000). Sublanguage Dependent Evaluation: Toward Predicting NLP Performances. In *Proceedings of the Second International Conference on*

Language Ressources and Evaluation (LREC), pages 1251–1254, Athens, Greece.

Kahane, S. (2000). Les grammaires de dépendance. *Revue TAL*, 41(1):318. Hermes Science Publication, Paris, France.

Kilgarriff, A. and Grefenstette, G. (2003). Introduction to the Special Issue on the Web as Corpus. *Computational Linguistics*, 29(3):333–347.

King, M. and Maegaard, B. (1998). Issues in Natural Language System Evaluation. In *Proceedings of the First International Conference on Linguistic Resources and Evaluation (LREC)*, volume 1, pages 225–230, Granada, Spain.

Lin, D. (1998). Dependency-Based Evaluation of MINIPAR. In *Proceedings of the Workshop on Evaluation of Parsing Systems*, pages 33–39, Granada, Spain.

Manning, C. D. and Schütze, H. (2002). *Foundation of Statistical Natural Language Processing*. Massachusetts Institute of Technology Press, 5th edition.

Mapelli, V., Nava, M., Surcin, S., Mostefa, D., and Choukri, K. (2004). Technolangue: A Permanent Evaluation & Information Infrastructure. In *Proceedings of the Fourth International Conference on Language Resources and Evaluation (LREC)*, pages 381–384, Lisboa, Portugal.

Marcus, M., Santorini, B., and Marcinkiewciz, M. (1993). Building a Large Annotated Corpus of English: The Penn Treebank. *Computational Linguistics*, 19:313–330.

Mikheev, A. (2000). Tagging Sentence Boundaries. In *Proceedings of the North American Chapter of the Association for Computational Linguistics (NAACL)*, pages 264–271, Seattle, USA.

Monceaux, L. (2002). *Adaptation d'un niveau d'analyse des interventions dans un dialogue – Application à un système de question – réponse*. Thèse de doctorat, Université Paris XI, France.

Monceaux, L. and Vilnat, A. (2003). Multi-analyse, vers une analyse syntaxique plus fiable. In *Actes de la 10ᵉ Conférence Annuelle sur le Traitement Automatique des Langues Naturelles (TALN)*, pages 215–222, Batz-sur-Mer, France.

Musillo, G. and Simaán, K. (2002). Toward Comparing Parsers from Different Linguistic Frameworks – An Information Theoretic Approach. In *Proceedings of the Workshop Beyond Parseval – Towards Improved Evaluation Measures for Parsing Systems at the Third International Conference on Language Resources and Evaluation (LREC)*, pages 44–51, Las Palmas, Gran Canaria, Spain.

Oepen, S., Netter, K., and Klein, J. (1996). Test Suites for Natural Language Processing. In Nerbonne, J., editor, *Linguistic Databases*, pages 13–36, Center for the Study of Language and Information (CSLI) Publications, Stanford, California, USA.

Paek, T. (2001). Empirical Methods for Evaluating Dialog Systems. In *Proceedings of the Workshop on Evaluation Methodologies for Language and Dialog Systems*, pages 1–8, Toulouse, France. Annual Meeting of the Association for Computational Linguistics (ACL).

Paroubek, P. and Rajman, M. (2000). Multitag une ressource linguistique produit du paradigme d'évaluation. In *Actes de la 7ème Conférence Annuelle sur le Traitement Automatique des Langues Naturelles*, pages 297–306, Lausanne, Switzerland.

Resnik, P. and Yarowsky, D. (1997). A Perspective on Word Sense Disambiguation Methods and their Evaluation. In *Proceedings of the ACL SIGLEX Workshop on Tagging Text with Lexical Semantics: Why, What and How?*, pages 79–86, Washington, USA.

Roark, B. (2002). Evaluating Parser Accuracy Using Edit Distance. In *Proceedings of the Workshop Beyond Parseval – Towards Improved Evaluation Measures for Parsing Systems at the Third International Conference on Language Resources and Evaluation (LREC)*, pages 30–36, Las Palmas, Gran Canaria, Spain.

Schmid, H. (1995). Improvements in Part-of-Speech Tagging with an Application to German. In *Proceedings of the 14th International Conference on Computational Linguistics*, pages 172–176, Kyoto, Japan.

Sparck Jones, K. and Galliers, J. R. (1995). *Evaluating Natural Language Processing Systems*. Springer Verlag, Heidelberg, Germany.

Srinivas, B., Doran, C., Hockey, B. A., and Joshi, K. (1996). An Approach to Robust Partial Parsing and Evaluation Metrics. In Carroll, J., editor, *Proceedings of the Workshop on Robust Parsing*, pages 70–82, ESSLI, Prague, Czech Republic.

Srinivas, B., Sarkar, A., Doran, C., and Hockey, B. (1998). Grammar and Parser Evaluation in the XTAG Project. In *Proceedings of the Workshop on Evaluation of Parsing Systems*, pages 63–69, Granada, Spain.

Tesnière, L. (1966). *Élements de syntaxe structurale*, Klincksieck, Paris, France.

Tufis, D. (1999). Text Speech and Dialog. In *Tiered Tagging and Combined Classifier, Lecture Notes in Artificial Intelligence*, volume 1692, pages 28–33. Springer.

Tufis, D. and Mason, O. (1998). Tagging Romanian Texts: A Case Study for QTAG, a Language Independent Probabilistic Tagger. In *Proceedings of the First International Conference on Language Resources and Evaluation*, pages 589–596, Granada, Spain.

van Halteren, H. (1999). Performance of Taggers. In *Syntactic Wordclass Tagging*, pages 81–94, Kluwer Academic Publishers, Dordrecht, The Netherlands.

Vergne, J. (2002). Une méthode pour l'analyse descendante et calculatoire de corpus multilingues – application au calcul des relations sujet-verbe. In *Actes de la 9ᵉ Conférence Annuelle sur le Traitement Automatique des Langues Naturelles (TALN)*, pages 63–74, Nancy, France.

Vilnat, A., Paroubek, P., Monceaux, L., Robba, I., Gendner, V., Illouz, G., and Jardino, M. (2003). Easy or How Difficult Can It Be to Define a Reference Treebank for French. In *Proceedings of the Second Workshop on Treebanks and Linguistic Theories (TLT)*, pages 229–232, Växjö, Sweden.

Wehrli, E. (1997). *L'analyse syntaxique des langues naturelles: problèmes et méthodes*. Masson, Paris, France.

Xia, F. and Palmer, M. (2000). Evaluating the Coverage of LTAGS on Annotated Corpora. In *Proceedings of the Workshop on Using Evaluation within HLT Programs: Results and Trends, at the Second International Conference on Language Ressources and Evaluation (LREC)*, pages 1–6, Athens, Greece.

Chapter 5

GENERAL PRINCIPLES
OF USER-ORIENTED EVALUATION

Margaret King

ISSCO – School of Translation and Interpretation, ETI
University of Geneva, Switzerland

Maghi.King@gmail.com

Abstract   This chapter is concerned with a particular perspective on the problem of evaluation design. User-oriented evaluation takes as primary some user or set of users who need to accomplish some task, and sets out to discover through evaluation whether a given software system will help them to do so effectively, productively, safely, and with a sense of satisfaction. (Note that, following ISO, user here is used in a very wide sense and encompasses much more than what has conventionally been called end-user.) There is a clear tension between taking specific user needs as primary and seeking common principles for the evaluation of particular software applications. The chapter suggests that this tension may be resolved by using an ISO standard for the evaluation of software as an appropriate level of generalization (ISO 9126). Quality models reflecting the characteristics of specific software applications (machine translation, document retrieval, information extraction systems, etc.) are then built on the skeleton set out in the ISO standard. Particular user needs are taken into account by picking out those parts of the appropriate quality model which reflect the needs, where necessary imposing a relative order of importance on the parts picked out. Execution of the evaluation then concentrates on the parts of the quality model chosen as pertinent to the user and the context of work. The focus of the chapter is on general design questions rather than on the strengths and weaknesses of specific metrics. However, there is some discussion of what it means for a metric to be valid and reliable, and of the difficulty of finding good metrics for those cases where system performance and human performance in interaction with the system are inextricably linked. A suggestion is made that it might be possible to automate an important part of the process of evaluation design, and an attempt to do this for the case of machine translation evaluations is briefly sketched.

Keywords   User-oriented evaluation; Quality models; ISO.

L. Dybkjær et al. (eds.), Evaluation of Text and Speech Systems, 125–161.

1   A Historical Note

I could not claim personal authorship of any of the ideas put forward in this chapter: they are the fruit of an effort started over 10 years ago through the launch by the European Commission of a series of initiatives whose main aim was to stimulate the production of linguistic resources for the European languages. This was to be achieved by creating standards, so that resources could be shared. The initiatives were the two EAGLES[1] initiatives (1993–1996 and 1997–1999), which were followed by the ISLE[2] project (1999–2002), a joint project of the European Union and the National Science Foundation of the United States. Swiss participation in all three initiatives was directly funded by the Swiss Federal Office for Education and Science.

EAGLES took the form of a number of working groups, who essentially organized their own work. Some of the working groups operated in areas which were ripe for standardization, such as the collection of speech data or written corpus collection: others were asked to do preliminary investigations, working towards pre-normative guidelines in a specific area. One of these latter was the working group on evaluation, whose remit was to find a general methodological framework for the evaluation of human language technology products and systems. The first EAGLES initiative set out a general framework which recurs throughout this chapter (EAGLES Evaluation Working Group, 1996). The second EAGLES initiative organized a series of workshops through which knowledge of the basic framework was disseminated and further refinement of it took place. The EAGLES work concentrated on relatively simple language technology products such as spelling checkers, grammar checkers, and translation memory systems as test beds for the evaluation methodology. The ISLE project moved on to more complex systems, concentrating on the construction of an evaluation framework for machine translation systems. This fairly substantial, but still incomplete, example of an evaluation framework can be found at the following URL: http://www.issco.unige.ch/femti.

Work on the machine translation framework (baptized FEMTI) is being carried on through a project of the Swiss National Science Foundation which began in early 2005.

The ISLE project continued the tradition of organizing workshops where intermediate results could be discussed and new ideas put forward. Several of these workshops were "hands-on" workshops where the participants worked directly on specific problems of evaluation or on constructing parts of the framework. Some of the preparatory documents for various workshops can be found at http:/www.issco.unige.ch/projects/isle/. Over the years, well over 100 people must have been actively involved in EAGLES or in ISLE work, and since most of the effort was collaborative, it would be almost impossible to say who first suggested some new idea. It is for this reason that the present author, who was chair of the evaluation working group throughout its lifetime, claims only to be the reporter of common work and not its originator.

Another historical and intellectual debt is very important in the work reported here. ISO/IEC published in 1991 the first of its standards concerning the evaluation of software (ISO-9126/91). The normative part of this document set out a quality model for the evaluation of software. It also contained pre-normative guidelines for how the process of evaluation should be defined. The standard was brought to the attention of the first EAGLES evaluation working group by Kirsten Falkedal, one of its members, and subsequently became a primary inspiration for EAGLES work. The link with ISO work on evaluation was consolidated during the second EAGLES initiative, with the technical editor of the standard participating directly in an EAGLES workshop and contributing to the draft final report. The evaluation framework for machine translation systems produced as part of the ISLE project is structured around the quality model set out in the ISO 9126 standard. Recently, ISO/IEC has published two new series of standards on software evaluation (see bibliography for full ISO references). Defining the quality model and metrics related to it has now been separated out from defining the process of evaluation, giving rise to a revised 9126 series (quality model and metrics) and the new 14598 series (evaluation process and management).

Both the ISO work itself and the EAGLES work based on it were influenced by work on quality assurance in the software industry: one assumption here is that the sort of thinking underlying the assessment carried out in the context of producing a piece of software carries over to evaluation in a wider context. Work on evaluation of software in the context of technology acquisition around the time of the EAGLES projects also brings out the importance of how the software will be used and in what context, thus falling into the user-oriented philosophy. (See, e.g., Brown and Wallnau, 1996). This general intellectual current is reflected too in the similarity between the general philosophy of user-oriented evaluation and recent developments in software design, as typified by the formulation and deployment of use cases in drawing up software specifications in languages like the Unified Modeling Language (UML; see, e.g., Booch et al., 1999).

Much of the rest of this chapter is intended to be directly based on the ISO standards, although of course only the author is responsible for any misrepresentation of them.

In the specific context of this chapter, I would like to thank the two anonymous reviewers, whose perceptive and helpful remarks have, I hope, contributed to the improvement of the first draft.

Finally, I want to acknowledge a personal debt to two of my ISSCO/TIM colleagues, Andrei Popescu-Belis and Nancy Underwood. Over the past several years we have spent much time in discussion of evaluation questions: they have been generous with their time and with their insights.

2   What is User-Oriented Evaluation?

Many academic evaluation exercises concentrate on a software system taken in isolation, looking primarily at what it is supposed to do, and ignoring the context in which it will do it. User-oriented evaluation adopts a radically different perspective, taking as primary a user or set of users who need to accomplish some task and asking whether the system will help them to do so effectively, productively, safely, and with a sense of satisfaction. This implies looking at a large and complex set of factors which will contribute to whether, in the end, a decision to acquire and deploy the system will seem to have been a good decision. Frequently, the factors involved are not independent of one another, either conceptually or in the ways that each factor may contribute to an overall judgement. Thus, an evaluation designer working in the user-oriented perspective may often find himself/herself saying something like "well, it would be nice to have x, but if not, y might compensate for the lack, but whatever happens with x and y we must have z".

This implies that right from the start evaluation cannot be seen as a search for a single magic metric that will tell all that needs to be told about the system or systems being considered and which, when used alone, will allow direct comparison of competing systems.

Because of this chapter's focus on the philosophy and design of user-oriented evaluations there is very little direct discussion of particular metrics. Some metrics will be used as illustrations of specific points and will be briefly described, but no metric will get the thoroughgoing discussion of its strengths and weaknesses that a proper account focusing on the definition and choice of metrics would deserve. In mitigation of this weakness, most metrics are really only of direct interest to someone involved in the process of concrete evaluation design for a particular application of language technology – summarization, information retrieval, term extraction, or any other of the by now very many applications available. Such a person needs a detailed analysis and critical discussion of the specialized metrics applicable in his/her area of interest, and such a discussion can best and most easily be found in the technical literature, where interest in evaluation and in suitable metrics has been constantly expanding in the past few years.

Making a conscious decision not to treat specific metrics in any detail should not be interpreted as dismissing the importance of metrics: indeed, it will be argued later that it is the choice of metrics which determines the operational content of any specific evaluation, and a sister paper to this one (King, 2005) has much to say about that. But what concerns us here is all that has to happen before the evaluation designer can even begin to think about what metrics he/she will choose. This preliminary – very great – labour will be set out in the form of a number of principles underlying evaluation design in the user-oriented perspective.

3   A First Principle: Quality is Decided by Users

In the vast majority of cases, it is impossible to say in absolute terms whether something of its kind is or is not good. This is true of objects, processes, study programmes – of almost anything we can think of. In the case of software this otherwise rather sweeping statement can be justified fairly easily. Software is not created for its aesthetic value: it is meant to help in achieving some task, and its value is to be judged precisely in terms of whether it does so. There is thus always a user of the software, someone or some process who needs to get something done, and who makes use of the software as a means to that end.

Users can come in all shapes and sizes: they are not necessarily what are conventionally thought of as "end-users". Drawing up an exhaustive list of people who might be users in some given situation is not a practical proposition, so let me illustrate this with a few examples. Quite obviously, as I sit typing this into a text processor, I am a user, both of the text processing system itself and of the whole platform in which it is embedded, and, in this case, I am also an end-user. But imagine now the university computer committee who decides what hardware to buy and what software to put on it. They too are users in the sense of this section. They use the computer facilities they have decided to purchase by putting them at the disposal of a community of end-users, and, just as I may be more or less satisfied with what I am using, they may be more or less satisfied with the provision they have made.

Other users may not be using a commercial product at all. If a research worker is developing a research prototype, he/she is a user of that prototype and of the modules that go to make it up: as such, he/she will be more or less satisfied with the prototype or its modules. It could even be plausibly argued that if one of the modules of his/her research prototype makes use of input provided by another module or interacts with it in some other way, the module of the prototype is itself a user. It cannot of course feel satisfaction, but an analogue to satisfaction can be formulated in terms of whether it gets the right input or the appropriate interaction.

An early ISO discussion illustrated the variety of potential users rather graphically by listing the users of an aeroplane, who include the cockpit crew who fly it, the passengers who travel in it, the cabin crew who look after the passengers, the company to which the aeroplane belongs, and even the control tower staff who give instructions for landing and take off. All of these have very different requirements which the aeroplane should fulfil.

Those who find this ISO-influenced extension of the sense of "user" rather counter-intuitive might feel more comfortable with a word like "stakeholder", as one of the reviewers suggests: indeed, the FEMTI evaluation framework described later quite consciously uses "stakeholder" in order to avoid some possible confusions between stakeholders in a general sense and users, who are seen as a subset of stakeholders. Whatever the word, the essential point is that the entities whose needs are to be satisfied or whose concerns have to be taken into consideration when designing an evaluation may be many and various: the evaluation designer should be very clear about whose needs and concerns are reflected in the evaluation design.

A user or stakeholder then is someone or something that has a set of needs: quality is to be judged in terms of whether or not those needs are satisfied. The goal of evaluation is to gather the data which will be analysed in order to provide a sound basis for that judgement. It follows from this that the first task of an evaluator is to find out what the needs of the particular user or users implied in the particular evaluation are. The second task is to formulate criteria reflecting those needs. On that foundation, the evaluator can decide what metrics, when applied correctly, will measure system performance with respect to the chosen criteria and work out the most reliable way of applying the metrics. The results of their application, when analysed and presented informatively and perspicaciously, will allow final judgement to be made.

4 A Second Principle: Users do not Have the Same Needs

4.1 Different Tasks, Different Needs

It is self-evident that a user may need different pieces of software in order to fulfil different tasks: a spelling checker cannot be expected to solve polynomial equations, or a search engine to play music. But it is slightly less obvious that different users may have different requirements even of the same piece of software. Machine translation systems can be used to illustrate this idea.

Let us imagine that I am thinking of hosting a future Olympic Games, and want to find out from the press what Greeks felt about Greece having hosted the games in 2004. Essentially, I need to comb the Greek newspapers looking for articles which report on popular reaction. I do not speak Greek, but I do have a limited budget to help in my search. I probably do not want to spend all my budget on hiring Greek speakers to check as many papers as they can before the money runs out; I would be much better off finding some cheap way to identify those articles particularly relevant to my search and using my budget to have their contents summarized. In this situation, a machine translation system may help: it can be used to produce a rough translation from which pertinent articles can be identified. The translation produced by the software has to be only good enough to allow identification of interesting articles. In other words, the most important needs here are for speed (there are a lot of newspapers) and economy (the budget is not enormous) rather than for high-quality translation; in fact, measuring translation quality in this case can be reduced to discovering whether or not the machine translation output does indeed permit a satisfactorily large percentage of relevant articles to be identified as such.

Contrast this with the situation where my proposal has been accepted and I must now host the games. Athletes from all over the world will come to compete, and they will all need to be provided with information in a language they can understand, ideally their own. It may be quite difficult to find human translators with the necessary language combinations to produce this information, so I may once again have recourse to machine translation. But in this context, the needs have changed dramatically. The translation must be good enough to avoid problems of misunderstanding or the risk of giving offence, speed is less important given that there have been several years in which to plan the organization, and even, in all likelihood, economy is less important since the amount of work to be done is decided by the languages in which information will be provided, not by how many newspaper articles can be treated before the budget runs out.[3]

This is of course rather an extreme example, but the same reasoning can be applied to much more modest situations and much less complex software.[4] Translation students when working on a translation tend to get very indignant about spelling checkers which do not pick up as unidentified words slang and borrowings from other languages. When they are writing letters to their friends, a spelling checker that did pick up those same barbarisms would probably prove very exasperating.

On top of all this, even when the task remains unchanged, different users may have different needs simply because they are different users, with different backgrounds, different expertise, and different expectations.

In summary, the set of needs pertinent to an evaluation is decided by a combination of the users concerned and of the task or tasks they want to accomplish.

4.2 Different Evaluation Purposes, Different Needs

Furthermore, evaluations themselves are meant to respond to a set of needs, and those needs encompass more than just finding out whether a piece of software does or does not do a specified set of tasks. In early EAGLES work, we distinguished different purposes behind carrying out an evaluation, each of which imposes its own requirements on the evaluation design.

First, there is the kind of evaluation familiar to any programmer or system designer: the main focus of the evaluation is on discovering why the software behaves as it does and, in particular, what causes things do go wrong. We call this *diagnostic evaluation*. An example in practice comes from rule-based parsing systems. In the early 1990s a lot of effort went into the creation of test suites, sets of artificially created inputs to a parsing system where the aim was for each input to test the system's behaviour with respect to a single well-defined linguistic phenomenon (King and Falkedal, 1990; Lehmann et al., 1996). Thus, by looking at the output from running the test suite, the system designer could see, for example, whether simple noun groups were being properly treated, or whether sentences containing passives were causing problems. In the particular case of parsing systems, knowledge of what inputs were not properly dealt with could point directly to what linguistic rules were not functioning properly.

Test data can take many forms, and some of those forms also serve as the basis of one kind (there are others) of *comparative evaluation*. In this scenario, a collection of data which has been agreed upon as appropriate for the system being evaluated is typically divided into two parts. One part, the training data, is used to guide the development of the systems to be evaluated. The other part of the data serves as test data: the same inputs are given to a number of different systems, and their ability to treat the inputs appropriately examined. Both inputs and expected outputs are specified as part of the test; by definition the specified outputs are the "right" answers given the specified inputs: they constitute a "gold standard" against which any particular set of input/output pairs produced in practice may be assessed. When we discuss metrics, we shall return to the use of gold standards of this kind in evaluation.

This is the basic principle behind the vast majority of the evaluation campaigns organized by DARPA/ARPA and others, where system designers and constructors compete to produce the "best" results from a common set of data (see the bibliography for references to the MUC, TREC, ATIS, and MT campaigns, for example). The primary aim of such a campaign is usually stated to be the advancement of core technology in a particular area, coupled with the creation of a research and development community working in that same area.

It goes without saying that diagnostic evaluation based on test data and comparative evaluation based on test data are two very different things. In the case of diagnostic evaluation, using test data to probe for where a system breaks down is meant to help in identifying a deficiency in its working. In the case of comparative evaluation as defined here, test data serve as a way of quantifying to what extent a system succeeds in producing the results it has been designed to produce – they tells us nothing of any other virtues or weaknesses. Indeed, using test data in this way has sometimes been stigmatized as producing the illusion that apples can be usefully compared to pears.

Within the human language technology field, test suites have also been frequently used to measure progress in the development of a system: an increase in the number of test items successfully dealt with provides a measure of how much the system has progressed towards the ultimate goal of being able to deal with every item in the test suite. Another way of carrying out *progress evaluation* of this kind is to collect together a corpus which is held to be representative of the text or language the system should be able to deal with. The fact that corpora are by definition texts which occur naturally has advantages in terms of economy and also produces the comfortable glow that comes from dealing with the real world instead of with an artificial academic construct. On the down side, a corpus used for testing is only informative if it is in fact representative of the real world which the system will be expected to deal with: ensuring representativity raises issues that are sometimes difficult to resolve. Furthermore, the use of a corpus as test material ties the evaluation (and its results) to a specific "real world": there can be no guarantee that the quality of results obtained in the context of use reflected by the choice of corpus will carry over to other contexts of use.

The final kind of evaluation distinguished by the early EAGLES group was called *adequacy evaluation*: the term was meant to capture a situation somewhat parallel to that of a consumer contemplating a major purchase. The consumer knows what is wanted in a proposed new washing machine or new car; a specific product is examined with a view to finding out whether it offers what the consumer wants. The parallel with software evaluation is not difficult. But it is perhaps worth pointing out that once again, different consumers, different users in the jargon of this chapter, may have very different views on what is wanted. Machine translation can again serve as a concrete illustration. Imagine a translation service contemplating the purchase of machine translation software. It may well be that the manager of the service wants a machine translation system which will deal with the language pairs where there is trouble recruiting good translators, whilst the translators already in the service want a system which will relieve them of some of the burden of translating the 500-page activity report which appears once every quarter and where over half the text remains unchanged from one edition to the next. And, of course, both manager and translators may be quite wrong in thinking that the answer to their problem is a machine translation system: an evaluation taking into account the whole work context may well reveal other and more productive options.

This last possibility brings us to another point about the variability of user needs, or rather, about the user's perception of his/her needs. The process of eliciting needs and making them explicit in the form of a set of user quality requirements may well contribute to a realization that needs should be refined, modified, or perhaps changed all together. There is nothing surprising about this: in fact discovering that one has misjudged or misstated a set of needs is a fairly common occurrence of daily life. (Who has not bought the wrong garment or ordered an ill-judged meal?) Elicitation and definition of needs is not, except in the simplest of cases, a linear process. This in itself constitutes a very strong argument for investing time and energy on drawing up explicit requirements based on acknowledged needs before expending the energy required to define ways of discovering whether a particular system can meet those needs.

The types of evaluation discussed in this section are not meant to be seen as impermeable categories. Diagnostic evaluation may be part of progress evaluation, comparative evaluation may be of two successive versions of a system and therefore also be progress evaluation, and it would be quite possible to see all the other types of evaluation as special cases of adequacy evaluation. The point in making the distinctions is twofold: first, to emphasize yet again that different contexts may impose very different requirements on both the software itself and on its evaluation; and second, to stress that defining the purpose of the evaluation is an essential preliminary to designing it.

On a more practical and even mundane level, it is also extremely important that all those involved in an evaluation share a common perception of its purpose. A stupid and rather costly mistake from my own experience will help to illustrate this somewhat obvious but too often neglected point. We had undertaken to build a system that would translate a limited set of sentences from German into French. This was in the days long before easy and convenient treatment of character sets, so our proof-of-concept demonstrator, whose evaluation was to determine whether we would continue with the project or not, made use of codes to replace the accented and special characters of the two languages. The evaluation was a disaster. We believed that its purpose was to show that we could in fact translate all the different linguistic phenomena contained in the agreed set of sentences, so using codes for French and German characters was irrelevant. The representative of the funding source thought that what had to be shown was that we could translate from German into French – and that we clearly could not do since we could not even deal with the appropriate character sets. Of course, anyone who knew about computing would simply say that our interlocutor did not understand the very minor importance of the character codes – but we still lost the contract. And, of course, this point carries through on a much larger scale once general management questions are an issue. To go back to our fictitious translation service, if the manager thinks the evaluation is being carried out in order to find out whether the service can offer new language pairs, but the translators think that the evaluation is aimed at finding out whether they can be replaced by a computer system, the potential for disaster is inescapable.

5 A Third Principle: Quality can be Characterized

5.1 Quality Models

Everything so far has been rather distressingly bottom-up. We have insisted on the idea that whilst quality can only be defined in terms of users, users have very different quality requirements, and we have aggravated the potential problems posed by that claim by adding that different kinds of evaluations designed with different aims in mind also affect the quality requirements which form the backbone of the evaluation design. The obvious conclusion is that every evaluation is necessarily a one-off exercise, carried out for a particular client in view of a particular set of user needs. If this were true, evaluation would also be a very costly exercise, since little if anything could be shared across evaluations.

The ISO 9126 standard constitutes a direct antidote to the slough of despond created by the idea of having to start afresh each time. The basic idea is that if we operate at a sufficiently high level of generality, there is a small set of characteristics of software which are likely to be pertinent to a judgement of quality in almost every case: listing these characteristics, breaking them down into sub-characteristics, and providing definitions of each item will provide the designer of an evaluation a way into examining the needs of particular (sets of) users and expressing their quality requirements in terms of the characteristics which make up part of the general quality model.

There is not enough space here to go into all the detail of the 9126 standard, but it is probably useful to give a brief summary, and some example definitions which are taken from ISO/IEC 9126 series, part 1, published in 2001.[5] The reader is urged to consult the standards directly for more detail and for further discussion.

ISO 9126 proposes six main quality characteristics of software. The first of these is functionality. Functionality is essentially concerned with what the software does, rather than how it does it. It is broken down into five sub-characteristics. The sub-characteristics of functionality are suitability, accuracy, interoperability, security, and compliance. We shall leave interoperability and security as intuitive notions, which will, of course, have to be fleshed out with concrete and detailed definitions in the context of any particular evaluation.

The distinction between suitability and accuracy, however, needs a little more commentary. Suitability is defined as "the capability of the software to provide an appropriate set of functions for specified tasks and user objectives", and accuracy as "the capability of the software product to provide the right or agreed results or effects": in other words, accuracy is based on whether the software conforms to its specifications. It is almost redundant to say that what results should be produced is a key component of the specifications. If the software does indeed produce the results its specifications say it should, by this definition the software scores well on accuracy. But high accuracy does not necessarily mean that the results produced are in fact useful to a particular user with a specific task to accomplish. In the worst case, the software designer has simply got wrong what might be helpful – market failures provide empirical verification of the existence of this possibility.

A concrete example may help in grasping the distinction. A major need in the translation world is for terminology extraction tools. Modern technology moves at such a rate that vast amounts of new terminology appear all the time, and even specialized technical translators cannot be expected to keep up with the development of terminology in their fields. At the same time, it is rare that a new term appears only once in a single document; most frequently, once the term has been coined it will be used almost simultaneously in a number of documents and may even find its way into a term bank before our hypothetical translator comes across it as a new term. A software tool which extracted from a text all the terms it contains would give the translator a head start in preparing the translation. The list of extracted terms could be compared to the contents of the term banks to which the translator has access, thereby isolating remaining problem cases. If the software could go one step further and not only isolate the new term but also identify its probable translation in any texts that had already been translated, the usefulness of the tool would be increased even further. There are softwares on the market which claim to be of assistance in identifying potential terms. The most simple of these operate on the assumption that a term is a string of words that will appear more than once in a document. They therefore list all the sequences of words which appear more than once in the text. (Most frequently, the user may decide the length of the sequence of words – for example, two words or more – and on a lower bound for how many times the sequence must appear in the text, e.g., twice or more.) Given these specifications for how to identify candidate terms, any piece of software that produces from a text a list of all and only those word sequences matching the parameters is accurate in the sense described here – it conforms to its specifications. But it takes very little reflection to see that the results will be pretty well useless to any translator or terminologist. Sequences such as "all the", "any piece", or "given that" will appear far too frequently, and the time taken to sift any potential real terminology from all the dross of useless suggestions will be so great that no user will contemplate the investment. To make matters worse, since no morphological analysis is carried out, "Internet technology" and "Internet technologies" may not be picked up as possible variants on a single term. And worse again, unless one or other of them occurs more than once, with the example parameters given, neither will be picked up at all. To couch this in the jargon of the well-known precision and recall metrics, there is both far too much noise and at least a strong risk of silence. In other words, the results, whilst totally accurate, are not suitable.[6] In user-oriented evaluation, suitability is likely to count for rather a lot more than conformity to specifications.

There are cases nonetheless where a failure to distinguish between accuracy and suitability may not be very important, simply because the nature of the software in question is such that the two do more or less coincide. A case in point is dictation software. Accuracy, in this case, is defined in terms of being able to transcribe correctly the words spoken by the user. For users who want to be able to dictate their text, it is a reasonable assumption that the fewer mistakes in transcription the software makes, the more suitable will they find the results. (A user may have other reasons of course to dislike the software, but in terms of this aspect of its functionality, all should be well.)

At the other extreme, software products are becoming available where the link between accuracy and suitability is far more problematic. A first example comes from search engines. Most of us have experienced the awful moment of being presented with a million or more results in response to a query. The search engine is perfectly accurate, however, according to its own specifications. The results are just not suitable once our information needs are taken into account. And, of course, the search engine cannot be blamed: the software has not functioned badly; we have failed to formulate our query in a satisfactory way. Less familiar examples are data-and text-mining softwares. They too deal with a very large mass of data, trying to find connections and associations that could not be found by any human. Such tools may well come up with totally accurate but completely uninteresting and therefore unsuitable insights, like an association between pregnant women and having children.

The problem is complicated by two further factors. The first is the quality of the data: if the data are poor, the software cannot be blamed for coming up with conclusions which are not very useful. The second is the competence and flair of the users. Typically, with these kinds of software, there is interaction between an expert user and the software in searching for a useful result: on the basis of a preliminary set of results the user will refine his search for information or instruct the software to ignore certain characteristics of the data. Some users are better at this than others. Once again, a piece of software cannot be blamed if a particular user cannot formulate and direct an information request appropriately. One of the current challenges in evaluation theory is to come up with a sound methodology for user-oriented evaluation of softwares where problems of this kind are inherent in the nature of the software (see King and Underwood, 2004 for more discussion).

A lot of time has been spent on only two sub-characteristics of functionality. Fortunately, the remaining quality characteristics and their sub-characteristics are intuitively more accessible, especially in these days of PCs and portable computers when many people serve as their own computer administrator. For this reason, Table 1 produces a summary of the six characteristics and their sub-characteristics. The right hand column gives a brief gloss of the definitions given in the ISO standard, leaving it to the reader to flesh out appropriate definitions for the terms used.[7]

Table 1. Summary of characteristics and sub-characteristics.

Quality characteristic	Sub-characteristics	Comments
1. Functionality		**Providing functions to meet needs**
	a. Suitability	Provision of an appropriate set of functions for specified tasks and user objectives
	b. Accuracy	Provision of the right or agreed on results
	c. Interoperability	Interaction with other specified systems
	d. Security	Protection of information and data
	e. Compliance	Adhesion to appropriate standards etc.
2. Reliability		**Maintaining performance**
	a. Maturity	Avoid failure as a result of faults in the software
	b. Fault tolerance	Maintain performance in spite of faults
	c. Recoverability	Re-establish performance and recover data in case of failure
3. Usability		**How easily can the user understand, learn, operate, and control the system? Is it attractive to users?**
	a. Understandability	Can the user understand whether the software is suitable, how it can be used for particular tasks, and what the conditions are for using it?
	b. Learnability	Can the user learn to use it?
	c. Operability	Can the user operate and control it?
	d. Attractiveness	Does the user find it attractive?
	e. Compliance	Adhesion to appropriate standards etc.
4. Efficiency		**Appropriate performance relative to resources used**
	a. Time behaviour	Response, processing, throughput
	b. Resource utilization	Amounts and types of resources (excluding human resources, which are part of quality in use)
	c. Compliance	Adhesion to appropriate standards etc.

5. Maintainability		**Correcting, improving, or adapting the software**
	a. Analysability	Can faults be diagnosed?
	b. Changeability	Can specified modifications be implemented (by a programmer or by the end-user or both)?
	c. Stability	Avoidance of unexpected side effects
	d. Testability	Can modified software be validated?
	e. Compliance	Adhesion to appropriate standards etc.
6. Portability		**Transferring the software from one environment to another**
	a. Adaptability	Adaptation to different specified environments
	b. Installability	Installation in a specified environment
	c. Coexistence	Coexistence with other independent software
	d. Replaceability	For example, is up-grading easy?
	e. Compliance	Adhesion to appropriate standards etc.

The glosses given here are meant only as mnemonics for the much fuller definitions of the standard. However, even in this very abbreviated (although, hopefully, not deformed) version it is immediately clear that the definitions are at a very high level of generality – they are, after all, meant to apply to any kind of software. But this means that they have to be made much more concrete in order to design an adequate evaluation for any particular type of software. We return to this issue in Section 5.3

Before moving on, the **Usability** quality characteristic deserves some commentary, if only because talk of user-oriented evaluation is so often misinterpreted as meaning evaluating usability. Usability, as shown in the table, breaks down into **understandability, learnability, operability, attractiveness**, and, as always, **compliance**. The notes given in the ISO standard on the various definitions make a number of interesting points. First, they make it clear that quality characteristics are interdependent. For example, some aspects of functionality, reliability, and efficiency will clearly affect usability, but are deliberately excluded from mention under usability in the interests of keeping the quality model tidy and well structured. Similarly, aspects of suitability (from functionality), changeability (from maintainability), adaptability (from portability), and installability (from portability), may affect the sub-characteristic operability found under usability. Trying to capture the intricate potential relationships between sub-characteristics would be very difficult, and especially so since often they are only potential rather than necessarily actual: when a specific evaluation is being designed, a potential relationship between two sub-characteristics may turn out not to exist in the particular context. Avoiding unnecessary complications in the interests of mental hygiene may impose a certain artificiality in the definition of a quality model.

This brings us to a central and critical point, which has already been hinted at: the real meaning of any quality characteristic or of its sub-characteristics is operational, and is given by the metrics used to measure system performance with respect to that characteristic. Furthermore, it is the decomposition of the top level characteristics and sub-characteristics in order to arrive at measurable attributes which allows the general quality model to be specialized for specific software applications. This will become clearer when we discuss the formal structure of a quality model in Section 5.2.

Second, the notes emphasize that usability issues affect all the different kinds of users: "Users may include operators, and users and indirect users who are under the influence of or dependant on the use of the software. Usability should address all of the different user environments that the software may affect, which may include preparation for usage and evaluation of results." This again emphasizes the great variety both of users and of the environments in which they work, stressing that there may well be users other than end-users whose needs have to be taken into account when designing an evaluation.

All of the quality characteristics making up the quality model contribute ultimately to what the ISO standard calls **quality in use**. This is the quality of a piece of software as it is perceived by an actual user, in an actual work situation trying to accomplish an actual task. ISO/IEC 9126-1/01 defines it as "the capability of the software product to enable specified users to achieve specified goals with effectiveness, productivity, safety and satisfaction in specified contexts of use". Quality in use can only really be evaluated in situ, although much effort is invested by manufacturers of commercial software into trying to control the eventual quality in use of a product before it is released on the market, and a central tenet of this chapter is that by careful examination of users and of the tasks they will perform it is possible to evaluate a piece of software in such a way as to be able to predict its potential quality in use.

Thus a basic assumption underlying both the ISO 9126 standard and the kind of evaluation discussed in this chapter is the existence of a sort of quality chain: good specifications will contribute directly to production of good code (internal quality), good code will contribute directly to good system performance in terms of the quality characteristics (external quality), and good system performance will contribute directly to good quality in use. The particular slant on this assumption in EAGLES and ISLE work is that by looking at a combination of user needs and system performance in terms of the quality characteristics, we can construct specialized quality models and thus, on the basis of an evaluation of external quality, go a long way towards predicting quality in use for the specific user.

5.2   Formalizing the Quality Model

The ISO quality model sketched briefly above is informal, in the sense that anything written in a natural language is informal: it names quality characteristics and sub-characteristics, and provides definitions in English for them. Both names and definitions are therefore open to different interpretations by different readers; this is not a fault in the standard, but a problem inherent in the use of natural language.

A major aim of the EAGLES work was to impose a more formal structure on the quality model with the double aim of facilitating clear thinking about quality models for particular types of software and of defining a structure which could serve as the basis for computer implementations of evaluation schemes based on the quality model principle.

Within EAGLES, a quality model was defined to be a hierarchical structure. The top-level nodes in the structure are the quality characteristics themselves. The sub-characteristics are daughter nodes of the top-level characteristics. The ISO definition legislates for only these two levels. The EAGLES version, however, allows sub-characteristics to be broken down in their turn, with the hierarchy descending to whatever level is needed to bottom out into attributes to which at least one metric can be associated. In other words, the leaves of the structure must contain attributes which are measurable.

Each node in the hierarchy is then defined to be a feature/value pair of the sort familiar from computational linguistics. The name of the quality characteristic or sub-characteristic is the name of the feature. When an evaluation is executed, the value of the feature is obtained by propagating values upwards from the leaves of the tree. The values on the leaves are obtained by applying the metric associated with that leaf. (For simplicity, we shall imagine that there is only one metric associated with each level: it is a fairly simple step to generalize to the case where more than one metric is associated). Values on higher nodes are obtained by combining the values from the next hierarchical level down according to a combining function which is part of specifying the particular evaluation.[8]

Perhaps the most interesting feature of this formalization is that the quality model has now gained a precise semantics. Where just saying that part of functionality is suitability does not say much and does not say it unambiguously, once suitability is tied directly or indirectly through a branch of the hierarchical structure to a metric or metrics, it acquires a clear and unambiguous interpretation: its meaning is given by how its value is to be obtained from the lower nodes in the quality model. This is what was meant by saying that the semantics of an instantiated quality model was operational, and determined ultimately by the choice of metrics. To this we should now add "and by how the values obtained through applying those metrics are combined to give values for upper nodes in the structure". The quality model can still of course be ill-conceived, but we are now much more likely to discover that it is, and discussion about its correctness or incorrectness is anchored in empirical observation.

5.3   From the General to the Particular: Specializing a Quality Model

The quality model defined by the ISO standard is situated at a very generic level. In order to produce from it a model useful for a particular evaluation we need to make it more concrete. This involves first specializing the model to take into account the particular kind of software to be evaluated and secondly making it more concrete by relating the model to the specific needs of a user.

If we look at the names and definitions of the ISO quality characteristics, functionality leaps out as the characteristic needing further specification in terms of the particular type of software to be evaluated. As the reader will remember, its sub-characteristics are suitability, accuracy, interoperability, security, and compliance. Of these, accuracy seems most closely to reflect the nature of the software to be evaluated, and it is therefore perhaps no accident that the majority of evaluation campaigns concentrate on evaluation of accuracy almost exclusively.

To start illustration with a fairly simple case, accuracy for a spelling checker plausibly breaks down into two sub-characteristics. The first of these is being able to identify strings of characters which do not constitute legal words of the language in question, signalling them and only them as potential spelling mistakes. The second is being able to propose plausible corrections. Proposing plausible corrections in its turn breaks down into two sub-characteristics. The first concerns whether the checker proposes the right correction; the second concerns the position of the right correction in the list of suggestions, assuming that more than one suggestion is made. With recent spelling checkers, a third sub-characteristic of accuracy might be the ability to identify correctly the language of a passage of text.

All of this sounds relatively straightforward, and we can rather easily imagine completing the model by associating metrics to the terminal nodes. For example, we might create a list of words, generate from that list a set of mistaken words, and use the list of mistakes to discover what percentage of our mistaken words are identified as such. Then, using the original list of words to provide us with a definition of what the right answer should be, we can discover in what percentage of cases the right word is proposed. It is a relatively

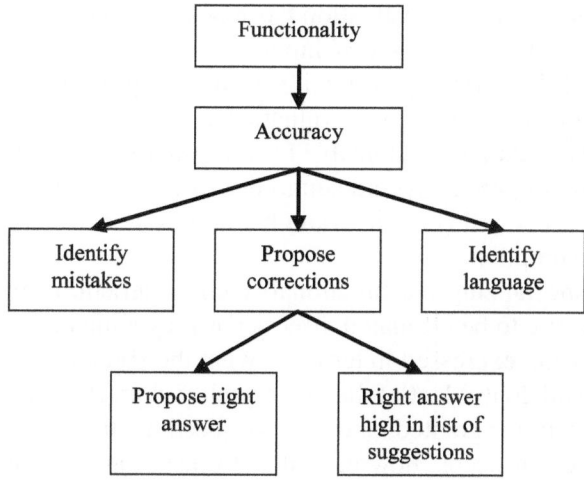

Figure 1. Substructure for the fragment of the quality model.

easy matter to check what position in the list of suggestions is occupied by the right proposal.[9] Finally, we can construct a text composed of fragments of text of a reasonable length for each of the languages which interests us, and use that as test data to discover whether the languages are correctly identified (for actual evaluations along these lines, see TEMAA, 1996 and Starlander and Popescu-Belis, 2002).

This gives us the substructure for the fragment of the quality model we are currently concerned with (Figure 1).

Unfortunately, even though superficially this looks convincingly tidy, defining accuracy for human language technology software is seldom as straightforward as it seems. What counts as a legal word of the language is mainly built into the software when it is released: in the most common case the software consults a built-in dictionary of legal words and if the string in the text does not correspond to an entry in the list, it is signalled as a mistake. Thus, accuracy in the ISO sense of conforming to specifications only depends on the software being able to identify correctly words which are not in the dictionary. But in the caricature case, the dictionary of legal words may be so impoverished as to be practically useless, thus rendering the software unsuitable for a large class of users. So, even in this apparently very simple case, accuracy in a user-oriented evaluation is considerably less important than suitability. (Fortunately, the metrics proposed can be implemented in such a way that they reflect user needs through an appropriate choice of words included in the test material.)

All we are really doing here, of course, is reinforcing a point already made at some length in Section 5.1. The main reason for labouring the point is that, as we noted there, academic evaluation has tended to concentrate on accuracy, usually defined in terms of a set of inputs and related outputs. (I have even heard it claimed that limiting evaluation in this way is the only respectable way for an academic to work on evaluation). To adopt the limitation does, however, assume that those responsible for the system specifications have been successful in forcing accuracy and suitability to coincide: they have correctly predicted what users will need. It would be an unwise evaluator who failed to examine this assumption.

So even in specializing the functionality characteristic to take account of the type of software to be evaluated, user needs play a major role. But the user needs are still being expressed in terms of what the software should do, rather than how it should do it. Most of the other quality characteristics take what the software should do for granted, and look at questions like how fast it is, what memory resources it needs, how easy it is to install and maintain, how easy it is to learn and to use, and so on – all issues of obvious importance when specializing the model to account for a particular user's needs.

An interesting exception for human language technology is maintainability, where a note to the ISO definitions makes it clear[10] that maintainability includes adapting a piece of software to meet end-user requirements. Many language technology products critically include adapting the software to meet specific needs. A spelling checker allows the user to enter items in a personal dictionary, thus avoiding new terminology, being constantly flagged as unknown. A dictation system usually gives best results if trained to a particular voice. The results of an alignment algorithm improve if the user is allowed to specify a list of abbreviations which should not cause segmentation to take place. A machine translation system performs better if the user can influence the contents of the dictionary. None of these change the basic functioning of the software, and so are not, in that sense, part of functionality. In a way, they are simply more radical examples along a continuum that starts with being able to customize software by changing colours or creating personalized tool bars, but they have a more direct influence on suitability: they offer a first example where some might find the classification under a particular quality characteristic rather arbitrary.[11]

Other examples where an evaluator might be unsure as to where an attribute fits in the quality model can be found if we think about particular applications. For example, one feature of machine translation systems which is likely to be of interest to many users is the speed with which the translation is produced. Put like that, this attribute looks as though its natural place is a sub-characteristic of efficiency, under time behaviour. But then, if we take into consideration that the time to produce a usable (for whatever purpose) translation may have to include reading through the output and perhaps modifying it to improve translation quality, it begins to seem that the interesting metric is not how many words an hour of raw output can be produced, but how many words of usable output. And once that move has been made, there will be some who think that how quickly usable output can be produced is part of suitability rather than efficiency, or others who think that two attributes are needed rather than one.

This latter stance is reflected by those who have used two metrics, the first typically measuring the number of words of raw output produced in some specific period of time, the second measuring how long it takes to produce useable output. The first of these metrics is rather easy to define, but it might be worth anticipating some later discussion by dwelling briefly on the difficulty of defining the second. The problem is twofold: first someone has to decide what counts as usable output; second, producing useable output (under any definition) from raw machine translation output necessarily requires human intervention, and human behaviour is affected by physical and emotional condition as well as by attitude to the task in hand. (An anecdote once popular amongst machine translation evaluators recounts that it was possible to reverse human judgements about which translations had been produced by a machine and which by humans simply by presenting the former beautifully typed on A4 paper and the latter badly laid out on line printer paper.) In practice, the two problems have usually been confounded and compounded: the most usual definition of a metric based on the time needed to produce useable output requires human beings to edit the raw output in order to produce what in their opinion is useable output, and measures the time they take to reach this goal. (Discussion of this and related questions can be found in Slocum et al., 1985). We shall come back to the difficulties posed by metrics which inherently require human involvement in a later section.

To return to quality models at a more general level, it has already been pointed out (Section 5.1) that mental hygiene does indeed impose a certain artificiality on the structure of quality models, but it is far more important in these cases to insist yet again that the real meaning of any substructure of the hierarchy is given by the metrics associated with the terminal nodes. The names of the features are, as a philosopher once said in a slightly different context, merely pegs on which to hang descriptions, the descriptions being the expression of a node by the nodes depending on it and, ultimately, by the measurable attributes found on the terminal nodes.

5.4 Combining Metrics in a Quality Model

It may seem that some of the quality characteristics have received very cavalier treatment so far, having been dismissed with a remark that they constitute constraints on the acceptable performance of the system rather than a description of what the system actually does. They come into their own when we start to consider the final way of tailoring the quality model to reflect specific user needs, since they carry the main burden of capturing the specific intended context of use.

The key notion here is that of the relative importance of nodes at the same level in the hierarchical structure. As a straightforward example, let us take the quality of portability and its sub-characteristic replaceability, where replaceability covers the capability of the software to be used in place of another software product for the same purpose in the same environment, e.g., when a software is upgraded. Some companies producing translation memory software produce new versions of their software at very frequent intervals. Translation memory systems make use of an archive of previous translations, where each sentence translated is linked to its translation. These translation archives represent an investment of considerable value: there is a direct relationship between the richness of the memory and the productivity gains resulting from using the memory for translation. If, then, installing a new version of the system means that memories created with the previous versions can no longer be used, no matter what other advantages the new version might offer, changing to the new version loses much of its attraction.[12] In other words, replaceability becomes a critical attribute, whose value may even determine the outcome of the evaluation as a whole. Of course, for someone who is thinking of buying his/her first translation memory software and who has no resources to exploit, replaceability is of no importance at all: what may be critical for one user may be totally irrelevant for another.

The combining function mentioned briefly in Section 5.2 is meant to allow expression of this notion of relative importance. For the user for whom replaceability is critical, the evaluation designer will give it a combining value such that it outweighs any other sub-characteristics. For the user for whom it does not matter at all, he will give it a value equivalent to saying that it should be neglected in the evaluation. Thus, part of tailoring the evaluation to the needs of the specific user is defining how the values from each level of the quality model are to be combined in order to pass them to a higher level. By definition, the combining function is specific to a particular evaluation: it is only the existence of such a mechanism which forms part of the definition of the model itself under the EAGLES extension. In terms of the ISO standards, the definition of a combining function corresponds to a part of defining the process of evaluation, as set out in the ISO/IEC 14598 series. It is part of the step described there as specifying the evaluation, where, after metrics have been chosen, rating levels for those metrics are established and criteria for assessment are also established. We discuss this step in Section 5.5. We shall come back to the discussion of metrics in more detail in Section 6.

5.5 Relating Performance to User Satisfaction

A very common type of metric typically involves producing a score on some scale, reflecting the particular system's performance with respect to the quality characteristic in question. This score, uninterpreted, says nothing about whether the system performs satisfactorily. To illustrate this idea, consider the Geneva education system, where marks in examinations range from 1 to 6. How is it possible to know, other than by being told, that 6 is the best mark and 1 the worst? In fact, most people from other systems will probably have guessed that it is so: they may then have difficulty in some other cantons where 1 is the highest mark. (I have been told that the lack of consistency in how examination marks are awarded in Switzerland is at the root of an urban myth about Einstein's performance in secondary school.) Establishing rating levels for metrics involves determining the correspondence between the un-interpreted score and the degree of satisfaction of the requirements.

Not all attributes acquire a numerical value when their metrics are applied. For example, the attribute reflecting which language pairs a machine translation system covers has a non-numerical value, as does the attribute covering what platform the software needs. Rating levels are also a way of ironing out differences in type across metrics that have to be combined. Since quality refers to given needs, there can be no general rules for when a score is satisfactory. This must be determined for each specific evaluation.

Each measure, interpreted by its rating level, contributes to the overall judgement of the product, but not necessarily in a uniform way. It may be, as we have seen earlier, that one requirement is critical, whilst another is desirable, but not strictly necessary. In this case, if the system performs badly with respect to the critical characteristic, it will be assessed negatively no matter what happens to all the other characteristics. If it performs badly with respect to the desirable but not necessary characteristic, it is its performance with respect to all the other characteristics which will determine whether the system is acceptable or not.

This consideration is familiar from discussion of the EAGLES/ISLE combining function. In ISO 14598 it feeds directly into establishing criteria for assessment, which involves defining a procedure for summarizing the results of the evaluation of the different characteristics, using, for example, decision tables or weighting functions of different kinds.

6   A Fourth Principle: Quality can be Measured

6.1   Defining and Validating Metrics

By now, the reader will need very little persuading that the utility and worth of a quality model depends critically on the metrics associated with the measurable attributes forming the terminal nodes of the quality model structure.

A primary constraint on a metric is that it should be valid, i.e., it should in fact measure what it purports to measure. This sounds blindingly obvious, but the evaluation literature abounds in metrics which fail to meet this stipulation. The social sciences literature is rich in discussion about validity. One distinction made there which was picked up by early EAGLES work is a distinction between internal validity and external validity. A metric is internally valid if its validity is guaranteed by the nature of the metric itself. It is externally valid if the results obtained by applying the metric correlate with the feature of interest without directly measuring it. An informal example of an internally valid metric is given by the way reading ages are tested. Reading age is first extensionally defined by drawing up lists of the words a child should be able to read at a given age. The reading age of a given child is then determined by asking him to read aloud texts which contain the vocabulary defining a specific age. His ability to do so determines whether he has reached the reading age defined by the vocabulary. The definition, in other words, is circular: reading age is defined by being able to read a certain set of words, and is tested for by asking that those words be read: validity is internal to the metric. An informal example of an externally valid metric comes from the questionnaires that life insurance companies ask potential customers to fill in. They clearly cannot sensibly ask how long the person to be insured will live, so they ask what his weight is, whether he smokes, if he has diabetes, if he has ever had major surgery, and so on – all factors which correlate closely with average life expectancy.

In human language technology evaluation, the word error rate metric used with speech recognition systems seems to offer a clear example of a metric which relies on internal validity. The speaker speaks a known word: if that word is correctly transcribed, the system produces the right answer. The number of right answers out of the total test set determines the system's score. In evaluation jargon, there is a gold standard which determines what the right answer should be.

Most evaluation campaigns have been based on the creation of gold standards. Their production is frequently a costly and contentious business, simply because there are relatively few applications where the right answer is easily defined. A couple of examples will illustrate this. Fact extraction systems take text as input and produce as output information extracted from that text, often in the form of a template where the system's task is to fill in slots in an appropriately chosen template. For example, from the sentence "The minister for foreign affairs will visit Paris on January 4th", a system might be expected to produce a structure[13] like:

```
(ACTION: visit
AGENT: minister for foreign affairs
LOCATION: Paris
DATE: January 4th)
```

The system would probably be expected to produce the same template from the sentence "January 4th is the date set for the visit by the minister for foreign affairs to Paris" or even from "A visit to Paris on January 4th is part of the schedule planned for the minister for foreign affairs". A collection of texts and a set of filled templates based on those texts constitute the gold standard for the evaluation of such systems.

The problem is obvious: how is it decided what templates should exist, what slots they should have, and what the fillers for those slots should be? Furthermore, how are the limits on what the system can be expected to do decided? If the sentence is "Utopia's most notorious minister is expected to cause major controversy by visiting the capital of France on the 4th of next month", can the system still be expected to extract the same slot fillers? Within an evaluation campaign, a common solution is to seek consensus amongst interested parties in these cases (Lehnart and Sundheim, 1991 discuss some of the issues raised by consensus seeking). Creating the test data is in itself expensive: when the cost of producing consensus is added in, test data of this kind can become a resource of considerable monetary value. Expense also helps to explain why test data is frequently reused.

Similar problems arise with applications like document retrieval, where judging the relevance of a retrieved document is of major importance in evaluating the system's success. Relevance judgements can be challenged, so some way of convincing both evaluators and those being evaluated of their acceptability has to be found. The TREC conferences[14] have been prolific in discussion of this issue and ingenious in ways of getting round it (see, e.g., Voorhees, 2000, 2003; Sparck Jones, 2001).

The root of the problem, of course, is that there is, in these cases, no answer which is indisputably right. The gold standard is achieved not by looking for absolute truth, but by seeking a wide enough agreement on what will count as right. Nonetheless, once the consensus has been achieved, the gold standard forms an intrinsic part of the metrics using it: the metrics achieve an internal validity.

There are, however, applications where even creating a right answer by consensus is problematic. One such is machine translation. It is in the nature of translation that there can be no single correct translation of a source text: the chances that any two human translators would come up with exactly the same translation for a sentence of reasonable length are very slim, but both their translations may be equally acceptable.

For this reason, most of the metrics historically used in machine translation evaluation have tended to rely critically on human judgement. Many ask human subjects to give a score to a segment (usually a clause or a sentence) of machine translation output based on a judgement of its intelligibility, fluency, accuracy, or some similar characteristic. These metrics suffer from several weaknesses. First, there is the problem we have already alluded to: human beings are not robots. They are impatient when they get tired, they may love or hate machines, they may resent having to take part in an exercise where they think they already know the outcome, they may believe that their future employment depends on the outcome of the evaluation exercise – the number of factors which might influence their behaviour is so large and so various that it is almost impossible to control for. Second, the instructions on how to apply the metrics are usually expressed in natural language and therefore interpretable by different people in different ways. Even if the decision is seemingly quite simple, in the style of "score 1 if the output is intelligible, 0 if it is not" experience has shown that intersubject reliability is far from guaranteed. A growing awareness of such problems (discussed, e.g., in King, 1996a, b, 1997) led to attempts to circumvent some of the problems by asking subjects to read the raw output and then to complete a comprehension test where the questions were based on the content of the original texts (see, e.g., White and O'Connell, 1994) . Even these metrics, however, are not exempt from the human interference syndrome: at the very least, comprehension tests are used in other areas in order to assess general intelligence. By definition then, some humans will be better at working out the correct answers than others, even when the machine translation output is unchanged.

And of course all these metrics suffer from one great weakness: they are expensive to implement. Setting up the tests cost money, human subjects have to be found and perhaps paid for their participation and human analysis of the raw results is required and must be paid for.

A number of recently proposed metrics, foreshadowed in Thompson (1992) but in practical terms starting with the BLEU metric (Papinieni et al., 2001), try to overcome the problems sketched above by applying quite complex statistical analysis to determine how close a candidate translation is to a set of what are called reference translations. Essentially, the metric looks at small stretches of the machine translation output (typically three or four words) and determines whether the stretch being examined also occurs in the reference translation(s). The overall score for the candidate translation is based on how many small stretches have their equivalent in the reference.[15]

It is clear even from this very brief and informal description that BLEU and other measures like it which depend on comparison with a (set of) reference translations do not really resolve the problem of finding a gold standard metric for translation quality, since the validity of the metric depends critically on the quality of the reference translation(s): in terms of earlier discussion, the validity of the metric is internal – if all (or even some of) the translations in the reference set are poor, the scores produced by applying the metric will not reflect what would normally be thought of as acceptable quality in the translation. For this reason, there has been much interest in checking, for particular evaluations, whether the results correlate with human judgement of the same machine translation outputs,[16] thus bringing us back to issues of intersubject reliability and economy.

Sidestepping the translation quality issue by using a set of reference translations is the real potential merit of these metrics, but in turn raises the practical problem of acquiring multiple reference translations in the appropriate domain, style, and register. This, of course, is not a new problem; it is closely akin to the problem of acquiring suitable training corpora for any empirically based system. But that it can be hard to solve is shown by the fact that theoretical work on the metrics has sometimes been forced to use literary or religious texts, and the perception is reinforced by the number of applications of the metrics which in the end use only one, or at best a very small number of, reference translations.

BLEU and related metrics are far from universally accepted for other reasons too: sentence length may adversely affect their general validity, and relatively little work has so far been done on how they function with languages where word order is free, making it more unlikely that even a short segment of the candidate translation text will exactly correspond to a segment of the reference translations. Thus, there is still much controversy about these metrics, as can be seen from the proceedings of almost any recent conference on machine translation.[17]

So far, the problems we have discussed come from the nature of the application. Other problems come from the data over which a software system is supposed to work. Document retrieval on the web offers a familiar example. A search engine responds to a query by searching the web for documents which match the query terms. Neither user nor evaluator can know what documents are available: the web is both vast and shifting – what is there in the morning may be gone by the afternoon, and new documents will certainly have appeared. A consequence of this is that although it is possible (at least in theory) to check that all the documents retrieved by the search engine do in fact match the query terms, it is not even theoretically possible to determine whether there were other documents available at the time of the search which should have been retrieved and were not.[18] If called upon to evaluate a search engine, all we can do is constrain the document collection, as is conventionally done in the evaluation of document retrieval systems, and assume that by external validity behaviour over the constrained collection correlates with behaviour over the unconstrained set of documents available (see TREC-2004 web track for an example of this strategy).

Another issue raised by a document collection which is constantly changing is that of reliability: a metric should be reliable in the sense that if it is applied in the same context on different occasions, it should produce the same result – in experimental jargon, the results should be replicable. The problem with searching on the web is exactly that we cannot guarantee that the context will remain the same. Once again, we are forced to constrain the context artificially in order to ensure reliability of the metric.

Reliability is a general issue which deserves much more discussion than the brief mention it will get here. We shall only add that pilot testing can help to ensure that a metric has no intrinsic reliability weaknesses, and paying particular attention to reliability issues when execution of the evaluation is being planned can help to eliminate practical problems.

6.2   Interaction between Humans and Metrics

Both validity and reliability are involved in the very delicate issue, already referred to, of human participation in defining and applying metrics. The problem is brutally simple: human beings are neither standardized nor automata. Behaviour varies from one human to another and even a single individual will perform differently depending on his/her state of health, how tired he/she is, and other inescapable natural factors. We have already discussed this problem to a certain extent, using metrics from machine translation evaluation as examples, such as metrics based on humans completing comprehension tests (see White and O'Connell, 1994 for discussion of these and similar issues). In that same discussion we pointed out that evaluators have often sought to eliminate human participation from their metrics. But it is not always possible to do so, essentially for two reasons. The first is that, as we have already mentioned, there are softwares which depend on interaction with a human; they are simply not designed to produce satisfactory results without the intervention of a human to guide their functioning. In these cases it is a major challenge to devise metrics that test the performance of the software independently of the ability of the human partner. In many cases, all that can be done is to be aware of the problem and to choose the population of human partners very carefully. Second, there are quality characteristics which cannot be measured at all without making use of humans. How, for example, can attractiveness (a sub-characteristic of usability) be measured except by asking humans for their judgement? In these cases too, all the evaluation designer can do is to be aware of potential problems and define a population of test subjects accordingly.

The choice and definition of metrics is a very thorny business about which much more deserves to be said than there is space for here. The recent publications in the ISO 9126 series have much to say on the matter, and discussion of a set of formal coherence criteria for metrics can be found in Hovy et al. (2002b).

Discussion of particular metrics can be found widely in almost any recent conference on computational linguistics or on applications of human language technology. Discussion of machine translation metrics in particular can be found in the documents pertaining to the ISLE workshops, available at http://www.issco.unige.ch/projects/isle.

7 Combining the Particular and the General: The Ideal

Sections 3 and 4 laid emphasis on the need to take into account the quality requirements of individual users. Section 5 then tried to compensate for a strongly bottom-up flavour by suggesting that a quality model conceived at a sufficiently high level could be designed, and that such a model could offer the evaluation designer a way into being systematic about defining what a particular user might need.

This section attempts to pull these two strands of thought together, by suggesting that by thinking in terms of classes of users, it should be possible to create a fully worked-out quality model that would in some sense be the union of the needs of all users. Designing a particular evaluation would then become a question of picking out from the general model just those requirements which are relevant to the specific evaluation being designed in order to create a tailor-made evaluation – a little like the pick n' mix sweet counters in the supermarket.

This is exactly the idea behind the FEMTI model for evaluation of machine translation systems, mentioned in Section 1. FEMTI sets up two taxonomies. The first is a classification of contexts of use in terms of the user of the machine translation system and the translation task to be accomplished, including characteristics of the input to the system. The second is a classification of the quality characteristics of machine translation software, detailed into hierarchies of sub-characteristics and attributes, bottoming out into metrics at the terminal nodes. The upper levels coincide with the ISO 9126 characteristics. The model is completed by a mapping from the first classification to the second, which defines (or at least suggests) the characteristics, sub-characteristics, and attributes or metrics that are most relevant for each context of use. The nodes of the two taxonomies frequently contain additional information in the form of bibliographic references or explicit mention of the type of user or stakeholder whose interests might be represented by the node.

In an ideal world, the structure described briefly above would be entirely automated. An evaluation designer would click on a section of the user needs/context of use taxonomy and would thereby bring up the relevant nodes from the quality characteristics taxonomy, together with a choice of relevant metrics. All he/she would have to do to complete the evaluation design would be to reply, when prompted, with information on the rating levels for this particular evaluation and on the combining function. Estrella et al. (2005) give a more detailed account of FEMTI and of preliminary work on establishing links between the two taxonomies.

At the moment, this is a utopian dream. Constructing even the current sloppy version of FEMTI has been long and arduous, and its constructors are well aware of lacunae and the continuing existence of inconsistencies. Perhaps even worse, in its current state it is almost totally uncritical about the metrics attached to the terminal nodes: the metrics have simply been collected from the literature and very little has been done to validate them or to investigate relationships between them – this is on the agenda for the next round of work.

There is also a strong sense, of course, in which work on defining such generic quality models can never be finished. Technology moves at ever-increasing speed, and systems change in consequence. Interest in the development of new metrics and their validation has not ceased to grow over the last few years, and with the economic stakes growing ever larger as systems become evermore complex, there is no reason to think that this interest will wane.

Nonetheless, it is by striving towards the construction of the utopia that we deepen our knowledge of what evaluation is all about.

8   Conclusion

The direction in evaluation work reflected in this chapter started with a desire to share expensive resources. The obvious question as we reach the end of the chapter is whether that has in any way been achieved by the work reported on here. I think it cannot be denied that the EAGLES-inspired work on user-oriented evaluation has been stimulating to the large community of research workers and other interested parties who have participated in it: empirical reinforcement of this claim comes from the fact that there is never any lack of potential participants whenever a new workshop is announced. The most obvious result is the growth of a common framework for thinking about evaluation which goes further than concentrating on what the software is supposed to do. Then too, the scientific community has become much more sophisticated about metrics and their application over the last decade or so, partly under the influence of a continuing interest in evaluation campaigns, partly through discussion stimulated by work in the EAGLES, and other similar contexts. We have not found any magic recipes for evaluating natural language software: it would have been naive to imagine that we might. We have made a lot of progress towards being able to justify or criticize a particular evaluation on reasoned and reasonable grounds, and we have made it easier for the evaluation designer to set about his/her job in a systematic fashion, with the confidence that what he/she is doing is grounded in accepted standards.

Notes

1. Expert Advisory Groups for Language Engineering Standards.

2. International Standards for Language Engineering.

3. To foreshadow later discussion, it is perhaps interesting to notice here already that the change in needs has direct consequences on what metrics might be suitable. In particular, a measure of translation quality based on whether or not relevant newspaper articles can be identified is, in this new context, useless.

4. The examples here are complete systems, but in a context like that of a research the same reasoning would apply to individual modules of the overall system; what would change would be the kinds of users.

5. Quotations from ISO/IEC documents are made with ISO permission, granted in the context of the EAGLES and ISLE projects.

6. This is of course the caricature case. Products actually on the market use a variety of devices to cut down the noise and avoid silence. Even so, producing suitable results remains a major issue for current terminology extraction tools, and even more so when they also try to extract a potential translation.

7. Whilst encouraging him, of course, to consult the more detailed definitions of the ISO standard itself.

8. The combining function is not as simple as it is being made to seem here.

9. This is very similar to the word error rate metric (see Section 6).

10. By pointing out that if the software is to be modified by the end-user, changeability may affect operability.

11. A point reinforced by one of the reviewers suggesting that a clearer distinction between maintainability (in the sense of it being possible for people other than those who wrote the original code to make straightforward adjustments to it) and adaptability (in the sense of being able to extend the software to do things that were not originally foreseen) is required. The ISO definition of maintainability includes both as part of the same sub-characteristic, the notes on that characteristic making it clear that this is a deliberate choice.

12. The TMX exchange format standard for translation memories was developed in order to avoid this kind of problem.

13. This example has been invented for the purposes of exposition here: any correspondence to the structures produced by a particular system is entirely accidental.

14. Text Retrieval Conference (TREC) TREC-9 Proceedings are available electronically at http://www.trec.nist.gov.trec9.t9-proceedings.

15. This is a ridiculously simplified account. The reader is referred to the literature for a more accurate and more detailed description.

16. See Lin and Och (2004) for a discussion of several automated machine translation metrics and of how they correlate with human judgements, together with a proposal for evaluation of the metrics themselves. A comparison of a number of metrics and their results when applied to working systems can also be found in Surcin et al. (2005).

17. Proceedings available electronically at http://www.amtaweb.org/summit/MTSummit/papers.html.

18. To state this in terms of well-known evaluation metrics: precision, first used as metric in document retrieval, is based on what proportion of the documents retrieved are actually relevant to the search request. In the context described here, it is theoretically (if not always practically) possible to measure precision. Recall, on the other hand, is based on measuring how many, out of all the relevant documents existing in the document set being searched, are actually retrieved. Measuring recall is not even theoretically possible in the web context: there is no possible way of knowing either what the collection of documents being searched over is, or what the relevant documents in that collection are.

References

AMTA (1992). MT Evaluation: Basis for Future Directions (Proceedings of a Workshop held in San Diego, California, USA). Technical report, Association for Machine Translation in the Americas.

Ankherst, M. (2001). Human Involvement and Interactivity of the Next Generation's Data Mining Tools. In *Proceedings of the DMKD Workshop on Research Issues in Data Mining and Knowledge Discovery*.

Blair, D. C. (2002). Some Thoughts on the Reported Results of TREC. *Information Processing and Management*, 38(3):445–451.

Boisen, S. and Bates, M. (1992). A Practical Methodology for the Evaluation of Spoken Language Systems. In *Proceedings of the Third Conference on Applied Natural Language Processing (ANLP)*, pages 162–169, Trento, Italy.

Booch, G., Rumbaugh, J., and Jacobson, I. (1999). *The Unified Modeling Language: User Guide*, Addison Wesley, Reading, USA.

Bourland, P. (2000). Experimental Components for the Evaluation of Interactive Information Retrieval Systems. *Journal of Documentation*, 56(1): 71–90.

Brown, A. and Wallnau, K. (1996). A Framework for Systematic Evaluation of Software Technologies. *IEEE Software*, 13(5):39–49.

Canelli, M., Grasso, D., and King, M. (2000). Methods and Metrics for the Evaluation of Dictation Systems: A Case Study. In *Proceedings of the Second International Conference on Language Resources and Evaluation (LREC)*, pages 1325–1331, Athens, Greece.

Church, K. W. and Hovy, E. H. (1993). Good Applications for Crummy MT. *Machine Translation*, 8:239–258.

Cowie, J. and Lehnert, W. (1996). Information Extraction. *Communications of the ACM, Special Edition on Natural Language Processing*, pages 80–91.

Doyon, J., Taylor, K., and White, J. S. (1998). The DARPA MT Evaluation Methodology: Past and Present. In *Proceedings of the Association for Machine Translation Conference (AMTA)*, Philadelphia, USA.

EAGLES Evaluation Working Group (1996). EAGLES Evaluation of Natural Language Processing Systems. Final report, Center for Sprogteknologi, Copenhagen, Denmark.

Estrella, P., Popescu-Belis, A., and Underwood, N. (2005). Finding the System that Suits You Best: Towards the Normalization of MT Evaluation. In *Proceedings of the 27th International Conference on Translating and the Computer (ASLIB)*, London, UK.

Falkedal, K., editor (1994). *Proceedings of the Evaluators' Forum*, ISSCO, Les Rasses, Switzerland.

Flickinger, D., Narbonne, J., Sag, I., and Wasow, T. (1987). Toward Evaluation of NLP Systems. Technical report, Hewlett Packard Laboratories, Palo Alto, USA.

Grishman, R. (1997). Information Extraction: Techniques and Challenges. International Summer School on Information Extraction (SCIE). New York University, New York, USA.

Hartley, A. and Popescu-Belis, A. (2004). Evaluation des systèmes de traduction automatique. In Chaudiron, S., editor, *Evaluation des systèmes de traitement de l'information*, Collection sciences et technologies de l'information, pages 311–335, Hermès, Paris, France.

Hawking, D., Craswell, N., Thistlewaite, P., and Harman, D. (1999). Results and Challenges in Web Search Evaluation. *Computer Networks*, 31(11-16): 1321–1330.

Hirschman, L. (1998a). Language Understanding Evaluations: Lessons Learned from MUC and ATIS. In *Proceedings of the First International Conference on Language Resources and Evaluation (LREC)*, pages 117–123, Granada, Spain.

Hirschman, L. (1998b). The Evolution of Evaluation: Lessons from the Message Understanding Conferences. *Computer Speech and Language*, 12:281–305.

Hovy, E. H., King, M., and Popescu-Belis, A. (2002a). Computer-Aided Specification of Quality Models for Machine Translation Evaluation. In *Proceedings of the Third International Conference on Language Resources and Evaluation (LREC)*, pages 729–753, Las Palmas, Gran Canaria, Spain.

Hovy, E. H., King, M., and Popescu-Belis, A. (2002b). Principles of Context-Based Machine Translation Evaluation. *Machine Translation*, 16:1–33.

ISO/IEC 14598-1:1999. Information Technology – Software Product Evaluation, Part 1: General Overview. International Organization for Standardization and International Electrotechnical Commission, Geneva, Switzerland.

ISO/IEC 14598-2:2000. Software Engineering – Product Evaluation; Part 2: Planning and Management. International Organization for Standardization and International Electrotechnical Commission, Geneva, Switzerland.

ISO/IEC 14598-3:2000. Software Engineering – Product Evaluation, Part 3: Process for Developers. International Organization for Standardization and International Electrotechnical Commission, Geneva, Switzerland.

ISO/IEC 14598-4:1999. Software Engineering – Product Evaluation, Part 4: Process for Acquirers. International Organization for Standardization and International Electrotechnical Commission, Geneva, Switzerland.

ISO/IEC 14598-5:1998. Information Technology – Software Product Evaluation, Part 5: Process for Evaluators. International Organization for Standardization and International Electrotechnical Commission, Geneva, Switzerland.

ISO/IEC 14598-6:2001. Software Engineering – Product Evaluation, Part 6: Documentation of Evaluation Modules. International Organization for Standardization and International Electrotechnical Commission, Geneva, Switzerland.

ISO/IEC 9126-1:2001. Software Engineering – Product Quality, Part 1: Quality Model. International Organization for Standardization and International Electrotechnical Commission, Geneva, Switzerland.

ISO/IEC 9126:1991. Information Technology – Software Product Evaluation, Quality Characteristics and Guidelines for Their Use. International Organization for Standardization and International Electrotechnical Commission, Geneva, Switzerland.

ISO/IEC CD 9126-30. Software Engineering – Software Product Quality Requirements and Evaluation, Part 30: Quality Metrics – Metrics Reference Model and Guide. International Organization for Standardization and International Electrotechnical Commission, Geneva, Switzerland. In preparation.

ISO/IEC TR 9126-2:2003. Software Engineering – Product Quality, Part 2: External Metrics. International Organization for Standardization and International Electrotechnical Commission, Geneva, Switzerland.

ISO/IEC TR 9126-3:2003. Software Engineering – Product Quality, Part 3: Internal Metrics. International Organization for Standardization and International Electrotechnical Commission, Geneva, Switzerland.

ISO/IEC TR 9126-4:2004. Software Engineering – Product Quality, Part 4: Quality in Use Metrics. International Organization for Standardization and International Electrotechnical Commission, Geneva, Switzerland.

King, M. (1996a). Evaluating Natural Language Processing Systems. *Special Edition of Communications of the ACM on Natural Language Processing Systems*, 39(1):73–79.

King, M. (1996b). On the Notion of Validity and the Evaluation of MT Systems. In Somers, H., editor, *Terminology, SLP and Translation: Studies in Honour of Juan C. Sager*, pages 189–205, John Benjamins, Amsterdam, The Netherlands.

King, M. (1997). Evaluating Translation. In Hauenschild, C. and Heizmann, S., editors, *Machine Translation and Translation Theory*, pages 251–263, Mouton de Gruyter, Berlin, Germany.

King, M. (1999). Evaluation Design: The EAGLES Framework. In Nübel, R. and Seewald-Heeg, U., editors, *Evaluation of the Linguistic Performance of Machine Translation Systems, Proceedings of Konvens'98, Bonn*, Gardezi Verlag, St. Augustin, Germany.

King, M., editor (2002). *Workbook of the LREC Workshop on Machine Translation Evaluation: Human Evaluators Meet Automated Metrics*, Las Palmas, Gran Canaria, Spain.

King, M. (2005). Accuracy and Suitability: New Challenges for Evaluation. *Language Resources and Evaluation*, 39:45–64.

King, M. and Falkedal, K. (1990). Using Test Suites in Evaluation of MT Systems. In *Proceedings of the International Conference on Computational Linguistics (COLING)*, volume 2, pages 211–216, Helsinki, Finland.

King, M. and Maegaard, B. (1998). Issues in Natural Language System Evaluation. In *Proceedings of the First International Conference on Linguistic Resources and Evaluation (LREC)*, volume 1, pages 225–230, Granada, Spain.

King, M., Popescu-Belis, A., and Hovy, E. H. (2003). FEMTI: Creating and Using a Framework for MT Evaluation. In *Proceedings of MT Summit IX*, pages 224–232, New Orleans, USA.

King, M. and Underwood, N., editors (2004). *Proceedings of the LREC Workshop on User Oriented Evaluation of Knowledge Discovery Systems*, Lisbon, Portugal.

Kuralenok, I. E. and Nekrestyanov, I. S. (2002). Evaluation of Text Retrieval Systems. *Programming and Computing Software*, 28(4):226–242.

Lehmann, S., Oepen, S., Regnier-Prost, S., Netter, K., Lux, V., Klein, J., Falkedal, K., Fouvry, F., Estival, D., Dauphin, E., Compagnion, H., Baur, J., Balkan, L., and Arnold, D. (1996). TSNLP – Test Suites for Natural Language Processing. In *Proceedings of the International Conference on Computational Linguistics (COLING)*, pages 711–716.

Lehnart, W. and Sundheim, B. (1991). A Performance Analysis of Text-Analysis Technologies. *AI Magazine*, 12(4):81–94.

Lin, C.-Y. and Och, F. J. (2004). ORANGE: A Method for Evaluating Automatic Evaluation Metrics for Machine Translation. In *Proceedings of the International Conference on Computational Linguistics (COLING)*, pages 23–27, Geneva, Switzerland.

Minker, W. (2002). Overview on Recent Activities in Speech Understanding and Dialogue Systems Evaluation. In *Proceedings of the International Conference on Spoken Language Processing (ICSLP)*, pages 337–340, Denver, Colorado, USA.

Nomura, H. and Isahara, J. (1992). JEIDA Methodology and Criteria on MT Evaluation. Technical report, Japan Electronic Industry Development Association (JEIDA).

Paggio, P. and Underwood, N. (1998). Validating the TEMAA Evaluation Methodology: A Case Study on Danish Spelling Checkers. *Natural Language Engineering*, 4(3):211–228.

Papinieni, K., Roukos, S., Ward, T., and Zhu, W.-J. (2001). BLEU: A Method for Automatic Evaluation of MT. Research report, Computer Science RC22176 (W0109-022), IBM Research Division, T. J. Watson Research Center.

Slocum, J., Bennett, W. S., Whiffin, L., and Norcross, E. (1985). An Evaluation of METAL: The LRC Machine Translation System. In *Proceedings of the Second Conference of the European Chapter of the Association for Computational Linguistics (EACL)*, pages 62–69, Geneva, Switzerland.

Sparck Jones, K. (2001). Automatic Language and Information Processing: Rethinking Evaluation. *Natural Language Engineering*, 7(1):29–46.

Sparck Jones, K. and Galliers, J. R. (1996). *Evaluating Natural Language Processing Systems: An Analysis and Review*. Number 1083 in Lecture Notes in Artificial Intelligence. Springer-Verlag, Berlin, Germany/New York, USA.

Sparck Jones, K. and Willet, P., editors (1997). *Readings in Information Retrieval*, Morgan Kaufman, San Francisco, USA.

Starlander, M. and Popescu-Belis, A. (2002). Corpus-Based Evaluation of a French Spelling and Grammar Checker. In *Proceedings of the Third International Conference on Language Resources and Evaluation (LREC)*, pages 262–274, Las Palmas, Gran Canaria, Spain.

Surcin, S., Hamon, O., Hartley, A., Rajman., M., Popescu-Belis, A., Hadi, W. M. E., Timimi, I., Dabbadie, M., and Choukri, K. (2005). Evaluation of Machine Translation with Predictive Metrics beyond BLEU/NIST: CESTA Evaluation Campaign #1. In *Proceedings of the Machine Translation Summit X*, pages 117–124, Phuket, Thailand.

TEMAA (1996). TEMAA Final Report. Technical Report LRE-62-070, Center for Sprogteknologi, Copenhagen, Denmark.

Thompson, H. S. (1992). The Strategic Role of Evaluation in Natural Language Processing and Speech Technology. Technical report, University of Edinburgh, UK. Record of a workshop sponsored by DANDI, ELSNET and HCRC.

VanSlype, G. (1979). Critical Study of Methods for Evaluating the Quality of MT. Technical Report BR 19142, European Commission, Directorate for General Scientific and Technical Information Management (DG XIII). http://www.issco.unige.ch/projects/isle.

Voorhees, E. (2000). Variations in Relevance Judgements and the Measurement of Retrieval Effectiveness. *Information Processing and Management*, 36:697–716.

Voorhees, E. (2003). Evaluating the Evaluation: A Case Study Using the TREC 2002 Question Answering Track. In *Proceedings of the HLT-NAACL*, pages 181–188, Edmonton, Canada.

White, J. S. and O'Connell, T. A. (1994). The DARPA MT Evaluation Methodologies: Evolution, Lessons and Future Approaches. In *Proceedings of the First Conference of the Association for Machine Translation in the Americas (AMTA)*, Columbia, Maryland, USA.

Yeh, A. S., Hirschman, L., and Morgan, A. A. (2003). Evaluation of Text Data Mining for Data Base Curation: Lessons Learned from the KDD Challenge Cup. *Bioinformatics*, 19(suppl. 1):i331–i339.

A note on the bibliography: Evaluation campaigns and projects can span many years and give birth to numerous publications. Here, only one reference is given to any single long-term effort, even though other publications may contain discussion which has been picked up here. The reference chosen is usually either the most recent or a retrospective summary. A much more detailed bibliography can be obtained directly from the author or from http://www.issco.unige.ch/.

Chapter 6

AN OVERVIEW OF EVALUATION METHODS IN TREC AD HOC INFORMATION RETRIEVAL AND TREC QUESTION ANSWERING

Simone Teufel

Computer Laboratory
University of Cambridge, United Kingdom

Simone.Teufel@cl.cam.ac.uk

Abstract   This chapter gives an overview of the current evaluation strategies and problems in the fields of information retrieval (IR) and question answering (QA), as instantiated in the Text Retrieval Conference (TREC). Whereas IR has a long tradition as a task, QA is a relatively new task which had to quickly develop its evaluation metrics, based on experiences gained in IR. This chapter will contrast the two tasks, their difficulties, and their evaluation metrics. We will end this chapter by pointing out limitations of the current evaluation strategies and potential future developments.

Keywords   Information retrieval; Question answering; Extrinsic evaluation; Intrinsic evaluation; Precision; Recall; Accuracy; MRR; Composite evaluation metrics.

1   Introduction

Why is evaluation of systems in natural language processing and related fields important? Language-related tasks are cognitively hard; for tasks which are interesting, systems do not perform anywhere near the 100% mark. Typically, one cannot assess if an increase in quality has taken place by subjectively looking at the output of two systems (or a possibly improved system and its predecessor). More complicated, objective evaluation strategies for monitoring performance differences are needed, and community agreement on these strategies is also important. For instance, the existence of an objective, agreed-upon, simple evaluation metric (namely word error rate, or WER) in the field of

163

L. Dybkjær et al. (eds.), Evaluation of Text and Speech Systems, 163–186.
© 2007 *Springer.*

automatic speech recognition (ASR) has substantially helped monitor progress in the task, and thus advance the field: the WER of the state-of-the-art ASR systems continues to go down year by year, for harder and harder sub-variants of the original task. Similar situations have arisen in optical character recognition (OCR) and information extraction. Evaluation can also direct future research: it can signal when a certain ceiling has been reached (i.e., when all state-of-the-art systems perform similarly), and can help define interesting new tasks. For instance, the filtering task in information retrieval (IR), a recent version of the ad hoc search task discussed here, models IR on a life information feed. Its evolution went hand in hand with a new evaluation track in a competitive evaluation conference series called Text Retrieval Conference (TREC) (see below). Similarly, the TREC web track fostered research into the evaluation of web search engines.

We will look at IR and question answering (QA) in the context of the most successful and largest-scale evaluation conference series to date, TREC (Harman, 1993; TREC, 2004), which has been run by NIST since the early 1990s. Other large-scale evaluation efforts for IR include the Cranfield experiment (Cleverdon, 1967), and recently NTCIR (NTCIR, 2005) in Asia and CLEF (CLEF, 2005) in Europe. Experience has shown that competitive evaluation exercises can act as a driving force for finding an objective and meaningful evaluation, for establishing good practice in evaluation, and thus for measuring and fostering progress. The continuity that these exercises bring has also encouraged research teams to make the investment of participating. When TREC emerged in the early 1990s, it marked a new phase in IR evaluation; 2005 was the 15th annual conference. In contrast, QA, a far newer task than IR, has only been run (as a track within TREC) since 1999. QA systems and evaluation strategies have evolved fast in those few years (e.g., three different evaluation measures have been experimented with since 1999). Nevertheless, those two tasks and their evaluation methods are very naturally connected, and we will now review both tasks in more detail.

1.1   The Tasks

1.1.1   Ad hoc Information Retrieval.   *Information Retrieval* (IR) is the task of finding documents from a large document collection which are relevant to a user's query. The query can be expressed as a set of keywords or as a natural language description. Figure 1 shows a sample TREC query, asking for documents about diseases which cause hair loss. Different levels of detail are given by the fields `title`, `desc`, and `narr`.

This task where systems return entire textual documents as their output is technically called *document retrieval*; it is the most well-known and popular subtype of IR. There are other subtasks of IR such as retrieval of speech, video, music, and retrieval on text passages (Callan, 1994); this chapter,

```
<num> Number: 508
<title> hair loss is a symptom of what diseases
<desc> Description:
Find diseases for which hair loss is a symptom.
<narr> Narrative:
A document is relevant if it positively connects the loss of
head hair in humans with a specific disease. In this context,
"thinning hair" and "hair loss" are synonymous. Loss of body
and/or facial hair is irrelevant, as is hair loss caused by drug
therapy.
```

Figure 1. Sample TREC query.

however, only considers document retrieval, and in particular, ad hoc document retrieval. Ad hoc IR is the one-time (batch-based) retrieval of documents that are relevant to a query, which is issued once and can not be refined. This is opposed to interactive search (where a user can iteratively refine queries), or filtering, where the definition of relevance might change over time, e.g., after the first relevant documents have been seen. Ad hoc retrieval also assumes a fixed document collection as opposed to a dynamic one such as the web. It is thus the simplest, most clear-cut definition of the document search task and also the most well-studied form of IR. We concentrate on it here because it allows for the basic concepts of IR to be presented without interactions with more complicated factors introduced by variant tasks.

Most modern IR evaluation set-ups, including TREC, rely on so-called "laboratory-style" performance evaluation: queries are generated by humans and formulated in natural language; subsequently a judge decides which documents (given a fixed, finite document set) are relevant to the query, a task called *relevance decision*. These decisions are used as fixed, a priori gold standard, which each system's result is compared to. Laboratory-style performance evaluations are easier to control, because the factors around the main problem in IR evaluation, the subjectivity of relevance decisions, are kept constant and thus as controllable as possible. The entire test collection consists only of three components: the queries, the relevance decisions, and the document set. During the construction of the collection, the abstract operational set-up is "frozen": practical details such as the kind of presentation of query results, which is known to potentially influence the results considerably, is factored out. This is done by choosing one particular feature (in this case, one particular presentation format), which is then kept constant. The advantage of such a set-up is the repeatability of experiments under different conditions. For instance, TREC produced 50 queries and relevance judgements per year, at considerable cost. But once this frozen document collection is created, any research group can use TREC queries and relevance judgements without having to recreate the exact conditions of the human judges and their interaction with one particular IR system.

However, such a set-up can only test a subset of the parameters that could be changed in an IR system – namely the so-called system parameters. System parameters tested include the following: how the documents are indexed (i.e., assign keywords to them that best describe the contents of the document), which query language is used (a query language is a set of keywords and some rules about how these can be combined), and which retrieval algorithm is used (how are terms in the query matched to index terms – there are different ways of manipulating terms and different mathematical models to calculate the best fit). A system parameter not tested in the classic laboratory model is how to present the results to the user (e.g., as a long unordered list of documents, as a ranked list, or arranged in a graphical way). Sparck Jones and Galliers (1995) list many aspects of the overall information system that could and should be evaluated but lie outside the laboratory-style model, such as the influence of the static document collection containing the universe of documents that can be queried, and of the user who formulates a query in a given query language, thus translating his or her information need into this query language. Such remit aspects (i.e., aspects of motivation, goal, and manner of the evaluation, specifically the environment variables of the influence of the document collection and the user query) are not normally explored; a notable exception to this is the study by Saracevic et al. (1988) which considers environment variables in detail.

1.1.2   Question Answering.   *Question Answering* (QA) is the task of returning a short piece of text as an answer to a question which is given in natural language. As search ground, a large collection of documents is used, from which the answer is selected. What counts as an answer is defined below; though it *may* in principle be an entire document, in most cases the answer is a much smaller unit, typically in the order of a sentence or a phrase. In TREC-QA, there are limitations on the type of question which is used: the question has to be factual (not involving any explicit opinion), and it has to be answerable within a short textual piece.

In comparison to the well-established evaluation of IR, the evaluation of QA is still in its infancy. Since 1999, NIST has prepared material for measuring system performance on the task of returning short answer passages (or, recently, exact answers) to a question formulated in natural language (Voorhees and Tice, 2000). This evaluation is run as a track in TREC (TREC-QA, 2004), attracting 20–36 participant groups in the following years. Figure 2 shows example questions from the first three TREC-QAs.

There is a human manual check on all returned system answers to see if they constitute a "correct" answer, under the assumption that there is not just one correct answer in the document collection. This manual check makes QA evaluation even more expensive than IR evaluation. One problem for the evaluation

TREC-8	How many calories are there in a Big Mac?
	Where is the Taj Mahal?
TREC-9	Who invented the paper clip?
	Where is Rider college located?
	What is the best-selling book?
TREC-10	What is an atom?
	How much does the human adult female brain weigh?
	When did Hawaii become a state?

Figure 2. Example TREC questions.

is that it is often unclear what should count as an answer. Answer generality or granularity can pose a problem, for instance, when a question asks for a point in time: while most assessors would judge "the nineties" as too general an answer to the question "When did Princess Diana die?", it is unclear what the right level of generality is in general (in this particular case, the day should probably be given; the time of day is too specific).

There are different question tasks in TREC-QA: factoid questions, list questions, definition questions, context questions, and reformulations of questions in different words.

The simplest and largest part of the questions are factoid questions, which ask for simple, factual information such as "how many calories are there in a Big Mac". Opinion questions, such as "what is the greatest film ever made?" are explicitly excluded.

List questions ask for several instances of one type. Examples from TREC-10 include: 4 US cities that have a "Shubert" theater; 9 novels written by John Updike; 6 names of navigational satellites; 20 countries that produce coffee. In order to qualify as a list question, the answers must not be found in one document; systems should be encouraged to assemble the answers from different documents. In later TRECs, the target number is no longer given; systems are required to find *all* instances of a certain type (see Figure 3).

Definition questions such as "Who is Colin Powell?" and "What is mould?" were used in every TREC-QA apart from TREC-11. They were always controversial, because it is extremely hard to assess what a good answer would be: answers could have more or less detail and be directed at different target users. However, TREC-12 brought definition questions back because they are very prevalent in real search engine logs. Due to space limitations, this chapter

| 1915: List the names of chewing gums. |
| Stimorol, Orbit, Winterfresh, Double Bubble, Dirol, Trident, Spearmint, Bazooka, Doublemint, Dentyne, Freedent, Hubba Bubba, Juicy Fruit, Big Red, Chiclets, Nicorette |

Figure 3. Answer list for list question 1915 (names of chewing gums found within the AQUAINT corpus).

cannot go into the specifics of their evaluation, which is based on "information nuggets" – however, it is important to note that definition questions were the only type of question in TREC-QAs so far for which the evaluation was not stable (Voorhees, 2003).

The context task in TREC-10 was a pilot evaluation for QA within a particular context. The task was designed to simulate the kind of dialogue processing that a system would need to support an interactive user session. Unfortunately, the results in the pilot were dominated by whether or not a system could answer the particular type of question the context question set started with: the ability to correctly answer questions later in a series was uncorrelated with the ability to correctly answer questions earlier in the series. Thus the task was discontinued.

Apart from question type, there are other dimensions of difficulty. For instance, the source of the questions has a strong impact on the task. In TREC-8, questions were formulated *after* an interesting fact was randomly found in a newspaper text: this meant that the formulation (or re-engineering) of the question was influenced by the actual answer string, making it likely that the answers and the questions are textually similar. Later TRECs used more realistic models of question source, by mining them from web logs. Such "real" questions are harder on assessors and systems, but more representative for those systems which use training; it is easier to find similar questions on the web, but competing systems need to care more about synonymy, polysemy, and other phenomena of superficial (string) differences between question and answers.

Since TREC-10, the organisers no longer guarantee that there is an answer in the document collection; in fact, 10% of the questions on average have no answer (i.e., the assessor did not find the answer and inspection of all system results also did not find an answer). In this case, the correct system return was "NIL". The lack of an answer guarantee makes the task harder, as the systems need an internal measure of their confidence in an answer (only 5 systems in TREC-10 had a NIL precision >0.25; this remained similar in later years).

Document collections for the early TREC-QAs were the same as for the main TREC (979,000 articles). In TREC-11, the collection was changed to the AQUAINT-collection (1,033,000 documents), which covers a more recent time frame (1998–2000). This collection consists of documents from the Associated Press news wire, the New York Times news wire, and the (English portion of the) Xinhua News Agency. The move to the new corpus partially addressed the timeliness problem: TREC rules state that any external sources such as the Internet can be used as long as the answer is reported in connection with a document from the document collection supporting the answer. From TREC-11 onwards systems started using the Internet and projected the answers found in the web back into the (aged) TREC document collection. In one case at TREC-11, a system which returned the objectively correct answer to a question asking for the current governor of Texas did not receive the credit as only the governor of Texas ruling in the late 1980s (the old TREC collection) could be counted as the correct answer.

The QA task is often thought of as a continuation of IR: even if the task is to pinpoint the right answer rather than finding generally relevant documents, some kind of IR must be performed first to find relevant documents. QA is also considered "harder" than IR at least in one aspect – it needs to perform deeper natural language analysis of the texts, and importantly, more complex query understanding. For instance, in the question "When did Princess Diana die?", an IR search engine would drop question words such as "when", whereas a QA system would use them to determine the correct answer type.

2   Evaluation Criteria

Evaluation criteria define the properties we are looking for in an ideal system output. The ideal IR system will return "relevant" documents, whereas the ideal QA system will return "correct and exact answers". The following sections give an overview of the difficulty in defining these properties operationally.

2.1   Ad Hoc IR: Relevance in Document

Ad hoc IR has been studied since the 1960s. The core problem the field had to solve was the fact that both information needs and perceived relevance are situation-dependent. Firstly, information needs are unique to a particular person at a particular time. The answer of modern evaluations such as TREC is sampling: collecting many different queries from many humans addresses one aspect of this problem, with the aim to sample enough of the entire range of "possible" queries to allow to draw conclusions about how the systems would perform on other, yet unknown queries.

Secondly, there is the relevance problem in IR: even within one information need, relevance of documents to a query, as perceived by a user, is situational and thus inherently subjective. It will differ over time for the same person, and it will differ between different humans even more. One factor influencing relevance is novelty: a document may be perfectly relevant to a query but a user who already knows it might not judge it as relevant because it is not immediately *useful* to him/her. Other factors have to do with the way in which a document is relevant: it may contain the answer itself, it may *point* to a different document that contains the answer, it may remind the user of a source or document that contains the answer, it may provide some relevant background to a question without really containing the information the user was looking for, etc. However, in an operational environment such as TREC, it cannot necessarily be guaranteed that one person will judge all necessary documents, and no particular order can be imposed in which documents are judged.

The challenge for setting up an objective and operationally viable evaluation is thus to find rules about relevance which make relevance decisions as context-independent as possible. In TREC, users were asked to judge whether each given document *in isolation* is relevant to the query, independently of the novelty of that document to the judges. Relevance should thus in principle be an objective property between each individual document and the query. The assumption that judges can mentally cancel previous context is probably not particularly realistic; however, the advantage of creating a (theoretically) situation-independent test collection outweighs these considerations.

2.2 QA: Relevance in Exact Answer String

While relevance in ad hoc IR is well discussed, defining the notion of a "correct answer" is a new challenge for QA evaluation. One of the problems is that there may be more than one right answer, and even a continuum in quality between answers. Interestingly, there is a correlation between the prescribed answer length and these problematic factors. Early TRECs allowed for 250 bytes or 50 bytes answers, but now exact answers are required. Figure 4 illustrates possible problems with non-exact answer decisions. It gives real example strings submitted to a TREC-9 question, in decreasing order of quality. Human annotators have to make a judgement as to which answers still count as "good enough".

The context of the answer is important. For that reason, systems return [docid, answer string] pairs (five per question in early TRECs, one per question since TREC-11). The document is to "support" the answer in that somewhere in the document the connection between the question and the answer must be present. For systems B, C, and D in Figure 4, the connection is already clear in the answer string. For the other systems, whether or not an answer is supported is judged by the human annotators after reading the submitted document. This makes the answer judgement an especially expensive task.

```
         What river in the US is known as the Big Muddy?
System A: | the Mississippi                                        |
System B: | Known as Big Muddy, the Mississippi is the longest     |
System C: | as Big Muddy , the Mississippi is the longest          |
System D: | messed with . Known as Big Muddy , the Mississip       |
System E: | Mississippi is the longest river in the US             |
System F: | the Mississippi is the longest river in the US         |
System G: | the Mississippi is the longest river(Mississippi)      |
System H: | has brought the Mississippi to its lowest              |
System I: | ipes.In Life on the Mississippi,Mark Twain wrote t     |
System K: | Southeast;Mississippi;Mark Twain;officials began       |
System L: | Known; Mississippi; US,; Minnesota; Cult Mexico        |
System M: | Mud Island,; Mississippi; ``The; history; Memphis      |
```

Figure 4. Example answers.

The requirement that answer strings have to be extracts (i.e., they have to be found verbatim in a document), in place since TREC-12, simplifies answer judgement and discourages "answer stuffing" (a practice where several suspected answers are appended into the result string, cf. systems K–M in Figure 4).

Each answer is independently judged as correct, unsupported, or incorrect by two human assessors. When the two judgements differ, an adjudicator makes the final decision. An answer is judged correct if it contains a right answer to the question, if the document from which it is drawn makes it clear that it is a right answer, and if the answer is responsive. Responsive extracts are non-ambiguous (they must not contain multiple entities of the same semantic category as the correct answer), and, for numerical answers which contain units, the answer string must contain that unit. An answer is judged unsupported if it contains a right answer and is responsive, but the document from which it is drawn does not indicate that it is a right answer. Otherwise, an answer is judged as incorrect. Answers supported by a document are accepted even if the answer is "objectively" wrong – in the closed world of the TREC-QA exercise, answers are correct if they are correct according to at least one document in the fixed collection. As mentioned above, another problem concerns answer granularity. Assessor opinion also differs with respect to how much detail is required to answer a question.

Answer judgement is expensive – for instance, in TREC-10, the mean answer pool per question judged was 309 document/answer pairs. This expense could be kept lower with a fixed gold standard agreed before the competition and simple string matching. However, TREC-QA style evaluation (where each returned answer is manually judged) ensures a higher quality of the evaluation, because systems could potentially return answers that are not yet in the gold standard. The decision not to use a gold standard – as is used in IR evaluations – is an important one, which may be partially responsible for the overall higher numerical results in QA in comparison to IR.

An important design criterion of the TREC-QA data-set is that it should be reusable for the training of later systems. Therefore, each year's TREC-QA answers and questions are made available in the form of a set of possible answer patterns, which simulate the manual checking of submitted answers, e.g., Figure 5, which gives known answers to the question "Who was Jane Goddall?". The patterns are expressed as `perl` regular expressions. Evaluation against frozen patterns is a suboptimal solution: false negatives are possible (e.g., some document might exist describing Jane G. which is not covered by these strings, which would be unduly penalised), and false positives are equally possible ("anthropologist" might occur in a non-Jane-G situation, which would be unduly rewarded). The patterns also cannot penalise "answer stuffing", or check for supportedness of answers. Nevertheless, patterns can be useful if

```
naturalist                chimpanzee\s+ researcher
anthropologist            wife.*van\s* Lawick
ethnologists?             chimpanzee\s* -?\s+ observer
primatologist             animal behaviou?rist
expert\s+ on\s+ chimps    scientist of unquestionable reputation
chimpanzee\s+ specialist  most\s recognizable\s+ living\s+ scientist
                          pioneered\s+ study\s+ of\s primates
```

Figure 5.   Example answer patterns for question "Who was Jane Goddall?".

their limitations are understood, as system rankings produced by *lenient* annotator assessment and pattern-based results are highly correlated: Kendall's τ of
0.944 for 250 bytes and 0.894 for 50 bytes. (Lenient assessment, given up after
TREC-9, treated unsupported answers as if they were fully correct.)

After discussing the theoretical evaluation problems in the two fields, we
will now turn to the actual evaluation metrics used.

3   Evaluation Metrics

3.1   Evaluation Metrics in IR

3.1.1   Recall, precision, and accuracy.   Given a test collection,
the main metrics used in IR evaluations are precision and recall, and several
summary metrics derived from these point-wise metrics.

Consider Figure 6, which defines the categories for precision, recall, and
accuracy. What is relevant or non-relevant is decided by the human judge (our
definition of "truth", also called a gold standard), whereas what is retrieved or
not retrieved is decided by the system.

Recall is defined as the proportion of retrieved items amongst the relevant
items ($\frac{A}{A+C}$); *precision* is defined as the proportion of relevant items amongst
retrieved items ($\frac{A}{A+B}$); and *accuracy* is defined as the proportion of correctly
classified items, either as relevant or as irrelevant ($\frac{A+D}{A+B+C+D}$). Recall, precision, and accuracy all range between 0 and 1.

Even though IR can in principle be seen as a classification task (documents
are classified as either relevant or non-relevant), it turns out that accuracy, the
evaluation metric of choice for classification tasks, is not a good measure for
IR. This is because it conflates performance on relevant items (A) with performance on irrelevant items (D) – which are numerous but less interesting for
the task. Due to artificially inflated numbers in any real situation, even systems
with a very real quality difference are nearly indistinguishable on account of
accuracy.

Figure 7 gives an example of how precision and recall can be used to judge
two systems against each other.

Our entire document set in this case is 130 documents (A+B+C+D). For one
given query, there are 28 relevant documents (A+C, shaded in light grey). Let

	Relevant	Non-relevant	Total
Retrieved	A	B	A+B
Not retrieved	C	D	C+D
Total	A+C	B+D	A+B+C+D

Figure 6. Categories for precision, recall, and accuracy.

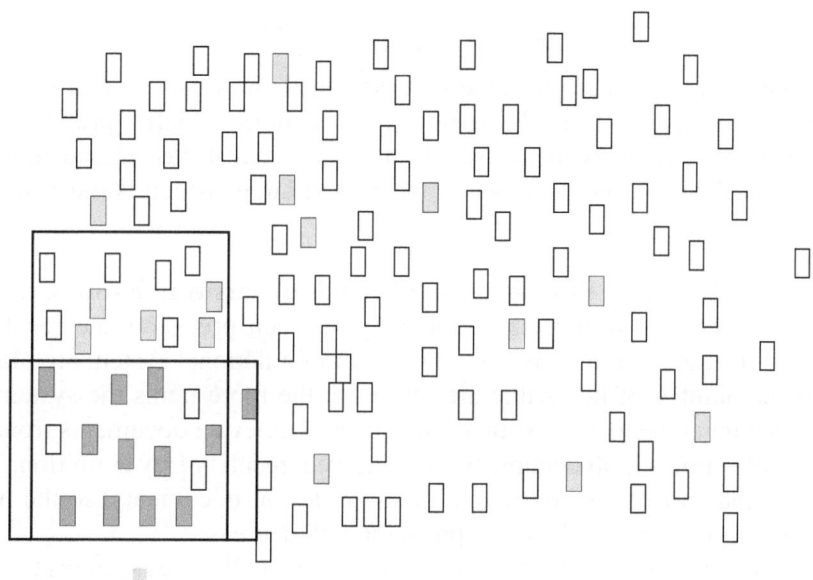

Figure 7. Example of the use of precision and recall.

us now assume that one fictional system, System 1, retrieves the 25 items given in the upper rectangle $((A+B)_1)$. Of these retrieved items, 16 are relevant (A_1). Precision, recall, and accuracy of System 1 can thus be calculated as follows (consider that with realistically large collections, accuracy would be close to 100% for all systems):

$$R_1 \ = \ \frac{A_1}{A+C} = \frac{16}{28} = 0.57 \qquad (6.1)$$

$$P_1 \ = \ \frac{A_1}{(A+B)_1} = \frac{16}{25} = 0.64 \qquad (6.2)$$

$$A_1 \ = \ \frac{A_1 + D_1}{A+B+C+D} = \frac{16 + 93}{130} = 0.84 \qquad (6.3)$$

Another system, System 2, might retrieve the 15 items given in the lower rectangle $(A+B)_2$; out of the retrieved items of System 2, 12 happen to be relevant ($A_2 = 12$); we can thus calculate the performance of System 2 as follows:

$$R_2 \;=\; \frac{12}{28} = 0.43 \tag{6.4}$$

$$P_2 \;=\; \frac{12}{15} = 0.8 \tag{6.5}$$

$$A_2 \;=\; \frac{12+99}{130} = 0.85 \tag{6.6}$$

System 2 has a higher precision than System 1: it is more "careful" in retrieving items, and as a result, its return set contains a higher proportion of relevant items (which is measured by precision), but it has missed more of the relevant items in the document collection at large (which is measured by recall).

3.1.2 Relation between recall and precision; F-measure.

In general, there is an inverse relationship between precision and recall, as Figure 8 illustrates. Here, precision and recall of a fictional system are plotted versus the number of items that are retrieved: the more items the system returns, the higher the likelihood that it will retrieve relevant documents from the overall collection – if all documents are retrieved, recall is 1 by definition. This comes at the cost of also retrieving many irrelevant documents, so the more documents are retrieved, the more precision will decrease.

The inverse relationship between precision and recall forces systems to compromise between them. But there are tasks which particularly need good precision whereas others need good recall. An example of a precision-critical task

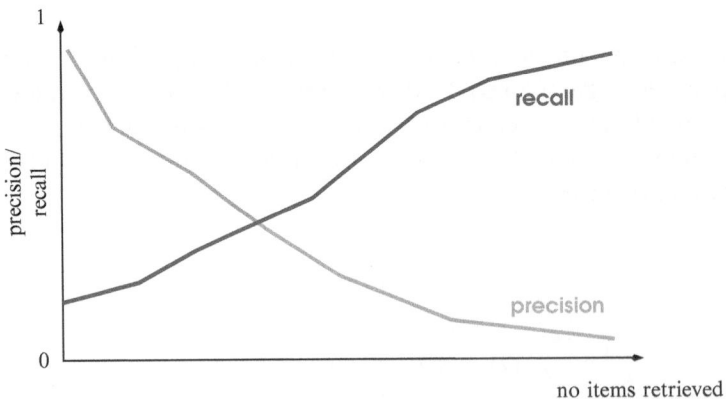

Figure 8. Inverse relationship between precision and recall.

are quick web searches, where little time is available, and where more than one relevant document exists which can answer the information need, due to the redundancy inherent in the web. That means that a full recall of *all* relevant documents is not required, and that the user would not want to consider non-relevant documents – full recall of all documents is not required, as at least one relevant document is expected to come up in a high rank anyway. An example of a recall-critical task is a patent search, where the worst-case scenario (with costly consequences) would be to miss even one single relevant document; time is less of an issue in this scenario.

Figure 9 shows the relationship between precision and recall in a more standard form, namely as precision plotted against recall (the so-called precision–recall curve). Data points are gained by manipulating the number of items retrieved, as in Figure 8 (but in contrast to Figure 8, this number cannot be directly read off here). Ideal systems, which combine high precision with high recall, will show curves that stretch as far as possible into the upper right corner. The precision–recall graph is related to the so-called receiver operating characteristic (ROC) graph known from the life sciences, which plots the hit rate (A in Figure 6) versus the false alarm rate (B) – in this graph, ideal curves stretch in the upper left corner.

Because of the inverse relationship between precision and recall, it is not obvious how the overall performance of a given system can be estimated. One could consider many possible precision/recall data points for any query, as arbitrarily many different cut-offs could be used with relevance-weighted IR engines – this is in opposition to Boolean systems, which always return

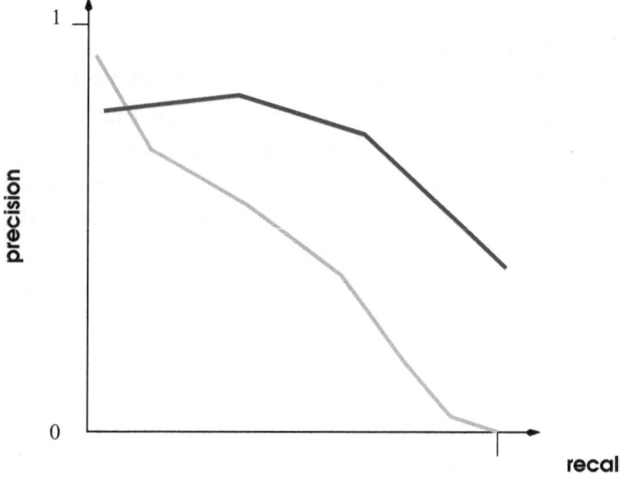

Figure 9. Two precision–recall curves.

a fixed set of documents. One possible answer is to consider the area under the precision–recall curve as an estimate of system performance. However, in a practical setting, one does not want to manipulate a system's retrieval set, plot a precision-recall curve, and then estimate the area under the curve. Two simpler estimations are to empirically determine the crossing-over of precision and recall, or to calculate the F-measure.

F-measure (van Rijsbergen, 1979) is defined as the weighted harmonic mean of precision and recall:

$$F_\alpha = \frac{PR}{(1 - \alpha)P + \alpha R} \qquad (6.7)$$

α is a parameter that allows to vary the relative importance of recall versus precision (a high *alpha* means that precision is more important and vice versa). The F-measure is most commonly used with $\alpha = 0.5$:

$$F_{0.5} = \frac{2PR}{P + R} \qquad (6.8)$$

The maximum value of $F_{0.5}$-measure (or F-measure for short) for a system is a good indication of the best compromise between precision and recall.

TREC also uses precision at a certain document rank (cut-off; e.g., P(r = 200) is the precision at rank 200, i.e., after the top 200 documents are considered), and precision at a certain level of recall (example: P(R = 0.2) is the precision at that point when a recall of 0.2 has been reached).

All these measures, however, assume that we can always determine recall exactly, but this is not so.

3.1.3   The recall problem.   The IR recall problem concerns the impossibility of collecting exhaustive relevance judgements in a realistically large document set. In order to be absolutely sure that no potentially relevant documents have been missed when making relevance judgements, judges would have to go through the entire document set of nearly a million documents, which is infeasible (for each individual query, it would take an estimated 6,500 hours to judge all documents in the TREC collection – and this would be at an unrealistically high speed of only 30 seconds per document). Therefore, methods are desirable which can determine a smaller set of documents to be judged manually in such a way that it is unlikely that other relevant documents exist outside this set. *Pooling* (van Rijsbergen and Sparck Jones, 1976) is one such method: the document pool to be manually judged is constructed by putting together the top N retrieval results from a set of n systems (in TREC $N = 100$). Humans judge all the documents in the pool, and documents outside the pool are automatically considered to be irrelevant. Pooling works best if the systems used are maximally different, and if many systems are available, as is

the case in TREC. It was also found that there is a large increase in pool quality if humans additionally do manual recall-oriented searches, using an IR system and the best queries they can think of, e.g., involving synonyms. Fortunately, there is considerable overlap in returned documents: the pool is smaller than the theoretical maximum of $N \cdot n$ systems (around one-third the maximum size).

3.1.4 **11-point average precision.** Another dimension of difficulty becomes apparent when we consider IR measures which can average over more than one query. The problem is that queries can have different numbers of relevant documents and that it is not possible to set a fixed threshold such that systems can achieve the theoretically possible maximal values under all conditions. For instance, for any query with more than 10 relevant documents, full recall could by definition never be achieved if the cut-off were set at 10 documents; for any query with less than 10 relevant documents, full precision could never be reached. Thus, more complicated joint measures are required.

11-point average precision is one of these, defined as:

$$P_{11} = \frac{1}{11} \sum_{j=0}^{10} \frac{1}{N} \sum_{i=1}^{N} \tilde{P}_i(r_j) \qquad (6.9)$$

with $\tilde{P}_i(r_j)$ being the precision (interpolated or measured) at the jth recall point for the ith query (out of N queries). $r_0, r_1, ...r_{10}$ are the 11 standard recall points ($r_j = \frac{j}{10}$). The precision we can *measure* is $P_i(R = r)$: the precision at the point where recall has first reached r. The reason why the $\tilde{P}_i(r_j)$ often has to be interpolated is that the measured recall points r do not in general fall onto a standard recall point (only when $r = \frac{j}{10}$)). There are many interpolation methods such as the following one:

$$\tilde{P}_i(r_j) = \begin{cases} max(r_j \leq r < r_{j+1})P_i(R = r) & \text{if such } r \text{ exists} \\ \tilde{P}_i(r_{j+1}) & \text{otherwise} \end{cases} \qquad (6.10)$$

Note that with interpolation it does not matter that the two queries have different numbers of relevant queries (and that the last relevant document occurs at different ranks): we still get exactly 11 precision – recall points per query, as required. The final calculation is the average of all $\tilde{P}_i(r_j)$ (1.00, 1.00, 1.00, 0.84, 0.67, 0.59, 0.59, 0.30, 0.23, 0.23) over 11, resulting in a $\tilde{P}_{11}$ of 0.61.

In Figure 10, $\tilde{P}_i(r_j)$ values have been interpolated, and $P_i(R = r)$ values have been exactly measured. Figure 11 gives the precision – recall curve for

$P_1(r_i)$ $P_2(r_i)$

Query 1				$P_1(r_i)$ values		$P_2(r_i)$ values		Query 2		
#		R		$\tilde{P}_1(r_0)=1.0$ → **1.0**	← $\tilde{P}_2(r_0)=1.0$					
				$\tilde{P}_1(r_1)=1.0$ → **1.0**	← $\tilde{P}_2(r_1)=1.0$					
1	X	.2		$P_1(R=.2)=1.0$ → **1.0**	← $\tilde{P}_2(r_2)=1.0$			Query 2		
2				$\tilde{P}_1(r_3)=.67$ → **.84**	← $\tilde{P}_2(r_3)=1.0$			R		#
3	X	.4		$P_1(R=.4)=.67$ → **.67**				.33	X	1
4										2
5				$\tilde{P}_1(r_5)=.5$ → **.59**	$\tilde{P}_2(r_4)=.67$			.67	X	3
6	X	.6		$P_1(R=.6)=.5$ → **.59**	← $\tilde{P}_2(r_5)=.67$					4
7					$\tilde{P}_2(r_6)=.67$					5
8										6
9				$\tilde{P}_1(r_7)=.4$ → **.30**	← $\tilde{P}_2(r_7)=.2$					7
10	X	.8		$P_1(R=.8)=.4$ → **.30**	← $\tilde{P}_2(r_8)=.2$					8
11										9
12										10
13										11
14				$\tilde{P}_1(r_9)=.25$ → **.23**	← $\tilde{P}_2(r_9)=.2$					12
15										13
16										14
17				**.23**	← $P_2(R=1)=.2$				X	15
18										
19										
20	X	1		$P_1(R=1)=.25$ → **.61**						

Figure 10. Example calculation: 11-point average precision, for two queries.

this example (bold circles for measured data points; thin circles for interpolated data points; dark for Query 1; light for Query 2).

3.1.5 Mean average precision (MAP).

There is a second, simpler composite measurement which generalises over different queries, called *Mean Average Precision* (MAP), which is sometimes also referred to as *mean precision at seen relevant documents*. Precision is calculated at each point when a new relevant document is retrieved (using P = 0 for each relevant document that was not retrieved). The average is then determined for each query. Finally, an average over all queries is calculated.

$$MAP = \frac{1}{N} \sum_{j=1}^{N} \frac{1}{Q_j} \sum_{i=1}^{Q_j} P(rel=i) \tag{6.11}$$

with Q_j being the number of relevant documents for query j; N the number of queries, and $P(rel=i)$ the precision at ith relevant document.

Again, an example MAP calculation for the two queries in Figure 10 would return 5 data points for Query 1: 1.00 (at rank 1), 0.67 (at rank 3), 0.5 (at rank 6), 0.4 (at rank 10), and 0.25 (at rank 20), averaging to 0.564 for Query 1; and 3 data points for Query 2: 1.0 at rank 1, 0.67 at rank 3, and 0.2 at rank 15, averaging to 0.623 for Query 2. This results in an overall MAP of $\frac{0.564+0.623}{2} = 0.594$.

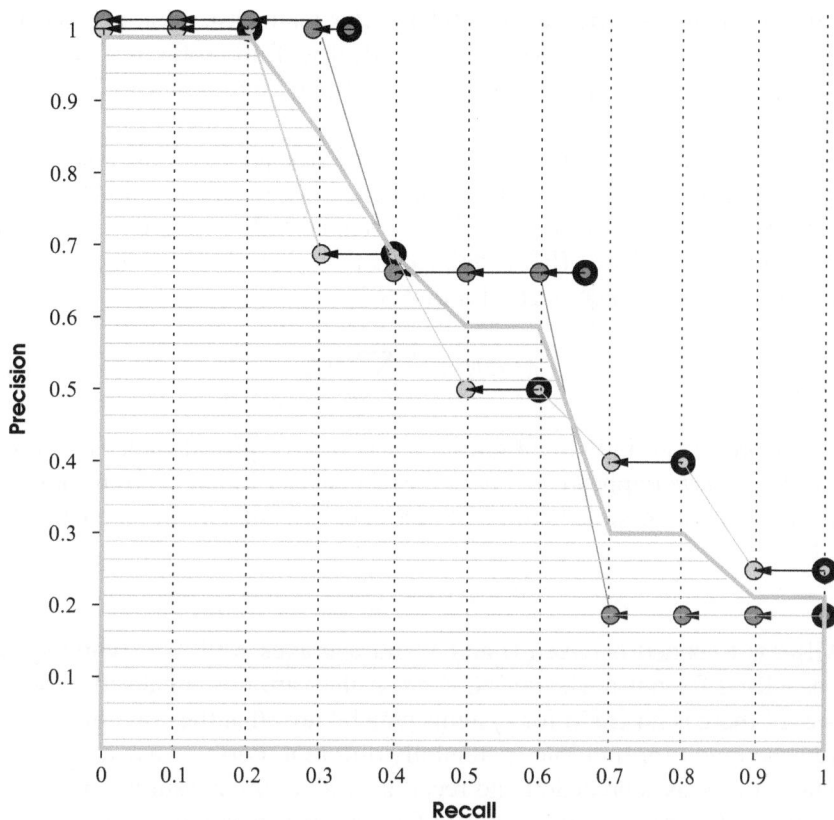

Figure 11. Precision – recall curve for the example calculation.

Mean precision at seen relevant documents favours systems which return relevant documents *fast*; it is therefore precision-biased. TREC publishes many composite precision/recall-based performance measures per run because in order to gain insight into what the system is doing overall, it is necessary to look at more than one metric. TREC has been criticised for putting too much emphasis on recall, given that most of today's IR requirements are precision-based and given that recall-oriented test collection preparation is very time- intensive (see above). This is one of the reasons why many researchers prefer mean precision over 11-point average precision as an overall summary IR measure.

3.2 Evaluation Metrics in QA

There has been experimentation in TREC with three different evaluation metrics: mean reciprocal rank (MRR), weighted confidence, and average accuracy. Average accuracy is the simplest evaluation metric and has been the official evaluation metric since 2003 for the main task. For list questions, precision and recall had to be adapted to deal with the difficulty of different numbers of return items for different list questions. Additionally, NIL accuracy is calculated.

In the case of MRR, each system returned five answers, in rank of confidence of their correctness, for each question. It was decided to look at the top five answers only, as the task is precision-oriented and lower ranks are assumed not to be of interest. The MRR is defined as the mean of the inverse rank of the first correct answer, taken over all n questions:

$$MRR = \frac{1}{n} \sum_{i=1}^{n} RR_i \qquad (6.12)$$

The score for an individual question i is the reciprocal rank r_i where the first correct answer appeared (0 if no correct answer in top five returns). Thus, there are only six possible reciprocal ranks per question: 0, 0.2, 0.25, 0.33, 0.5, and 1.

$$RR_i = \frac{1}{r_i} \qquad (6.13)$$

MRR is bounded between 0 and 1 and averages well, and while systems are penalised for not retrieving an answer, they are not penalised unduly so. However, there is no credit for systems which know that they do not know, and there is no credit for multiple (potentially different) correct answers.

The list task uses precision and recall as evaluation measures. The instance precision (IP) and instance recall (IR) for a list question can be computed from the final answer list and the assessor's judgement. Let S be the size of the final answer list (i.e., the number of known answers), D the number of correct, distinct responses returned by the system, and N the total number of responses returned by the system. Then $IP = \frac{D}{N}$ and $IR = \frac{D}{S}$. Precision and recall were then combined using the F-measure with equal weight given to recall and precision ($F = \frac{2*IP*IR}{IP+IR}$), and the average F-score over all list questions is reported.

In TREC-11, the evaluation metric was changed to *confidence-weighted score*, designed to reward systems for their confidence in their answers, and only one answer per question was returned. Within the submission file, systems had to rank their answers to the 500 questions according to their confidence in that answer, with the answer they were most confident with ranked highest in the file. Confidence-weighted score is defined as $\frac{1}{Q} \sum_{1}^{Q} \frac{\text{\# correct in first } i}{i}$ (Q being the number of questions). With this measurement, it is possible for two systems with the same answer strings for every question to score considerably differently, if the answers are ranked (confidence scored) differently.

In TREC-12, evaluation was changed once more (Voorhees, 2003). The new main evaluation score for a passages task run is surprisingly simple:

accuracy, the fraction of questions judged correct (with one answer per question). In comparison to MRR, this measure assumes that the user is only really interested in the first answer, which must be correct for any score to be given to that question.

Also reported are the recall and precision of recognising when no answer exists in the document collection (called NIL recall and NIL precision). Precision of recognising no answer is the ratio of the number of times NIL was returned and correct to the number of times it was returned; recall is the ratio of the number of times NIL was returned and correct to the number of times it was correct.

3.3 Scalability and Stability of the Measures

In the early days of IR, there was little concern about scalability of IR performance, and thus small document collections and small numbers of queries were generally accepted (cf. the Cranfield 2 experiments which operated on only 1400 documents, albeit with 279 queries; Cleverdon:67). As discussed above, the current consensus is that a large number of queries (as well as a large document collection) is necessary in order to capture user variation, to support claims of statistical significance in results, and to demonstrate (for commercial credibility) that performance levels and differences hold as document collection sizes grow. There are practical difficulties in obtaining large document collections, which is why the current TREC collection is not a balanced corpus: it contains those newspapers which were easy to incorporate for unrelated reasons, e.g., because they operated without copyright restrictions. This is acceptable for the experiment, but ideally, one would wish for a balanced corpus (reflecting all types of texts typically encountered by humans in their daily life). Additionally, the cost of collecting large amounts of queries and relevance judgements is very high. But over the years, the TREC collection has proved to be an extremely valuable and frequently used collection for the IR community, supporting many experiments since it became available.

There have also been experiments to test the effect of IR ad hoc query size (long, medium, short queries). The best results are achieved for long queries, for which the systems were clearly optimised; all performed worse for shorter, more realistic queries. This showed that, not surprisingly, automatic query expansion in systems deployed today is not perfect yet (the additional information in the long queries lists additional relevance conditions). In QA, this is correlated to the difference in performance between factoid questions (which systems are generally better at) and definition questions (which are harder to do, and which are also harder to evaluate).

Scalability also concerns the number of participants. The fact that TREC has many participants is important for two practical reasons: firstly, the quality of the document pool in pooling is dependent on the number of systems, particularly those using different technologies. Secondly, one needs a reasonable number of systems (i.e., data points) to prove stability of the evaluation (inter-annotator agreement), because correlation measures between results by different judges (such as Kendall's tau) require a reasonable number of data points to be statistically significant.

Voorhees (2002) found that the comparative effectiveness of different retrieval methods is stable in the face of changes to the relevance judgements. This means that even though TREC annotators show relatively low agreement in their relevance judgements, and even though, as a result, the numerical performance measures of a system (e.g., MAP) differ considerably when relevance judgements by a different annotator are used, the *ranks* given to systems according to different annotators did not substantially differ (Kendall's tau was over 0.9). Voorhees' results show that no interaction occurs (no annotator's relevance decision favours any system over any other). This property is called *stability* of judgements. This is a very positive result for TREC evaluations, where the relative ranking of systems matters more than any absolute system results, and where there are many systems such that the rank vector is large enough to be meaningful. However, it is worth keeping in mind that the subjectivity of relevance judgements remains a problem – if we wanted to make statements about the absolute results of competing systems (and absolute differences between them), current TREC judgements are not stable enough to support these.

Results about stability in QA are similar: Low inter-assessor agreement on question correctness meant that absolute MRRs were not stable, but *relative* MRRs (i.e., their ranks) were (Voorhees and Tice, 2000). Voorhees (2002) showed that relative confidence-weighted score is stable at Kendall's tau of above 0.9, but definition questions are not stable. Concerning assessor disagreement, the TREC-QA organisers decided that it was not only impossible to force agreement among TREC assessors, but also undesirable because it would not address the problem of measuring success rate of deployed systems.

4   Real-World Performance

4.1   TREC Ad Hoc IR

Sparck Jones (1995, 2000) provides insightful detailed summaries of the results of TRECs over the years. The most important lessons from these observations can be summarised as follows: of those systems which performed fully automatic searches in TREC-7 and TREC-8 (the last two "ad hoc" TREC conferences in 1997 and 1998), the best results were in the range of 0.40–0.45 (in terms of precision at document cut-off 30). These systems mostly achieve these results only when using long queries and narratives, but one team in TREC-7 managed results in the 0.40–0.45 range even for the short queries.

All systems performed worse for shorter queries. Generally, the best systems are statistically not significantly different, which points to the fact that an apparent plateau has been reached (at least if measured with the current, stringent and gold standard – based evaluation). Manual searches resulted in best results in the range of 0.55–0.60. Comparison of the TREC results over the years shows that the 0.40–0.45 result achieved in TREC-7 and TREC-8 was the highest fully automatic IR result ever measured for short and medium-length queries (apart from one occurrence at TREC-4). TREC-3 was exceptional in that its highest automatic results were in the 0.55–0.60 range – however, this was achieved only for long queries. At cut-off 10, several systems achieved almost 50% precision in automatic searching even with very short queries, and several exceeded 50% with the medium-length queries. (Manual searching under these conditions can lead to 70%, but with additional time and effort required.) Performance in the "middle" TRECs (4, 5, and 6) declined under much less favourable data conditions (less relevant documents available, less information on topics given). The better performance in TREC-7 and TREC-8 must be attributed to superior systems, as the manual performance has remained on a plateau.

4.2   TREC QA

Results of the top-scoring systems in the early TRECs are: 0.66 (27% questions unanswered) for TREC-8, 0.58 for TREC-9, 0.68 for TREC-10 (for 50 bytes); for the 250 bytes the results were 0.65% in TREC-8 and 0.75% in TREC-9. Interestingly, in 55% of cases where the answer was found in the first five answers, this answer was in rank 1 (TREC-9, average over all systems). This was part of the reason of the TREC-QA organisers for moving to evaluation metrics, which consider only one answer per question.

The highest scores for the TREC-11 factoid task (confidence-weighted score) were 0.86, 0.69, and 0.61, for the list task the results were 0.65, 0.15, and 0.11. For the TREC-12 list task the numbers were 0.396, 0.319, and 0.134 (all in average F-scores). The list task can therefore be seen as a task which is much harder than the factoid task.

Highest scorers for the TREC-12 passage task achieved 0.685 accuracy (with the second best system at 0.419), whereas the highest entry in the exact (factoid) main task was as high as 0.700 (with the second best system at 0.622).

5   Conclusion

Numerically, the results for TREC-QA are consistently higher than those for adhoc IR. While the evaluation measures are not directly comparable, we can still observe that the best systems in QA are close to the maximal possible value, but the best systems in IR, a much maturer field, are relatively poor compared to the maximal value. This could be a side effect of the evaluation design, as well as an indication that QA is somehow a "simpler" (or better-defined) task than IR, due to IR's problems with relevance. In TREC-QA system output is not compared against a fixed gold standard; instead judges assess the actual system output. In this setting, humans are well-known to be more lenient judging something that is suggested as correct than choosing answers/documents for a fixed gold standard. Thus, it is possible that gold standard–based evaluations are inherently harsher.

In summary, ad hoc IR evaluation as done by TREC only covers one small part of the spectrum of IR evaluations, using laboratory conditions, precision and recall measured from large, fixed test collections. Real users in natural interaction with their IR system are not involved. A host of sophisticated performance metrics is available, e.g., 11-point average precision and mean average precision. There is a theoretical problem with the subjectivity of relevance, but it turns out that this problem is partially solvable by extensive sampling (cf. Section 2.1). There is also a recall problem, but it too is solvable, by pooling (cf. Section 3.1.3). The evaluation methodology used is provably stable towards human judgement differences. Thus, we can consider IR evaluation as mature. However, one of the big problems is the high cost of these evaluations, in terms of preparing collections and relevance judgements. There is current research into how this cost could be reduced. For instance, one could interpret the observable actions of Internet users as implicit relevance decisions: how long is a document looked at after search; is it saved; which action follows? These actions, however, are psychologically and practically very complex and not very well researched at this point.

Over the years and across systems, TREC performance in ad hoc retrieval has reached a plateau, possibly quite close to the best performance currently reachable with word-based statistical methods. Thus, interest in ad hoc IR has waned, and recently, new and related IR tasks have been tested in TREC "tracks" (such as filtering and web-based retrieval) – these new tasks are harder, but more realistic, and some of them require new evaluation measures. Future developments could concern evaluation metrics that mirror user satisfaction in a dynamic IR set-up – where the definition of the task, the information need, and even the collection are changing during a run, where extremely large-scale document collections are used, and where success and failure of personalised searches are evaluated.

QA, on the other hand, is a task that has only appeared in the last 5 years but that has been the object of a major evaluation effort in the framework of TREC. The main evaluation metrics changed from mean reciprocal rank, via a weighted confidence measure, to simple accuracy of answer return on a single answer, which is currently considered as fully appropriate to assess system performance for this task. Answers are individually judged, rather than compared to a gold standard. There has been an enormous human effort in question creation and answer judgement.

The questions used in current TREC-QA are factual and simple, and there has been some debate about whether the field is ready to move to harder tasks. Undoubtedly, Deep Natural Language Processing (NLP) (e.g., comparison on the basis of logical form) helps for QA: those systems which use deeper processing (Harabagiu et al., 2003) consistently performed very well in all TREC-QAs. However, there have been competitor systems which use very little deep processing, and which rely on heuristics and redundant data on the web instead. While they could not rival the NLP-based systems, they nevertheless performed in mid-field, which was seen as a surprising success, given the very short development time when compared to the years of effort going into "deeper" systems. However, this also brought up questions about the goal of QA evaluation in general. Is the aim of QA evaluation to measure performance of the mundane task of answering simple, factual questions? Then today's QA systems have (almost) reached that goal; once redundancy/data-based systems can perform this task as well as deep NLP systems, a plateau will be reached. If, however, the aim of the QA task is to act as a diagnostic tool for how far the field has advanced in the overall goal of "intelligent" text understanding, the task may have to be made much harder, for instance, by using harder question types and requiring more detailed reasoning behind the answers.

However, overall the evaluation of QA can be considered a task which has managed to find its defining coordinates in a short time. The evaluation has constantly been adjusted, following system developments and factors which could not be known beforehand. In only 5 years of evolution, a satisfactory solution has been found, leading to a generally accepted evaluation methodology. The history of QA evaluation also shows how research in a certain direction can be fostered by directly manipulating the evaluation rules and metrics to encourage desirable properties of systems.

References

Callan, J. P. (1994). Passage-Level Evidence in Document Retrieval. In *Proceedings of the Annual International Conference on Research and Development in Information Retrieval (SIGIR)*, pages 302–310, Dublin, Ireland.

CLEF (2005). Cross Language Evaluation Framework, http://www.clef-campaign.org/.

Cleverdon, C. W. (1967). The Cranfield Tests on Index Language Devices. *Aslib Proceedings*, 19(6):173–194.

Harabagiu, S., Moldovan, D., Clark, C., Bowden, M., Williams, J., and Bensley, J. (2003). Answer Mining by Combining Extraction Techniques with Abductive Reasoning. In Voorhees, E. M. and Buckland, L. P., editors,

Proceedings of the Twelfth Text REtrieval Conference (TREC-12), pages 375–382, Department of Commerce, National Institute of Standards and Technology.

Harman, D. (1993). The First Text REtrieval Conference (TREC-1). *Information Processing and Management*, 29(4):411–414.

NTCIR (2005). NII Test Collection for IR Systems, http://research.nii.ac.jp/ntcir/.

Saracevic, T., Kantor, P. B., Chamis, M. A. Y., and Trivison, D. (1988). A Study of Information Seeking and Retrieving. Parts I–III. *Journal of the American Society for Information Science*, 39(3):161–216.

Sparck Jones, K. (1995). Reflections on TREC. *Information Processing and Management*, 31(3):291–314.

Sparck Jones, K. (2000). Further Reflections on TREC. *Information Processing and Management*, 36(1):37–85.

Sparck Jones, K. and Galliers, J. (1995). *Evaluating Natural Language Processing Systems*. Springer Verlag, Berlin, Heidelberg, Germany.

TREC (2004). The Text REtrieval Conference, official website, http:// trec.nist.gov/.

TREC-QA (2004). The Text REtrieval Conference, Question Answering Track, http://trec.nist.gov/data/qa.html.

van Rijsbergen, C. J. (1979). *Information Retrieval*. Butterworth, London, UK, 2nd edition.

van Rijsbergen, C. J. and Sparck Jones, K. (1976). Information Retrieval Test Collections. *Journal of Documentation*, 32:59–75.

Voorhees, E. (2000). Variations in Relevance Judgements and the Measurement of Retrieval Effectiveness. *Information Processing and Management*, 36:697–716.

Voorhees, E. (2002). Overview of the TREC 2002 Question Answering Track. In Voorhees, E. M. and Buckland, L. P., editors, *Proceedings of the Eleventh Text REtrieval Conference (TREC)*, Department of Commerce, National Institute of Standards and Technology.

Voorhees, E. (2003). Overview of the TREC 2003 Question Answering Track. In Voorhees, E. M. and Buckland, L. P., editors, *Proceedings of the Twelfth Text REtrieval Conference (TREC)*, pages 54–68, Department of Commerce, National Institute of Standards and Technology.

Voorhees, E. and Tice, D. (2000). Building a Question Answering Test Collection. In *Proceedings of the Annual International Conference on Research and Development in Information Retrieval (SIGIR)*, pages 200–207, Athens, Greece.

Chapter 7

SPOKEN DIALOGUE SYSTEMS EVALUATION

Niels Ole Bernsen, Laila Dybkjær

Natural Interactive Systems Laboratory
Odense, Denmark

nob@nis.sdu.dk, laila@nis.sdu.dk

Wolfgang Minker

Department of Information Technology
University of Ulm, Germany

wolfgang.minker@uni-ulm.de

Abstract   This chapter first provides a brief introduction to evaluation methods and criteria and then presents two very different spoken dialogue research prototype systems and their evaluation. The first prototype is the non-task-oriented, multimodal Hans Christian Andersen (HCA) system for edutainment, the second prototype is the task-oriented, multimodal SENECA onboard system in the car. The systems were tested with representative users in the laboratory and in the field, respectively. For both systems we describe rationale for the chosen evaluation method, evaluation process, evaluation criteria, and evaluation results.

Keywords   Evaluation; Spoken dialogue systems; Methods; Criteria.

1   Introduction

Evaluation is an important part of the software life cycle and is interwoven with development in complex ways. Its function is to provide iterative feedback on the quality of each system component, as well as of the entire system throughout the development process. Evaluation is crucial to ensure, e.g., system correctness, appropriateness, and adequacy.

For spoken dialogue systems (SDSs) and their components and aspects, including speech recognition, natural language understanding, dialogue

L. Dybkjær et al. (eds.), Evaluation of Text and Speech Systems, 187–219.

management, response generation, speech synthesis, system integration, and human factors, there has been extensive work on evaluation as documented in, e.g., the EAGLES guidelines (Gibbon et al., 1997) and the DISC Best Practice Guide (http://www.disc2.dk), both of which provide useful information on technical and usability evaluation, and in the US DARPA Communicator project, which used the (Paradigm for Dialogue System Evaluation) PARADISE framework (Walker et al., 1997) for usability evaluation, see (Dybkjær et al., 2004) for an overview.

However, the SDSs field is rapidly developing in new directions. Task-oriented unimodal systems are becoming increasingly sophisticated and are now often used in mobile environments. Multimodal task-oriented SDSs have become popular, not least in research. Mobile multimodal aspects will be illustrated in Section 4. A new breed of non-task-oriented SDSs is emerging. A multimodal example is the conversational Hans Christian Andersen (HCA) system to be discussed in Section 3. These developments continue to pose new challenges to research into the evaluation of SDSs.

The aim of this chapter is to give the reader some insight into the evaluation of SDSs, which have the challenging characteristics just mentioned. Through presentation of two concrete and very different examples, we try to demonstrate how advanced SDSs could be evaluated in practice and explain what the considerations behind the selection of evaluation methods and criteria have been. Before presenting the examples, we discuss evaluation methods and criteria in order to provide a frame of reference for what follows (Section 2). The first example (Section 3) is from progress evaluation of a non-task-oriented, multimodal SDS for edutainment for use in a stationary environment. The second example (Section 4) is an evaluation of a task-oriented multimodal on-board system in the car. In presenting these examples, our aim is not to give a complete overview of existing evaluation methods and criteria for SDSs but, rather, to focus on actual evaluation practice in research prototyping. Section 5 concludes the chapter.

2   Evaluation Methods and Criteria

According to development best practice, evaluation should be done throughout the software life-cycle. A broad selection of evaluation methods is available. These methods are general and can be used largely independently of whether the SDS is unimodal or multimodal, task-oriented or non-task-oriented, for mobile or non-mobile use, etc. Some methods are mainly applied in particular life cycle phases while others are used throughout. In all cases some model of the system is required. By a system model we understand the current version of the evolving system no matter if it only exists as hand-made drawings or scribbles, is fully implemented, or is anything in between.

2.1   Some Terminology

Before describing some frequently used evaluation methods we present some central terms related to evaluation. *Technical evaluation* concerns technical properties of the entire system, as well as of each of its components. Technical evaluation should be done by developers or by a professional evaluation team through *objective evaluation*, i.e., evaluation, which is as far as possible independent of the personal opinions of the evaluators.

Usability evaluation of a system very often involves representative users. To some extent, the evaluation team may draw upon objective evaluation metrics but a substantial part of usability evaluation is done via *subjective evaluation*, i.e., by judging some property of a system or, less frequently, component, by reference to users' personal opinions.

We are aware that some people consider the term "objective evaluation" imprecise because there is always a human in the loop and therefore one might claim that there is always some amount of subjectivity involved in the evaluation even if only in the choice of the quantitative metrics (not) to apply. Nevertheless, we prefer the term objective to other terms, such as "expert evaluation" or "instrumental evaluation". These terms are more precise but also more narrow which means that we would need several terms to cover what we mean by objective evaluation. For similar reasons, we shall use the term usability evaluation rather than, e.g., "user oriented evaluation". Usability evaluation may be narrow and, e.g., concern only the naturalness of the speech synthesis, or it may be broad and concern many different aspects of the overall system as measured both objectively and subjectively. Usability evaluation need not involve test users but may be done by usability experts, cf. below.

Objective, as well as subjective evaluation can be both quantitative and qualitative. *Quantitative evaluation*, when objective, consists in counting something and producing a meaningful number, percentage, etc. In subjective quantitative evaluation, there are at least two possibilities: non-expert personal opinions are expressed as quantitative scores of some kind, or such opinions are expressed as numbers or percentages, e.g., regarding the perceived number of times the user requested help. *Qualitative evaluation* consists in estimating or judging some property by reference to expert standards and rules or to one's personal opinion.

2.2   Evaluation Methods

When constructing software there is a number of software tests one may consider to use to ensure that the software actually runs robustly and has the specified functionality. The list of such test methods is long and we don't have space to go into details, so we just briefly describe a few frequently used methods, including unit test, integration test, and function tests in terms of blackbox and glassbox. A *unit test* is applied to a, typically small, system component called a unit, and is written and carried out by the code developers. It is based on test suites, which may be prepared even before the code is written. The test suites are meant to be run again and again (regression test) as the code develops in order to check the functionality of the unit. An *integration test* is a test of whether two or more modules actually work together when integrated. The purpose of a *function test* is to systematically test if system functions work. It is normally carried out on an integrated system, which may be the entire system or some large module, e.g., a natural language understanding module. While a *glassbox test* focuses on the code and tests the internal logic of the system, a *blackbox test* focuses on the system's input/output behaviour to see if it is in accordance with specifications and descriptions in manuals. The code itself is not considered but is viewed as a black box.

All methods just mentioned are closely related to the code development process. Assuming an iterative life-cycle model, their primary use is therefore in the construction phase, and they mainly help evaluate certain technical aspects. There is another set of evaluation methods, which focus on interaction and, which are mainly applicable to other life-cycle phases. There are also many of these. Figure 1 shows some of the most frequently used methods, cf. (Bernsen and Dybkjær, 2007). Data collected with these methods may serve both as a basis for technical evaluation and for usability evaluation.

The methods in Figure 1 apart from walkthrough and guideline-based evaluation – typically involve representative users. Most evaluations with representative users are carried out in the lab and are often *controlled tests* in the sense that users are given precise tasks (scenarios) to carry out. Lab tests with users have much in common as regards how they are prepared and run, no matter which method is used and which development stage the system model is at.

To ensure data reliability, it is important that the users involved in an evaluation are representative of the target user group and that they jointly represent the diversity of properties characterising the target group.

Development stage	Early	Middle	Late
Evaluation methods	Walkthrough		
	Low-fidelity prototyping		
	Guideline-based evaluation		
	Wizard of Oz		
	High-fidelity prototyping		
			Field test
	Think-aloud		
	Interview		
	Questionnaire		

Figure 1. Frequently used interaction evaluation methods.

Low-fidelity prototypes (or *mock-ups*) and *walkthroughs* are mainly used early in the life cycle. These methods only require some preliminary model of the evolving system, such as a paper sketch (mock-up) or a dialogue model graph. Their results provide early input on, e.g., missing system functionality and interaction design problems. While prototype evaluation normally involves users, walkthroughs are often carried out by the development team.

Guideline-based evaluation is mainly used in the early life-cycle phases. Guideline-based evaluation does not require user involvement but does require a system model and a set of guidelines. Some weaknesses of guideline-based evaluation are that detailed and reliable sets of guidelines often do not exist (yet), especially for advanced types of system, multimodal or otherwise, and that focus during guideline application tends to be narrowly fixed on what the guidelines recommend. On the other hand, reliable guidelines reflect good practice and, if available, it makes good sense to try to follow them. Guideline-based evaluation is done by a person, often from the development team, who is able to apply the guidelines. There is a related method called *expert evaluation*, which is carried out by an (external) expert who is familiar with existing practice for the task or domain in question. *Heuristic evaluation* is sometimes taken to mean guideline-based evaluation and is sometimes used synonymously with expert evaluation.

Wizard-of-Oz simulation in which one or more persons act as the system in interaction with users, is useful primarily when a near-complete design of (central parts of) the system model is available to serve as basis for simulation. The method can provide very detailed feedback on the designed functionality and usability. As long as the system as a whole or part(s) of it has not been implemented, design revisions can be made without code (re-)writing.

A *high-fidelity prototype* is a prototype, which has an interface similar to that of the planned final system. High-fidelity prototypes can be used throughout the life cycle since there need not be much functionality behind the interface before the prototype can be used to generate useful information for the development team by letting users interact with it. High-fidelity prototypes are often used in controlled lab tests, i.e., in a controlled environment with invited users who often follow scenarios. In a *field test*, users are not controlled but use the system in, or from, their own environment, e.g., their office, whenever it suits them. A field test is typically used towards the end of development when the system is close to being finalised. It serves to reveal errors and weaknesses that were not detected in previous tests.

The *think-aloud method* is often used in combination with a controlled lab test based on some prototype (low or high-fidelity) with which users interact while they try to phrase their thoughts. Think-aloud may reveal where users have problems due to inadequate interface design.

Questionnaires and *interviews* are often used before and/or after users interact with some model of the system, i.e., questionnaires and interviews may accompany or complement use of any of the above methods involving users. While interviews may capture the users' immediate reactions to a system, questionnaires leave time for the users to organise their thoughts and think about how to express them. Interviews are more time-consuming to use because they require the presence of an interviewer and some post-processing of interview notes. Questionnaires may be made electronically available to minimize the post-processing.

All evaluation methods generate data, which may be captured and used for later analysis and evaluation. Depending on the nature of the data collected, this data may serve as basis for technical evaluation, usability evaluation, or both.

2.3   Evaluation Criteria

Evaluation criteria concerning technical, as well as usability aspects may be established and applied to the collected data with various purposes in mind, such as evaluation of system quality and conformance to specifications, comparison of the system with other systems, or evaluation of progress during system development. The difficult question is exactly which evaluation criteria to apply at any point, not least when it comes to usability evaluation. For instance, in most cases it may be rather straightforward to evaluate efficiency of interaction by measuring time to task completion but, as regards, e.g., user satisfaction there is no simple quantitative measure to rely on.

Technical evaluation, on the other hand, is well developed for several aspects of SDSs and their components. For instance, there is broad agreement on key evaluation criteria for some basic qualities of speech recognisers. These criteria include, e.g., word and sentence error rate, vocabulary coverage, perplexity, and real-time performance, cf., e.g., the DISC dialogue engineering model at http://www.disc2.dk/slds/.

There are ongoing standardisation efforts. For example, the International Telecommunication Union ITU-T SG12 (Study Group 12 on performance and quality of service, http://www.itu.int/ITU-T/studygroups/com12/index.asp) has issued recommendations on how to evaluate spoken dialogue systems and some of their components, cf. ITU-T Rec. P.85 and P.851, and the National Institute of Standards and Technology (NIST) develops evaluation protocols and benchmark tests (http://www.itl.nist.gov/iad/894.01/).

Standards facilitate use of a common set of evaluation criteria or, rather, perhaps, some subset of common criteria, in each specific case. Technical sophistication differs dramatically among unimodal, as well as multimodal SDSs, which means that the same set of evaluation criteria cannot be applied to all.

From the point of view of usability, system differences include, e.g., the fact that the skills and preferences of the target users differ widely from one system to another. This and other parameters, such as application type, task, domain, and use environment, must be taken into account when designing for, and evaluating, usability no matter the technical sophistication of the system.

As experience is being gathered on technical solutions for spoken multimodal systems, it seems that a major part of the focus in research is currently on how to evaluate the usability of these systems, cf., e.g., (Minker et al., 2005a). One reason may be that there are more unknown usability factors than technical factors involved; another, that the novel usability and qualitative evaluation issues raised by this kind of systems are being addressed at an earlier stage than the majority of novel quantitative and technical issues.

3 Evaluation of the NICE Hans Christian Andersen Prototype

Our first evaluation example is the first research prototype of a multimodal non-task-oriented SDS, the NICE Hans Christian Andersen (HCA) SDS, which was developed as part of the European Human Language Technologies NICE project (2002–2005) on Natural Interactive Communication for Edutainment. The evaluated prototype was the first of two prototypes, which we shall call PT1 and PT2, respectively. We first briefly describe the system and then present our evaluation of PT1. Although we describe the actual test set-up, focus in what follows is not on evaluation *process* but on the *methods and criteria*, which were applied, as well as on the test *results* achieved.

3.1 Description of the First HCA Prototype

The main goal of the HCA system is to enable edutaining conversation with 10 to 18 year-old children and teenagers in museums and other public locations. There, users from many different countries are expected to have non-task-oriented conversation with HCA in English for an average duration of, say, 5–15 minutes. In generic terms, the system is a new kind of computer game, which integrates spoken conversation into a professional computer games environment. The user communicates with HCA using spontaneous speech and 2D pointing gesture. 3D animated, embodied HCA communicates with the user through speech, gesture, facial expression, and body movement. In the first prototype, communication takes the form of limited mixed-initiative spoken conversation.

The event-driven, modular architecture of the system is shown in Figure 2 and described in more detail in (Bernsen et al., 2004a). The speech recogniser is hatched in the figure because it was not integrated in the first prototype.

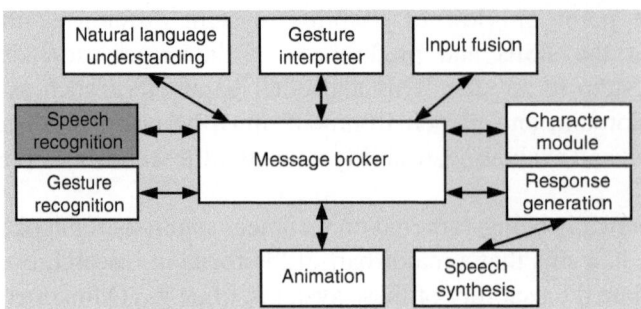

Figure 2.   General HCA system architecture.

While most of the modules are self-explanatory, it may be mentioned that the character module is the system's conversation manager and that the message broker manages XML-format message passing between all system modules.

Norwegian Information Security Laboratory (NISLab) has developed HCA's natural language understanding, character module (Bernsen and Dybkjær, 2004a), and response generation (Corradini et al., 2005) components. The other components shown in Figure 2 have been developed by other project partners or are (based on) freeware (gesture recognition, message broker), or off-the-shelf software (speech synthesis from AT&T). The speech recogniser is the commercial SpeechPearl recogniser from Scansoft (now Nuance) trained on non-native English speech from children. For gesture recognition, gesture interpretation, and input fusion, see (Martin et al., 2006). For animation, see (Corradini et al., 2004). The project partners are: TeliaSonera, Sweden, Liquid Media, Sweden, Scansoft, Belgium, and LIMSI/CNRS, France.

HCA's domains of knowledge and discourse include his fairytales, his childhood in Odense, Denmark, his persona and physical presence in his study, getting information about the user, his role as "gatekeeper" for a fairytale games world developed by project partner TeliaSonera and not described here (Gustafson et al., 2004), and the "meta" domain of resolving miscommunication problems. These domains are probably among those which most users would expect anyway. Users meet HCA in his study (Figure 3), which is a rendering of his actual study on display in Copenhagen, modified so that he can walk around freely and with a pair of doors leading into the fairytale world (not visible in the figure). Pictures relating to HCA's knowledge domains have been hung on the walls. The user may point to them and ask questions about them. HCA can tell stories about the pictures and about other objects in his room, such as his travel bag.

Lacking locomotion autonomy in the first prototype, HCA's locomotion is controlled by the user who is also in control of four different virtual camera angles onto his study. In PT1, the animation engine only allowed HCA to display

Figure 3. HCA gesturing in his study.

one movement at a time, which means that he could, e.g., blink but then could not move his mouth at the same time. Basically, this means that he behaves somewhat rigidly because he is quite far from acting like a human being when speaking.

3.2 Evaluation of the First HCA Prototype

The first integrated HCA prototype (PT1) was tested in January 2004 with 18 users from the target user group of 10 to 18-year-olds. In the user test set-up, the recogniser was replaced by a wizard who typed what the user said. The rest of the system was running. The speech recogniser still needed to be trained on 40–50 hours of speech data recorded with mostly non-native English speaking children.

The test users used the system in two different conditions. In the first 20 minutes condition, they had unconstrained conversation with HCA based only on instructions on how to change the virtual camera angles, control HCA's locomotion, and input speech and gesture. This enabled them to become familiar with the system. In the following, second test condition and after a short break, the users spent 20 minutes trying to solve as many problems as possible from a hand-out list, which included 13 problems, such as "Find out if HCA has a preferred fairytale and what it is" and "Tell HCA about games you like or know". The reason for this dual-condition test protocol was to make sure that, in the second test condition, users would put a strong "initiative pressure" upon the system during conversation due to the fact that the users had an agenda of their own, even if, in the first condition, they might tend to obediently follow HCA's lead during conversation.

Each user was interviewed immediately after the second-condition interaction with HCA. The semi-structured interviews were based on a common set of questions. In total, each session had a duration of 60–70 minutes.

Users arrived in parallel, so there were two test rooms, two wizards doing recogniser simulation, and two interviewers. The wizards were trained transcribers who had also been specifically trained for the PT1 test. In one room, the user had a mouse and a touch screen for gesture input, whereas in the other room only a mouse was available as pointing device. In the room with the touch screen, the user could also watch HCA on a 42" flat-panel screen. An observer was present in this room as well. An experimenter took care of guiding and instructing the users and a technician was around for handling any technical problems arising. Everybody involved had a dedicated, printed instruction sheet to follow. In addition, system developers would come and go discretely, discuss their observations, assist the technician when needed, etc.

As we will not return to this topic below, it may be mentioned here that the different set-ups in the two test rooms did produce interesting differences in user behaviour. While we did not observe any differences related to display size, the availability of the mouse in both set-ups made the users click "like crazy" whilst talking to HCA and tended to alienate them to the touch screen alternative, when available. These effects disappeared completely in the PT2 test in which only touch screens could be used for deictic gesture input (Martin et al., 2006). All interactions with PT1 were logged, audio recorded, and video recorded. In total, approximately 11 hours of interaction were recorded on audio, video, and logfile, respectively. In addition, 18 sets of semi-structured interview notes were collected. This data served as our basis for evaluating PT1 according to criteria, which had been agreed early in the project.

3.2.1   Choice of evaluation method.

The PT1 evaluation addressed a fully implemented system except that the recogniser was not yet hooked up as explained above. Thus, the evaluation method to look for should be one, which is well-suited for the first integration phase of the software life-cycle in which progress evaluation is not possible because there are no previous system versions to compare with; in which we wish to establish if the prototype performs adequately according to development plans; and, not least, in which we want to get input from representative users. We decided on a controlled laboratory test using a high-fidelity prototype bionic Wizard-of-Oz set-up in which a wizard replaced the speech recogniser.

The reason why we chose to evaluate HCA PT1 with target group users in a controlled laboratory setting rather than in the field, is the following. A field test, e.g., in a museum, is much harder to control than a laboratory test. It is difficult or impossible to: instruct users adequately in the field to ensure a strict dual test condition experimental regime, to interview the users, and to video record the users in action with all that this entails in terms of informed consent, permission signatures, and rights to use the recorded data for purposes explicitly agreed upon. When conducting costly testing of a first system prototype, it is critically important to collect data, which is optimised for the purpose of obtaining the interaction information, which is most needed in order to judge how the system performs and is perceived by users. Analysis of this data is crucial to the processes of functional extension, re-specification, and redesign, which are normally planned to follow a first-prototype user test. To ensure full control of the corpus collection process, a controlled laboratory test seemed to be the only viable approach in our case.

3.2.2 Requirements to test users. The test plan established early in the project included a number of requirements to test users of the HCA prototypes. These requirements are listed below followed by a comment on how they were met in the evaluation of PT1.

- Each prototype should be evaluated by at least 12 test users. This was a pragmatic estimate of the minimum number of users we would need to obtain a fair amount of speech data and sufficient data to get a reasonably reliable idea of which improvements to make. PT1 was evaluated with 18 users.

- Age. At least eight users should belong to the primary target group. Since the target environment for the system is museums and the like, there may well be users present who do not belong to our primary target group. We would therefore accept up to one-third of test users not belonging to the primary target group, although we would prefer all users to be children and youngsters to collect as many relevant speech data as possible. All 18 users belonged to the primary target group of 10 to 18-year-olds with an age range of 10–18 years and an average age of 14.3 years.

- Both genders should be represented approximately equally. The test group included nine girls and nine boys.

- User background diversification. The user group shows a good spread in computer game literacy, from zero game hours per week to 20+ hours. All users were schoolchildren. We did not collect data on other diversification factors, such as general computer literacy or experience with educational computer programs.

- Language background diversification. The reason for this requirement is that the system is aimed for use in museums, which attract an English-speaking audience from across the world. Only a single user, an 18-year-old Scotsman, was not Danish and had English, the language of conversation with HCA, as first language. However, a large-scale (approximately 500 users) Wizard-of-Oz study conducted in the field in the summer of 2003 at the HCA Museum included users of 29 different nationalities (Bernsen et al., 2004b). Thus we felt that we already had voluminous data on the differential behaviour in conversation of users with different nationalities and first languages.

3.2.3   Technical evaluation criteria.   A set of technical evaluation criteria had been defined for the system as a whole (Table 1), as well as for its individual components (Table 2). The primary purpose of the technical system evaluation criteria was to test if the system has (i) the specified overall technical functionality, and (ii) the technical robustness required for users to interact with it smoothly for usability evaluation to make sense. In all cases, objective measures can be applied. Table 1 lists the technical system evaluation criteria used for both PT1 and PT2. The table indicates for each criterion whether evaluation is quantitative or qualitative and explains what we understand to be measured by the criterion. The evaluation result per criterion is shown and so is an annotated qualitative score value or comment for each PT1 result. "1" is the lowest score, "5" the highest. It should be noted that the score values allocated in Tables 1 and 2 are strongly relative to what could be expected of the first prototype given the development plans. When evaluating the second system prototype (PT2), the scores would be replaced by scores which adequately reflect the quality of the system per aspect evaluated.

The results were derived from the data collected during the user test of PT1. Mainly the test logfiles were used together with technical knowledge about the system, e.g., regarding the number of emotions, which could be expressed in principle.

Table 1. Technical evaluation criteria for the HCA system.

Technical criterion	Explanation	Evaluation	Score 1–5
Technical robustness	Quantitative; how often does the system crash; how often does it produce a bug, which prevents continued interaction (e.g., a loop)	Some crashes and a number of loops, improvement needed	3 acceptable
Handling of out-of-domain input	Qualitative; to which extent does the system react reasonably to out-of-domain input	System has only few reaction possibilities. Further improvement needed	2 acceptable

Real-time performance, spoken part	Quantitative; how long does it usually take to get reaction from the system to spoken input	OK, natural language understanding is fast; recogniser not tested	5 very good
Real-time performance, gesture part	Quantitative; how long does it usually take to get reaction from the system to gesture input	Too slow due to a designed delay of several seconds to wait for possible spoken input. Further improvement needed	3 basic
Barge-in	Is barge-in implemented	No barge-in in PT1	As planned
Number of emotions	Quantitative; how many different emotions can in principle be conveyed	4 basic emotions	4 good
Actual emotion expression	Quantitative; how many different emotions are actually conveyed verbally and non-verbally	1 basic emotion. Much improvement needed, particularly in rendering capabilities: scripts, synchronous non-verbal expressions, speed, amplitude	1 as planned
Number of input modalities	Quantitative; how many input modalities does the system allow	3, i.e., speech, 2D gesture, user key haptics for changing virtual camera angle and making HCA walk around (inconsistent with character autonomy)	As planned
Number of output modalities	Quantitative; how many output modalities does the system allow	Natural interactive speech, facial expression, gesture. More rendering capability needed	As planned
Synchronisation of output	Qualitative; is output properly synchronised	Speech/gesture/facial OK. More rendering capability needed. No lip synchronisation	As planned
Number of domains	Quantitative; how many domains can HCA talk about	6, i.e., HCA's life, fairytales, physical presence, user, gatekeeper, meta	As planned

Table 2. Technical evaluation criteria for the HCA system components.

Technical criterion	Explanation	Score 1–5
Speech recogniser		
Word error rate	No speech recognition in PT1	N/A
Vocabulary coverage	No speech recognition in PT1	N/A
Perplexity	No speech recognition in PT1	N/A
Real-time performance	No speech recognition in PT1	N/A
Gesture recogniser		
Recognition accuracy regarding gesture shape	84% of a total of 542 shapes measured on 9 hours of user test data	As planned
Natural language understanding		
Lexical coverage	66%	Ahead of plan
Parser error rate	16%	Ahead of plan
Topic spotter error rate	Not evaluated for PT1	As planned
Anaphora resolution error rate	Not in PT1	As planned
Gesture interpretation		
Selection of referenced objects error rate	30 (26%) of 117 results were erroneous, measured on 2 hours of user test data	Basic
Input fusion		
Robustness to temporal distortion between input modalities	No semantic fusion in PT1. No fusion of data structures because no waiting function for NLU input when gesture input	Behind plan
Fusion error rate	No semantic fusion in PT1	Behind plan
Cases in which events have not been merged but should have been	No semantic fusion in PT1	Behind plan
Cases in which events have been merged but should not have been	No semantic fusion in PT1	Behind plan
Recognised modality combination error rate	No semantic fusion in PT1	Behind plan

Character module

Meta-communication facilities	Handling of user input: repeat, low confidence score, insults	As planned
Handling of initiative	Limited free user initiative; no user initiative in mini-dialogues	As planned
Performance of conversation history	Support for meta-communication and mini-dialogues	As planned
Handling of changes in emotion	HCA's emotional state updated for each user input	As planned
Response generation		
Coverage of action set (nonverbal action)	Approximately 300 spoken output templates and 100 primitive non-verbal behaviours	2 acceptable
Graphical rendering (animation)		
Synchronisation with speech output	Works for a single non-verbal element at a time. No lip synchronisation	As planned
Naturalness of animation, facial	Overlapping non-verbal elements missing. Limited number of animations	As planned
Naturalness of animation, gesture	Overlapping non-verbal elements missing. Limited number of animations	As planned
Naturalness of animation, movement	Somewhat rigid HCA walk	As planned
Text-to-speech		
Speech quality	OK	4 good
Intelligibility	Some syllables "swallowed"	4 good
Naturalness	OK	4 good
Non-speech sound		
Appropriateness in context of music/sound to set a mood	Not in PT1	N/A
Integration		
Communication among modules	PT1 is reasonably well-tested with respect to inter-module communication	4 good
Message dispatcher	OK	4/5 good
Processing time per module	Real-time overall, except for gesture modules	5/3 fine/basic

Focus in the NICE project was not on thorough and exhaustive technical evaluation. Rather, the idea has been to keep the technical evaluation of components at a limited though reasonably sufficient level. This is reflected in Table 2, which includes relatively few but important criteria per component. The evaluation results in Table 2 are mainly based on analysis of logfiles from the user test of PT1 and technical knowledge of the components. If nothing else is indicated, the results refer to the user test material as a whole. See also (Martin et al., 2004a; Martin et al., 2004b) concerning gesture recognition and interpretation. The "mini-dialogues" mentioned in the table are small hard-coded dialogue structures plugged into Andersen's conversation management structure at points where he is expected to go in more depth with some topic.

Overall, as suggested by Tables 1 and 2, PT1 conformed reasonably well to the PT1 requirements and design specification. On some points, PT1 functionality and performance was better than planned. For instance, the natural language understanding module had been integrated and could be tested ahead of plan. On other points, PT1 functionality and performance was worse than planned. For instance, input fusion had not been implemented.

3.2.4   Usability evaluation criteria.   While the focus on technical evaluation is limited in the NICE project, usability evaluation plays a central role because little is known about the usability aspects of spoken computer games for edutainment. The usability evaluation criteria adopted in the evaluation plan include state-of-the-art criteria, as well as new criteria that we anticipated would be needed and had to be developed in the project itself.

We divided the usability evaluation criteria into two groups. One group includes what we call basic usability criteria (Table 3), i.e., criteria that we consider basic to usability. If one of these criteria produces a strongly negative evaluation result, this may mean that the module(s) responsible must be improved before further evaluation is worthwhile. For example, if speech recognition adequacy is very bad this means that, basically, the user is not able to communicate with the system until recognition has been improved. Technical evaluation measures of, e.g., speech recogniser performance, gesture recogniser performance, and parser performance are objective metrics, which may be compared to perceived subjective recognition and understanding adequacy.

The second group of criteria (Table 4) includes the criteria, which we consider essential to the evaluation of the NICE prototypes. Several of these are new and may need subsequent re-definition in order to serve their purposes.

Most parameters in Tables 3 and 4 must, as indicated in the second column, be evaluated using a subjective method, such as questionnaire or interview. Like Tables 1 and 2, Tables 3 and 4 list the core evaluation criteria to be applied to both PT1 and PT2. The tables explain what we understand to be measured

Table 3. Basic usability evaluation criteria for the HCA system.

Basic usability criterion	Explanation	Evaluation	Score 1–5
Speech understanding adequacy	Subjective; how well does the system understand speech input	Quite well; but fairly often HCA does not answer the user's question but says something irrelevant; vocabulary seems too small	3 acceptable
Gesture understanding adequacy	Subjective; how well does the system understand gesture input	Reaction to gesture input too slow. This perceived slowness is due to a one-second delay set in the system to allow the input fusion module to wait for possible linguistic input following the gesture. This delay will have to be reduced. It would be nice if HCA could tell about more things in his study than a few pictures	3 basic
Combined speech/ gesture understanding adequacy	Subjective; how well does the system understand combined speech/ gesture input	No semantic input fusion in PT1	Behind plan
Output voice quality	Subjective; how intelligible and natural is the system output voice	Mostly OK, intelligible, not unpleasant, modest syllable "swallowing"	4 good
Output phrasing adequacy	Subjective; how adequate are the system's output formulations	Mostly OK, no user remarks	4 good
Animation quality	Subjective; how natural is the animated output	A couple of annoying errors (HCA could walk on the ceiling and in furniture). Basically animation was OK although HCA could be more lively and he walks in a strange way	3 acceptable
Quality of graphics	Subjective; how good is the graphics	Rather good, only a (true) user remark on too dark graphics due to the study light sources	4/5 very good

Table 3 – Continued

Basic usability criterion	Explanation	Evaluation	Score 1–5
Ease of use of input devices	Subjective; how easy are the input devices to use, such as the touch screen	Microphone, mouse, touch screen, keyboard: users generally positive	4/5 very good
Frequency of interaction problems, spoken part	Quantitative; how often does a problem occur related to spoken interaction (e.g., the user is not understood or is misunderstood)	A larger number of bugs, primarily loops, found than expected. A total of 13.3% of the output was found affected by bugs. Non-bugged interaction, on the other hand, showed better performance than expected	Bugged interaction: 2 barely adequate. Non-bugged interaction: 3/4 acceptable
Frequency of interaction problems, gesture part	Quantitative; how often does a problem occur related to gesture interaction	No figures available but mouse-pointing users continued to create a stack problem due to multiple fast mouse clicks causing a number of interaction problems. By contrast, the touch screen users emulated human 3D pointing during conversation	3 basic
Frequency of interaction problems, graphics rendering part	Quantitative; how often does a problem occur related to graphics	Two serious generic bugs found: most users got lost in space outside HCA's study at least once, HCA sometimes got immersed in furniture	2 barely adequate
Sufficiency of domain coverage	Subjective; how well does the system cover the domains it announces to the user	HCA does not have enough answers to questions; there is enough about fairytales but not about his life	3/4 acceptable
Number of objects users interacted with through gesture	Quantitative; serves to check to which extent the possibilities offered by the system are also used by users	21 pointable objects in HCA's study: in general, users pointed to most of them and to many more as well	3 acceptable
Number of topics addressed in conversation	Quantitative; serves to check how well the implemented domains cover the topics addressed by users	All generic topics (approx. 30) addressed; some topic details (approx. 10) addressed but not covered	As expected

Table 4. Core usability evaluation criteria for the HCA system.

Core usability criterion	Explanation	Evaluation	Score 1–5
Conversation success	Quantitative; how often is an exchange between the user and the system successful in the discourse context	Most users pointed out that HCA's responses were sometimes irrelevant. Work on quantitative metrics in progress	3 acceptable
Naturalness of user speech and gesture	Subjective; how natural is it to communicate in the available modalities	Very positive user comments overall although some users said they had to get used to talking to a computer	4/5 very good
Output behaviour naturalness	Subjective; character believability, coordination and synchronisation of verbal and non-verbal behaviour, display of emotions, dialogue initiative and flow, etc.	Very complex criterion, hard to score. Still, users were surprisingly positive, not least about HCA's physical appearance	3/4 quite acceptable
Sufficiency of the system's reasoning capabilities	Subjective; how good is the system at reasoning about user input	No reasoning available in PT1. Needs identified for reasoning about implications of user input	As planned
Ease of use of the game	Subjective; how easy is it for the user to find out what to do and how to interact	Reasonably easy. Main difficulties due to HCA's limited understanding abilities and users' limited English, e.g., few knew the names of HCA's fairytales in English	3 acceptable
Error handling adequacy, spoken part	Subjective; how good is the system at detecting errors relating to spoken input and how well does it handle them	Limited. Main complaint is that HCA often does not answer the user's questions but keeps talking about whatever he is talking about or says something irrelevant	2 acceptable
Error handling adequacy, gesture part	Subjective; how good is the system at detecting and handling errors relating to gesture input	No error handling involving gesture	Behind plan

Table 4 – Continued

Core usability criterion	Explanation	Evaluation	Score 1–5
Scope of user modelling	Subjective; to which extent does the system exploit what it learns about the user	No user comments. User age, gender and nationality collected; age information used once in an HCA question	As planned
Entertainment value	Subjective; this measure includes game quality and originality, interest taken in the game, feeling like playing again, time spent playing, user game initiative, etc.	User test very positive	4 good
Educational value	Subjective; to which extent did the user learn from interacting with the system	User test very positive. As (user) self-assessment is occasionally misleading, we might have added some recall questions relating to what HCA told each particular user	4 good
User satisfaction	Subjective; how satisfied is the user with the system	User test very positive	4 good

by each criterion. The evaluation result per criterion is shown and so is an annotated score value or comment for each of the PT1 results. Each allocated score relates to what we believe should be expected of PT1. For instance, in PT1, one is entitled to expect a better approximation to real-time performance than to perfect handling of non-task-oriented conversation, the latter being one of the main research challenges in the HCA project. If real-time performance is a serious problem in PT1, we may have an unpleasant and unexpected problem on our hands at this stage, whereas if conversation management is not perfect in PT1, this is only what everyone would be entitled to expect. More generally speaking, and with the exception of real-time performance, we consider a score of "3" for all main challenges addressed in the HCA system clearly adequate at this stage of development. Still, we need to stress the judgmental nature of many of the scores assigned in Tables 3 and 4. The results are mainly based on our interpretation of the data collected in the interviews during the user test of

PT1. Bernsen and Dybkjær (2004b) provide details about the questions asked to users during the interviews and users' answers to each of the questions. In Table 4, "Scope of user modelling" refers to HCA's collection of information provided by the user, which he then makes use of later on during conversation.

3.2.5 Conclusion on PT1 evaluation.

Despite its shortcomings, not least in its capability to conduct human-style spoken conversation, PT1 was received remarkably well by the target users in the test. Note, however, that it is common to find some amount of uncritical positive user bias in tests of new technology with exiting perspectives, especially when users have never interacted with the technology before. We would have preferred a smaller number of bugs than was actually found with respect to (a) spoken interaction and (b) the workings of the rendering when users made HCA do locomotion in his study. The system clearly does have edutainment potential, which serves to validate its underlying theory of non-task-oriented conversation for edutainment (Bernsen and Dybkjær, 2004b). In view of these evaluation results, we decided to focus work on PT2 on basic improvements in the system's spoken and non-verbal conversational abilities. The – now completed – PT2 features a completely redesigned conversation manager for full mixed-initiative non-task-oriented conversation, ontology-based natural language understanding and conversation management, speech recognition, a better speech synthesis, and multiple synchronous non-verbal output streams, including audiovisual speech and facially expressed emotion reflecting the character's current emotional state.

4 Evaluation of the SENECA Prototype

Our second evaluation example is of a task-oriented multimodal SDS for a wide range of entertainment, navigation, and communication applications in mobile environments. The research has been carried out in the EU Esprit and Human Language Technologies (HLT) project SENECA (1998–2002) on Speech control modules for Entertainment, Navigation and communication Equipment in CArs (Gärtner et al., 2001). Project partners were: The Bosch Group, Germany; Daimler-Chrysler, Germany; Daimler Benz Aerospace, Germany; Motorola Germany; Motorola Semiconductor, Israel; Centro Ricerche Fiat, Italy; and Renault Recherche Innovation, France.

The goal of the project was to integrate and further develop SDS technology for use in cars up to an almost commercial level. The usability of the SENECA prototype system has been evaluated in different development cycles by means of user tests collecting objective and subjective data. With speech input, road safety, especially for complex tasks, is significantly improved. Both objectively and as perceived by the driver, humans are less distracted from driving when using speech input for on-board devices than if using manual input as in standard remote-controlled navigation systems (Gärtner et al., 2001; Green, 2000). In the following, focus is on description of the *evaluation set-up*, the *usability criteria*, and some evaluation *results*.

4.1   Description of the SENECA Prototype System

A large variety of electronic systems are now available in the car for comfort, ease of driving, entertainment, and communications. Some of these systems, notably for navigation and entertainment, require rather complex human-computer interaction, which increases the risk of driver distraction.

The SENECA prototype system whose architecture is shown in Figure 4, represents a step towards close-to-the-market technologies enabling drivers to interact with on-board systems and services in an easy, risk-free way. The head unit of the system – for the driver and front passenger, the COMAND head unit represents the central operating and display unit for numerous functions and devices – is linked via an optical D2B (Domestic Digital Bus) to the GSM module, the CD changer and the (Digital Signal Processing) (DSP) module. The latter contains the signal and D2B communication software. A notebook computer contains the SENECA SDS software, i.e., all the modules that are subject to research, including speech recognition, dialogue management, and access to different databases. DSP and notebook computer are connected via a serial link. In the context of a research project, such a partial software solution conveniently enables optimisation and evaluation. The SENECA SDS prototypes developed for French, German, and Italian languages allow control of entertainment (i.e., radio), navigation, and communication (i.e., telephone) equipment using command and control dialogues combined with speech and

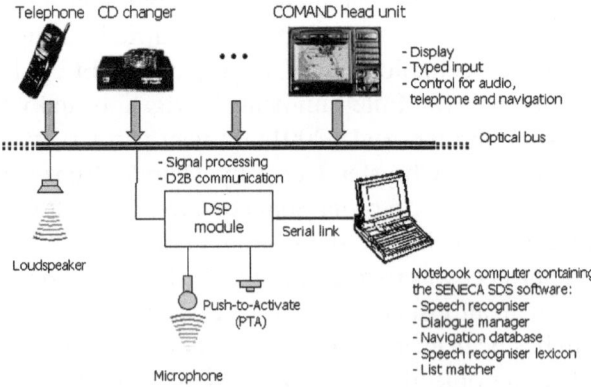

Figure 4.   Architecture of the SENECA prototype system.

text output. A more detailed description of the SENECA SDS prototype system for the German language can be found in (Minker et al., 2005b). In the following, we focus on the German prototype.

4.2 Evaluation of the SENECA Prototype System

The German SENECA prototype has been evaluated early and late in the development process, namely at the *concept demonstrator* and *system demonstrator* stages. In both tests, based on an identical evaluation set-up, system operation using speech input and output was compared to functionally equivalent haptic input operation using the COMAND head unit so as to be able to demonstrate the quality of the respective input modalities and their impact on driving safety and quality.

Since industry is primarily interested in high usability and acceptance rates of their future products and since the SENECA project was intended to develop close-to-the-market prototypes, usability field tests have been carried out with mainly core criteria defined on the basis of the project's needs, including quantitative and qualitative elements. These field tests will be described in the following sections.

4.2.1 Evaluation set-up and criteria. The basic components of the experimental set-up employed for the in-field usability evaluation of the German concept and system demonstrators include a passenger car, the standard COMAND head-unit, a second set of pedals, the SENECA prototype, an additional notebook computer with event keys and clock, a video system (three cameras, multiplexer, and digital video recorder), and a set of microphones. Three seats were taken by the driver, a professional driving assessor and the principal investigator, respectively, and one seat was used for the testing equipment.

The notebook computer and the video-recording system were installed in a rack on one of the back seats (Figure 5). Three softkeys of the notebook computer were used for time event recording. A logfile was created for each test person. The notebook computer's display with the system's clock was combined with the camera recordings in order to obtain a time reference for processing the video data.

The video system was connected to three cameras, which recorded the forward traffic scene, the driver's face, and the COMAND head unit display, respectively (Figure 6). The signals from the cameras and the display image of the additional notebook computer were mixed and digitally recorded by a Digital Video Walkman. In addition to the SENECA SDS prototype microphone,

Figure 5.   SENECA test car equipment (Mutschler and Baum, 2001).

Figure 6.   Camera and microphone positions in the test car (Mutschler and Baum, 2001).

a microphone was installed under the car roof to capture comments made by the passengers, especially the driver. The comments were recorded synchronously with the video data.

The driving assessor noted driving errors and rated the test person's driving skills using a specially designed recording device. In dangerous situations, the driving assessor warned the test person or even intervened by using the second set of pedals or by taking hold of the steering wheel. This seemed particularly important since users had to perform the manual input tasks whilst driving, which is normally prohibited.

The principal investigator was responsible for the organisation and monitoring of the experimental set-up. He announced the tasks for the test person to perform. He also recorded the start and end of the task, as well as special unforeseen events by pressing predefined keys on the notebook computer. Two driving assessors and two experimenters were employed.

The evaluation trials took place on a 46 km long course near a middle-sized city in Germany. The course was composed of express roadways, highways, entrances/exits, and streets across cities and villages. The test persons drove the course twice to cover both experimental conditions (speech mode/manual mode). Prior to the first experimental trial, a separate training phase was performed on a partly different course while the test person was practicing the handling of the car and several exemplary tasks in the respective input modalities. A set of nine tasks that were representative of manipulating entertainment, navigation and communication equipment was carried out in both experimental conditions, including destination entry (city and street names), activating stored destinations, telephone number dialling, activating stored numbers, etc. The tasks required typical operating actions, namely activating a main function or sub-function, selecting an item from a list, as well as spelling characters. The tasks had to be performed on pre-defined route segments. Assistance was given if necessary and noted by the experimenter. If a task was not completed at pre-defined points, it was declared aborted.

The entire trial sequence comprised written and verbal instructions, a pre-experimental questionnaire, training of SENECA/COMAND operations before the test trial, the test trial on the course, post-trial interviews, and a post-experimental questionnaire. A complete trial took about 3 hours. The Task Completion Rate (TCR) was calculated from the logfile data containing all interesting event times, as well as the speech recogniser transcripts. A task was completed when correctly and completely solved within a scheduled segment without any essential assistance. The duration of the different operations required for task completion was documented by the experimenter. The driving assessor recorded the driving errors and judged the driving quality on a six-point scale.

The driving errors were categorised into the following seven main categories: too low speed, too high speed, too low longitudinal and lateral distances to other cars, inexact lane keeping, insufficient observation of the traffic scene, no indication of change of driving direction, and sudden/late braking. The corresponding times of the driving errors made were recorded automatically. Glances to the display, speedometer/steering wheel, rear mirror, aside (including the outside mirrors) were extracted from the video data.

In a subjective evaluation, the test persons were asked about driving safety, system handling when alternatively using speech and haptic input, appropriateness of the command and control vocabulary, as well as their acceptance and preference of input modalities. The test persons had to compare the speech-based interface to other extra car devices with respect to driving safety and driver comfort on a six-point scale. The difficulty with the performed field tests relies in the fact that the tasks were not counterbalanced in any way, which makes the interpretation of results somewhat more difficult (e.g., are variations due to task, or to sequence effects). Another difficulty is the time and resource-consuming, and hence rather expensive, evaluation set-up. Therefore, the number of test persons had to be limited. In the German system demonstrator evaluation thus only 16 test persons participated.

4.2.2   Concept demonstrator evaluation.   As mentioned, the SENECA prototype has been evaluated at different stages of the project. Usability tests with the *concept demonstrator* version of the prototype allowed to identify implementation-related problems and conceptual weaknesses of the system early in the development process. Such proper diagnostics of system shortcomings can be fed back into system improvement. For instance, the dialogue was sometimes interrupted by the system itself without any traceable reason. Conceptually, test persons found it distracting to have to recall the – not always natural and intuitive – command and control vocabulary. They also criticised the sometimes short vocal prompts and the lack of spoken feedback. In terms of dialogue flow management, the system frequently required users to remember previous system manipulations in order to confirm their input. The system-driven dialogue strategy thus seemed to demand a considerable mental load of the user. Finally, the incoherent dialogue flow strategies between applications (navigation, telephone, and radio) were also judged as inconvenient by the users.

For the evaluation of the final *system demonstrator*, the project partners took the concept demonstrator evaluation results into account in order to improve the system. Also as an outcome of the concept demonstrator evaluation, a long-term user evaluation has been suggested. Analyses of the subjective evaluation data from the interviews have shown that participants would need more time to memorise commands than the 3 hours scheduled for the test trial. In a long-term evaluation, it would be possible to analyse a wider range of functions and evaluate the system, its recognition capabilities, and driver satisfaction in a more reliable way. Such a long-term user evaluation has been performed by a number of selected test persons but cannot be reported here for confidentiality reasons.

4.2.3   System demonstrator evaluation.   The system demonstrator evaluation was carried out by the end of the SENECA SDS prototype development cycle. With a technically improved prototype system, quantitative results including TCR and driving error measures, as well as subjective usability evaluations were in focus.

4.2.4   Quantitative usability evaluation results.   Most of the tasks showed a markedly lower TCR with speech input compared to haptic input. Averaged over all tasks, the TCR was 79% for speech input and 90% for haptic input. Incomplete speech tasks mostly occurred due to forgotten commands.

In terms of input times, speech input took 63 seconds compared to haptic input requiring 84 seconds (averaged over all tasks). In terms of input accuracy, the most important user errors with speech were vocabulary errors (e.g., wrong commands). Some input spelling errors occurred as well. Errors also occurred when users did not follow the pre-defined dialogue flow, such as when a user, instead of only confirming the ability to provide additional information with a yes/no reply, provided this information directly. Push-to-activate (PTA) errors, i.e., missing or inappropriate PTA activation, were rather sparse, which may be due to learning effects. All these user-induced errors increased the input time and reduced the TCR. However, the long-term evaluations of the SENECA SDS with selected users in France have shown the impact of learning effects: for experienced users using speech input, the TCR attained almost 100% for the navigation task. This task, requiring input of city and street names, may incite the most complex user operations for in-vehicle infotainment systems. In general, with speech input there has been a higher score for driving skills and there are fewer driving errors as compared to manual input, particularly for destination input tasks.

The evaluations in Italy have shown that the SENECA SDS reduces differences between different age groups. Comparison has shown that it is only for young users that the haptic input modality proved to be more efficient. This is probably due to the fact that youngsters have more experience in using technical devices and to their higher dexterity in interacting with them.

4.2.5   Subjective usability evaluation results.   Safety and comfort of SENECA compared with other car devices were individually assessed by the test persons on a six-point scale using questionnaires. SENECA was estimated to provide almost a top level of safety and comfort.

Concerning the safety implications, speech input was judged to be below well-established devices, such as ESP (Electronic Stability Program) and the multifunction steering wheel, and to be in the range of automatic transmission. In terms of comfort, speech input was judged to be below air conditioning and in the range of automatic transmission and the multifunction steering wheel. In the Italian2 evaluation, participants were asked if the SENECA SDS was above, below, or equivalent to their expectations. Of the test persons, 47% judged the system to be equal to or above their expectations (compared to 7% for the haptic interface).

To get a general idea of user satisfaction, the test persons were asked what they like about using SENECA. Six test persons assessed speech input to be simple and comfortable. Three test persons mentioned the hands-free/eyes-free aspect. Other positive statements concerned ease of learning, little prior knowledge necessary, speech output, and the good readability of text output.

The advantage of speech input is reflected in the answers to the question about the subjective feeling of driving safety and comfort: 11 test persons mentioned "Higher distraction and less attention to traffic/higher concentration required when using haptic input". In addition to these basic disadvantages, many design aspects of the haptic system were criticised. To the question "What did you dislike about speech input?" only three test persons noted the speech misrecognitions.

Table 5 summarises the most important quantitative and subjective usability criteria and evaluation results for the SENECA prototype systems.

Table 5. Basic and core usability evaluation criteria for the SENECA prototype system.

Usability criterion	Explanation	Evaluation	Score
User satisfaction	Subjective; how satisfied is the user with the system in general	User satisfaction is quite high with the speech-based interface	Good
Task completion rate (TCR)	Quantitative; measure of the success in accomplishing the task in a given time window in either input modality (speech and haptic)	Most of the tasks showed a markedly lower TCR with speech input compared to haptic input	79% averaged over all tasks for speech input, 90% for haptic input
Input times	Quantitative; the duration of completing the task in either input mode (speech and haptic) was measured by the experimenter	Speech input required less time on average than haptic input	63 seconds averaged over all tasks for speech input, 84 seconds for haptic input
Accuracy of inputs	Includes vocabulary errors, orientation errors, spelling errors, open microphone errors	Not explicitly calculated, but affects task completion rate and input times	N/A

Driving performance	Quantitative; a professional driving assessor noted the number of driving errors and rated the test person's driving skills	Significantly less driving errors occurred when using speech input, notably in the categories *inexact lane keeping* and *speed too low*	Number (frequency) of errors averaged across subjects: Inexact lane keeping: 6.6 for speech input; 13.9 for haptic input; speed too low: 2.9 for speech input, 5.9 for haptic input
Glance analysis	Quantitative; glances to the display, speedometer/steering wheel, rear mirror, and aside were extracted from the video data and counted by the experimenter	For low-complexity tasks, the total number of display glances per task for speech and manual input are equal. For complex tasks, speech input required less short and long glances than haptic input	Cannot be reported for confidentiality reasons
Acceptance and preference of input and output modes	Subjective; test persons were asked what they (dis-)liked with speech/haptic input; assessed on a six-point scale	Test persons preferred speech input. They estimated speech output to be very helpful	Cannot be reported for confidentiality reasons
Driving comfort and safety	Subjective; the feeling of the test persons of being comfortable or distracted when manipulating the device using either input modality; assessed on a six-point scale	Test persons felt more comfortable and less distracted when using SENECA compared to using the haptic system	Cannot be reported for confidentiality reasons
Comparison with other car devices	Subjective; how is the speech-based interface judged with respect to other infotainment and entertainment systems in the car in terms of comfort and safety	SENECA was estimated to provide almost top level of safety and comfort	5 on a six-point scale with 1 being the lowest score

4.3   Conclusion on the Evaluation of the SENECA Prototype System

The scientific community is well aware that speech in cars is the enabling technology for interactively and selectively bringing news and information to mobile environments without causing a safety hazard. We have presented the SENECA spoken language dialogue system demonstrator. It provides speech-based access to entertainment, navigation and communication applications in mobile environments. The SENECA SDS demonstrators have been evaluated by real users in the field. The results show that the TCR is higher with haptic input and that with speech input, road safety, especially in the case of complex tasks, is significantly improved. The SENECA project consortium consisted mainly of industry partners that aimed at developing a close-to-the-market prototype. The SENECA evaluations focused on safety, usability, user acceptance, and potential market of the future product. Therefore, technical evaluation criteria have been judged less important. The SENECA evaluations have also demonstrated the rather time and resource-consuming experimental set-up that may be required for specific application domains, such as mobile environments. Given these important constraints, only a limited number of test persons could be recruited for the evaluation, which may have influenced the statistical significance of the results.

5   Conclusion

Having initially described the large variety of established methods available to testers and evaluators of SDSs, this chapter proceeded to illustrate the "real life" on the shop floor of testers and evaluators of today's advanced multimodal SDSs. Our first example described progress evaluation of a forefront research, first prototype embodied conversational agent system, using a controlled laboratory test. The second example described selected aspects of two successive, controlled infield evaluations of a close-to-exploitation task-oriented SDS for in-car use. Depending on how one wishes to count SDS system generations, the two systems are two or three generations apart. The SENECA system uses a command-and-control vocabulary, the dialogue is thoroughly system-driven, and the system is used to solve particular, rather well-circumscribed tasks. The HCA system uses fully spontaneous spoken input, aims – however imperfectly – to enable fully mixed-initiative conversation, and does not enable the user to solve a task at all. The SENECA system was tested in its real environment albeit in a controlled setting, whereas, for the HCA system, developers had to use laboratory testing for testing their first, even incomplete, prototype. Even some of the SENECA findings were predictable from the literature, such as that users were likely to have difficulty learning the command keywords and phrases required for operating the system (Bernsen et al., 1998).

Still, the SENECA results reported are not entirely unambiguous. Speech input is still more error-prone than typing and it is perfectly understandable that the SENECA consortium chose to subject the system to a further, long-term user trial in which they have investigated the long-term learning effects on users who had to keep using the command keywords and phrases until they, perhaps, did manage to control the system without problems of memorising what to say to it. Thus, even with relatively familiar technology and carefully prepared user trials, it is quite possible to have to conclude that the trials made were inconclusive due to their design and that new trials are required.

The differences in the challenges addressed by the two systems are also apparent in the evaluation criteria applied. For SENECA, it was possible to apply, from the start, a series of familiar evaluation criteria, including those applied in order to evaluate various aspects of comparison between using remote-control typed input spelling for navigation and using spoken input, respectively. For the HCA system, on the other hand, we were partly groping in the dark. For instance, how does one grade conformance to specification of a first prototype when the specification was always focused on the *second* prototype and when too little was known in advance about what the first prototype could be made to do? Conversely, not being able to grade with relative exactitude conformance to specification of the first prototype runs the risk of failing to develop the second prototype to specification. Maybe we should have tried to specify both prototypes equally precisely. In another example, how can we evaluate one of the key properties of the HCA system, i.e., conversation success, when too little is known about what conversation success is (Traum et al., 2004)? The closest analogy to conversation success in the SENECA system is TCR but this is of little help since there is no task in the HCA system.

By way of conclusion, we may claim to have illustrated, at least, that (i) even if the choice of evaluation methodologies is often reasonably straightforward even for the evaluation of advanced state-of-the-art systems and components, art, craft skills, and even luck are still required for optimising the choice of evaluation criteria needed for assessment in the light of the data gathered; (ii) new generations of SDSs are likely to keep us occupied for a long time to come in order to invent, apply, discard, revise, and iteratively tune new evaluation criteria in order to optimise our – always costly – evaluations.

Acknowledgements   The NICE project was supported by the European Commission's HLT under Grant IST-2001-35293. The SENECA project was supported by the European Commission's 4th framework ESPRIT programme "System Integration and Applications" under HLT (Contract number ESPRIT 26–981). The support is gratefully acknowledged. The authors want to thank all partners and colleagues involved in the projects.

References

Bernsen, N. O., Charfuelán, M., Corradini, A., Dybkjær, L., Hansen, T., Kiilerich, S., Kolodnytsky, M., Kupkin, D., and Mehta, M. (2004a). First Prototype of Conversational H.C. Andersen. In Costabile, M., editor, *Proceedings of the International Working Conference on Advanced Visual Interfaces (AVI)*, pages 458–461, Association for Computing Machinery (ACM), New York, USA.

Bernsen, N. O., Dybkjær, H., and Dybkjær, L. (1998). *Designing Interactive Speech Systems. From First Ideas to User Testing.* Springer Verlag.

Bernsen, N. O. and Dybkjær, L. (2004a). Domain-Oriented Conversation with H. C. Andersen. In *Proceedings of the Tutorial and Research Workshop on Affective Dialogue Systems (ADS)*, volume 3068 of *Lecture Notes in Artificial Intelligence*, pages 142–153, Springer Verlag, Heidelberg, Germany.

Bernsen, N. O. and Dybkjær, L. (2004b). Evaluation of Spoken Multimodal Conversation. In *Proceedings of the Sixth International Conference on Multimodal Interfaces (ICMI)*, pages 38–45, Association for Computing Machinery (ACM), New York, USA.

Bernsen, N. O. and Dybkjær, L. (2007). *Multimodal Usability.* To appear.

Bernsen, N. O., Dybkjær, L., and Kiilerich, S. (2004b). Evaluating Conversation with Hans Christian Andersen. In *Proceedings of the Fourth International Conference on Language Resources and Evaluation (LREC)*, volume 3, pages 1011–1014, European Language Resources Association (ELRA), Paris, France.

Corradini, A., Bernsen, N. O., Fredriksson, M., Johanneson, L., Königsmann, J., and Mehta, M. (2004). Towards Believable Behavior Generation for Embodied Conversational Agents. In *International Conference on Computational Science (ICCS), Workshop on Interactive Visualisation and Interaction Technologies (IV&IT)*, volume 3038 of *Lecture Notes in Computer Science*, pages 946–953, Springer Verlag, Heidelberg, Germany.

Corradini, A., Mehta, M., Bernsen, N. O., and Charfuelán, M. (2005). Animating an Interactive Conversational Character for an Educational Game System. In Riedl, J., Jameson, A., Billsus, D., and Lau, T., editors, *Proceedings of the 2005 International Conference on Intelligent User Interfaces (IUI)*, pages 183–190, ACM Press, New York, USA.

Dybkjær, L., Bernsen, N. O., and Minker, W. (2004). Evaluation and Usability of Multimodal Spoken Language Dialogue Systems. *Speech Communication*, 43(1–2):33–54.

Gärtner, U., König, W., and Wittig, T. (2001). Evaluation of Manual vs. Speech Input When Using a Driver Information System in Real Traffic. In *Online Proceedings of International Driving Symposium on Human Factors in Driver Assessment, Training and Vehicle*

Design, Aspen, USA. http://ppc.uiowa.edu/Driving-Assessment/2001/Summaries/Downloads/download.html

Gibbon, D., Moore, R., and Winski, R. (1997). *Handbook of Standards and Resources for Spoken Language Systems*. Mouton de Gruyter, Berlin.

Green, P. (2000). Crashes Induced by Driver Information Systems and What Can Be Done to Reduce Them. In *Proceedings of the Convergence Conference*, pages 26–36, Society of Automotive Engineers, Warrendale, USA.

Gustafson, J., Bell, L., Boye, J., Lindström, A., and Wiren, M. (2004). The NICE Fairy-tale Game System. In *Proceedings of the Fifth SIGdial Workshop on Discourse and Dialogue*, pages 23–26, Association for Computational Linguistics, Boston, USA.

Martin, J.-C., Buisine, S., and Abrilian, S. (2004a). Requirements and Design Specification for Gesture and Input Fusion in PT2 HCA Study. NICE Project Deliverable D1.1-2a Part 2, LIMSI-CNRS, Paris, France.

Martin, J.-C., Buisine, S., Pitel, G., and Bernsen, N. O. (2006). Fusion of Children's Speech and 2D Gestures when Conversing with 3D Characters. *Multimodal Human-Computer Interfaces. Special Issue of Signal Processing*, 86(12):3596–3624.

Martin, J.-C., Pitel, G., Buisine, S., and Bernsen, N. O. (2004b). Gesture Interpretation Module. EU HLT NICE Project Deliverable D3.4-2, LIMSI-CNRS, Paris, France.

Minker, W., Bühler, D., and Dybkjær, L., editors (2005a). *Spoken Multimodal Human-Computer Dialogue in Mobile Environments*, volume 28 of *Text, Speech and Language Technology*, Springer.

Minker, W., Haiber, U., Heisterkamp, P., and Scheible, S. (2005b). Design, Implementation and Evaluation of the SENECA Spoken Language Dialogue System. In Minker, W., Bühler, D., and Dybkjær, L., editors, *Spoken Multimodal Human-Computer Dialogue in Mobile Environments*, volume 28 of *Text, Speech and Language Technology*, pages 287–310, Springer.

Mutschler, H. and Baum, W. (2001). Evaluation of the System Demonstrator - German Results. Final SENECA Project Deliverable, Robert Bosch, Hildesheim.

Traum, D., Robinson, S., and Stephan, J. (2004). Evaluation of Multi-party Virtual Reality Dialogue Interaction. In *Proceedings of the Fourth International Conference on Language Resources and Evaluation (LREC)*, pages 1699–1702, Lisbon, Portugal.

Walker, M. A., Litman, D., Kamm, C. A., and Abella, A. (1997). PARADISE: A General Framework for Evaluating Spoken Dialogue Agents. In *Proceedings of Annual Meeting of the Association for Computational Linguistics (ACL/EACL)*, pages 271–280, Madrid, Spain.

Chapter 8

LINGUISTIC RESOURCES, DEVELOPMENT, AND EVALUATION OF TEXT AND SPEECH SYSTEMS

Christopher Cieri

University of Pennsylvania, Department of Linguistics, Linguistic Data Consortium
Philadelphia, USA

ccieri@ldc.upenn.edu

Abstract   Over the past several decades, research and development of human language technology has been driven or hindered by the availability of data and a number of organizations have arisen to address the demand for greater volumes of linguistic data in a wider variety of languages with more sophisticated annotation and better quality. A great deal of the linguistic data available today results from common task technology evaluation programs that, at least as implemented in the United States, typically involve objective measures of system performance on a benchmark corpus that are compared with human performance over the same data. Data centres play an important role by distributing and archiving, sometimes collecting and annotating, and even by coordinating the efforts of other organizations in the creation of linguistic data. Data planning depends upon the purpose of the project, the linguistic resources needed, the internal and external limitations on acquiring them, availability of data, bandwidth and distribution requirements, available funding, the limits on human annotation, the timeline, the details of the processing pipeline including the ability to parallelize, or the need to serialize steps. Language resource creation includes planning, creation of a specification, collection, segmentation, annotation, quality assurance, preparation for use, distribution, adjudication, refinement, and extension. In preparation for publication, shared corpora are generally associated with metadata and documented to indicate the authors and annotators of the data, the volume and types of raw material included, the percent annotated, the annotation specification, and the quality control measures adopted. This chapter sketches issues involved in identifying and evaluating existing language resources and in planning, creating, validating, and distributing new language resources, especially those used for developing human language technologies with specific examples taken from the collection and annotation of conversational telephone speech and the adjudication of corpora created to support information retrieval.

221

L. Dybkjær et al. (eds.), Evaluation of Text and Speech Systems, 221–261.

© 2007 *Springer.*

Keywords   Language resources; Data; Data centres; Common task evaluation; Specification; Collection; Segmentation; Annotation; Intellectual property rights; Informed consent; Conversational telephone speech; Human subject behaviour; Quality assurance; Inter-annotator agreement; Adjudication; Distribution.

1   Introduction

The material for this chapter comes from lecture notes for a 2002 ELSNET Summer School with the goal of sketching the issues involved in identifying and evaluating existing language resource and in planning, creating, validating, and distributing new language resources especially those used for developing human language technologies. The workshop discussed these issues in the particular context of the common task technology development and evaluation programs that characterized human language technology research in the United States in the decade prior to the writing of this chapter. In preparing this chapter for publication, issues with momentary relevance for the ELSNET student but no general relevance were removed and facts, figures, and arguments were updated and generalized. The sections that follow begin with a description of the current linguistic resources landscape including the impact of common task programs and the role of data centres. After defining some terms, the discussion moves to planning resources for technology development including both technical and legal issues. After a brief discussion of how to find linguistic resources in the current context, the second half of the chapter details the issues involved in building language resources with emphasis on data collection.

2   The Linguistic Resource Landscape

Over the past several decades, research and development of human language technology has been driven or hindered by the availability of data.

> Modern speech and language processing is heavily based on common resources:
> raw speech and text corpora, annotated corpora and treebanks, standard tagsets
> for labelling pronunciation, part-of-speech parses, word-sense, and dialogue-
> level phenomena. (Jurafsky and Martin, 2000)

This dependence upon data is due in part to the shift toward probabilistic approaches and machine learning.

> By the last five years of the millennium it was clear that the field was vastly
> changing. First, probabilistic and data-driven models had become quite standard
> throughout natural language processing. Algorithms for parsing, part-of-speech
> tagging, reference resolution and discourse processing all began to incorpo-
> rate probabilities and employ evaluation methodologies borrowed from speech
> recognition and information retrieval. (Jurafsky and Martin, 2000)

Although research continues on making the best use of limited data in statistical tasks, such as are common in speech recognition and natural language processing, we will argue that the need for linguistic resources in human language technologies is inevitable whether the research is statistical or rule governed. There is ample evidence that research communities and commercial developers of language technologies agree. COCOSDA (http://www.cocosda.org/), the International Committee for the Coordination and Standardization of Speech Databases and Assessment Techniques, established to promote cooperation in spoken language processing, emphasizes resources in its mission statement:

> COCOSDA supports the development of spoken language resources and speech technology evaluation. For the former, COCOSDA promotes the development of distinctive types of spoken language data corpora for the purpose of building and/or evaluating current or future spoken language technology.

Although the past 15 years has seen the birth of more than a dozen organizations that create or distribute language data, demand continues to outpace supply. ELSNET (http://www.elsnet.org/), the European Network of Excellence in Human Language Technologies, began receiving funding from the European Commission in 1991 to advance human language technologies by offering "an environment that allows for optimal exploitation of the available human and intellectual resources". The Linguistic Data Consortium (LDC (http://www.ldc.upenn.edu)) was founded in 1992 to support language-related education, research and technology development by sharing linguistic resources. The European Language Resources Association (ELRA (http://www.elra.info/)) was established as a non-profit organization in 1995 to make language resources available for language engineering. The Bavarian Archive for Speech Signals (BAS (http://www.phonetik.uni-muenchen.de/Bas/)) was founded in 1995 to distribute databases of spoken German to the speech science and engineering communities and has since added 17 corpora to its catalogue. Between 1991 and 1994, a consortium led by Oxford University Press built the 100 million word British National Corpus (http://www.natcorp.ox.ac.uk/). Planning for the American National Corpus (http://americannationalcorpus.org/) began in 2001 with the first release becoming available in 2003 and the second release in 2005.

Many teaching and research groups have contributed valuable language resources. The Center for Spoken Language Understanding (CSLU (http://cslu.cse.ogi.edu/)) at the Oregon Graduate Institute of Science and Technology seeks to teach and conduct basic research and technology development and to help other teachers, researchers, and businesses build and use spoken language technology. They have created 20 different corpora since 1992. The Johns Hopkins Center for Language and Speech Processing (CLSP (http://www.clsp.jhu.edu)), established in 1992, promotes research and education in language and speech technologies and develops one or more databases each year, in particular as a product of its annual summer workshops. The Institute for Signal and Information Processing (ISIP (http://www.isip.msstate.edu/)) of the Mississippi State University was founded in 1994 to develop public domain speech recognition software and has contributed several important data resources including JEIDA [ISBN: 1-58563-093-4, ISBN: 1-58563-099-3], a corpus of southern accented speech and the resegmentation of the Switchboard [ISBN: 1-58563-121-3] corpus.

The current landscape for language resources is characterized by individual researchers, small and large research groups, and data centres all striving to create data and yet failing to keep pace with the demand for greater volumes of data in a wider variety of languages with more sophisticated annotation and better quality. As of the writing of this chapter, "large scale" data collection might be defined as billions of words of text, tens of thousands of hours of broadcast speech, thousands of hours of conversational telephone speech, and hundreds of hours of meeting recordings. For part of speech, entity, and syntactic tagging projects, "large scale" is currently defined as a million or more words of tagged text.

When we speak of a wider variety of languages, we mean that several research communities working in speech and text engineering have begun to move beyond the dozen most commercially viable languages that have often been the subject of intensive resource development and toward those languages that are sometimes called *low density* not for the number of native speakers but rather for the scarcity of publicly available resources. In some circles, the term *"low density languages"* has been replaced by the term *"less commonly taught languages"* but even the latter must be understood to mean less commonly taught outside the countries where they are national or regional languages of importance. In the current landscape, English, especially American English is the language for which exist the greatest number and variety of language resources of the greatest volume. There also exist impressive lists of resources for many of the languages of Europe, including Eastern Europe, though not always to the same degree. Beyond the largest languages of North America and Europe, Mandarin Chinese, Modern Standard Arabic, and Japanese are now well represented. Beyond that, however, there are few languages with adequate resources to support the comprehensive development of language technologies. Recent years have seen some attention focused on languages such as Bengali, Cebuano, Hindi, Punjabi, Tagalog, Tamil, Tigrinya, Urdu, Uzbek, and Yoruba with large populations of native speakers, writing systems, a press, and an Internet presence but with very little in the way of publicly available language resources to support technology development.

With each passing year, new research communities embrace an approach to empirical analysis that is both computer-based and collaborative. At the same time, research communities that have traditionally used digital data now demand data in new orders of magnitude. We can see evidence for the former in the experiences of the TalkBank Project (http://www.talkbank.org), an inter-disciplinary research project funded by a 5-year grant from the U.S. National Science Foundation (BCS- 998009, KDI, SBE) to Carnegie Mellon University and the University of Pennsylvania. The project's goal was to foster funda-mental research in the study of communication by providing standards and tools for creating, searching, and publishing primary materials via networked computers. The TalkBank principals identified and collaborated with 15 disciplinary groups of which seven received focused attention: Animal Com-munication, Classroom Discourse, Conversation Analysis, Linguistic Explo-ration, Gesture, Text, and Discourse. The Talkbank principals have observed growing demand for shared data resources and common tools and formats among all of the Talkbank areas. Ten years ago the list of publicly available digital linguistic resources was dominated by resources for speech recogni-tion, speaker verification, information retrieval, and natural language process-ing with ACL/DCI [ISBN: 1-58563-000-4], TIMIT [ISBN: 1-58563-019-5], TIDIGITS [ISBN: 1-58563-018-7], ECI [ISBN: 1-58563-033-3], Switchboard [ISBN: 1-58563-121-3], ATIS [ISBN: 1-58563-001-2], YOHO [ISBN: 1-58563-042-X], and Penn Treebank [ISBN: 1-58563-163-9] perhaps the most well-known data-sets, of that era. Today, due in part to the efforts of the Talkbank Project, the list of publicly available data-sets is much more var-ied and addresses the needs of communities that were not well represented in 1995. The Talkbank Corpora include: the FORM1 and FORM2 Kinematic Gesture corpora [ISBN: 1-58563-299-6, 1-58563-269-4], Grassfields Bantu Fieldwork: Dschang Lexicon and Dschang and Ngomba Tone Paradigms [ISBN: 1-58563-255-4, 1-58563-254-6, 1-58563-216-3], the SLx Corpus of Classic Sociolinguistic Interviews [ISBN: 1-58563-273-2], and the Santa Barbara Corpus of Spoken American English, Parts 2, 3, and 4 [ISBN: 1-58563-272-4, 1-58563-308-9, 158563-348-8] and Field Recordings of Vervet Monkey Calls [ISBN: 1-58563-312-7]. The research community work-ing on the quantitative analysis of linguistic variation, which has been devoted to empirical methods since William Labov's seminal work *The Social Strati-fication of English in New York City* (Labov, 1966), has not traditionally pub-lished data-sets. This practice began to change with Gregory Guy's (1999) workshop on publicly accessible data and has borne fruit with the publication of the SLx corpus [ISBN: 1-58563-273-2] of classical sociolinguistic inter-views collected by Labov and his students and transcribed, time-aligned, and annotated for examples of sociolinguistic variation by LDC.

While new communities join the ranks of those that work with digital language corpora, communities that worked with digital language data 10 years ago have continued to demand greater volumes of data. The resources created by the DARPA TIDES (http://www.darpa.mil/IPTO/Programs/tides) (Translingual Information Detection, Extraction and Summarization) and EARS (http://www.darpa.mil/IPTO/Programs/ears) (Effective Affordable Reusable Speech-to-Text) research communities offer an example. These include Gigaword News Text Corpora in English, Chinese, and Arabic [ISBN: 1-58563-271-6, 1-58563-230-9, 1-58563-260-0 respectively] with roughly a billion words in each, parallel and translated text corpora now measured in the hundreds of millions of words and the Fisher English corpora (Cieri et al., 2004) that now consist of approximately 4,000 hours of conversational telephone speech of which about two-thirds are publicly available [ISBN: 1-58563-313-5, 1-58563-314-3, 1-58563-335-6, 1-58563-336-4] at the time of writing.

Every speech and language researcher is not only a potential user but also a potential creator of linguistic resources thanks to desktop computing that has advanced to support both collection and annotation of text, audio, and video in amounts measured in the hundreds of gigabytes. Unfortunately, data creation and annotation require skills that are not adequately taught in the typical graduate programs in Electrical Engineering, Computer Science, Linguistics, or Computational Linguistics. Medium to large-scaledata collection and annotation further require specific technological infrastructure and management. International language resource centres such as the LDC and increasingly the ELRA maintain stable infrastructure and manage medium to large-scale language resource efforts. Together they have published more than 600 data-sets of which more than half have been donated by other organizations or individuals.

Simultaneous with the demand for increases in volume and language variety have been demands for more challenging data with annotations of greater sophistication. Speech recognition has seen the progression in its scope from a small vocabulary of words and short phrases to read speech, broadcast news, telephone conversation, speech in noisy environments and, most recently, speech during meetings. Treebanks have been re-annotated to create Proposition Banks and Charles University has produced Dependency Treebanks with tectogrammatical annotation, that is annotation at the level of meaning abstracted from the variations in linguistic form that appear on other linguistic levels. Treebanks have also moved from the realm of text to conversational speech, including languages such as Levantine Colloquial Arabic that lack the standardizing effects of a broadly accepted writing system. Part of speech tagging has evolved to include morphological analysis and gloss in the case of the LDC Arabic Treebank [ISBN: 1-58563-261-9, 1-58563-282-1, 1-58563-341-0, 1-58563-343-7]. The Automatic Content Extraction (ACE (http://www.nist.gov/speech/tests/ace/)) community has developed, from what was simple named entity tagging, a new specification for text tagging that includes entities, relations, events, and coreference. Video has been tagged for text recognition, entity recognition and tracking, and the physics of gesture.

2.1 Common Task Research and Technology Evaluation Programs

A great deal of the linguistic data available today have been created as a result of *common task* technology evaluation programs. Mariani (2002) sketches the history of speech and language technology evaluation in the United States giving the origin:

> Evaluation as a theme was introduced after the first DARPA programme on Speech Understanding Systems (SUS), which lasted from 1971 to 1976. The main conclusion of SUS was - that it was impossible to compare systems which were developed on different tasks, with different languages of various levels of difficulty.

the point at which common task evaluation became a regular theme:

> Evaluation was subsequently included as a theme in the following DARPA programme which started in 1984, but work was not initiated until 1987. The evaluation campaigns were open to non-US laboratories in 1992, and Philips Speech Processing (Germany), Cambridge University Engineering Department (UK) and LIMSI-CNRS (France) participated in the evaluation on that year, with excellent results.

and a mention of what is probably the most inclusive and international evaluation program:

> The Text Retrieval Evaluation Conference (TREC) programme started in 1992. It was opened to the international community from the very beginning and more than 120 groups have participated in this programme since. Both spoken and written language processing were addressed in the evaluation-based programmes.

The common task evaluation program is an implementation of a research management paradigm that has proven itself over the past decades. Under this model, multiple organizations work together to solve research and development problems while benefiting from shared infrastructure that may include task definitions, evaluation metrics and procedures, data and software components. Common task programs often involve direct sponsorship of participants but that is not always the case. Every year dozens of organizations participate in common task evaluation programs organized by the United States National Institute of Standards and Technologies (NIST (http://www.nist.gov)) without direct sponsorship finding that the opportunity to collaborate and have their technology evaluated objectively is a benefit worth the effort required by the evaluation. Common task programs may have one or more tasks required of all participants, one or more optional tasks and even some tasks that are site-specific. Examples of common tasks include automatic speech recognition of read speech, broadcast news, conversational telephone speech and meetings, identification of the languages spoken in a corpus of telephone calls, speaker identification from telephone calls, translation of news stories, identification of all stories in a corpus that discuss a topic, extraction and categorization of entities, relations and events in a corpus, the compression of one or more news stories into a headline or into summaries of varying length, and the development of two-way speech-to-speech translation.

Common task evaluation programs as practiced in the United states typically involve objective measures of system performance on a benchmark corpus that are compared with human performance over the same data. Examples of such metrics include word error or word accuracy rate in which system generated transcripts are compared to human transcripts of the same speech and points are deducted for every reference word missing from, added to, or replaced in the system transcript. Another, more controversial, metric is the Bleu score (Papinieni et al., 2002) in which translation systems are graded on the overlap between the word n-grams in their output and those in a set of independent human translations. The number of reference translations and the length of the n-grams can vary.

Mariani (2002), writes: *"The [European] projects are based on concept of co-operation among consortia, not on competition."* US common task programs have sometimes been criticized for being too competitive. Where common task evaluations measure participant performance directly via stable data and evaluation metrics, competition is inevitable. However, the concept of "competition with cooperation" is prominent in many US programs. Sites share data, discoveries, and software and join to form mini-consortia. Furthermore, in most common task evaluation projects data, evaluation metrics, and research results are published. Meetings are completely open or else include international observers. Research sites are also free to publish their own results at international conferences. It is important to note that different program managers have configured their programs to vary competitiveness. Naturally, if the goal is to identify the site with the highest performing system in order to award a contract for further development or creation of a production system, then research sites will be inclined toward competition and away from cooperation. Compare this with the DARPA EARS program in which annual performance goals were considered very challenging but in which the program required just one site to meet each goal with a system that could be composed of components from other sites. The effect of this approach was that many groups participated in multi-site teams and some participated in more than one such team. Intense cooperation among international research teams continues in the DARPA GALE (http://www.darpa.mil/IPTO/Programs/gale) program among others.

Task definitions originate with the program manager who seeks to accelerate research and development on pre-commercial technologies in order to respond to a government need. The program manager, researchers, resource and evaluation providers all refine the task definitions before they are formalized in an evaluation specification. The community also identifies resource needs and develops a schedule typically at a kick-off meeting. Infrastructure groups create resources and implement evaluation methods, negotiating with the community on any modifications. Evaluation is generally the responsibility of an organization that is independent of sponsors and all sites. In the United States, NIST, part of the Department of Commerce, is the most common evaluation group.

Shared resources lower the barrier of entry to all program participants and reduce the duplication of effort. One or more of the research sites may supply data or an independent organization may be contracted to create data specifically for the program. The LDC hosted at the University of Pennsylvania has been archiving and distributing language resources for common task evaluation programs since 1993 and has been creating them since 1995. In Europe, ELRA fulfils a similar function.

Most US common task programs distinguish two or three kinds of data. *Evaluation Data*, is carefully constructed specifically for the measurement of system performance. At evaluation time, research sites receive raw data and are required to process it and produce output compliant with the evaluation specification. The evaluation group then compares system outputs to human outputs produced according to the same, or else compatible, specifications. In many cases the human outputs are created ahead of time for all benchmark data and held in reserve until system outputs have been submitted. However, human annotators sometimes adjudicate sites' results either as a replacement for or as a complement to up-front annotation. Technology developers are typically unaware of the composition or time epoch of the evaluation data. The difference between evaluation data and *Training Data* may be varied to focus attention on the technology's generality or alternatively on its suitability to a specific task. In other words, technology developers build their rules or statistical models upon training data that may be matched or intentionally mismatched to the evaluation data. The size of the evaluation corpus will depend upon the technology and conditions being evaluated. However evaluation sets are generally sized to be the minimum that will provide robust, statistically significant technology evaluation. Funding for evaluation data is generally reserved before any is allocated to other kinds of data. However, the creation of evaluation data may occur after all other data is created. This is because many evaluation programs seek to take evaluation data from an epoch that is separate and preferably later than the epochs of other kinds of data. Doing so gives an opportunity to evaluate how technologies will fare when dealing with the new vocabulary that inevitably arises over time. Although it is possible to take evaluation data from a later time epoch and still create it early in an evaluation cycle, the desire to have the entire data-set be as fresh as possible, thus making it interesting for purposes of demonstrating technologies, means that data collection is often ongoing during an evaluation cycle and that evaluation data is often created after the other types, indeed just in time for its use in an evaluation.

Some but not all common task programs create a third kind, *Development/Test Data*, generally similar to evaluation data differing only in that development/test data is provided directly to sites for their own internal evaluation of the generality of their technologies. In multi-year programs, previous years' evaluation data is frequently reused as development test data.

In common task evaluation programs, such as those organized by DARPA and NIST, all three data types as well as the specifications for creating data and for evaluating systems, sites' system descriptions, and NIST's reports of results are published on an annual basis. In some cases, evaluation corpora are held in reserve until they can be replaced by newer evaluation corpora. This allows NIST to evaluate the systems of research sites who seek to enter the program mid-year.

Mariani (2002) provides a European perspective on common task evaluation programs. On the difference between US and European sponsored research, he writes: *"Simply stated, the US focuses on fewer but larger-size projects, whereas European funding is spread thinner over a larger number of projects and players."* Further contrasting the availability of infrastructure for evaluation, he writes:

> The main actors in this framework are: the National Institute for Standards and Technology (NIST) as the organiser - defining the calendar, the protocols, the metrics, organising workshops and meetings; the Linguistic Data Consortium (LDC) as the Language Resources provider; several technology developers, both from the public and industrial sectors. The tasks addressed in this framework were made more and more difficult with time.

and then: *"... there is no infrastructure for evaluation in the EU, and the definition of the measure of success is still open."* Seeing this as a major obstacle to progress, Mariani writes:

> The question arises, therefore, whether it is acceptable that European technology development and applications are conducted in Europe, with a dependence on technology assessment in the US, due to a lack of proper evaluation infrastructure in Europe. [...] "As for EU-US co-operation in Human Language Technologies, especially in Standards, Resources and Evaluation, this appears to be working well at present. The consensus is that it is well worth investing future effort in this direction for all concerned."

Over the past 5 years, the EU has sought to correct the situation Mariani mentions, in part due to his own efforts. Quite recently, ELRA has begun to evaluate technology in EU sponsored programs.

Mariani concludes with a set of common challenges for European and American technology development:

> Multilingualism is a major challenge on both sides of the Atlantic, for very different reasons. In Europe, there is a need to address all languages of EU citizens, for cultural and political reasons. In the USA, they feel that they have a strong strategic disadvantage: everyone understands English but they don't understand other languages. Therefore they cannot get the information from abroad!

From a contemporaneous American perspective, we report on the results of a breakout group on innovation and infrastructure held during the 2000 NIST Transcription Workshop. Participants acknowledged the benefits of shared task definitions, data, and evaluation metrics as reference points for comparison and noted that they function as a driving force for research agendas and tend to encourage solutions that tune to one task. Some researchers noted that they spent considerable time duplicating others' approaches in order to maintain competitive scores rather than focusing on innovation. The fundamental challenges they identified at the time, understanding signal characteristics, localization, speaker variability, lack of data, lack of sharing of tools and components, improvement of diagnostics beyond word error rate, and information transfer across linguistic levels, have since become the focus of intensive research. DARPA EARS devoted considerable energy into creating a large corpus of conversational telephone speech that represents the differences in regional accent, as well as age and sex that characterize American speech. The EARS community also developed a stable benchmark corpus and rules for its use that supported the measurement of progress from year to tear. The Novel Approaches working group in EARS developed a new set of features used in acoustic decoding of speech. The research management innovations continue in the DARPA GALE program where large, multi-site teams collaborate intensively to reduce the pressure on each participant to reproduce technological innovations developed by all other participants.

Researchers also sought to lower barriers to enter into the community in order to increase the size of the gene pool. They suggested a reinforcement of the idea of hub and spoke design, whereby a small number of required evaluation conditions made it possible to evaluate all systems on a consistent basis while optional tasks allowed researchers to pursue their own areas of inquiry. Similarly a mixture of large and small tasks would allow teams of different size to focus their efforts appropriately. Finally they lauded events such as the training workshops coordinated by the Johns Hopkins University and Mississippi State as ways to bring new researchers into the community. They recommended that future programs focus on tool and component sharing. Researchers generally agreed that well annotated, stable data, formal evaluation specification, and the knowledge transfer that takes place at workshops sponsored by the evaluation community were crucial to progress.

2.2   The Role of Data Centres

Data Centres play an important role in enabling education, research, and technology development. Within the United States, several multi-site, common task research programs have collaborated with the LDC to meet their data needs. LDC began in 1992 with the goal of serving as an archive and distribution point of corpora for technology development and evaluation. Over time the mission of the LDC has expanded either in response to or in anticipation of growing needs. In 1995, LDC began its first data collection projects when it became clear that there were not enough other labs to meet the growing demand. By 1998, it was clear that demand would continue to grow and data collection and annotation became a central focus for LDC. That same year, LDC also began to focus on infrastructure and tool development to support data collection and annotation. At the time of writing, LDC has grown to include 43 full-time employees and a transient staff of part-time annotators that has been as large as 65. 2019 unique organizations in 89 countries have used LDC data. To date, LDC has released 31,269 copies of 558 titles including more than 2500 copies of more than 160 titles within common task programs. The data produced for common task programs may be held in reserve to support evaluation before it is eventually released generally.

LDC is an open consortium that unites researchers in the non-profit, commercial, and government sectors with a common interest in language research, teaching, and technology development. The basic model is that organizations join the consortium on a yearly basis paying a membership fee that supports consortium operations. In return they receive rights to no-cost copies of all data released during the years in which they were members. Membership is open to any organization. Rights are ongoing and can be exercised at any time. For example, 1993 members may still request data under their membership for that year. The membership fees have never increased since they were set in 1992 by a board of overseers that included participants from the government, commercial, and non-profit sectors. Although preferable, it is not strictly necessary for an organization to become an LDC member. Many corpora may be licensed to non-members. To support new entrants into human language research communities, LDC also allows current members to acquire data from previous membership years at reduced rates.

As mentioned above, LDC serves as both a centralized distribution point and an archive. Every corpus ever released is still available. In some cases, newer versions with additional data or bug fixes replace old ones. However, where

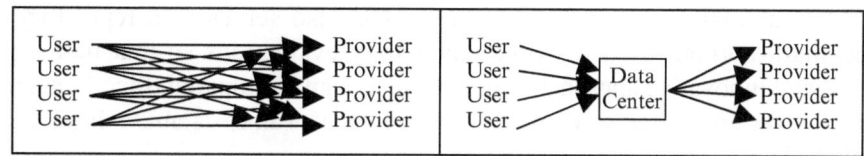

Figure 1. Data Centres serve as intellectual property intermediaries, reducing the number of user-provider negotiations necessary.

corpora have served as evaluation benchmarks they are preserved in exactly the same form in which they were originally released. This stability in the data is necessary to allow comparison of system performance over time. Where errors are discovered in benchmark corpora they are documented without being repaired.

LDC also acts as an intellectual property intermediary thereby reducing the amount of negotiation involved in resource sharing. Figure 1 demonstrates the benefit of such an arrangement. In order for a group of users to acquire rights to data directly from each of a group of providers, the number of agreements would be the product of the number of users and providers. Data centres acting as intermediaries provide a level of abstraction whereby each user signs one user agreement and each provider signs one provider agreement with terms that have been coordinated. The total number of agreements needed is just the sum, not the product, of the number of users and providers. More importantly, researchers gain consistent rights regardless of their negotiation skills and providers reduce the effort they spend to support research. This is especially important for commercial providers because they receive little or no direct revenue from supporting research.

There are additional advantages to the centralization of data resources. To the extent that resources are centralized, potential users have a smaller number of places they must search. LDC corpora are identified by catalogue number and ISBN, and their authors and titles are given within the catalogue. Centralized corpora can also be better standardized both in terms of structure and format and in terms of content and quality. Corpora published through the LDC are checked for quality and released in a consistent form, to the extent allowed by the variation in their target audiences.

Data centres consolidate resources from a multitude of disciplines in a single location. The LDC Catalogue, for example, contains resources that were developed to support research in: speech recognition under a variety of circumstances (including broadcast news, conversation telephone speech, and meetings), speech synthesis, language and acoustic modelling, information retrieval, information extraction, summarization, natural language processing, machine translation and speech-to-speech translation, and dialogue systems.

ELRA's catalogue has similar diversity. LDC also serves as a repository of benchmark corpora used in NIST technology evaluations so that new algorithms and innovative approaches may be tested and compared directly against state of the art systems whose scores on these same database have been published.

In its role as data centre, LDC strives to address the needs of its research communities. In part this has meant distributing and in many cases creating corpora in a greater variety of languages with more sophisticated annotation for use in an expanding number of disciplines. It has also meant creating and distributing data collection and annotation tools and corpus standards, and integrating data creation and technology development. Specifically, over the past few years LDC has increased collaboration with the beneficiaries of its data in order to use their technologies and technology evaluation tools to improve corpus creation. In the commonest cases, LDC corpora are often dually annotated and then scored for consistency using the same tools that score system performance against a benchmark corpus.

A corpus contains data selected and prepared for a specific purpose. However, it is sometimes possible to create a corpus that supports more than one kind of research. For example, in December of 2004, LDC received a request for conversational telephone speech that was dense in named entities and therefore useful for projects focusing on information extraction, such as the Automatic Content Extraction (Doddington et al., 2004) program. Having met the goals of a phase of the Fisher English (Cieri et al., 2004) collection of conversational telephone speech supporting speech-to-text technology evaluation, LDC was able to change the topics assigned to subjects in order to highlight people and places in the news. Topics were formulated to remind subjects of the important persons and places associated with each event. The results were conversations that were certainly useful for the original goals but were also much richer in entities and events, and therefore able to serve the ACE project as well.

Over the past dozen years, several other data centres have begun to perform functions similar to LDC with models that are similar but not identical. The ELRA also serves as an archive and repository of language data. Under their model, members receive discounts on licensing fees. Where LDC and NIST have specialized to focus on data and technology evaluation respectively, ELRA has recently begun to handle both functions for European programs.

3   Background on Linguistic Data and Annotation

A *corpus* is any body of raw data selected, sampled, formatted, and annotated for a specific purpose. The terms *language data*, *linguistic data*, and *raw data*, here refer to recorded observations of any performance or experiment involving a spoken, written, or signed language or communicative system. *Annotation* is any process of adding value to raw data through the application of human judgement. For example, an audio recording of a telephone conversation is raw data. A transcript of that same conversation encodes subtle human judgement about what was said, and in some cases intended, and is thus annotation.

Annotation may be accomplished with direct human effort or mediated by some technology based upon rules or statistical observation. Morphological analysis, in particular generating one or more analyses of a surface form, is frequently rule-based while part of speech-tagging, particularly selecting the most probable analysis from among several possibilities, is frequently based upon statistical models. Other examples of annotation include transcription, segmentation, part-of-speech tagging, parsing, entity, relation, event and co-reference tagging, sense disambiguation, topic categorization, summarization, and translation.

Segmentation, a very specific type of annotation, involves dividing some larger unit of observation into smaller pieces to facilitate future annotation, search, or analysis. For some purposes it may be necessary to segment by actually cutting a recording, for example, a large audio or video file, into pieces and storing them separately. However, segmentation can generally be accomplished by storing the time stamps that mark the beginning and end of significant events in a separate annotation file in order to preserve the integrity of the original recording. Recordings of conversations might be segmented at speaker changes, breaths, or pauses. News broadcasts might be segmented at speaker changes or story boundaries.

In-line annotations are embedded within raw language data. Though very common, especially in text, in-line annotations can be problematic for several reasons. Although there are formats that permit raw data and annotations of different modes to be mixed in the same file, this practice may compromise the integrity of the raw data. In many cases the formats that allow mixed modes to be embedded in the same file are proprietary and reduce the generality of access. Multi-tiered annotation, in-line, can make data unreadable. Finally, the distribution rights for raw text and annotation are frequently very different. Reliance on in-line annotation reduces the ability to distribute by multiplying the restrictions that may apply to the raw data and its annotation.

Stand-off annotations are separate from the signal and refer to it or portions of it via time codes, byte offsets or word offsets, for example. Stand-off annotation is widely recognized as the best option for those who work with audio and video data. Stand-off annotation is equally effective though less common when working with text. In the simplest cases, where the signal is text and there is a single layer of annotation, stand-off can be slightly more complicated to parse than in-line. However, even in this case there are advantages of stand-off annotation, which can be associated equally well with text, audio, or video without changing the raw data in any way and can be used to maintain separate layers of annotations.

It is important to reiterate that a corpus contains data selected for a specific purpose. Selection is an important part of corpus creation. The match or mismatch between the data in a corpus and the technology or application for which it is used may have a large impact on the success of the venture. To give some simple examples, a speech recognition system trained on broadcast news will not fare as well when tested on conversational telephone speech as would the same engine trained on matching data. Unfortunately, many research communities lack the specific data they need to conduct research and technology development and must settle for, or choose to settle for as a cost-saving measure, data that was developed for some other purpose. The Switchboard [ISBN: 1-58563-121-3] corpus for example, was originally developed to support research in speaker identification and topic spotting but has been re-annotated to support research in everything from speech recognition to natural language processing and parsing. The Topic Detection and Tracking 2 (TDT-2) [ISBN: 1-58563-183-3] corpus has similarly been re-purposed for speech recognition and spoken document retrieval.

It should be clear by now that *time* is an important dimension in spoken linguistic data. Time is evident in recordings of live linguistic performance such as conversations or monologues. In written language, *sequence* replaces time as a significant dimension. Text need not be written or even read in the order in which the final version appears. Writers are free to edit and reorder their writings and readers are free to progress through a text in some non-linear fashion. Nonetheless, the sequence of words on a page or in a file represents the author's deliberate intent and thus forms a dimension upon which subsequent analysis is based. Of course, not all linguistic data need be ordered along a chronological or even sequential dimension. In lexicons, for example, the order of entries means something entirely different than the order of written words in a text or spoken words in a conversation.

Speech and gesture are necessarily captured as the communicative performance takes place with time playing a major role in the analysis of these modes. Time is generally represented as the offset from the starting time of the event recording not as absolute time. However, in some cases the absolute starting time of the recording of the event is present either in metadata or encoded in the file name of the recording or both. This is desirable. Now that desktop computing makes it possible for individual researchers to collect and annotate small to medium sized corpora, the number of collection projects has grown creating opportunities to study phenomena across corpora. With time playing such a crucial role in the introduction of new vocabulary, especially named entities, the encoding of absolute time in data collection offers the possibility of placing recordings from multiple sources on a single timeline.

The recording of written language on the other hand generally does not preserve the order in which the components, words or characters, of the communication were produced. This may be because the recording technology, stone tablets, papyrus, or sheets of paper, lacked the ability to represent time or because, as is the case with modern word processing technology, time is ignored. In the recorded version, written communications order language according to the author's desires, which may be very different from the order in which it was produced. One exception is handwriting which, like gesture, may be recorded via motion capture devices such that timing information is available. For handwriting a combination of stylus and writing surface translate handwriting into time-sequenced movement data. In the case of gesture, motion may be captured, for example, by a combination of transmitters placed on a subject's joints and receivers placed at the corners of a three-dimensional bounding box or may be interpolated from two-dimensional video. Although the grammars of spoken, written, and gestured language differ significantly from one another and although there is a common association between written language and text and between spoken language and audio, one should not conclude that all text encodes written language or that all audio encodes speech. One may read written material aloud and transcribe spoken material proving that the mode of recording language does not guarantee the type of language recorded.

4   Data Planning for Technology Development and Evaluation

Data planning for technology or application development and evaluation depends upon a number of factors including the purpose of the project, the linguistic resources needed, the internal and external limitations on acquiring them, availability of data, bandwidth and distribution requirements, available funding, the limits on human annotation, the timeline, the details of the processing pipeline including the ability to parallelize or the need to serialize steps.

4.1   Technical Issues

Planning for corpus creation involves matching the types and volume of raw data and the complexity and coverage of their annotation to the needs of the human language technology, such as speech-to-text, and sometimes to an application using that technology, such as a voice mail transcription system. Basic speech-to-text technologies require audio recordings of speech with time-aligned annotation. Acoustic modelling requires a close alignment of the speech signal with symbolic labels. Were it not for phonetic variation and differences between orthography and phonetic reality, a single layer of time-aligned orthographic transcription, which would thus also be phonetic, would be sufficient. However, because writing systems often differ from phonetic reality, transcriptions need to be mediated either through a second layer of annotation or through a pronouncing lexicon. The lexicon generally contains an entry for each surface form showing its alternate pronunciations, possibly its morphological analysis in morphologically complex languages, its part of speech and preferably its frequency in different domains. The former approach involves creating two or more tiers of transcription in which the tiers are aligned to each other and the audio. One tier provides an orthographic transcription and the other a phonetic transcription. It should be noted that the two-tiered transcription is a kind of contextualized version of the pronouncing dictionary.

Another difference to consider in comparing corpora is the variability potentially present in the raw data. Language varies according to region. Regional varieties of a language are generally called dialects. However, the reader is cautioned that the meaning of the term changes with the situation. Linguists use the term dialect to refer to mutually intelligible varieties of the same language. When varieties become mutually unintelligible they are considered different languages. However, there is great variation in usage; varieties sometimes labelled dialects, such as the dialects of Chinese, evince less mutual intelligibility than varieties traditionally considered different languages, such as Swedish and Norwegian. The situation is further complicated in dialect continua, chains of regional dialects in which adjacent pairs are mutually intelligible while varieties separated by greater space are not. Although there has been some work done on cross-dialectal training of human language technologies, this work is still in its early stages so that it remains important to match the dialects of training data to dialects targeted by the technology or application. Variation in spoken and written language may also be conditioned by social factors, time, register, domain, and mode. Vocabularies may be general, technical, literary, or conversational. Speaking and writing are different modes of communications marked by different grammar.

We can elucidate the process of analyzing needs for technology or application development through an example, a system designed to gather information for purposes of evaluating the merits of accusations of fraud in the stock market or other illegal business practice. Such a system might process multiple sources of information in order to help investigators find correlations between events and trading or business activities. The sources of information might be news text and press releases present on the World Wide Web or available via subscription feeds, news broadcasts and cable news programmes; wire taps and corporate email archives of companies under surveillance or investigation; video recordings of their meetings and of depositions of their employees, partners, and customers, financial analyses, transaction reports and filings. The system would help answer a number of questions using this data. For example, within the telephone conversations, one would like to know who speaks, what they say both in summary and in detail, whether they mention the company under investigation or its employees regardless of whether that mention used a fully specified name or a nickname. In meeting video, one would also like to analyze gesture, gaze, and body language in order to help determine the power relations among the participants and their disposition toward each other and toward the topics discussed. These needs suggest a number of technologies already under development including speaker recognition, summarization, information extraction, speech recognition, video and gesture analysis, and information each of which have their own data requirements.

4.2 Intellectual Property Rights and Informed Consent

The acquisition of intellectual property rights and the informed consent of human subjects are important parts of the data planning process and the responsibility of the collection team. Where a technology development effort benefits from existing data, these issues have generally been handled though their impact may show in the cost of licensing the corpus. A complete review of the legal issues goes beyond the scope of this work. Here we will simply discuss representative issues taking examples from the current situation in the United States noting that laws and practice differ from country to country.

Within the United States, the creator of an original work is owner of that work and the only one who has the right to copy and distribute. The creator can assign copyright by contract and employers generally arrange to acquire copyright for the work done by their employees. To support research and teaching, the principle of *fair use* permits copying for those purposes. US law provides the parameters with which fair use is evaluated but does not actually define the space. The parameters include: the use of the material whether for commercial purposes or for education and research, the size of the material used relative to the entire body of work from which it is extracted, the degree to which the data is transformed before use, and the probable impact the use will have on the owners' ability to derive income from the material. The interpretation of fair use is left to the discretion of courts. In practice, organizations typically define safe harbours in which they believe they can operate with reasonable assurance of avoiding charges of copyright violation. Given the uncertainty surrounding copyright law, the LDC normally acquires explicit rights to distribute the data in its corpora.

Much of the data used in human language technology development comes from news publishers and broadcasters. That data is intrinsically interesting and has a broad vocabulary due to the variety of topics covered in the news. Other benefits of news text and broadcast news are that the data is broadly available, that they can be licensed for research use without unusual limitations and that licensing costs are reasonable given creation costs. Some sources are willing to share their data for research use without cost. For example, some governments, including the US government, consider their publications to be in the public domain. Other sources have offered data centres deep discounts off their normal licensing fees. In negotiating rights for language data, LDC generally seeks non-exclusive, perpetual, worldwide, royalty free license to distribute to both LDC members and non-members who sign an agreement limiting their use of the data to linguistic education, research, and technology development without limitation as to quantity. These conditions are motivated by the use of corpora as benchmarks for evaluating new technologies. Distribution restrictions that limit distribution either by number of copies, time, or region limit the usefulness of the data for technology evaluation.

For conversational and meeting speech, the primary issue is *informed consent*. Within the United States, research that involved human subject must proceed according to a collection protocol approved by an Institutional Review Board (IRB). These boards, apparently designed to regulate clinical medical trials, review collection protocols for their risk versus the benefit presumed to result from the research. For Human Language Technology (HLT) research and development, the risks are generally no greater than those subjects encounter in their everyday lives. In most data collection efforts, subjects are simply asked to talk or write or to make judgements about language. One area of concern, however, is the risk to anonymity. Collection efforts maintain the anonymity of human subjects by separating the identifying information used to contact and compensate subjects from the actual recordings of speech or decisions. For many linguistic research projects the benefits to human subjects are also minimal compared, for example, to the benefits of having access to experimental pharmaceuticals in clinical trials. However, this minimal benefit to the individual is acceptable given the minimal risk and the potential benefit to society resulting from the creation or improvement of technologies that become part of our everyday lives.

5   Finding Resources

One of the first decisions one must make is whether to use existing resources or else build them to specification. Found resources are generally less expensive and may have the virtue of being previously used, discussed, and improved. However they may not necessarily be ideal for the target use. Resources built to specification are optimized for the target use but with added cost and time. Finding digital linguistic resources is somewhat more difficult than finding books due to the distributed nature of their publication and the lack of a single catalogue. In order to find resources published directly by their creators, one must know the creators in advance, learn about them via published papers, request advice from experts using networked discussion lists, or perform Internet searches by resource type and language. Resources that are distributed via data centres, such as the LDC or the ELRA are somewhat easier to find due to their centralization and due to the catalogues the centres maintain.

At the time of writing, the ELRA (http://catalog.elda.org) catalogue allowed full text search with the user entering one or more search terms and specifying whether those terms were to be matched exactly, in conjunction or in disjunction. The search engine responds with a hit list containing brief descriptions of matching corpora and links to fuller descriptions. Available information includes pricing information and, for selected corpora, additional documentation, samples, a validation report, a description of the design of the database, and a list of known bugs. Pricing information is distinguished along three dimensions, whether the organization is an ELRA member or not, whether the organization is commercial or not, and whether the use is commercial or not.

The LDC catalogue (http://www.ldc.upenn.edu/Catalog), at the time of writing, can be browsed by data type, data source, and release year and can be searched using full text search and fielded records in any combination. The fields: catalogue number, corpus name, authors, and corpus description can be searched with keywords. The fields for languages, data types, associated research projects and recommended applications have controlled vocabularies that are selected from a pick list. The user can specify whether to conjoin multiple fields with Boolean AND or OR. The search engine responds with a hit list containing pointers to the full catalogue entries for each item. Catalogue entries include the corpus name, authors, the catalogue number and ISBN number, release date, data type, data source, associated programs, recommended applications, languages and ISO language codes, distribution media, licensing information, links to online documentation, and samples. Once licenses are properly executed, LDC data are distributed on media, CD, DVD, or hard drive or via HTTP transfer depending upon the size of the corpus.

The Open Language Archives Community (OLAC (http://www.language-archives.org/)) indexes 33 different collections of language data, including the holdings of the LDC and ELRA, as a union catalogue of language resources. OLAC separates the function of hosting data from the functions of hosting, indexing and searching metadata. Participating archives export their metadata to search providers who index and maintain search engines. For example the advanced search functions hosted by the LinguistList (http://linguistlist.org/olac/) allow keyword searching in the title, creator/ contributor and corpus description fields and searching with controlled vocabulary among the language, type, and discourse type fields. Queries against the LinguistList search engine return hit lists with links to fuller catalogue records. The contents of these fuller descriptions vary from one data provider to another. The OLAC metadata language accommodates most of the metadata types needed by its constituent data providers and is extensible. Metadata types include creator, contributor, publisher, title, coverage, date, description, format including encoding and markup, identifier, language, relation to other resources, rights, source, subject, functionality, and linguistic type.

6   Building Resources

The actual steps in building language resources include planning, creation of a specification, collection, segmentation, annotation, quality assurance, preparation for use, distribution, adjudication, refinement, and extension. We have already discussed planning, including planning for the acquisition of distribution rights and consents. The sections that follow cover the other steps with particular emphasis on collection.

6.1   Specification

During the course of a corpus creation project, a multitude of decisions are made and implemented. Unless the project has a very short life cycle or the principals have exceedingly good memories, some decisions will be forgotten, reviewed, and possibly revised though not always with the effect of improving the effort. A corpus specification describing the overall use of the corpus, the raw data used as input, the collection and annotation processes including dependencies among parts of the process, the output formats, and assumptions about all of the above, can help stabilize and coordinate such effort. The specification contributes to planning, training of collection and annotation staff, and documentation of the final products. It also reminds internal staff, sponsors, and potential users of the decisions made.

6.2   Collection

In preparation for the development or evaluation of language technologies, one may collect data representing spoken, written, or gestured communicative modes that may be captured as audio, text, or video.

6.2.1   Collection parameters.   Before beginning, one must determine the parameters of collection. Here we will discuss two such parameters *sampling resolution* and *quantization*. Sampling resolution is the frequency with which an analogue signal is sampled to produce a digital artefact. The sampling of two-dimensional graphics, for example, is measured in dots per inch. Video is generally sampled at roughly 30 frames per second. Speech is sampled as it is digitized at rates that tend to range from 8 to 48 thousand cycles per second or kilohertz (kHz). The range of frequencies involved in spoken language (0–8 kHz) and the frequencies the human ear can detect (0–11kHz), as well as the need to double sampling frequencies in order to avoid aliasing, have figured historically in the selection of sampling rates for digital technologies and formats. The most common sampling rates are: 8, 11, 16, 22, 44, and 48 kHz. Quantization refers to the range of values any single sample may have. For example, common quantizations for two-dimensional images range from two bits, representing just black and white dots, to 32 bits representing more than 4 billion colours or shades of grey. Speech is typically quantized in 8, 16, 20, or 24 bits. The greater dynamic range offered by 20 and 24 bit quantization reduce the probability of reaching the sample peak (clipping) when increasing microphone gain or when dealing with an audio signal that has especially great or especially variable amplitude.

Deciding upon a sampling rate and quantization often involves compromise. The principle of full information capture (Chapman and Kenney, 1996) states that sampling and quantization should be fine enough to capture the smallest detail considered significant. In image digitization this might involve reviewing an image with a jeweller's loupe to identify the smallest detail to be preserved, measuring that unit and then setting resolution to assure capture. In the domain of spoken language, full information capture might be interpreted as recording the highest frequencies used in human language in which case audio sampling rates of 16 kHz would be adequate. Another approach sets capture parameters at the limits of the biological system. In the case of audio data for human listening, 22 kHz sampling reflects this thinking. Current needs also play a role in setting collection parameters. A collection designed to provide training data for a technology that expects data at a certain sampling rate may reasonably decide to collect at just that rate. This approach optimizes for short-term gain and may prove problematic if current needs prove less demanding than future needs. In LDC's experience, data have a protracted job cycle being re-annotated and reused far beyond original intent. Other constraints include available time and funding to conduct the data collection and the capacity of available technologies at the time. Following Moore's Law, we expect the capability of computer technology to increase and its cost to decrease. As a result, constraints based upon technical capacity and cost tend to loosen over time. A nearly ideal situation exists when affordable technology is capable of collecting data that not only meets current needs but satisfies the principle of full information capture and exceeds the ability of the biological system. We have reached that state with respect to collection of digital text and audio. A billion words of text in a language that averages six characters per word encoded as two bytes per characters would require 12 gigabytes of storage if uncompressed. Even inexpensive notebook computers generally have that

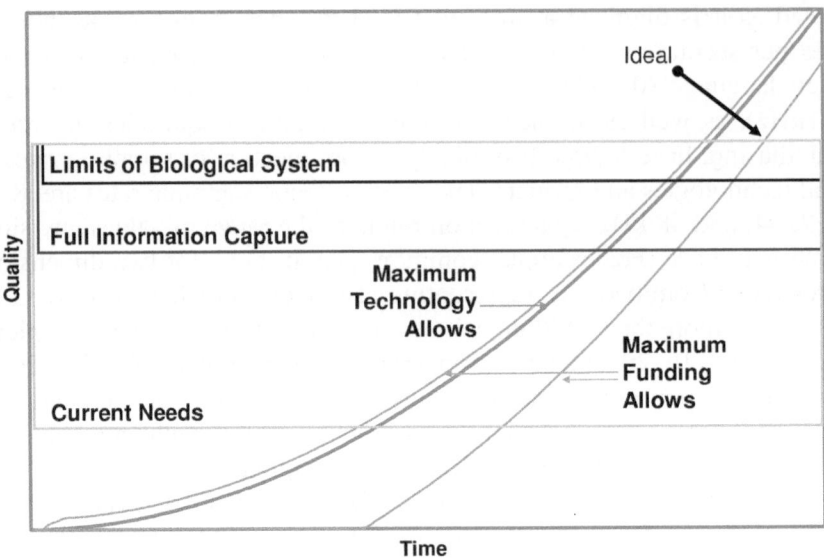

Figure 2.   Factors influencing data collection parameters.

much storage to spare. Similarly, an hour of single channel audio sampled at 22 kHz with 16 bit quantization requires about 150 MB (megabytes) of storage per hour of recording. Although current notebook computers lack the capacity to store, say, 1,000 hours of such data, desktop computers and external drives for notebook computers can easily store this much data at costs that range from one-half to US\$2 per gigabyte. The situation for digital video is not quite so far along. Large collections of high quality video still require storage solutions that, while possible, are not standard on average desktop computers. Figure 2 presents these factors graphically. Note that the principle of full information capture need not require lower quality than is imposed by the limits of the biological system though the graph presents them in that relationship.

6.2.2   Text.   The volume of text corpora is typically measured in bytes or words. Because the number of bytes per word varies from language to language even when a general purpose encoding such as Unicode is used, byte counts can only be compared where the texts are in the same language and encoding. The number of characters per word varies by language, while the number of bytes per character varies by language and encoding. In languages such as Chinese, where words are not generally space separated, and where the conceptualization of word does not benefit from centuries of space separated writing, segmentation, and thus word count vary with the counter. Furthermore it is important to note whether word counts include tags that can comprise a considerable percentage of the tokens in the text especially in those harvested from web pages. Consider the following *New York Times* article excerpted below. The complete document contains 467 space separated tokens of which 35 are tags and 30 are non-text tokens. That leaves just 402 text tokens or 86% in a news story that appears to have very little extraneous mark-up.

```
<DOC>
<DOCNO> NYT20000101.0002 </DOCNO>
<DOCTYPE> NEWS STORY </DOCTYPE>
<DATE_TIME> 2000-01-01 00:21 </DATE_TIME>
<HEADER>A3886 &Cx1f; taf-zu a BC-NYTIMES-ISSUE-NUMBER-
01-01 0415 </HEADER>
<BODY>
<SLUG> BC-NYTIMES-ISSUE-NUMBER-NYT </SLUG>
<HEADLINE>A CORRECTION: WELCOME TO 51,254 </HEADLINE>
(1h)
c.1999 N.Y. Times News Service
<TEXT>
<P>NEW YORK _ For those who believe that in the good old days _
before calculators, before computers _ people were better at
mental arithmetic, The New York Times offers a sobering New
Year's message: Not necessarily.</P>
<P>On Feb. 6, 1898, it seems, someone preparing the next day's
front page tried to add 1 to the issue number in the upper left
corner (14,499) and came up with 15,000. Apparently no one
noticed, because the 500-issue error persisted until Friday
(No. 51,753). Saturday The Times turns back the clock to
correct the sequence: this issue is No. 51,254.</P>
<P>Thus an article on March 14, 1995, celebrating the arrival
of No. 50,000 was 500 days premature. It should have appeared
on July 26, 1996.</P>
<P> As for the other number on the front page _ the volume,
in Roman numerals _ it remains CXLIX. It will change to CL on
Sept. 18, when The Times enters its 150th year.</P>
</TEXT>
</BODY>
<TRAILER>NYT-01-01-00 0021EST &QL; </TRAILER>
</DOC>
```

Standard desktop computing is more than adequate to support small- and medium-sized text collections. The specialized tools, such as leased lines and dedicated modems, previously used to distribute newswire are rapidly being replaced by distribution via the Internet using ftp, http, and rss protocols. If large-scale text collection remains challenging, the cause is not the network bandwidth or storage capacity of desktop computers but rather the long-term commitment required. The largest news text corpora now exceed one billion words; for example, the second edition of the English Gigaword News Text [ISBN: 1-58563-350-X] corpus contains 2.3 billion words of text selected from both daily distributions and archives of several major news providers covering a 12-year period.

Parallel Text, that is text and its translation into another language, is generally measured in words of *source language* text. Source refers to the language in which the text was originally written while *target* refers to the language into which it is translated. In some cases it will be difficult to distinguish the source and target languages because that information is not provided with the text. The form of the text itself may provide hints. For example, in parallel text involving English, non-native use of the determiner "the" will suggest the text was translated, imperfectly, into English. In parallel text produced by multilingual publishers such as the United Nations and many international news sources, original text may have been written in any of the several languages. The largest parallel text corpora contain tens of millions of words of text in the source language. Examples include the Hong Kong Parallel Text [ISBN: 1-58563-290-2], Arabic English Parallel News, Part 1 [ISBN: 1-58563-310-0], and UN Parallel Text Complete [ISBN: 1-58563-038-1] corpora.

6.2.3   Speech.   In studies of speech conducted over the past decade, audio recordings of spoken language have included isolated words, short phrases selected at random or selected to be phonetically rich or balanced, read speech, task-oriented dialogues among humans or between humans and machines, broadcast news, conversations, and meetings. Some collections, particularly those involving broadcast news and meetings have included video. Although not strictly necessary for all applications, audio collections are frequently accompanied by time-aligned transcriptions, which may be orthographic, phonetic or some hybrid.

Corpora that support speech-to-text systems typically include audio recordings of speech in the language and preferably in an acoustic environment and genre that match the target application. A voice mail transcription system would need to be able to handle telephone speech characterized by reduced bandwidth and multiple encodings and decodings, compressions and decompressions of the signal as it passes over landlines, cellular networks, or even the Internet. In addition there is variability at the handsets of both talkers, which may be traditional handsets with carbon button microphones, head mounted headphone/microphone combinations, or speaker phones and which may involve additional retransmission of the signal if the handset is cordless. In just the few examples given above, distance from mouth to microphone may vary from a few centimeters to a few meters. Because of the severe differences in spectral properties, telephone speech, broadcast speech, and broadband speech, are generally treated separately.

The increasing integration of speech-to-text with other technologies has increased the requirements for raw data and annotations. Where video accompanies audio, researchers have investigated the fusion of lip shape recognition with speech recognition to improve accuracy. Similarly, optical character recognition of text appearing in broadcast video, face and object recognition, and tracking and related technologies enrich the information that can be extracted from broadcast. However, the development of these technologies requires the collection of other types of data, as well as new annotations.

In contrast, data for text-to-speech systems generally include carefully produced speech, recorded in a quiet environment with high quality microphones. The speech is commonly read from prompts and may include words, short phrases and sentences, and nonsense syllables selected to give the best possible coverage of the language's phonotactics. Sentences may be written to be phonetically rich at the risk of sounding unnatural. Alternatively, sentences of actual text may be selected for their coverage of the consonant and vowels combinations, prosodic features and the like.

Speech corpora are measured in hours of recording. Hours of actual speech will be somewhat less because stretches of silence do occur in conversational corpora, and stretches of music and commercials occur in broadcast. Speech corpora may also be measured in the number of words contained in their transcripts. Of course, the number of words per minute of speech varies by language, speaking style, speaker, and format. In the CallHome English [ISBN: 1-58563-112-4] transcript, of which a small piece is presented below, 32% of the tokens are something other than words.

```
825.89 828.31 A: Oh. How's he doing?
827.81 828.48 B: And he's had
829.40 835.67 B: Well he's working for an American firm
over here, and he's doing very very well. %um, and his wife
just had their fourth child.
835.80 836.63 A: Wow.
836.34 838.15 B: A little boy. &Benjamin. yeah.
838.51 839.22 A: Wow.
838.82 842.10 B: %um, about, %uh, t- two weeks ago maybe.
842.12 842.64 A: %huh.
842.33 842.85 B: Tops.
843.76 846.20 B: And I got a card from, you remember &Amy
&XXX?
846.10 846.60 A: yeah.
847.25 849.27 B: yeah. Well she just had a baby a couple of
849.62 850.44 B: (( ))
850.63 851.50 A: heard that.
851.38 852.65 B: Well this is this is number two.
```

The largest corpora of conversational telephone speech, for example, the Fisher English corpus parts 1 and 2 [1-58563-313-5, 1-58563-335-6] are now measured in the thousands of hours.

High-end systems for collecting conversational telephone speech may consist of a server augmented by the same kind of telephony hardware and software used to manage interactive phone systems. These systems can both initiate and accept calls. With custom-written software they may be programmed to acquire informed consent, authenticate and pair subjects, describe the collection protocol, guide subjects through a session, ask questions, accept answers as speech or as selections from multiple choices with the help of push button tones, and record speech either separating or mixing the audio from the participants. Lower end solutions exist. However, those that collect speech at the phone of one of the participants reduce the mobility of the effort by forcing one participant to always be at the collection point or else to carry the collection system with her. Such systems add unwanted variability to the quality of the collection by recording one side of the conversation at the source and the other after transmission through a telephone network. Some may mix the near and far sides of the conversation into a single stream loosing the ability to separate them subsequently.

In contrast, low-end systems for collecting broadcast speech may be quite effective. Digital video recorders have, at the time of writing, become popular on the consumer market due to the broad availability of digital video and large capacity hard drives. Although many consumer-oriented systems prevent access to the video signal, there are now dozens of video tuner boards, digital video cameras-and software interfaces that allow digital video to be streamed directly to computer disk and accessed independently. For large-scale collection, a more customized solution may be desirable. For example, LDC's current broadcast collection system includes satellite dishes and receivers to capture both proprietary signals and standard C and Ku band signals, as well as wideband and shortwave antennae and cable television. Each of the dishes and antennae are connected to one or more receivers whose output is routed through an audio- video matrix to a number of processors. Servers stream digital audio and video to disk or else digitize analogue signal and then store it. Closed caption decoders extract captions from the video signal and write them to disk as a rough time-aligned transcript of some broadcast sources. Audio is also streamed to systems running best-of-breed commercial speech to text software in order to provide time-aligned transcripts. Video, audio- and transcripts are stored on spinning disk with coordinated file names and are written to tape as a back-up. The entire operation is automated by a master computer that maintains a database of programs to record, the times and channels on which they appear, instructions for tuning dishes and receivers, and indications of whether closed captioning is to be extracted or automatic transcripts created. This system automates broadcast collection so that it runs over nights, weekends, and holidays without human intervention. However, it is important to note that such automation requires ex post facto human auditing since programs may be pre-empted and programming schedules may change.

6.2.4 Communicative interactions in data supporting speech technology development.

Speech data from broadcast news, telephone conversations, and multiparty meetings vary significantly along a number of other dimensions. Figure 3 lists several interactions and indicates how they affect the difficulty each presents to human annotators and speech systems.

The three speech types differ with respect to the degree of variability present in the physical environment and in the audio capture equipment used. In broadcast news, most speech takes place in the studio environment where high quality equipment and quiet prevail. When news broadcasts contain audio of correspondent reports, telephone calls, or satellite transmissions, humans notice the difference in quality and the performance of speech-to-text systems degrade. Recognition of telephone speech suffers from the greater variability present in the physical environment in which the speakers find themselves. Broadcast news and telephone conversations also differ with respect to both movement in situ and change of location as factors affecting the ability to recognize speech. Broadcast news personalities tend to sit in a single place and minimize movements that would create noise. Conversational speech lacks this level of discipline. Not only may participants generate additional noise through movements but they may also change their location relative to the data capture devices either by moving a phone away from their mouths, by walking out of range of a wireless phone base or, in the meeting environment, by

	Broadcast	Telephone	Meetings
Variable Environment		░	▓
Variable Capture		░	▓
Movement		░	▓
Change of Location		░	▓
Multimodality	▓		▓
Informality		▓	▓
Impromptu Speech		▓	▓
Overlapped Speech			▓
External Apparatus	░		▓
Multiple Speakers	░		▓
Information Handicap	░		▓
Observer's Paradox			▓
Readable Transcript	░	░	▓

Increasing Challenge =>		░	▓

Figure 3. Comparison of human interactions underlying three speech data types.

walking alternately toward and away from room microphones. Broadcast news does present a greater challenge than telephone conversation in its multimodal signal. The modern television broadcast may contain not only the video of the on-air personality but also background images, closed captioning, sidebar text, and the horizontally scrolling text, or "crawl", that CNN, for example, conspicuously employs. Integrating these sources of information is an open research problem for information management technologies. Broadcast news speech, relatively formal and well-rehearsed, contains a narrower variety of linguistic styles, and fewer disfluencies and rapid speech phenomena than conversational speech. In telephone conversations the number of speakers is usually small and fixed while in broadcast news there may be studio guests, call-ins, and man-on the-street interviews. *Information handicap* refers to the paucity of information the annotator or recognition system has relative to the participant in a communicative interaction. During telephone conversation, a recognition system has as much signal data as the interlocutors. However in meetings and broadcast television, the facial expressions, maps, visual aids, etc. that help to disambiguate the audio for participants are lacking in the audio signal generally provided to systems. The *Observer's Paradox* states that in order to understand human communication one must study it even though the very act of observation affects the phenomena under study. Broadcasters know they are being watched for their news content and their register is formal as a result. Observation by speech researchers has no additional impact in this case. Among LDC telephone collections, there is both evidence that participants believe they should monitor their speech and evidence that they sometimes forget to do so. The effect of observation has the potential to be the most profound in meetings where special rooms may be required and where microphones may be in plain sight.

Case Study: Collection of Conversational Telephone Speech

This section summarizes observations from LDC's experience covering five phases of Switchboard collections (Cieri et al., 2003), four Fisher collections and two Mixer collections (Cieri et al., 2006). All three types of collection recruit large numbers of subjects to complete conversations on assigned topics with other subjects in the study. In Switchboard studies, subjects are encouraged to participate in up to 10 six-minute telephone conversations. Because, Switchboard has been used primarily to support speaker identification technology development during a time when the research focused on low level acoustic features, not all of the Switchboard data has been transcribed. On the other hand, special care was taken to verify speaker identity. The behaviour of the robot operators that enable the studies differs somewhat in each case. The Switchboard robot operator, waits for an incoming call from one of the subjects at which time it initiates outbound calls, using a single line, to a series of participants until one accepts the call. The Fisher robot operator takes control of the call flow by initiating calls simultaneously to a number of subjects pairing them as soon as it has two on hold who agree to participate. In Mixer studies, the robot operator operates similarly but the goals of the collection, speaker recognition in a multilingual, multi-channel environment, led to changes in the types of subjects recruited, in collection parameters such as the increase in the number of calls a subject could make and in equipment aspects, such as the microphones and handsets used.

Conversational telephone speech proceeds in two phases, recruitment and collection. The importance of recruitment is sometimes overlooked. Without participants, there is no data. Experience from previous studies has shown that several factors in the recruitment process can have profound effects on the collection's outcome. These include the time of year in which the collection takes place. For example, in Switchboard Cellular Phase I (1999–2000), the requirement that participants make a minimum number of calls from locations outdoors led to the study beginning 3 months earlier than planned simply to avoid the winter months. It was also observed that restricting the hours during which participants can make calls raised the probability that they would actually reach another available participant by concentrating call activity into a small number of hours. In most cases, recruitment must begin several weeks prior to the beginning of collection. When recruitment occurs too far in advance, participant interest wanes prematurely. When collection begins too soon, the lack of a critical mass of available participants may frustrate callers. The best recruitment efforts, however, are only as good as the technology that supports them. Recruitment requires a reliable database of participants and a user-friendly interface to support the recruitment team. Subject data generally includes: name, gender, age, education, occupation, location born and raised, and where appropriate, ethnicity. For purpose of payment and participant care, contact information and identifying numbers, such as social security numbers in the United States are also crucial. Generally speaking, this data is collected during the initial discussion between the participant and the recruitment staff. Indeed, that may also be the only time the recruiters speak directly with a participant.

LDC generally advertises via print media and electronic announcements. Potential participants contact the LDC via phone or e-mail, or by completing electronic forms whence they learn: (1) that speech will be recorded for research and educational purposes, (2) that personal information will be kept confidential, not be released with the data, (3) when the study begins and ends and how to participate, (4) how, how much, and when they will be compensated.

Registered participants receive detailed written instructions that reiterate everything discussed in person and sketched on the project's web pages. In telephone studies, the instructions include a person identification number (PIN) and the series of prompts that participants will hear. Some conversational studies (Switchboard, Mixer, Fisher) require a critical mass of recruits before they can begin. In other protocols (CallHome) a participant can begin immediately after registering. In either case, participant compliance is closely monitored to ensure a successful study. If a study does not proceed according to plan, adjusting study parameters including the number of recruits, their demographics, and their compensation may prove helpful.

Collection systems must be accurate, reliable, economical, and capable of delivering real world data. For broadcast, telephone, and meeting speech, LDC has developed robust systems that leverage off-the-shelf hardware. The telephone system consists of customized software, telephony hardware, and a project database and can record multiple simultaneous conversations with no need for operator intervention. The database contains demographic information and call activity statistics for each participant and supports all recruitment, collection and reporting. Call activity is logged each time a participant tries to make a call, or receives one.

The LDC's meeting recording system can record 16 tracks of digital audio from a mixture of wireless and far-field wired microphones. Lavalier or head-mounted microphones are used for close recording. Room microphones, including a microphone array and PZM, omnidirectional and directional microphones are also used. The meeting recording system consists of a digital mixer, a multi-track digital tape recording deck, wireless microphone receivers, a microphone preamplifier, and a multi-channel digital audio computer interface. Meeting sessions are recorded as 16 bit/44 kHz PCM audio.

6.2.5   Human subject behaviour.   The goal of Switchboard Cellular Phase I, was to collect 10 six-minute calls from 190 GSM cellphone users balanced by gender. The most successful recruiting effort involved employees of a local GSM provider, in which 293 participants were recruited. Unfortunately calls to many of the registered phones went unanswered during times the subjects had agreed to receive calls. This proved to be a result of participants' habit of turning off their cellphones when not using them. To counter this problem and to generally improve customer care, LDC initiated multiple participant call-backs and mailings and a participant lottery for those who completed the study. Although this study had a high rate of success in terms of subjects who completed the required number of calls, it was very labour-intensive. Switchboard Cellular Phase II included several adjustments to these challenges.

The goal in Switchboard Cellular Phase II was 10 calls each from 210 participants balanced by gender with no restriction on cellular network. LDC recruited 591 participants and instituted a sliding pay scale that covered subject costs for each call while simultaneously providing strong incentives to

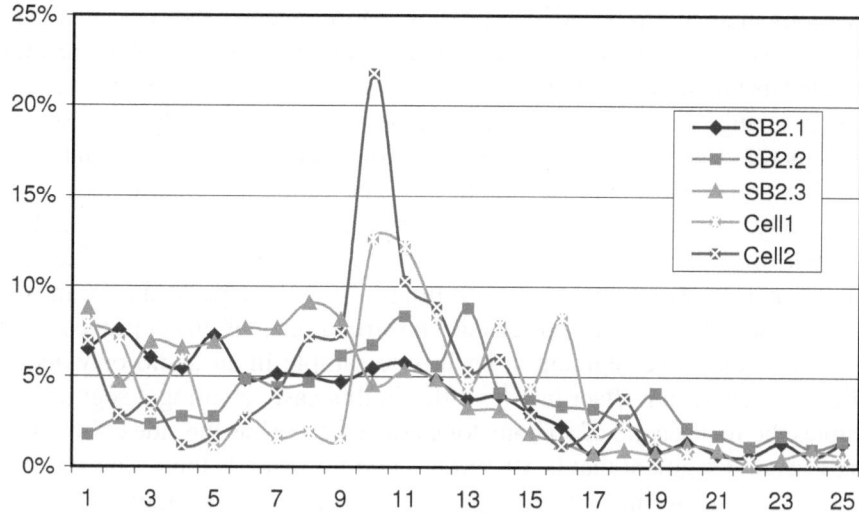

Figure 4. Switchboard call summary. The vertical axis shows the number of participants who made the number of calls on the horizontal axis.

complete the study. As a result of these measures, LDC was able to complete Switchboard Cellular II in about 1 month. Figure 4 shows participant behaviour in each of the Switchboard collections. Switchboard Cellular 2 has the tightest distribution of subjects around the goal of 10 calls. For Switchboard 2.1–2.3, the goal was to collect an **average** of 10 calls per participant. Although these studies eventually met their goals, Figure 4 shows a very diffuse distribution of participant performance. In the Cellular studies, the goal became having a minimum number of subjects who participated in at least 10 calls. The labour-intensive approach adopted in Switchboard Cellular 1 produced a funny distribution of subject performance and was costly in terms of recruiter effort. The approach used in Switchboard Cellular 2 produced a distribution that is very tightly centred around a mode at 10 calls and was in every other way, more efficient.

6.3 Segmentation

As noted previously, *segmentation* is the actual or virtual division of a recording of communicative performance into pieces to facilitate annotation, search or analysis. Similar to records and fields in a structured database or chapters and sections in a book, time-aligned segments allow the user to zoom in on target phenomena, for example, by searching the transcript and then using the time stamps to play the corresponding audio. Segments may correspond to pause or breath groups in conversational speech, speaker turns in conversation or broadcast news and to stories in a news text collection, speaker turns, stories, or sections in an audio or video collection. More recently the segments correspond to "SU"s, extents whose syntactic and semantic properties suggest they be treated as units. The granularity of segments will depend upon intended use and may change over time. Stand-off segmentation is generally more suitable and adaptable to change both because it allows for multiple segmentations of these files and because it preserves the first generation digital artefact.

Naturally, most annotation is dependent upon segmentation. Formalisms and tools may have a constraining effect on annotation possibilities. For example, some assume that each recording of linguistic performance must be uniquely and exhaustively segmented. The strong form of this approach allows for one and only one segment at each time sample in an audio or video file and at each character offset in a text file. In this case, creating a segment that occupies the first second of an hour-long conversation has the side effect of creating a second segment that is 59 minutes and 59 seconds long. The start time of the first segment must be zero, the end time of the last segment must be 60 minutes 0 seconds, and the end time of any segment after the first must be equal to the start time of the following segment. This approach is problematic for speech involving more than one speaker where overlaps occur. A weaker form of the same approach applies the same constraints within an annotation tier but allows for multiple tiers. This approach accommodates overlapping speech but is still awkward for partially annotated files because it forces the portions that are not annotated to be either included in nonce segments, increasing segment count or else attached to annotated segments increasing the duration of segments unnecessarily. The alternative approach is to allow segments to be independent of each other. The strong form of this alternative approach allows multiple tiers of annotation and removes the constraints that govern start and end times of adjacent segments thus allowing some to overlap and allowing gaps between others; segments are no longer forced to abut. The disadvantage of this approach is that an error in which a human annotator fails to include interesting material in a defined segment results in that material being overlooked during annotation by default. Annotation projects that use this approach to segmentation need a quality control pass in which annotators or systems look for annotatable material between defined segments.

6.4   Annotation

As previously noted, we define annotation as any process that adds value to raw data through the application of human judgement. That judgement may be applied either directly by human annotators or automatically with humans specifying the rules that systems implement. Bird and Liberman's (2001) survey of a multitude of annotation practices showed a common theme. Formally, annotation may be seen as the attachment of one or more category/value pairs to segments of a corpus. Categories indicate the type of annotation. Each type may have one or more values. For example, a two layer orthographic and phonetic transcription of prompted speech, such as we find in the TIMIT corpus (Garofolo et al., 1990), might have two categories, *word* and *phone*. For an utterance of the word "So", annotations would include *word=so* and *phone=s*. The duration of the segments ranges from relatively small to relatively large. There are several TIMIT phone tags per second of speech. On the other end of the spectrum, categorizations of an entire recording may be formalized as metadata or, to keep the formalism consistent as annotations with time spans that equal the length of the recording. Where a category may have only one value, either the category or value label may be excluded. Where a corpus contains a single kind of annotation, bare values without category labels are often given.

Annotation varies with respect to the expertise required and the variability expected. *Expert annotation* requires specific background and advanced skills. The syntactic annotation of Treebanks and the entity, relation, event, and co-reference tagging of the ACE program are examples of expert annotation. In the former case, the successful annotators have generally been college graduates, graduate students, or post-doctoral researchers whose secondary education included a specialization in the syntax of the language under study where that language was also the medium of instruction. Even such highly skilled scholars spend months perfecting their knowledge of the specification before they can be fully productive annotators. Although individual variation plays some role in the quality of expert annotation, one expects inter-annotator agreement to increase with training and collaboration. *Intuitive annotation*, where the goal is to capture the judgement of an average speaker or potential technology user, requires less specific training. Sometimes native speaking ability in the target language is enough. The specification and tools are also generally simpler and one expects more variation among annotators. Translation in non-technical domains is a kind of intuitive annotation where variation may be extreme. In some cases, the annotator may also act as a user model for a given technology. Topic annotation within the Topic Detection and Tracking (TDT) and High Accuracy Retrieval from Documents (HARD) use the annotator as user model.

Linguistic Resources may also be differentiated as to whether they serve a very specific purpose such as the topic and entity tagging for information retrieval and extraction, or provide general knowledge such as part-of-speech tagged text, and translation lexicons.

6.5 Quality Assurance and Inter-Annotator Agreement

Annotation tasks naturally vary according to level of difficulty. The distinction between intuitive and expert annotation sketched above impacts both the amount of inter-annotator agreement and its importance to human language technologies.

The goal of some collection and annotation tasks is to sample the variability that exists in a human population. For example in the first months of DARPA TIDES' sponsorship of machine translation evaluation, a critical task was to develop an objective measure of translation quality knowing that for any source language text there may be many very different translations that are nonetheless equally valid. The solution adopted by the community was to create multiple human translations of the same source language text and, grossly speaking, credit systems that produced translations that were attested in any of the human translations. Human translators were given very few constraints. They were required to produce a direct translation, avoiding summary and exegesis, that was grammatical in the target language and as faithful to the original text and its cultural matrix as possible. Their atom was the sentence of source language text. They were required to produce one or more sentences of translation for each sentence of source. Otherwise, they were left to their own discretion. In this case, it is important to model inter-translator variation. However, any attempt to force the translators into greater conformity risks distorting the model and the resulting evaluation of system performance.

In contrast, the syntactic annotation of text or transcribed speech is an example of expert annotation in which there is generally assumed to be a right answer. Annotators are expected to be highly trained in general syntax, the syntax of the target language and the annotation specification and the quality of their work is expected to increase with training and experience assuming a positive disposition toward the work. Measures of inter-annotator agreement in syntactic annotation are useful in determining how difficult the task is. At the same time, ongoing training, error analysis, and similar measures that increase agreement are valid.

With that background in mind we distinguish four kinds of quality control (QC): precision, recall, discrepancy, and structure. *Precision QC* attempts to find incorrect assignments of an annotation. Annotators review each case in which a data span has been given an annotation and verify that the annotation is appropriate. Unless an annotator misunderstands the specification, mistakes of this kind, false alarms, should be relatively less common than the next type we will discuss. Where annotations are sparse, a greater percentage of annotation may be submitted to precision QC. For example, LDC reviewed 100% of all annotations in the TDT corpora where a small number of news stories will have been marked as relevant to a given topic. *Recall QC* attempts to find failed assignments of an annotation. Annotators review segments where an annotation was not applied to verify that it should not have been. Errors of this kind, misses, result from waning attention and are relatively more common among human annotators. The search for misses may employ computer assistance, for example, a search engine may identify documents with high relevance scores for a given topic for a human annotator to review. *Discrepancy QC* reviews annotations of the same data done by multiple independent annotators. Depending upon the nature of the annotation discrepancies may be used to calculate scores of inter-annotator agreement, to identify cases in which annotators misunderstand the specification, to identify cases in which the specification fails to treat specific phenomena, and to identify cases that require a judgement call. Naturally, some findings may lead to revision of the specification or scoring metric. Others may lead to remedial training of annotators. Generally, LDC performs discrepancy analysis on 5–10% of all annotated data using a double-blind protocol. Finally *Structure QC* uses facts about relations among annotations in order to identify suspect annotations. To take a simple example, in Arabic a prepositional phrase may occur within a noun phrase, as in "the woman from Tunis". However, structurally, the PP tag must actually be subjacent to the N tag not to the NP tag directly. In bracketed notation, this structure is (NP(N(PP...))) and any case of (NP(PP...)) is suspect. Once the rules have been established, Structure QC can generally be done automatically so that one expects 100% of all annotated data to be subject to this level of scrutiny. XML validation and checks of audio file headers are also species of Structure QC.

6.6 Preparation, Distribution, Adjudication

In preparation for release, corpora are generally associated with metadata and documented to indicate the authors and annotators of the data, the volume and types of raw material included, the percent annotated, the annotation specification, and the quality control measures adopted. Although authorship may seem the simplest of these for corpora of linguistic data it is often difficult to identify the author because corpus creation was, and often still is, viewed differently where authorship is concerned than writing academic papers or presenting at conferences. Furthermore, there is no standard for determining what kind of contribution to a corpus counts as authorship. For a corpus of annotated conversational telephone speech, the subjects, transcriptionists, other annotators, their immediate managers, senior managers or principal investigators, financial and contracting personnel, sponsors' technical representative, and their management will all have contributed to the realization of the corpus.

In some cases it may be necessary or just preferable to annotate data in a different format than the one in which it is distributed. To give a simple example, transcripts that include markup for disfluency, non-lexemes, partial words and the like will be more readable for humans if these items are tagged simply and in-line. On the other hand to permit robust processing of the transcripts, these simpler user tags may be converted into a mark-up language, for example, XML. In large-scale projects involving rotating teams of native speakers of different languages who must learn complex annotation specifications and execute them with consistency, LDC gives relatively high priority to simplifying annotation even if that means reformatting prior to release.

Despite multiple passes of quality control, errors still find their way into corpora. Adjudication processes may help reduce such error. Adjudication typically involves reviewing two or more independent annotations of the data to identify and resolve areas of disagreement. The independent annotations may involve humans or machines or both. During the creation of the TDT corpora, adjudication was used to identify human annotator errors in the assignment of documents to topic clusters. This process was implemented when the project abandoned *exhaustive* annotation in favour of *search-guided* annotation. *Exhaustive* annotation in the case of the TDT-2 corpus meant that each of more than 50,000 documents were compared against each of 100 topics yielding more than 5,000,000 decisions. In TDT-4 and TDT-5, exhaustive annotation was replaced by search guided annotation in which a search engine seeded with keywords from topic descriptions and text from on-topic documents, searched the corpus and returned a relevance ranked list of hits. Human annotators then reviewed those hits looking for truly on-topic documents and following consistent rules to decide how many documents to review. Because the success of this method could have been skewed by problems in the search engine, the results were adjudicated in the following way. Once the evaluation had taken place, the results from the tracking systems developed by the several research sites where compared to each other and to LDC's human annotators. Documents were ordered with respect to how many research systems disagreed with the human annotators. Human annotators then proceeded in priority order through the cases where the majority of systems disagreed. Figure 5 shows the results of this adjudication and confirms something that makes sense intuitively. Humans using search-guided annotation to decide whether a news story discusses a specific topic are more likely to miss relevant stories than they are to erroneously judge a story to be relevant. When all seven systems concluded that the LDC human annotator has missed a relevant story, the systems were correct 100% of the time. Otherwise the human, search-guided annotation generally made the right decision in the majority of cases. The human false alarm rate was very low. Even in the few cases in which all systems disagreed with the human judge who thought the story was on-topic, the human was generally correct. Naturally such adjudication can also be used to validate annotation based only on human effort. In some cases, for example, in the TREC cross-language document retrieval track, adjudication is used instead of human annotation of an evaluation corpus. In other words, the evaluation corpus is given

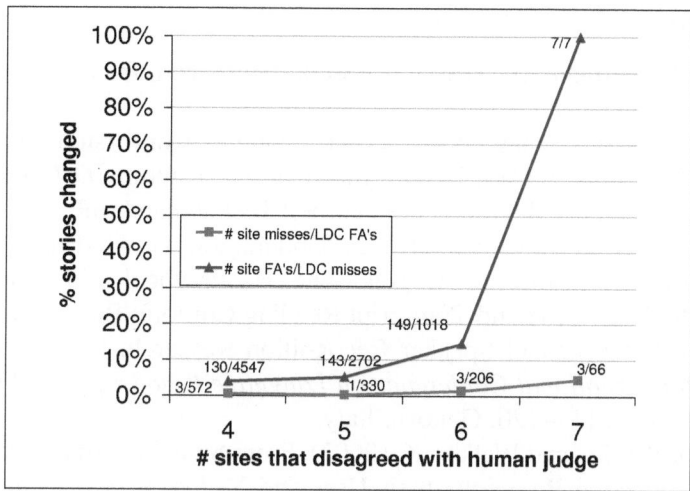

Figure 5. Results of human-system adjudication. In search-guided topic annotation of news, human errors are more commonly misses than false alarms.

to sites without annotation. System results are pooled using a process similar to the above and then adjudicated by humans to produce the final answer key and system scores.

7 Conclusion

This chapter has tried to give a perspective on the creation and sharing of language resources for purposes of technology development and evaluation informed by experience within the rubric of common task technology programs described above. It bears repeatation that there are other perspectives on language resource creation informed by other experiences and moulded by other approaches to research management. A theme that runs throughout the research communities working in linguistic education, research and technology development is the increasing use of language resources. Each year new communities embrace the practice of sharing language resources. The communities that had established that practice a decade or more ago, continue to rely upon shared resources of ever-increasing sophistication, diversity and volume. Technological advancements endow the average desktop with the ability to create and share small and medium-scale resources. Perhaps the greatest challenge currently facing HLT communities is the generalization of technologies developed for a small number of languages. Work in resource sparse languages also termed "low density" or "less commonly taught" offers both the difficulty of truly generalizing technologies to handle human languages of startling diversity as it also offers the rewards of improved communication and access to information leading to improved understanding.

References

Bird, S. and Liberman, M. (2001). A Formal Framework for Linguistic Annotation. *Speech Communication*, 33(1–2):23–60.

Chapman, S. and Kenney, A. R. (1996). Digital Conversion of Research Library Materials: A Case for Full Informational Capture. *D-Lib Magazine*. http://www.dlib.org/dlib/october96/cornell/10chapman.html.

Cieri, C., Andrews, W., Campbell, J. P., Doddington, G., Godfrey, J., Huang, S., Liberman, M., Martin, A., Nakasone, H., Przybocki, M., and Walker, K. (2006). The Mixer and Transcript Reading Corpora: Resources for Multilingual, Crosschannel Speaker Recognition Research. In *Proceedings of the Fifth International Conference on Language Resources and Evaluation (LREC)*, pages 117–120, Genova, Italy.

Cieri, C., Miller, D., and Walker, K. (2003). From Switchboard to Fisher: Telephone Collection Protocols, their Uses and Yields. In *Proceedings of the European Conference on Speech Communication and Technology (Eurospeech)*, pages 1597–1600, Geneva, Switzerland.

Cieri, C., Miller, D., and Walker, K. (2004). The Fisher Corpus: A Resource for the Next Generations of Speech-to-Text. In *Proceedings of the Fourth International Conference on Language Resources and Evaluation (LREC)*, pages 69–71, Lisbon, Portugal.

Doddington, G., Mitchell, A., Przybocki, M., Ramshaw, L., Strassel, S., and Weischedel, R. (2004). Automatic Content Extraction (ACE) Program - Task Definitions and Performance Measures. In *Proceedings of the Fourth International Conference on Language Resources and Evaluation (LREC)*, pages 837–840, Lisbon, Portugal.

Garofolo, J. S., Lamel, L. F., Fisher, W. M., Fiscus, J. G., Pallett, D. S., and Dahlgren, N. L. (1990). The DARPA TIMIT Acoustic-Phonetic Continuous Speech Corpus. [CD-ROM] US Department of Commerce, Gaithersburg, MD.

Guy, G., editor (1999). *Symposium on Public Access Data Bases, NWAVE 28: The 28th Annual Conference on New Ways of Analyzing Variation*, Toronto, Canada.

Jurafsky, D. and Martin, J. H. (2000). *Speech and Language Processing: An Introduction to Natural Language Processing, Computational Linguistics, and Speech Recognition*. Prentice-Hall, New Jersey.

Labov, W. (1966). *The Social Stratification of English in New York City*. Center for Applied Linguistics, Washington, DC.

Mariani, J. (2002). Are We Losing Ground to the US? A Contrastive Analysis of US and EU Research Frameworks on Human Language Technologies. http://www.hltcentral.org/page-975.0.shtml.

Papinieni, K., Roukos, S., Ward, T., and Zhu, W.-J. (2002). BLEU: A Method for Automatic Evaluation of Machine Translation. In *Proceedings of the 40th Annual Meeting of the Association for Computational Linguistics (ACL)*, pages 311–318, Philadelphia, USA.

Chapter 9

TOWARDS INTERNATIONAL STANDARDS FOR LANGUAGE RESOURCES

Nancy Ide
Vassar College, USA
ide@cs.vassar.edu

Laurent Romary
LORIA-INRIA, France
Laurent.Romary@loria.fr

Abstract   This chapter describes the Linguistic Annotation Framework (LAF) developed by the International Standards Organization TC37 SC4, which is to serve as a basis for harmonizing existing language resources, as well as developing new ones. We then describe the use of the LAF to represent the American National Corpus and its linguistic annotations.

Keywords   Language resources; Standards; Corpora; Linguistic annotation; ISO; American National Corpus.

1   Introduction

As noted in Cole et al. (1997), years of research and development in computational linguistics and language engineering have yielded many stable results, which have in turn been integrated into language processing applications and industrial software. Especially over the past 15 years, researchers and developers have increasingly understood the need to define common practices and formats for linguistic resources, which serve Human Language Technologies (HLT) development as the primary source for statistical language modelling. To answer this need, numerous projects have been launched to lay the basis for standardization of resource representation

L. Dybkjær et al. (eds.), Evaluation of Text and Speech Systems, 263–284.
© 2007 *Springer.*

and annotation – e.g., the Text Encoding Initiative (TEI) (http://www.tei-c.org), the Corpus Encoding Standard (CES and XCES) (http://www.xml-ces.org), the Expert Advisory Group on Language Engineering Standards (EAGLES) and the International Standard for Language Engineering (ISLE) (http://www.ilc.cnr.it/EAGLES96/home.html), as well as software platforms for resource creation, annotation, and use – MULTEXT (http://www.lpl.univ-aix.fr/projects/multext), LT XML (http://www.ltg.ed.ac.uk/software/xml), GATE (http://gate.ac.uk/), NITE (http://www.dfki.de/nite/main.html), ATLAS (http://www.nist.gov/speech/atlas/). However, although in practice consensus has begun to emerge, definitive standards have not yet been put in place. In large part this is as it should be: advances in technology together with the emergence of a solid body of web-based standards have dramatically impacted and redefined many of our ideas about the ways in which resources will be stored and accessed over the past several years. Perhaps more importantly, the ways in which language data – together with "communicative" data of any kind, including gesture, facial expression, and speech – are processed and analyzed will certainly continue to change, as more and more emphasis is put on immediate processing of (often multimodal) streamed data. Whatever the scenario, though, if we intend to make HLT work in the larger arena of universal availability and accessibility, data, its annotations, and processing results will have to be represented in some way that allows exploitation by the full array of language processing technologies.

It has been argued that attempting standardization for language resources and surrounding information is premature, and the evolving nature of the domain and technology certainly speaks to that claim. But the growth of the web and the explosion in the number of electronic documents to be handled and maintained within the industrial sector has created an immediate and urgent need for generic language processing components for document indexing and classifying, information extraction, summarization, topic detection, etc., in both mono- and multilingual environments, together with robust machine translation and facilities for man-machine multimodal communication. While progress will continue, the field has nonetheless reached a point where we can see clear to a reasonable representation and processing model that should fulfil the needs of HLT for at least the foreseeable future. Indeed, commonality that can enable flexible use and reuse of communicative data is essential for the next generation of language processing applications, if we are to build a global information environment. It is therefore critical at this time to move toward standardization, and in particular, to do this in an internationally accepted framework.

It is in this context that a committee of the International Standards Organization (ISO), TC 37/SC 4, has been established to develop standards for *language resources management*, with the aim of building on existing technologies and schemes to codify best practices as a set of standards for representing and processing language-related information, as a means to leverage the growth of language engineering. Fully aware that its activities will be necessarily on going and evolving, the committee has set out the following general goals:

- To provide means to use and reuse linguistic data across applications, at all levels of linguistic description from surface mark-up of primary sources to multilayered processing results

- To facilitate maintenance of a coherent document life cycle through various processing stages, so as to enable enrichment of existing data with new information and the incremental construction of processing systems

2   Background

Before initiating any standardizing activity, it is necessary to identify its scope and relation to past and/or ongoing activities. As a starting point, Figure 1 describes the general "ecology" of language resources and the interdependencies required for their management.

Primary resources may be texts, spoken data, multimodal data (e.g., hand motion, eye gaze, perceptual settings, etc.). *Linguistic information* consists of annotations (ranging from phonetic and morpho-syntactic annotation to discourse level annotations, such as reference chains, dialogue structure, etc.) associated with a segment or segments of a primary resource or other descriptive layer.[1] *Lexical and knowledge structures* may be linked to primary resources and annotations, or created from primary resources; they are most often used to support linguistic analysis, including annotation. As such, they often are the source of information that is used for linguistic annotation. *Metadata* can be regarded as another type of annotation associated with a document containing primary or annotation data, which identifies and describes the resource. Finally, *links* and *access protocols* provide the mechanisms for representing and accessing language resources.

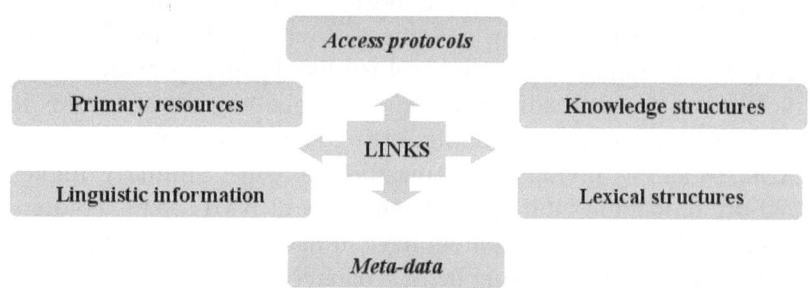

Figure 1.   Ecology of language resources.

Over the last 20 years, numerous projects and initiatives have worked towards the development of standards for one or more of the components pictured above, as well as for a general architecture that would enable efficient representation of the resources themselves together with the "links" establishing the interdependencies among them. Among the most notable are the TEI, CES, and XCES, and MATE/NITE for the representation of primary data and annotations; EAGLES/ISLE for annotation content; OLIF (http://www.olif.net/), SALT (http://www.loria.fr/projets/SALT/), and ISLE for various kinds of lexical/terminological data; RDF/OWL and Topic Maps for knowledge structures; Dublin Core and the Open Archives Initiative (OAI) (http://www.openarchives.org/) for general metadata; MPEG7, IMDI, and OLAC for domain-specific metadata; Corba (http://www.corba.org/) and the W3C's SOAP (http://www.w3.org/TR/soap/) and web services work for access protocols; and MULTEXT, Edinburgh's LT framework, TIPSTER (http://www.fas.org/irp/program/process/tipster.htm), GATE, and ATLAS for general architecture. Most of these projects actually address several of what we can regard as the multiple "dimensions" of language resource representation, including (at least) the following:

Rendering formats and mechanisms, such as SGML, XML, Lisp-like structures, annotation graphs, or a particular database format.

Annotation content, including categories of annotation information for linguistic phenomena (e.g., modality, aspect, etc.) and the values that can be associated with each category.

General architectural principles for language resources, such as the now widely- accepted notions of pipeline architecture and stand-off annotation.

Even here, there are interdependencies: for example, the choice of a representation format will have repercussions for content, first of all because relations among pieces of information may be expressed implicitly through the structures provided by the format, the most common of which is a hierarchical structure for grouping and/or defining part/whole relations. Some formats impose other constraints – for example, Lisp-like formats provide a hierarchical structure but do not readily accommodate labelling the structures to distinguish their function (e.g., grouping, listing alternatives, etc.), as one might do in XML by simply giving a tag a meaningful name. Similarly, implementing stand-off annotation with XML dictates use of XML paths, pointers, and links. As a result, format and content have in past projects often been treated as a whole, rather than addressing them separately.

Despite the numerous projects and initiatives that have sought to establish standards for various aspects of linguistic annotation, there remains no universally accepted set of practices and categories, and there continues to be considerable reinvention of the wheel within the international community. This begs the question: why should the ISO effort succeed where others have failed? There are several answers to this question, the most notable of which is the evolution of technology, both in terms of the availability of accepted frameworks that operate within the web context, including primarily World Wide Web Consortium (W3C) standards, such as XML and RDF/OWL, together with cross-platform/web-adaptable software development tools, such as Java. However, the technological advances resulting from development of the web has done more than provide us with widely accepted standards for language data representation. The shift from stand-alone applications to an environment where both data and software is distributed over the web has dramatically impacted the ways in which we create and represent language resources and their annotations, as well as the kinds of information we want to represent. The enhanced potential to exploit the web to share, merge, and compare language data has itself encouraged widespread adoption of W3C representation standards, and indeed, the web itself has come to be regarded as a virtually infinite "corpus" of multilingual and multimodal data. In addition, in the context of the web certain language processing applications – e.g., information retrieval and extraction, summarization, etc., together with applications that handle multimodal data – have taken the foreground, and the kinds of information that we are most interested in identifying and processing have evolved in tandem. The web has also spawned heightened interest in what we can regard as "on the fly" annotation and analysis for streamed data, and more generally, a need to support incremental annotation at various linguistic levels.

Attempts to standardize linguistic content categories and their values have always been plagued by the thorny problem of varying linguistic theories and application needs: some *de facto* standards, such as WordNet for semantic annotation, have emerged, but there is relatively little commonality in this area beyond these few exceptions despite massive efforts, such as the EAGLES/ISLE project. The forces driving new interest in harmonization of annotation content are similar to those driving standardization for data representation: the existence of the web and the promise of a "semantic web" demand common terminology for every level of description, as the recent efforts to develop standard metadata categories and ontologies demonstrate. The ontology efforts also show how difficult content standardization is to achieve. So, while we have increased motivation to develop linguistic content categories, and possibly a better base than at any time in the past from which to proceed, this aspect of language resource standardization can only be approached cautiously and, likely, far more slowly than resource representation.

With a sounder technological base and a clearer idea of where we need to go, yet another standardization effort seems to be in order. It is important to note, however, that the ISO effort builds to the extent possible on previous efforts, adopting the parts it can and extending or modifying them as seems necessary, and taking advantage of the incremental convergence of opinion on various aspects of the process that has directly resulted from attempts at standardization and/or commonality in the past. To this end, the ISO group has established collaborations with major standardizing groups, including most of the prior initiatives enumerated above, as well as others involved in standardization activities, in order to ensure that the development of ISO standards for language resource management both incorporates and reflects existing practice and informs ongoing work within these other groups. In addition, the ongoing work within the ISO committee is continually presented at major conferences and workshops so that the community is aware of our work and can comment and contribute to the effort.

The "incremental view" of standardization, wherein standards are developed over a series of iterations that potentially span decades, informs both the work within ISO/TC 37/SC 4 and the place of its work in the overall scheme. The standards developed by this ISO sub-committee may not be the final word on language resource representation and management, but they will, we hope, take a necessary step toward that goal. Our work, like the creation of the web-based infrastructure being developed by W3C and others, is best seen as part of a development process that can be compared to building a brick wall: we add brick by brick, layer by layer, and occasionally develop some infrastructural component that adds a significant piece to the overall construction. We are not sure when or where this process will end, but each effort is required for eventual completion.

3   The Linguistic Annotation Framework

The Linguistic Annotation Framework (LAF) is intended to provide a standard infrastructure for representing language resources and their annotations that can serve as a basis for harmonizing existing resources, as well as developing new ones.

Annotation of linguistic data may involve multiple annotation steps, for example, morpho-syntactic tagging, syntactic analysis, entity and event recognition, semantic annotation, coreference resolution, discourse structure analysis, etc. Annotation at lower linguistic levels typically serves as input to the higher-level annotation process in an incremental process. Depending on the application intended to use the annotations, lower-level annotations may or may not be preserved in a persistent format. For example, information extraction software often annotates linguistic features required to generate the final annotation, without preserving the intermediate information. In other situations, the annotation process may not be strictly incremental. For example, when handling streamed data (text, video, and audio, a stream of sensor readings, satellite images, etc.) the processor analyzes language data in a linear, time-bound sequence, and therefore annotations may be temporarily partial during processing if long-distance dependencies between seen and unseen segments of the data exist.

At present, most annotated resources are static entities used primarily for training annotation software, as well as corpus linguistics and lexicography. However, in the context of the Semantic Web, annotations for a variety of higher-level linguistic and communicative features will increasingly be preserved in web-accessible form and used by software agents and other analytic software for inferencing and retrieval. This dictates that the LAF not only relies on web technologies (e.g., RDF/OWL) for representing annotations, but also that "layers" of annotations for the full range of annotation types (including named entities, time, space, and event annotation, annotation for gesture, facial expression, etc.) are at the same time separable (so that agents and other analytic software can access only those annotation types that are required for the purpose, and mergeable (so that two or more annotation types can be combined where necessary). They may also need to be dynamic, in the sense that new and/or modified information can be added as necessary.

The LAF consists of two major components:

1. An abstract data model and a concrete representation format isomorphic to the model

2. A mechanism for defining and using linguistic categories and values

Each of these components is covered in the following sections.

3.1   Architecture and Abstract Model

In order to ensure that the LAF architecture reflects state-of-the-art methods drawn from consensus of the research community, a group of experts[2] was convened in November, 2002, to lay out its overall structure. The group, which included researchers with extensive experience in the development of annotation schemes at a variety of linguistic levels together with developers of major resource-handling software (GATE, ATLAS, Edinburgh LT tools), defined the general architecture pictured in Figure 2.

The fundamental principle underlying the LAF architecture is that the user controls the representation format for linguistic resources and annotations, using any desired scheme (XML, LISP structures, or any other format). The only restriction applied to the user format is that it must be mappable to an *abstract data model*. This mapping is accomplished via a rigid "dump" format, isomorphic to the data model and intended primarily for machine rather than human use.

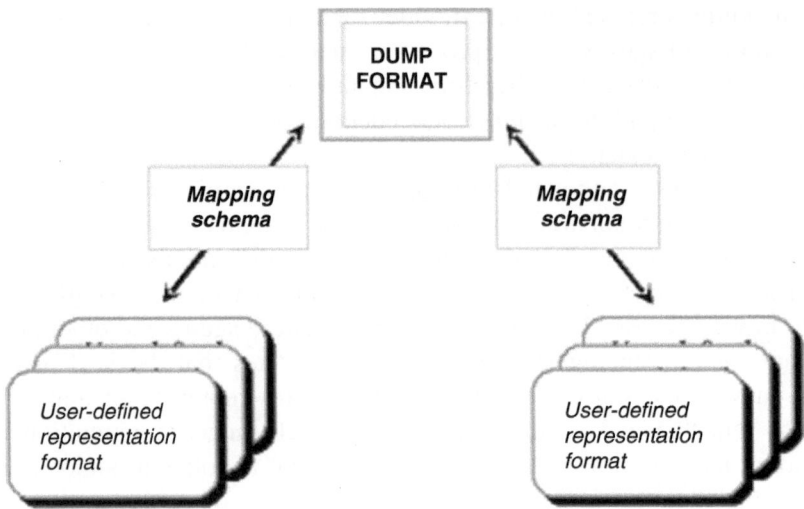

Figure 2.   LAF architecture.

To guide the LAF development, the following general principles were outlined by the group of experts:

- The data model and document form are distinct but mappable to one another.

- The data model is parsimonious, general, and formally precise.

- The document form is largely under user control.

- The mapping between the flexible document form and data model is via a rigid dump-format. The responsibility of converting to the dump format is on the producer of the resource.

- Mapping is operationalized via either a schema-based data-binding process or schema-derived stylesheet mapping between the user document and the dump format instantiation. The mapping from document form to the dump format is documented in an XML Schema (or the functional equivalent thereof) associated with the dump format instantiation.

- It must be possible to isolate specific layers of annotation from other annotation layers or the primary (base) data; i.e., it must be possible to create a dump format instantiation using stand-off annotation.

- The dump format supports stream marshalling and unmarshalling.

The dump format is isomorphic to the underlying abstract data model, which is built upon a clear separation of the *structure* of linguistic information (including annotations and knowledge structures) and *content*, i.e., the linguistic information itself. A document and its annotations form a directed graph capable of referencing *n*-dimensional regions of primary data, as well as other annotations. In the primary data, the nodes of the graph are virtual, located between each "character" in the primary data, where a character is defined to be a contiguous byte sequence of a specified length, as specified in ISO 10646/Unicode. When an annotation references another annotation document rather than primary data, the nodes are the edges within that document that have been defined over the primary data or other annotation documents. That is, given a graph, *G*, over primary data, we create an *edge graph G'* whose nodes can themselves be annotated, thereby allowing for edges between the edges of the original graph *G*. Edges are labelled with feature structures containing the annotation content relevant to the data identified by the edge. The choice of this model is indicated by its almost universal use in defining general-purpose annotation formats, including the Generic Modeling Tool (GMT) (Ide and Romary, 2001; Ide and Romary, 2002; Ide and Romary, 2004b) and Annotation Graphs (Bird and Liberman, 2001). All annotations are stand-off – i.e., represented in documents separate from the primary data and other annotations – in order to support incremental annotation and separability of different annotation levels.

The graph of feature structures contains elementary structural nodes to which one or more feature structures are attached, providing the semantics ("content") of the annotation. A small inventory of logical operations (e.g., disjunction, sets) over the feature structures is specified, which define the model's abstract semantics. These operations provide the same expressive power as those defined for general-purpose, typed feature structures. Semantic coherence is provided by a registry of features maintained in RDF/OWL format, as described in Section 3.2. Users may define their own data categories or establish variants of categories in the registry. In the latter case, the newly defined data categories are formalized using the same format as definitions available in the registry. A schema providing the mapping of categories used in the document to categories in the registry and the formal specification of newly-defined categories is associated with the dump format instantiation.

In the LAF scenario, the dump format is invisible to users; users work only with their own formats, and transduce to and from the dump format only for processing and exchange. Thus, each site need only define a mapping between an in-house format and the dump format in order to use resources produced by any other site.

3.2   Data Category Registry

It is important to note that in principle, the dump format places no restrictions on annotation content (i.e., the categories and values in an annotation); annotation content is effectively user-defined, taken directly from the user's original annotation. However, it is obvious that harmonization of content categories is a critical next step toward standardizing annotations. LAF is addressing this far more controversial and problematic issue separately. Two major activities within SC4 are aimed at harmonization of annotation content: (1) definition of user annotation formats for different annotation levels[3], and (2) creation of a Data Category Registry (DCR) containing pre-defined data elements and schemas that can be used directly in annotations (Ide and Romary, 2004a).

Differences in approach to language resources and among individual system objectives inevitably lead to variations in data category definitions and data category names. The use of uniform data category names and definitions within the same resource domain (e.g., among terminological, lexicographical, and text corpus resources), at least at the interchange level, contributes to system coherence and enhances the reusability of data. Procedures for defining data categories in a given resource domain should also be uniform in order to ensure interoperability.

We define a *data category* as an elementary descriptor used in a linguistic annotation scheme. In feature structure terminology, data categories include both attributes (hereafter called *type descriptors*), such as SYNTACTIC CATEGORY and GRAMMATICAL GENDER, as well as a set of associated atomic *values* taken by such attributes, such as NOUN and FEMININE. In both cases we distinguish between the abstraction (concept) behind an attribute or value, and its realization as some string of characters or other object. Figure 3 provides an overview of these relationships. Whereas there is only one concept for a given attribute or value, there may be multiple instantiations.

type descriptor	*value*	
GENDER	MASCULINE FEMININE NEUTER	*conceptual dimension*
ger.	{m,f,n}	*instantiation*
genre	{masc, fem, neut}	*instantiation*

Figure 3.   Data category overview.

The DCR under development within ISO/TC 37/SC 4 is built around this fundamental concept/instance distinction. In principle, the DCR provides a set of reference concepts, while the annotator provides a *Data Category Specification* (DCS) that comprises a mapping between his or her scheme-specific instantiations and the concepts in the DCR. As such, the DCS provides documentation for the linguistic annotation scheme in question. The DCS for a given annotation document/s is included or referenced in any data exchange to provide the receiver with the information required to interpret the annotation content or to map it to another instantiation. Semantic integrity is guaranteed by mutual reference to DCR concepts.

To serve the needs of the widest possible user community, the DCR must be developed with an eye toward multilingualism. The DCR will support multiple languages by providing the following:

- Reference definitions for data categories in various languages

- Data element names for the data categories in various languages

- Description of usage in language-specific contexts, including definitions, usage notes, examples, and/or lists of values (e.g., GENDER takes the values *masculine, feminine* in French; *masculine, feminine, neuter* in German)

In addition, to both accommodate archival data and ensure semantic integrity, a mapping of data categories instantiated in the DCR to categories and values in well-known projects and initiatives will be provided.

The creation of a single global DCR for all types of language resources treated within TC 37 provides a unified view over the various applications of the resource. However, for the purposes of both category creation and DCR access, the DCR will be organized according to *thematic views*, i.e., domains of activity, which include specialized subsets of the information in the registry. Given the ongoing activities within TC 37, we can envisage definable subsets of the DCR for at least the following: terminological data collection, various types of linguistic annotation (morpho-syntactic, syntactic, discourse level, etc.), lexical representation for both NLP-oriented and traditional lexicography, language resource metadata, and language codes.

Figure 4 illustrates the relationship between data category specifications and the DCR. The patterned cells correspond to individual DCSs. Some data categories are relevant to a single domain, while others are common to multiple domains: for example, *sense number* is probably specific to lexicographical resources, but linguistic categories, such as *part of speech, grammatical gender, grammatical number*, etc. have wider application. Each thematic domain contributes all its data categories the global DCR, while at the same time identifying those data categories that it shares with other domains.

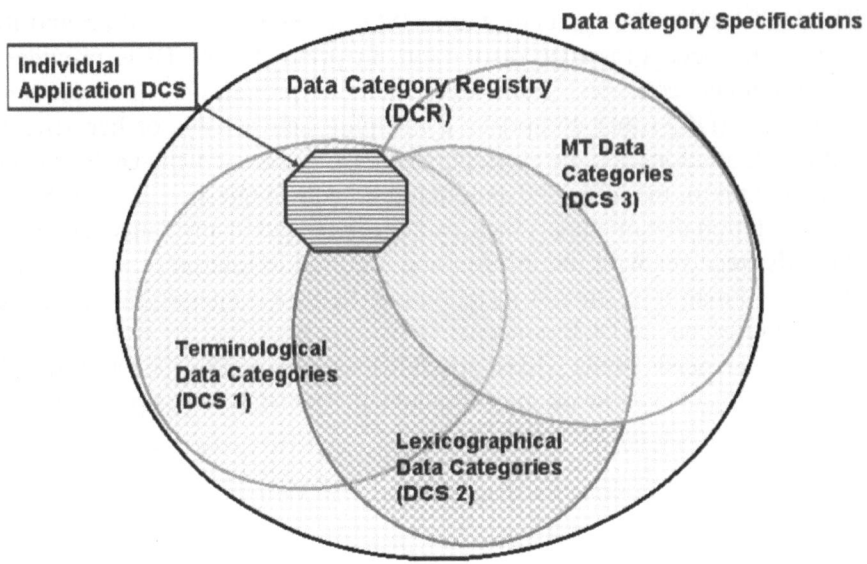

Figure 4.   Relation of data category selections to the DCR.

The oval shapes in the Venn diagram represent DCS subsets. A smaller sub-set can be selected from the domain DCS for use in a given application, as represented by the octagon in Figure 4. Note that while some of the data cat-egories contained in this subset are common to several different domains, this application is wholly contained within the DCS for terminological entries, so we can conclude that it is designed for use with a terminological application.

We intend to proceed cautiously, implementing categories that are widely used and relatively low-level, to ensure acceptance by the community. By building up slowly, the DCR should eventually contain a wide range of data categories, with their complete history, data category description, and attendant metadata. It would then be possible to specify a DCS (see previous section) for different thematic domains and an ontology of relations among them. In the short term, it is likely unreasonable to define such an ontology until there is greater awareness and consensus at the international level. No choice should be made in the definition of the DCR that would hamper further work in this direction.

So far, we have defined a preliminary template for data category definitions to be used as an underlying model for the DCR (ISO DIS 12620 under ISO committee TC 37/SC 3), which can also serve as a model for manipulation and transmission of proprietary data categories within the language engineering community. The heart of a data category description is the *Conceptual Entry* section, which we define to include the following fields:

ENTRY IDENTIFIER used for interchange of data category;

DEFINITION reference definition for the category, language, and theory neutral to the extent possible;

EXPLANATION additional information about the data category not relevant in a definition (e.g., more precise linguistic background for the use of the data category);

EXAMPLE illustration of use of the category, excluding language specific usages (documented elsewhere);

SOURCE may refine definition, explanation, or example to indicate the source from which the corresponding text has been borrowed or adapted;

STATUS may refine definition to indicate approval, acceptability, or applicability in a given context;

PROFILE relates the current data category to one or several views (e.g., Morpho-syntax, Syntax, Metadata, Language description, etc.);

CONCEPTUAL RANGE relates the category to the set of possible values (expressed as a list of data categories). A datatype may be provided instead of a list of values;

NOTE additional information excluding technical information that would normally be described within explanation;

BROADER CONCEPT generic pointer to a more general data category (e.g., from common noun to noun).

3.3   Using the DCR

The purpose of the DCR is to promote greater usability and reusability of annotated language resources and increased semantic integrity for information in annotation documents by providing a set of formally defined reference categories. "Formal definition" in this context includes natural language definitions for each category accompanied by specification of the possible values each category may take. At present, we envision instantiation of the DCR as a simple database in which each entry is either a type descriptor or value. Data categories will be referenced either by the DCR entry identifier, or, since the DCR will be publicly available online, via a URI.

Note that this simple instantiation of the DCR makes no distinction in terms of representation between type descriptors and values; each is considered as a data category and provided with an entry identifier for reference. Only minimal constraints on their use in an annotation are specified – i.e., constraints on descriptor/value combinations given in the descriptor entry. The broader structural integrity of an annotation is provided by placing constraints on nodes in the annotation graph (as defined in the LAF architecture) with which a given category can be associated. For example, the structural graph for a syntactic constituency analysis would consist of a hierarchy of typed nodes corresponding to the non-terminals in the grammar, with constraints on their embedding, and with which only appropriate descriptor/value pairs may be associated. Node types (e.g., NP, VP), as well as associated grammatical information (e.g., tense, number) may all be specified with data categories drawn from the DCR.

A more formal specification of data categories can be provided using mechanisms, such as RDF Schema (RDFS) and the Ontology Web Language (OWL) to formalize the properties and relations associated with data categories. For example, consider the following RDF Schema fragment:

```
<rdfs:Class rdf:about="#Noun">
  <rdfs:label>Noun</rdfs:label>
  <rdfs:comment>Class for
          nouns</rdfs:comment>
</rdfs:Class>
<rdfs:Property rdf:about="#number">
  <rdfs:domain
      rdfs:resource="Noun"/>
  <rdfs:range
      rdf:resource="rdfs:#Literal"/>
</rdfs:Property>
```

This fragment defines a class of objects called "Noun" that has the property "number". Note that the schema defines the classes but does not instantiate objects belonging to the class; instantiation may be accomplished directly in the annotation file, as follows (for brevity, the following examples assume appropriate namespace declarations specifying the URIs of schema and instance declarations)

```
<Noun rdf:about="Mydoc#W1">
    <number rdf:value="Plural"/>
</Noun>
```

where "Mydoc#W1" is the URI of the word being annotated as a noun. Alternatively, the DCR could contain instantiations of basic data elements, specifying values for properties, which can be referenced directly in the annotation. For example, the DCR could include the following instantiation:

```
<Noun rdf:ID="NMP">
    <number rdf:value="plural"/>
</Noun>
```

An annotation document could then reference the pre-defined instance as follows:[4]

```
<rdf:Description rdf:about="myDoc#W1">
    <POS rdf:resource="categories#NMS"/>
</rdf:Description>
```

An RDFS/OWL specification of data categories would enable greater control over descriptor/value use and also allow for the possibility of inferencing over annotations. RDFS/OWL descriptions function much like class definitions in an object-oriented programming language: they provide, in effect, templates that describe the properties of an object, specify constraints on which objects can provide the value for a given property, and specify super- and subclass relations among objects. For example, a general *dependent* relation may be defined for a verb object, which must have one of the possible values *argument* or *modifier*; *argument* can in turn have the possible values *subject*, *object*, or *complement*, etc., cf. the hierarchy in Figure 3, (Carroll et al., 2004). In a document containing a syntactic annotation, several objects with the type *argument* may be instantiated, each with a different value. Based on the RDFS/OWL definition, each instantiation of *argument* is recognized as a subclass of *dependent* and inherits the appropriate properties.

Definition of a precise hierarchy of linguistic categories and properties is a massive undertaking, and it is far from obvious that such a hierarchy could be agreed upon within the community. Therefore, we are proceeding cautiously to define hierarchical relations among categories, and leaving the bulk of this activity to users of the DCR. We will provide a library of RDF/OWL specifications describing hierarchical relations together with value constraints, interdependencies, etc., that can be used as desired by annotators. We expect that the library will be built up gradually from our initial descriptions and the contributions of users.

It cannot be overemphasized that the goal of the DCR is not to impose a specific set of categories, but rather to ensure that the semantics of data categories included in annotations are well-defined, either by referring to categories that are formally described in the DCR or by formal definition of new or variant categories. The DCR, at least at the outset, can only help us to move toward commonality in annotation content, which is becoming more and more essential as annotated language data is increasingly distributed over multiple sites and accessible via the web.

In the end, the DCR will come into widespread use only if it is easy for annotators to use and provides useful categories for various kinds of resource annotation. Ease of use can be assured by providing ready-to-use templates for reference to the DCR from within annotation documents, enabling immediate web access to definitions in a clear and concise format, and, perhaps above all, ensuring that at least a few highly visible projects use DCR references. The initial inclusion of categories that are for the most part relatively atomic and universally accepted is a move towards ensuring their usefulness for linguistic annotation, but, if the DCR is to be truly successful, it will also be necessary to include and demonstrate the use of categories that have become, for better or worse, *de facto* standards defined by widely used resources. The obvious example is WordNet: whatever its shortcomings for NLP, WordNet is the most universally used resource in the field, and there are now over 30 WordNets in different languages built around the same categories and concepts. One way to bring the DCR into general use is to implement a "DCR-aware" version of WordNet that specifies a mapping of WordNet categories to the DCR, and, on the other hand, ensure that WordNet-specific categories (e.g., synset) and all categories used in WordNet (e.g., meronym, hypernym, etc.) are in fact included in the DCR. Similarly, a mapping of categories in FrameNet, which is now also being replicated for other languages, and other existing or developing "standards", such as the EAGLES morpho-syntactic categories, TIME-ML (http://www.timeml.org), etc., can be made available via the DCR website. In this way, annotators will become aware of DCR categories and have real examples demonstrating DCR use.

4   Putting it All Together

To illustrate how the LAF principles are applied in practice, consider an interchange scenario between two users ("A" and "B"), each having his/her own annotation scheme for a given annotation layer, and a third user ("C") who wants to use both A's and B's annotations. Such a scenario is in fact typical within evaluation campaigns, such as PARSEVAL.

A and B apply LAF by mapping the descriptors used in their respective annotation schemes to categories in the DCR. The mapping is specified using an RDF/OWL schema, for which a template or automatic generation tool is available on the DCR website. If categories used in the user-specific annotation scheme are not included in the DCR, or if a DCR definition for a given category requires modification or extension, the new or variant categories are fully defined in the schema (again using a template or tool available on the DCR website).

Next, the user format is transduced to a LAF representation. The transduction may reveal that some of the annotation information in the user's scheme is implied by its structure; for example, in the Penn Treebank (PTB) syntactic annotation, the "subject" relation between a noun phrase and a verb phrase is implied by their relative positions in the parse tree represented by the LISP format, while the "object" relation is given explicitly (via an NP-Obj label) because the position of an NP in the tree is less definitively indicative of its semantic role. Similarly, embedded "S-units" in the PTB imply what is often called an "xcomp" relation, which in turn (implicitly, in the PTB) inherits its subject from the S-unit within which it is nested. In order to use such implicit information, the software must be aware that, for instance, the first NP within an S is to be considered the subject. However, it should not be expected that user C's software is designed to make this inference, and therefore LAF compliance requires that such information be made explicit by the creator of the original scheme when transducing to LAF format.[5]

The transduction process demands familiarity with the LAF XML format and moderate computational expertise to create a transduction script. LAF-compliaint annotations are represented in a generic XML format for specifying edges (using a <struct> element, historically so-named to stand for "structural node") and the associated feature structures; as such, the XML elements provide the structure of the annotation but do not include any information concerning annotation content. The actual content of the annotation is provided in the attribute/value pairs within the feature structure.[6]

The transduction process therefore involves user-specific structures (e.g., nested parentheses in the PTB LISP example) to XML <struct> elements, and filling attribute value slots in the feature structure encoding with the appropriate labels. Because all LAF annotation documents are stand-off, it also may involve disentangling data and annotations, and providing XPointer links from edges (<struct> elements) in the annotation document to the primary data.

An example of a PTB transduction to LAF format is given in Figures 5 and 6. Each <struct> element corresponds to an edge in the graph, traversing the indicated span in the primary data. <feat> elements provide the feature/value pairs associated with the immediate parent node.[7] Note that in this example, XML embedding of <struct> elements reflects the constituency relations among the edges, reflecting the LISP tree-structure. We take advantage of the fact that XML processors will reconstruct the implied tree structure from the embedding, while at the same time we are providing sufficient information to reconstruct it automatically from the values given in the TARGET attributes if XML processing is unavailable or inapplicable.

When user C obtains the LAF version of A's and B's annotations, the only processing requirement is that his tool understands the dump format to extract the annotation information in each one, either in order to use them directly in an application or transduce them to an in-house format of his own. Because

```
((S (NP-SBJ-1 Paul)
    (VP intends)
    (S    (NP-SBJ *-1)
       (VP  to
          (VP  leave
             (NP IBM))))
 .))
```

Figure 5.   PIB annotation of "Paul intends to leave IBM".

```
<struct target="xptr(substring(/p/s[1]/text(),1,26))">
 <feat type="syntacticCategory">S</feat>
 <struct id="s0" target="xptr(substring(/p/s[1]/text(),1,4))">
   <feat type="syntacticCategory">NP</feat>
   <feat type="syntacticFunction">subject</feat>
 </struct>
 <struct target="xptr(substring(/p/s[1]/text(),5,7))">
   <feat type="syntacticCategory">VP</feat>
 </struct>
 <struct target="xptr(substring(/p/s[1]/text(),12,12))">
   <struct target="s0"/>
   <struct>
    <feat type="syntacticCategory">VP</feat>
    <struct target="xptr(substring(/p/s[1]/text(),15,9))">
      <feat type="syntacticCategory">VP</feat>
      <struct target="xptr(substring(/p/s[1]/text(),21,3))">
        <feat type="syntacticCategory">NP</feat>
      </struct>
    </struct>
   </struct>
 </struct>
</struct>
</struct>
```

Figure 6.   Dump format instantiation of "Paul intends to leave IBM".

both user A and B have provided a mapping of their respective categories in the RDF/OWL schema that accompanies the LAF-compliant annotation documents, user C can readily translate scheme-specific categories, such as "NP" to his own category designation, if they differ. So, for example, if user A uses "NP" for noun phrases, and user B uses "Nominal", then if both A's and B's RDF/OWL schemas map these two designations to a common DCR category, user C knows that the two notations represent the same concept. User C, in turn, can map A's and B's notations to his own notation for that concept, if desired.

4.1   A Case Study: The ANC

The American National Corpus (ANC) project (http://AmericanNational Corpus.org), which is creating a 100 million word corpus of American English comparable to the British National Corpus, is representing its data and annotations in accordance with the LAF specifications. The ANC is being heavily annotated for a variety of linguistic information, including morpho-syntax, syntax, named entities, semantics (WordNet sense tags and FrameNet frames), etc., and the project is providing multiple alternative annotations at each level produced by different automatic annotation tools. In order to accommodate the layering of several different POS taggings, noun, and verb chunks, dependency and constituency parse annotation schemes, and named entity annotations, and in particular to enable merging annotations when desired, it is necessary to use a common representation that can accommodate many different kinds of annotation. Therefore, the ANC has chosen to represent all annotations in the LAF dump format. The annotation set for each ANC document includes the header for that document and the primary data with no internal mark-up, together with all applicable annotation documents. The header points to the primary data, as well as each annotation document; annotation documents are linked to the primary data.

The ANC's choice to use the LAF representation makes the data extremely flexible: the primary text can be used with no mark-up or annotations if desired (which is commonly the case for concordance generation, etc.), or the user can choose to deal with a particular annotation set independent of the text (e.g., to generate statistics for POS taggers or parsers). Furthermore, annotations of many different types, or several versions of a single annotation type (e.g., multiple part of speech taggings), can be provided without encountering the problems of incompatibility (in particular, the famous "overlapping hierarchy" problem that arises when different systems assign different boundaries to words or other elements in data). Most importantly, users acquire all annotations in a common format; if users were to generate annotations for the ANC data on their own, each annotation – including annotations of the same type – would be in a different format and require special processing. By rendering all annotations in LAF format, comparison and merging of annotations becomes a far simpler task.

At present, few software systems handle stand-off annotation, and those that do often demand computational expertise beyond what many ANC users – who include linguists, teachers of English as a second language, etc. – have access to. Therefore, the ANC project has developed an easy-to-use tool and user interface (http://americannationalcorpus.org/tools/index.html#xces-parser) (Suderman and Ide, 2006) to merge the stand-off annotations of the user's choice with the primary data and produce the merged document in any of several formats, including, at present, a well-formed XML document in XCES format (suitable for use with various search and access interfaces such as the BNC's XAIRA (http://sourceforge.net/projects/xaira)), Word-Smith/MonoConc Pro format, and text with part of speech tags appended to each word and separated by an underscore. The ANC merging tool implements the org.xml.sax.XMLReader, and therefore it is relatively trivial for users to provide their own interface in order to produce output in any format, or to perform other operations on the data (e.g., frequency counts, bigram generation, etc.). By using this tool, the ANC user need never deal directly with or see the underlying representation of the corpus and its stand-off annotations, but gains all the advantages that representation offers.

Because the DCR is still in its development phase, ANC annotation documents do not currently provide RDF/OWL schema mappings to DCR categories. Furthermore, because many ANC annotations are generated automatically using a wide range of freely available or contributed software, determining the mapping for each annotation document may be unfeasible. The ANC will, however, provide the DCR mapping for categories used to annotate its 10 million word "gold standard" sub-corpus, which includes hand-validated annotations for morpho-syntax, syntax, named entities, WordNet senses, and FrameNet frames. As such, the ANC should provide a proof of concept for the LAF architecture, and serve as a usage example upon which others can build.

5   Conclusion

The framework presented here for linguistic annotation is intended to allow for variation in annotation schemes, while at the same time enabling comparison and evaluation, merging of different annotations, and development of common tools for creating and using annotated data. We have developed an abstract model for annotations that is capable of representing the necessary information, while providing a common encoding format that tools can be adapted to manipulate and access, as well as a means to combine and compare annotations. The details presented here provide a look "under the hood" in order to show the flexibility and representational power of the abstract scheme; however, the intention is that annotators and users of syntactic annotation schemes can continue to use their own or other formats with which they are comfortable, and translation into and out of the abstract format will be automatic.

Our framework for linguistic annotation is built around some relatively straightforward ideas: separation of information conveyed by means of structure and information conveyed directly by specification of content categories; development of an abstract format that puts a layer of abstraction between site-specific annotation schemes and standard specifications; and creation of a DCR to provide a reference set of annotation categories. The emergence of XML and related standards, together with RDF/OWL, provides the enabling technology. We are, therefore, at a point where the creation and use of annotated data and concerns about the way it is represented can be treated separately – i.e., researchers can focus on the question of *what* to represent, independent of the question of *how* to represent it. The end result should be greater coherence, consistency, and ease of use and access for linguistically annotated data.

The abstract model that captures the fundamental properties of an annotation scheme provides a conceptual tool for assessing the coherence and consistency of existing schemes and those being developed. The model enforces clear distinctions between implicit and explicit information (e.g., functional relations implied by structural relations in constituent syntactic analyses) and phrasal and functional relations. It is alarmingly common for annotation schemes to represent these different kinds of information in the same way, rendering their distinction computationally intractable (even if they are perfectly understandable by the informed human reader). Hand-developed annotation schemes used in treebanks are often described informally in guidebooks for annotators, leaving considerable room for variation; for example, (Charniak, 1996), notes that the PTB implicitly contains more than 10,000 context-free rules, most of which are used only once. Comparison and transduction of schemes becomes virtually impossible under such circumstances. While requiring that annotators make relations explicit and consider the mapping to the abstract format increases overhead, we feel that the exercise will help avoid such problems, and can only lead to greater coherence, consistency, and inter-operability among annotation schemes.

Notes

1. In fact, the term "primary resource" is somewhat misleading, since each transcription or annotation level can be regarded as a primary resource for another level. This notion of multiple information layers is the underlying principle for stand-off mark-up.

2. Participants: Nuria Bel (Universitat de Barcelona), David Durand (Brown University), Henry Thompson (University of Edinburgh), Koiti Hasida (AIST Tokyo), Eric De La Clergerie (INRIA), Lionel Clement (INRIA), Laurent Romary (LORIA), Nancy Ide (Vassar College), Kiyong Lee (Korea University), Keith Suderman (Vassar College), Aswani Kumar (LORIA), Chris Laprun (NIST), Thierry Declerck (DFKI), Jean Carletta (University of Edinburgh), Michael Strube (European Media Laboratory), Hamish Cunningham (University of Sheffield), Tomaz Erjavec (Institute Jozef Stefan), Hennie Brugman (Max-Planck-Institut für Psycholinguistik), Fabio Vitali (Universite di Bologna), Key-Sun Choi (Korterm), Jean-Michel Borde (Digital Visual), and Eric Kow (LORIA).

3. Draft documents and working papers for the various areas, including morpho-syntactic annotation (ISO/TC 37/SC 4 document N225), syntactic annotation (ISO/TC 37/SC 4 document N244), word segmentation (ISO/TC 37/SC 4 document N233), etc. are available at http://www.tc37sc4.org/.

4. In these examples, *number* is given literal values. However, with OWL it is possible to restrict the range of possible values by enumeration.

5. It is of course possible to generate a LAF representation without making implicit information explicit, thus placing the burden of extracting the information on the user of the LAF instantiation. LAF guidelines can "require" explicitness in principle, but they cannot ensure that it is enforced.

6. A full description of the XML feature structure representation can be found in ISO standard 24610-1. See also the TEI guidelines, Chapter 16 (http://www.tei-c.org/release/doc/tei-p5-doc/html/FS.html).

7. The use of <feat> elements in this example shows the use of a simplified XML format for feature structures that is sufficient for many types of annotation information. In cases where the full power of FS representation is required, the TEI/ISO standard XML representation for feature structures can be used.

References

Bird, S. and Liberman, M. (2001). A Formal Framework for Linguistic Annotation. *Speech Communication*, 33(1–2):23–60.

Carroll, J., Minnen, G., and Briscoe, T. (2004). Parser Evaluation. In Abeillé, A., editor, *Treebanks: Building and Using Parsed Corpora*, pages 299–316, Kluwer Academic Publishers, Dordrecht, The Netherlands.

Charniak, E. (1996). Treebank Grammars. In *Proceedings of the Thirteenth National Conference on Artificial Intelligence (AAAI)*, pages 1031–1036, MIT Press.

Cole, R., Mariani, J., Uszkoreit, H., Zaenen, A., and Zue, V., editors (1997). *Survey of the State of the Art in Human Language Technology*. Cambridge University Press, first edition.

Ide, N. and Romary, L. (2001). A Common Framework for Syntactic Annotation. In *Proceedings of the 39th Annual Meeting of the Association for Computational Linguistics (ACL)*, pages 298–305, Toulouse, France.

Ide, N. and Romary, L. (2002). Standards for Language Resources. In *Proceedings of the Third Language Resources and Evaluation Conference (LREC)*, pages 839–844, Las Palmas, Gran Canaria, Spain.

Ide, N. and Romary, L. (2004a). A Registry of Standard Data Categories for Linguistic Annotation. In *Proceedings of the Fourth International Language Resources and Evaluation Conference (LREC)*, pages 135–139, Lisbon, Portugal.

Ide, N. and Romary, L. (2004b). International Standard for a Linguistic Annotation Framework. *Natural Language Engineering*, 10(3–4):211–225.

Suderman, K. and Ide, N. (2006). Layering and Merging Linguistic Annotations. In *Proceedings of the Fifth Workshop on NLP and XML (NLPXML)*, pages 89–92, Trento, Italy.

Index

Text, Speech and Language Technology

1. H. Bunt and M. Tomita (eds.): *Recent Advances in Parsing Technology.* 1996
   ISBN 0-7923-4152-X
2. S. Young and G. Bloothooft (eds.): *Corpus-Based Methods in Language and Speech Processing.* 1997
   ISBN 0-7923-4463-4
3. T. Dutoit: *An Introduction to Text-to-Speech Synthesis.* 1997 ISBN 0-7923-4498-7
4. L. Lebart, A. Salem and L. Berry: *Exploring Textual Data.* 1998
   ISBN 0-7923-4840-0
5. J. Carson-Berndsen: *Time Map Phonology.* 1998 ISBN 0-7923-4883-4
6. P. Saint-Dizier (ed.): *Predicative Forms in Natural Language and in Lexical Knowledge Bases.* 1999 ISBN 0-7923-5499-0
7. T. Strzalkowski (ed.): *Natural Language Information Retrieval.* 1999
   ISBN 0-7923-5685-3
8. J. Harrington and S. Cassiday: *Techniques in Speech Acoustics.* 1999
   ISBN 0-7923-5731-0
9. H. van Halteren (ed.): *Syntactic Wordclass Tagging.* 1999 ISBN 0-7923-5896-1
10. E. Viegas (ed.): *Breadth and Depth of Semantic Lexicons.* 1999 ISBN 0-7923-6039-7
11. S. Armstrong, K. Church, P. Isabelle, S. Nanzi, E. Tzoukermann and D. Yarowsky (eds.): *Natural Language Processing Using Very Large Corpora.* 1999
   ISBN 0-7923-6055-9
12. F. Van Eynde and D. Gibbon (eds.): *Lexicon Development for Speech and Language Processing.* 2000 ISBN 0-7923-6368-X; Pb: 07923-6369-8
13. J. Véronis (ed.): *Parallel Text Processing.* Alignment and Use of Translation Corpora. 2000 ISBN 0-7923-6546-1
14. M. Horne (ed.): *Prosody: Theory and Experiment.* Studies Presented to Gösta Bruce. 2000 ISBN 0-7923-6579-8
15. A. Botinis (ed.): *Intonation.* Analysis, Modelling and Technology. 2000
   ISBN 0-7923-6605-0
16. H. Bunt and A. Nijholt (eds.): *Advances in Probabilistic and Other Parsing Technologies.* 2000 ISBN 0-7923-6616-6
17. J.-C. Junqua and G. van Noord (eds.): *Robustness in Languages and Speech Technology.* 2001 ISBN 0-7923-6790-1
18. R.H. Baayen: *Word Frequency Distributions.* 2001 ISBN 0-7923-7017-1
19. B. Granström, D. House and. I. Karlsson (eds.): *Multimodality in Language and Speech Systems.* 2002 ISBN 1-4020-0635-7
20. M. Carl and A. Way (eds.): *Recent Advances in Example-Based Machine Translation.* 2003 ISBN 1-4020-1400-7; Pb 1-4020-1401-5
21. A. Abeillé: *Treebanks.* Building and Using Parsed Corpora. 2003
   ISBN 1-4020-1334-5; Pb 1-4020-1335-3
22. J. van Kuppevelt and R.W. Smith (eds.): *Current and New Directions in Discourse and Dialogue.* 2003 ISBN 1-4020-1614-X; Pb 1-4020-1615-8
23. H. Bunt, J. Carroll and G. Satta (eds.): *New Developments in Parsing Technology.* 2004 ISBN 1-4020-2293-X; Pb 1-4020-2294-8

Text, Speech and Language Technology

24. G. Fant: *Speech Acoustics and Phonetics.* Selected Writings. 2004
ISBN 1-4020-2373-1; Pb 1-4020-2789-3
25. W.J. Barry and W.A. Van Dommelen (eds.): *The Integration of Phonetic Knowledge in Speech Technology.* 2005   ISBN 1-4020-2635-8; Pb 1-4020-2636-6
26. D. Dahl (ed.): *Practical Spoken Dialog Systems.* 2004
ISBN 1-4020-2674-9; Pb 1-4020-2675-7
27. O. Stock and M. Zancanaro (eds.): *Multimodal Intelligent Information Presentation.* 2005   ISBN 1-4020-3049-5; Pb 1-4020-3050-9
28. W. Minker, D. Bühler and L. Dybkjaer (eds.): *Spoken Multimodal Human-Computer Dialogue in Mobile Environments.* 2004   ISBN 1-4020-3073-8; Pb 1-4020-3074-6
29. P. Saint-Dizier (ed.): *Syntax and Semantics of Prepositions.* 2005
ISBN 1-4020-3849-6
30. J. C. J. van Kuppevelt, L. Dybkjaer, N. O. Bernsen (eds.): *Advances in natural Multimodal Dialogue Systems.* 2005   ISBN 1-4020-3932-8
31. P. Grzybek (ed.): *Contributions to the Science of Text and Language.* Word Length Studies and Related Issues. 2006   ISBN 1-4020-4067-9
32. T. Strzalkowski and S. Harabagiu (eds.): *Advances in Open Domain Question Answering.* 2006   ISBN 1-4020-4744-4
33. E. Agirre and P. Edmonds (eds.): *Word Sense Disambiguation.* Algorithms and Applications. 2006   ISBN 1-4020-4808-4
34. J. Nivre (eds.): *Inductive Dependency Parsing.* 2006
ISBN 1-4020-4888-2
35. K. Ahmed, C. Brewster and M. Stevenson (eds.): *Words and Intelligence I.* Selected Papers by Yorick Wilks. 2007   ISBN 1-4020-5284-7
36. K. Ahmed, C. Brewster and M. Stevenson (eds.): *Words and Intelligence II.* Essays in Honor of Yorick Wilks. 2007   ISBN 1-4020-5832-2
37. L. Dybkjær, H. Hemsen and W. Minker (eds.): *Evaluation of Text and Speech Systems.* 2007   ISBN 1-4020-5815-2